Everyday
Forms of Whiteness

Perspectives on a Multiracial America series
Joe R. Feagin, Texas A&M University, series editor

The racial composition of the United States is rapidly changing. Books in the series will explore various aspects of the coming multiracial society, one in which European Americans are no longer the majority and where issues of white-on-black racism have been joined by many other challenges to white dominance.

Titles:

David J. Leonard and C. Richard King, *Commodified and Criminalized: New Racism and African Americans in Contemporary Sports*

Melanie Bush, *Breaking the Code of Good Intentions: Everyday Forms of Whiteness*

Amir Mavasti and Karyn McKinney, *Middle Eastern Lives in America*

Richard Rees, *Shades of Difference: A History of Ethnicity in America*

Katheryn Russell-Brown, *Protecting Our Own: Race, Crime, and African Americans*

Elizabeth M. Aranda, *Emotional Bridges to Puerto Rico: Migration, Return Migration, and the Struggles of Incorporation*

Victoria Kaplan, *Structural Inequality: Black Architects in the United States*

Angela J. Hattery, David G. Embrick, and Earl Smith, *Globalization and America: Race, Human Rights, and Inequality*

Pamela Anne Quiroz, *Adoption in a Color-Blind Society*

Adia Harvey Wingfield, *Doing Business with Beauty: Black Women, Hair Salons, and the Racial Enclave Economy*

Erica Chito Childs, *Fade to Black and White: Interracial Images in Popular Culture*

Jessie Daniels, *Cyber Racism: White Supremacy Online and the New Attack on Civil Rights*

Teun A. van Dijk, *Racism and Discourse in Latin America*

Melanie E. L. Bush, *Everyday Forms of Whiteness: Understanding Race in a "Post-Racial" World*, 2nd edition

Everyday Forms of Whiteness

Understanding Race in a *"Post-Racial"* World

Second Edition

Melanie E. L. Bush

ROWMAN & LITTLEFIELD PUBLISHERS, INC.
Lanham • Boulder • New York • Toronto • Plymouth, UK

Published by Rowman & Littlefield Publishers, Inc.
A wholly owned subsidary of The Rowman & Littlefield Publishing Group, Inc.
4501 Forbes Boulevard, Suite 200, Lanham, Maryland 20706
http://www.rowmanlittlefield.com

Estover Road, Plymouth PL6 7PY, United Kingdom

British Library Cataloguing in Publication Information Available

Library of Congress Cataloging-in-Publication Data
Bush, Melanie E. L., 1955-
  Everyday forms of whiteness : understanding race in a "post-racial" world / Melanie E.
L. Bush. -- 2nd ed.
    p. cm. -- (Perspectives on a multiracial America series)
  Previously published as: Breaking the code of good intentions, c2004.
  Includes bibliographical references and index.
  ISBN 978-0-7425-9997-0 (cloth : alk. paper) -- ISBN 978-0-7425-9998-7 (pbk. : alk.
paper) -- ISBN 978-0-7425-9999-4 (electronic : alk. paper)
  1. United States--Race relations. 2. United States--Ethnic relations. 3. Racism--
United States. 4. Whites--United States--Attitudes. 5. Minorities--United States--Social
conditions. 6. United States--Social conditions--1980- 7. National characteristics,
American. I. Bush, Melanie E. L., 1955- Breaking the code of good intentions. II. Title.
  E184.A1B917 2011
  305.800973--dc22

2010032814

To the universal spirits and ever-present souls all over the world who throughout history and the present day, passionately believe we can build a world based on peace and justice for all and who sustain strength, courage, hope, and love despite all odds;

To those who are not here to receive the recognition they deserve for teaching and giving so much, so often, and for always sharing joy, wisdom, compassion, and laughter: Momma Zoom, Liz, Juanita, Harriet, Soji, Barkoo, Vanda, Beth, Stanley, and Uncle Pete;

And to those who are my heart, my soul, my true lifetime spiritual collaborators and co-conspirators: Rod, Sarafina, Mom, Dad, E, Aunt Honey, Andree and Isabella!

Contents

Foreword

The perspectives of white students on inequality documented in this book re-mind me of the epigram attributed to Abraham Lincoln: "You may fool all the people some of the time; you can even fool some of the people all the time; but you can't fool all of the people all the time." After reading these student accounts, however, I would add a sadder phrase: "You can fool most of the people most of the time." This is especially true if the topics concerned are racial and class inequality and those being fooled are ordinary white Ameri-cans. Those doing this fooling are the wealthy white elites that still control U.S. society. This book demonstrates that these elites have largely succeeded in brainwashing the majority of ordinary whites into accepting a worldview that even contradicts the latter's self-interests.

In this informative, exciting, and well-theorized book, social scientist Melanie Bush probes deeply into understandings and rationalizations about racial and class matters held by many students at our largest urban public uni-versity, the City University of New York (CUNY). Bush's analysis of student views is in the tradition of classical social science studies that have described racial and class views of ordinary Americans, such as Gunnar Myrdal's pathbreaking analysis of racial ideology, *An American Dilemma* (1944), and Joe Feagin's pioneering analysis of anti-poor views, *Subordinating the Poor* (1975). Melanie Bush, like her predecessors, has described well the views that ordinary Americans, particularly white Americans, hold in regard to mat-ters of poverty, inequality, and race.

For this project, Bush interviewed students and staff from Brooklyn College, which educates a significant number of CUNY's more than two hundred thousand students. She used a variety of concatenated research methods—a survey of nearly five hundred students; focus groups with 131 students, faculty, and staff; interviews with seven faculty members; participant observation of thirteen student activities; and much archival data. Collected at the beginning of the twenty-first century, the survey data and focus group commentaries are examined in depth in order to offer a frequently original analysis of the ways in which ordinary Americans—particularly white Americans—make sense out of racial and class matters in their surroundings. In a detailed and nuanced analysis, we hear clearly the articulate voices of the hundreds of people, mostly young people, who participated in this research project.

Strikingly enough, the data show great ignorance, much misinformation, many misapprehensions, and an array of rationalizations about racial and class inequality. Thus, like numerous other researchers, Bush finds that most young whites believe the United States has mostly achieved racial equality, even though much research shows otherwise. Yet, these often woefully misinformed white students include some of this country's better-educated and relatively privileged youth. Indeed, within the general U.S. population, relatively few Americans—and only a minority of whites— have had the opportunity to devote several years of their lives to college studies exploring what the United States is about, historically and on the contemporary scene. Even with this advanced education, most remain seriously undereducated, even in regard to critical class and racial realities in their own everyday lives. One might reasonably conclude, as Bush does, that much of their ignorance and rationalizing misinformation has been generated, or reinforced, by the many educational settings within which they have already spent much of their lives.

Numerous social scientists have carefully documented the high level of class, racial, and gender inequality in U.S. society. The material reality is one in which the wealthy, whites, and men are at the top of well-entrenched class, racial, and gender hierarchies. Yet, as Bush demonstrates from her data, this large group of white students does not see these great inequalities, or does not see them as so great as to be problematical for what they, and most other Americans, view as the "world's greatest democracy."

The central issue of this book is the ideological rationalizing and framing that are deeply and routinely inculcated in the minds of average Americans, especially white Americans. Drawing in detail on rich survey and interview data, Bush limns an array of important ideological discourses and mechanisms by means of which youth, mainly white youth, interpret social inequalities. While she draws on other data periodically, Bush places heaviest emphasis on students' survey and interview data in showing their everyday understandings and identifying central mechanisms of ideological construction that support and reproduce the class and racial hierarchies of U.S. society.

One important interpretive mechanism involves students' naturalization and mystification of the poverty that they do see. Although most recognize that there still is poverty, they tend to be fatalistic about it or blame it on the lack of motivation of the poor. A second interpretive mechanism is related to this: Most of these white students—as well as many other Americans and people overseas—routinely view whiteness as normal and thus view "American" as a white identity. That is, for them the American identity does not really include Americans of color or those citizens born outside the United States. These views are clear examples of what Hernan Vera and I have described as "sincere fictions of the white self." They are typically held with sincerity if not fervor, yet they are deeply rooted in ethnocentrism and racial stereotyping about who is, and is not, virtuous and American.

Bush's data are rich and enable her to examine yet more mechanisms that help to reproduce patterns of racial and class inequality. One such mechanism takes the form of the "rigid regulation of discourse," that is, the unwillingness of most whites to allow serious questioning of standard interpretations of wealth, justice, and inequality issues. It is not simply that these white college students are misinformed or engaging in stereotypical thinking. Instead, they view their misunderstandings and stereotypes as true and correct—as, indeed, quasi-religious pieties whose orthodoxy should not be questioned. These students do not stand apart from the rest of the society, for most whites consider such establishment views as correct dogma. Such views are constantly reiterated as "truths" in the media, education, and the pulpit.

Two other interpretive mechanisms that these students use to present their stereotyped understanding of class and racial realities involve linguistic coding. They often use coded language to bring up racist views without seeming racist. Examples include coded references to Americans of color in the frequent use of such terms as "crime," "welfare," and "urban areas." (Thus when they speak of "crime," they likely do not have in mind embezzlement scandals involving leading corporate executives. Nor are they likely to include in "welfare" their grandparents who are getting social security.)

This terminology, like similar terminology used across white America, is specifically utilized to hide racial and class stereotyping just beneath the surface. The students also use racial narratives that regularly place positive judgments on whites and white behavior and negative judgments on people of color and their behavior, such as narratives suggesting that whites do not often commit murder or use drugs while Blacks and Latinos often do. The reality, of course, is that whites do much murder and are the major consumers of illicit drugs in the United States.

Bush identifies even more mechanisms that help to reproduce racial and class hierarchies. One is the typical life pattern reported by most students. Segregation is characteristic of most aspects of their daily living, so that most white students have limited contacts with people of color. Whites in academic and other settings often rationalize the social and residential segregation that whites have created, historically and currently, with the sincere fiction that people of color prefer to be "with their own kind." Coupled with these views is the naïve notion that racism exists now only because people of color keep talking about it. Other interpretive mechanisms reinforcing racial hierarchy include white students' misapprehension that it is now whites who are suffering from unfair advantages because of remedial programs that attempt to undo discrimination faced by Americans of color, along with the weight that students give to individualism and individual competition as being best for all and as leading to a fair society. This view, in turn, is often coupled with a commitment to the status quo, which includes stigmatizing resistance to it. Inegalitarian social realities, in their view, are naturally that way and cannot or will not be changed.

For the most part, the status quo ideology wins out. Most white students parrot what they have been taught by parents, media, church, and schools. As they speak in this book's chapters, we constantly see just beneath the surface four hundred years of class and racial oppression. They often speak in status-quo-affirming rationalizations. One cannot readily understand what they are saying without, as Bush demonstrates, understanding their historical and social contexts. It is these contexts that have created or reinforced misunderstandings and rationalizations of social inequality. The troubling views of these white students represent much more than a distorted "knowledge" into which they have been socialized; they reflect the way in which the dominant elite maintains its powerful position in entrenched hierarchies.

Knowledge is often an instrument of domination. Since these white students are young, they are, as Pierre Bourdieu might say, the "dominated among the dominant." They, as young whites, now mostly buy into a view of the United States that is often demonstrably false. Yet, the data strongly contradicting their stereotyped views rarely have an impact on the status quo ideology. In their views on the racial and class hierarchies that are central to U.S. society, with a few exceptions, these youth accept the rich white man's view of the world. Strangely enough, this ideology is so strong that the majority are unable even to understand the class-driven world that is hurting their, and their families', life chances. There is an extraordinary disconnect between what the country really is and what these students believe it to be.

This book is social science at its best, for it shows clearly that good social science not only tells us much about the empirical reality of society but also much about its moral realities and potential as well. Here, as elsewhere, excellent social science is oriented to moral and ethical issues. It helps us to see how we are dominated, and how to resist that domination. In that sense, good social science brings more freedom to a United States where the value of freedom is frequently parroted for the very purpose of suppressing the real freedom of U.S. citizens. While this is committed social science, it is also committed to demythologizing and democratizing an inegalitarian social world. Forces that try to dominate us and our youth are revealed, empirically, for what they are, and demythologized, to work toward a better democracy.

In spite of her generally negative portrait, Bush concludes with a more hopeful message, for she sees in many comments by the students glimmers of accurate understandings of social realities—and thus possibilities for change in the future. Fortunately, there are what Bush calls some "cracks in the wall of whiteness." As she sees it, there are times when these students test and contest the hierarchical world around them, however limited this testing may be. These are areas of thought and inclination that might be used to bring a change in how white youth view an inegalitarian world. They include their often strong beliefs in ideals of democracy and justice, at least at an abstract level, as well as their sometimes realistic, class-related understandings about their own financial insecurities and employment futures. There is also substantial critical reaction among them to the more extreme machinations of the rich, which have become more obvious in recent years. There is, too, some hope in the critical thinking that may come, for some at least, out of discussions in college courses. The broad educational goal is to foster and generate much more contestation of the class and racial hierarchies, and associated rationalizations, that dominate these students' lives.

While there is a certain difficulty in placing too much faith in such potential change, Bush is adamant about the need to challenge student rationalizations, misunderstandings, and stereotypes by many means, including more innovative and critical educational efforts. She is surely right that there is a great need to find many new ways to disrupt the unreflective understandings of racial and class matters among white youth and, indeed, many other Americans.

In the end, we come up against very hard questions about the likely future of U.S. society. Why do most white Americans and many other Americans cling to the firm belief that the United States is a model democracy without significant structural inequality in the face of overwhelming evidence to the contrary? Can the United States ever become truly democratic when many ordinary Americans, especially the white majority, accept an ideology that heavily benefits those who are the most powerful and the richest? These are enduring questions that must be answered by substantial citizen organization for progressive change, if the United States is ever to become in reality the democracy it loudly proclaims itself to be.

Joe R. Feagin
Ella McFadden Professor of Liberal Arts
Texas A&M University

Preface

Growing up in the 1960s, with parents active with the NYC schoolteacher's union, I heard firsthand about struggles for decentralization of educational system in Ocean Hill/Brownsville and the influence of the Black Panther Party. At an early age, I went door-to-door with my Dad, talking to neighbors about U.S. involvement in the war in Vietnam. The beat of the times conveyed that we were the makers of history and that the poverty, racism, and violence of U.S. society could and would be challenged and overcome. The fury and indignation of the late 1960s and 1970s rebellions against local, national, and global injustice inspired in me a vision of a better world. At the same time, ideological incongruencies were so glaring that the intersections and contradictions of race and class identity for ordinary white folks struggling to make ends meet collided with the righteous struggles for inclusion and equality of people of color. My awareness of the tenuous nature of class-consciousness and the way racial identity intersects and undercuts broader unity took root during this time.

I was in college at McGill University shortly after the Quebec State of Siege, studying world systems theory with Immanuel Wallerstein. I researched capital flows from the periphery to the core, investigating the notion of the United States as a benevolent savior, and simultaneously did community work, particularly with women in Montreal who were organizing around local issues. Thus began my intense simultaneous pursuits of intellectual understanding and grassroots activism. Such pursuits developed my social commitment and brought transcendent meaning to my everyday life, ultimately leading me to seek an understanding of the forces that underlay inequality. Every opportunity I received was a gift to pass on to others, and a compelling responsibility.

After college I spent ten years in the San Francisco Bay Area, doing full-time political work such as organizing "tax the corporations" initiatives, working for full employment in Oakland and against U.S. involvement in Southern Africa and Central America. By the 1980s Ronald Reagan was president, the air traffic controllers were fired, and the Nicaraguan contras were actively being supported by our tax dollars. We needed new intellectual leadership and activist vision. The beat of those times was foreboding and demanded serious reassessment about where we (both globally and nationally) were headed.

I returned home to New York City and once again tried to piece together an understanding of the world and a perspective on local issues. In 1990, I began working at Brooklyn College and became part of the extensive community of the City University of New York. While this provided many opportunities for thoughtful engagement, I increasingly felt overwhelmed by the centrality of racial animosity in daily life in NYC. Given the repeated incidents of racial brutality, Bumpurs, Hawkins, and Griffith[1] became household names. I found most troubling not only the irrational cruelty of the individuals involved but also that these incidents appeared justifiable in the eyes of many whites. This posed for me irresistible research questions about how everyday processes reproduce privileging and inequality. Why do otherwise intelligent, well-intentioned, and sensitive people, particularly whites, refute the reality of bias? How does someone struggling for an education despite continuous challenges become "lazy," "worthless," and unworthy of our support? How does a wallet become a gun?[2] And so, this project was formulated.

I have been blessed in so many ways by numerous experiences and exposure to people who have taught me much about our society, about racism, and how the presumption of white privilege functions constantly in a myriad of discrete and overt ways. This struggle and these blessings inspired this inquiry. I realize that, however big or small the privileging of any individual, the system of white supremacy offers little encouragement for questioning its cultural, ideological, and material base. However, somewhere deep inside I believe that we have no other choice but to work to expose the systems of domination and advantage that manifest in ways so subtle that people don't even realize they are colluding in them. This is a book about hope, about understanding, about education and awareness, about commitment, and about humanity. As Arundhati Roy recently said, "Another world is not only possible, she is on her way. On a quiet day, I can hear her breathing. . . ."[3]

Notes about the Second Edition

In the ten years since the original research was conducted, much has changed yet much has remained quite the same or in fact actually has become more difficult for most people. This second edition reflects recent opinion data as well as updated statistics. While most of the original analysis still holds, there are several new developments and ways to understand the reality of race in U.S. and global society in the year 2010. Post-racial? Most decidedly not. However, there are some differences in levels of willingness to engage in discussion about the structural and embedded nature of white supremacy.

There is certainly a broad sense that there is some sort of problem with the way society is organized though most people are not so sure what that problem exactly is nor what is to be done. The dynamics of racial antagonism have somewhat changed such that the "black-white" polarity is less prominent, primarily evident in discourse that continues to specifically pathologize and criminalize the Black experience. Negative stereotyping particularly of Latino immigrants and anyone of Arab, Muslim, or Middle Eastern descent has increased dramatically. These ideological frames are widespread and increasingly adhered to by all racial groups and the public at large. Race has become more focused on "immigration," "terrorism," identity and as a proxy for poverty despite the realities faced by most all people in the United States. These issues have been historically present in the discourse about race, but have become primary points of reference.

So are we facing the "perfect storm" in which demography, economics, and organizing among ordinary people provide the means for truly challenging the structural basis of the racial hierarchy? Is the historical world capitalist system truly at the end of its cycle, occurring simultaneously with a crisis in U.S. hegemony, and heightened instability of white supremacy? How will ordinary people, particularly whites, respond to these realities, at this moment in time? The mechanisms for sustaining historical patterns have multiplied, yet so have the "cracks" in the wall of whiteness. As the World Social Forum movement declares, "Another World is Possible" and the United States Social Forum movement calls out, "Another U.S. is Necessary." The future is uncertain; in whose interests will the path lead us? Are you ready for some action?

Melanie E. L. Bush

Acknowledgments

Many people made critical contributions, intellectually and spiritually, to the research and analysis that influenced this work. To acknowledge each and every one by name would not be realistic and to measure one person's role as more worthy of mention than another, impossible. So, as Tato Laviera beautifully stated, "With every word I write, I give thanks to fifty people," and that is easily an underestimate![1] I express tremendous gratitude to all of you.

For this second edition, acknowledgement first goes to all those noted in the first edition. You continue to be the foundation and inspiration for everything I do. I reiterate very special and profound appreciation to Rod and Sarafina, Mom, Dad, Ethan, Aunt Honey and Alfreda Adams, Raj and Athena, and the Bush, Tillman, Craddock, Levine, Okome, Chin, Tenemas-Chavez, Grant, Culley, Lee, Starr, Parker, Walters, Forsh, Zhang, Patterson, Lopez, and Finch families.

To all the many colleagues, students, and friends at Adelphi University, thank you so much for your support. In particular, Donna Truong, Lakeisha John, Mashal Hamidi for your research assistance and general support, the entire Sociology and Anthropology Department, Muriel Herring, and all those who patiently listened to me talk endlessly about this project over the last year and a half, for your encouragement. To name you all would take the whole book! To all involved with the Adelphi Collaboration Project, for your inspiration. To students who were in classes with me over the period during which I worked on the second edition, I hope you see your thoughts, ideas, and generosity reflected in this revision.

Much appreciation goes to those at Brooklyn College and in CUNY who provided unending support with the original and revisit research by providing information, access to classes, and encouragement.

Great appreciation is given to the many scholars who have been incredibly generous with ideas, feedback, and references and who provided the theoretical frameworks within which my thinking developed. If there was one person to thank it would be Leith Mullings, whose scholarly insight and moral wisdom guided the analysis. She provides an extraordinary role model as an engaged intellectual. She challenged me when my thinking or writing was lazy and has been a life anchor in so many different ways. I owe significant intellectual debts to many people, including though not limited to Elizabeth (Betita) Martinez, Immanuel Wallerstein, James Jennings, Joe Feagin, Manning Marable, Robin D. G. Kelley, David Roediger, Rose Brewer, and Steve Steinberg.

Thanks to the CUNY Dispute Resolution Consortium, the Hewlett Foundation, and Adelphi University for grants that made the research possible.

To Sarah Stanton and everyone at Rowman & Littlefield Publishers for patience in the book revision!

To all acknowledged in the first edition and many more this time round, thank you for taking this project and my ideas seriously. To everyone who gave generously as participants, supporters, critics, and intellectual and spiritual boosters and friends, for knowing we can make a difference and that we must, I acknowledge you and express deep appreciation for your support. Much gratitude and respect for all those named and unnamed.

Thank you all, profoundly.

1

The Here and Now

American Idealism . . . has always existed in a paradoxical linkage with greed, an alarming tolerance for social injustices and the racial blindness that allowed the same mind that shaped the Declaration of Independence to condone slavery.

—*New York Times*, editorial, 31 December 1999

The economic and political changes that occurred between the 1960s and the first years of the twenty-first century provided the social context, in the United States and globally, for the shift in public opinion from an assumption of collective responsibility for the common good and toward a belief in the social survival of the fittest. This book analyzes the role of race, racialization, and racism within this framework and in the process of uniting and dividing ordinary people. The second edition includes discussion of the changes in reality and in perception in the years that followed (2001–2010).

To what extent did the transitions of the late twentieth century that brought an end to the Second Reconstruction[1] and undermined the bargaining power of an increasingly global workforce also lead to an acute sense of white victimization, as is often portrayed by the media?[2] Has that changed in the last decade? What does it mean to be "white" in the twenty-first century? What role does the educational system play in shaping beliefs and attitudes about race and society; what role should it play?

Using research conducted first in 1998–2000 and then in 2009 at a college within the largest urban public institution of higher education in the nation, this book explores beliefs and attitudes about identity, privilege, poverty, democracy, and intergroup relations, illuminating the connection between everyday thinking and the institutions, policies, and programs that structure society. Examining views of ordinary people, I outline numerous mechanisms and dynamics of power that generate and reinforce dominant narratives about race and support structural hierarchies, as well as "cracks in the wall of whiteness" or potential opportunities to interrupt these processes.

EVERYDAY THINKING MATTERS

At the "United Nations World Conference against Racism," in 2001, Gay McDougall, chair of the Commission to End Racial Discrimination, was asked, "Who is responsible for racism and how do we change people's minds?" She responded: "Racism is more than about how one person treats another; racism is imbedded in our systems. It is not about changing minds; it is about changing institutions. We need to get beyond attitudes and get to the structures that have been in place from one generation to the next" (Secours 2001b).

However, I argue that the critical relationship between racial attitudes and social structures desperately needs to be examined if historical patterns of systemic racial inequality are to be challenged and overcome. It seems logical that heightened awareness of the expanding polarization of wealth over the last four decades among ordinary whites might influence their views about the root causes of sustained racial inequality. They themselves increasingly face the consequences of the economic constrictions of the base and the explosion of a part-time, temporary, and service-oriented workforce. Over 50 percent of workers say they are living paycheck to paycheck (Rivera et al. 2009, v) up from 25 to 30 percent just a decade ago (Schor 1998, 20).[3] Poor, working- and middle-class whites are experiencing economic pressures related to global restructuring that African Americans and Latinos have suffered for over two decades (Price 1995, 19).

"Roughly 40.3 million households spent more than 30 percent of their incomes on housing in 2008, while 18.6 million of these households spent more than half—up from 13.8 million in 2001."[4] In 2008, average pay for corporate executives soared to nearly 344 times that of the average worker (Anderson et al. 2008, 1). "An in-depth study in 2004 on the explosion of CEO pay revealed that, including stock options and other benefits, CEO pay is more accurately $500 to $1" (DeGraw 2010b). Wealth and income disparities between racial groups have been exacerbated by policies and practices such as sub-prime lending and housing foreclosures that have disproportionately affected communities of color. The current recession has already been experienced by many "Blacks in the US as a depression that, in terms of unemployment, equals or exceeds the Great Depression of 1929" (Rivera et al. 2009, iii).

Where do most whites place blame for the economic insecurity they are experiencing? Do they feel discriminated against, as white people? Dr. Jack Levin, director of the Brudnick Center on Violence and Conflict at Northeastern University, suggests that many do and that this resentment has led to an increased incidence of racially driven hate crimes on college campuses. He writes, "It's a defensive position from the point of view of these students, who are what used to be the proto-typical college student: white, male and Protestant. Now they have to share with people who are different—Black, Latino and Asian students—and they don't like losing their advantage and privilege" (Lords 2001, 10). The election of Barack Obama did not halt these incidents. In fact, some report an increase in hate crime, more than half involving race (Dervarics 2008). Exploring these questions allows us to better understand the way that ordinary whites think about the role of race in everyday life that perpetuates longstanding racialized patterns in workplaces, schools, housing, and other aspects of public policy.[5]

Increasing attention has been paid in the last few decades to addressing dynamics of race by examining "whiteness," a compilation of institutional privileges and ideological characteristics bestowed upon members of the dominant group in societies organized by the idea and practice of pan-European supremacy. This has been done through studies of racialized imagery (Chito Childs 2009; Yancy 2008; Morrison 1992; hooks 1995; Dyer 1997; Fine, Weis, Powell, and Wong 1997; Nakayama and Martin 1999), everyday thinking (Picca and Feagin 2007; McIntosh 1992; Wellman 1993; Feagin and Vera 1995; Frankenberg 1997; Shipler 1997; Lipsitz 1998; Berger 1999; Williams, L., 2000), theoretical notions of the construction of whiteness (Smith 2007; Saxton 1990; Allen 1994; Brodkin 1994; Roediger 1994, 2002, 2005; Ignatiev 1995) and structural patterns such as in schools (Leonardo 2009; Pollock 2008), cities (Shaw 2007), and the law (Haney-López 2006). Much of the recent literature has taken an explicitly anti-white supremacy or anti-racism stance (Tochluk 2008; Smith 2007; Harvey, Case, and Gorsline 2004), though with varied analyses and remedies. Scholar Joe Feagin has developed the concept of a "white racial frame" to describe the embeddedness of white supremacy in the development of a racialized United States. He explains that the use of stereotypes, metaphors, images, emotions, and narratives both emanate from and support systemic racism (Feagin 2009).

By linking the consciousness of ordinary people (particularly whites though not exclusively) and structural patterns of inequality, this book bridges the theoretical concepts, lived experiences, and implications of a racial hierarchy. The social reality of "race" (institutions, systems, structures) could not be maintained without widespread support for and/or complicity with ideological justifications for the system that places whites *as a group* in a distinctively higher position than all other racial groups along nearly all indicators of socio-economic status. Drawing on the beliefs, attitudes, and ideas of those who participated in this research, I outline fourteen mechanisms that reproduce racialized structures of power by eliciting ideological loyalty from ordinary people. I also describe nine "cracks in the wall of whiteness" that provide opportunities to challenge the racial status quo.

EQUALITY: MISPERCEPTION OR REALITY?

Why do most whites believe we have achieved racial equality in the United States, while social and economic measures indicate otherwise? A study conducted jointly in 2001 by the *Washington Post*, Henry J. Kaiser Family Foundation, and Harvard University found that 40 to 60 percent of all whites believe that the average Black is faring as well or better than the average white and that "African Americans already have achieved economic and social parity" (Morin 2001, A1). Since then, whites increasingly indicate they believe that we have achieved racial equality. In a poll conducted in January 2009 by the *Washington Post* and ABC News, 76 percent of whites reported that Blacks have achieved racial equality, or will soon achieve it.[6] Furthermore, 81 percent of whites reported that Blacks who live in their community have as good a chance as whites to get housing they can afford; 83 percent said Blacks in their community have as good a chance to get a job for which they are qualified (*Washington Post*-ABC News Poll 2009).

In another poll conducted in 2009 by CBS and the *New York Times*, 62 percent of whites versus 44 percent of Blacks thought both races had equal opportunity. Roughly 25 percent of whites versus 51 percent of Blacks said that whites have a greater chance at getting ahead. This difference in perception needs to be understood in relation to social, economic, and political indicators for these two communities. A report entitled "The State of the Dream 2009," published by United for a Fair Economy, indicates that 24 percent of Blacks and 21 percent of Latinos are living in poverty, versus 8 percent of whites (iii); median household incomes of Blacks and Latinos are $38,269 and $40,000, respectively, while the median household income of whites is $61,280 (18, 19). Only 18 percent of people of color have retirement accounts, compared to 43.4 percent of their white counterparts (23). On the *median*, for every dollar of white wealth, people of color have fifteen cents.

On average, people of color have eight cents for every dollar of white wealth (28) (Rivera et al. 2009).

What explains the differences in perception between Blacks and whites? Why are there such vast misperceptions by both groups about existing levels of inequality? The gap between the perception of equality and the reality of inequality has real consequences. One's degree of awareness about structural realities plays an integral role in everyday decisions made on the job, at the polls, in schools and stores, and in the choice of housing (Lipsitz 1998; Secours 2001a). If someone believes we have achieved equality, he or she is less likely to support measures to address inequality. To the extent that whites are aware of inequality, their beliefs about the underlying causes are significant.

For example, while housing segregation between whites and Hispanics and between whites and Asians exists, it does not appear to be due to negative beliefs about those communities. On the other hand, whites appear to avoid living in neighborhoods with more than a small Black population because they associate Blacks with high crime, low housing values, and low-quality education (Emerson, Chai, and Yancey 2001, 932).

In the range of 10 to 15 percent Black residents (in a neighborhood), whites state that they are neutral about the likelihood of buying a house. Above 15 percent Black, whites state that they are unlikely to buy the house. The strength of this stated unlikeliness increases with increases in the percentage of Black residents . . . even after responses are controlled for the reasons typically given for avoiding residing with African Americans (Emerson, Chai, and Yancey 2001, 931–32).

According to the 2000 Census, whites are more likely to be segregated than any other group (California Newsreel 2003, 19). In 2009, white households with children were indeed more segregated from Black, Hispanic, and Asian households than white households overall. Poor white households tend to display the highest levels of dissimilarity particularly with corresponding poor households of other racial and ethnic groups. White households with children are the least likely to live in integrated neighborhoods though the authors state that their study does not reveal whether whites chose the area because of services or race/ethnicity of the community (Iceland et al. 2009, 16).

When levels of inequality are misperceived, structural realities such as poverty become associated with communities of color as if they are cultural characteristics. This translates to a belief that there is no need for institutional redress through programs such as affirmative action. Racism is viewed as a problem of interpersonal relationships and not related to system-wide patterns that differentially position whites and people of color. The logic of discourse about "reverse" discrimination makes sense in this context because discrimination is analyzed ahistorically and out of the broader social context whereby redress can compensate for structural patterns.[7]

In other words, when decisions and actions are based on misperceptions, there are consequences. Formal research has been conducted on white attitudes toward Blacks on a regular basis since the first national survey in 1942 by the National Opinion Research Center at the University of Denver (now at the University of Chicago) (Smith and Sheatsley 1984, 14). The 2001 *Washington Post* survey found that whites who hold more accurate views of Black circumstances are more likely to believe the government has social obligations. These include the responsibility to ensure all schools are of equal quality (69 percent of whites with accurate views versus 57 percent of whites with misperceptions) and the responsibility to ensure that all races are treated equally by courts and the police (79 percent of whites with accurate views versus 60 percent of whites with misperceptions) (Morin 2001, A1). Table 1.1 provides additional information about gaps between perceptions and reality, in three domains.

Not only has there been no decline in the Black–white income gap, in 2004, a typical Black family had an income that was 58 percent of a typical white family's (Isaacs 2007) while in 1974, median Black incomes were 63 percent those of whites.[8] The proportion of Black per capita income today to that of whites is strikingly similar to the initial counting of Black slaves in the Constitution: three-fifths that of whites (Sklar 2003a, 56). In addition, whites are twice as likely to have money invested in stocks, bonds, or mutual funds and half as likely to have reported recent difficulties in paying their rent or mortgage (Morin 2001, A1).

Table 1.1   Whites' Perceptions of Racial Equality

Percentage of whites who hold perception	That the average Black compares to the average white in relation to:	Reality
61	Equal or better access to healthcare	Blacks are nearly twice as likely to have no insurance
49	Similar levels of education	17% of Blacks have completed college versus 28% of whites
42	Similar earnings	Black median income $27,910, 50% under $25,000; white median income $44,366, 30% under $25,000

Source: Richard Morin, "Misperceptions Cloud Whites' View of Blacks," *Washington Post* Final Edition (11 July 2001), A1.

Compounding these misperceptions is the notion that we are in a post-racial society and no longer need to calculate the racial impact of policy decisions, legislation, and programs. However, "when elected officials consciously consider racial impacts during the lawmaking and budget-setting processes, they have the opportunity to eliminate existing racial disparities and prevent unintended consequences" (Johnson 2010, 2). Given that how people think underlies how they act, it is critical to understand how beliefs and attitudes develop.

"WHITE BACKLASH" AND RACIAL CODING

These misperceptions directly relate to the sentiment among some whites in the United States (commonly termed "white backlash") that the liberal social policies established during the 1960s pandered to Blacks to the detriment of the well-being of whites. This perspective asserts that anti-colonial and anti-imperialist struggles for freedom and justice and against white supremacy, U.S. global domination, and hegemony went too far (Winant 2001, 148). Calling upon the United States to live up to its ideals was one thing; making those ideals a reality was another.

Although this type of white resentment surfaced in the 1960s, the civil rights movement, war on poverty, and discourse about the "Great Society" created an environment where social responsibility and expanded, democratic participation were encouraged. Society engaged in a widespread debate about the nature of poverty and the ideals on which the country was founded that led to "the elaboration of social policies based on vastly expanded notions of equality, democracy and social justice. . . . A mature global liberalism held sway, promising the spread of the good and then the great society to all Americans and eventually to all who followed our example and leadership" (Bush 2001).

This environment left many whites conflicted about their allegiances, yet the economy was still in a period of expansion, so white anger about the advances of Blacks, Latinos, and Asians did not dominate. It was not until the mid-1970s that their sense of victimization and resentment began to crystallize. "The emergence of conservatism as a political and intellectual force in the 1970s and 1980s was an important turning point in post-World War II American politics. Prior to the 1970s, conservatives had a limited influence in the shaping of domestic policies and programs. There were influential conservatives, but no dominant ideology that shaped political life" (Stafford 1992, 101).[9]

In the mid-1970s, working- and middle-class whites began to experience layoffs and the reconfiguration of their economic and political lives as the period of economic constriction commenced that extend into the crisis evident today. This experience led many whites to seek explanations for why they have such a difficult time staying afloat. Without the means to explicitly express feelings of blame, racialized coding has become a routine part of mainstream discourse. This allows for plausible deniability against claims of racism. An *Atlantic Monthly* cover story entitled "When the Official Subject is Presidential Politics, Taxes, Welfare, Crime, Rights or Values, The Real Subject Is Race" (Edsall 1991, 53–86) analyzed this coding as it developed. "In this cryptic vernacular we have a new and insidious form of race-baiting that is so well camouflaged that it does not carry the political liabilities" (Steinberg 1995, 214). However, "much of the way that race matters in politics occurs via a process of 'racial coding'" that influences voting practices (Bobo and Charles 2009, 253).

During this period, mainstream discourse flaunted images of successful Blacks and often portrayed interracial friendships as commonplace. Articulated particularly in media and political debates, this development provided some positive images of Blacks in contrast to the predominantly stereotypical depictions as criminals and athletes; however, these images also have had a detrimental influence. Numerous movies and television shows suggest that race in the United States is mediated solely through personal relations and that racial inequality and racism is a thing of the past. Early examples include *The Cosby Show*, *The Jeffersons*, *Forrest Gump*, *Pulp Fiction*, *White Men Can't Jump*, *Webster*, and *Diff'rent Strokes* (DeMott 1995, 12–13). More recent films include *Guess Who?*, *Daddy Day Care*, *Corrina, Corrina*, and *Hitch*, many of which involve interracial relationships (Chito Childs 2009).

At a time when historical and structural explanations for racial inequality are not readily accessible to the public at large, the perception of a wallet as a gun and the implicit acceptance that racialized fear justifies murder[10] stand as dramatic testaments to the continuing significance of race. The issue at hand is not solely whether people interact in a civil manner, nor whether we all "get along." Rather, this book focuses on everyday processes and discourses of power, linking agency and structure within a political and economic framework. Henry Giroux, author and scholar, said:

> There are too few attempts to develop a pedagogy of whiteness that enables white students to move beyond positions of guilt or resentment. There is a curious absence in the work on whiteness regarding how students might examine critically the construction of their own identities in order to rethink whiteness as a discourse of both critique and possibility. (Giroux 1997)

I do not however, subscribe to the notion that our primary task is to forge a positive white identity, because if race was constructed as a tool to dominate and subordinate, how can we render it positive? I focus on questions of

agency and optimism, process and structure, while recognizing simultaneous, contradictory, and sometimes competing forces as they are articulated
in everyday life.[11]

Social life *is* competitive for most people under capitalism.[12] For poor,
working- and middle-class whites, the desire for an upper edge flows from
a material sense of insecurity.[13] Media and popular discourse suggests that
their vulnerability is due to the increasing numbers and standard of living of
Blacks, Latinos, and Asians and not to the increasing power and wealth of
the rich though "The increase in incomes of the top 1 percent of Americans
from 2003 to 2005 exceeded the total income of the poorest 20 percent of
Americans. . . . This growing concentration of income at the top . . . had been
under way for more than 25 years" (Johnston 2007).

This book sheds light on a range of mechanisms that construct mainstream
narratives to explain history from the perspective of the rich and powerful,
hiding the material and structural realities faced by most people regardless
of community.[14] Studies comparing Blacks' and whites' attitudes about race
often conclude that divergent perceptions exist. Dissimilarities in attitude
are described as isolated differences of opinion and rarely are compared to
actual data. They less frequently offer an analysis about the reasons for, or
significance of, the disparities. The following excerpts demonstrate this point:
"*New York Times* and CBS News conducted a national survey in June 2000 to
ascertain the attitudes of Blacks and whites on the issue of race in America"
(Sack and Elder 2000). "It was concluded that even after the dismantling of
legal segregation thirty-five years ago, today Blacks and whites continue to
have starkly divergent perceptions on many issues pertaining to race and they
remain largely isolated from each other in their everyday lives" (Horton 2000,
35). Newer studies more often address the question of why the disparity in
perception exists.

Some suggest that the gap reflects the use of different reference points
for analysis (how far we've come or how far we have to go) (Eibach and
Ehrlinger 2006), or emanate from a notion of zero-sum possibilities for
equality between groups (Eibach and Keegan 2006). Others have found that
"people who were lower in prejudice perceived that less racial progress had
been made compared to those who were higher in prejudice . . . [and] more
strongly anchor their perceptions of racial progress on how far the US has
to go to achieve equality in the future" (Brodish, Brazy, and Devine 2008,
523). In this case, the difference in perceptions influences individual opinions
toward policies such as affirmative action.

It is also important to compare perceptions to realities as this allows us to
understand how patterns of inequality persist through the use of ideological
narratives that justify the status quo. When we expose the actual state of

racial inequality in society, both a "mechanism" and a "crack" are exposed. For example, when structural factors that underlie patterns of poverty and wealth within particular racial groups are mystified, it is difficult to challenge them. Identifying this mechanism and demystifying these systemic factors can provide the means to interrupt the patterns and transform the racialized structures.

POLITICAL AND ECONOMIC
TRANSITIONS IN THE PUBLIC SECTOR

This book focuses particularly on academia; however, similar racialized patterns can be found in the public sector overall, such as in health care, transportation, social services, libraries, and the justice system. For example, funding of prisons has directly increased in proportion to a decrease in funding to higher education; correspondingly, the jail and prison population of the United States has nearly quadrupled since 1980 at a cost of $25,000 a year per prisoner (Sklar 2003a, 56). Nationally, net cost at public four-year colleges grew from 39 to 55 percent of median family income from 1999–2000 to 2007–2008, for the lowest income quintile (The National Center for Public Policy and Higher Education 2008, 10). One might wonder whether a constricting job market for college graduates might have anything to do with these shifts (Romer 1999).

"From 1996 to 2005, government spending on criminal justice related expenses increased by 64 percent. . . . In 2005, the United States spent $213 billion on the criminal justice system. . . . By way of comparison, in 2005, state and local governments spent less than $42 billion on housing and $192 billion on higher education." "This was during a period when crime rates dropped to the lowest they have been in 30 years" (Petteruti and Walsh 2008, 7). "Between 1977 and 1999, total state and local expenditures on corrections increased by 946 percent—about 2.5 times the rate of increase of spending on all levels of education (370 percent). Researchers from Post Secondary Opportunities found that between 1980 and 2000 . . . corrections' share of all state and local spending grew by 104 percent and higher education's share of all state and local spending dropped by 21 percent" (Page, Petteruti, Walsh, Jason Ziedenberg 2007, 7). This is particularly significant since it is well documented that states with higher levels of educational achievement have lower rates of violent crime. "Of the 10 states that saw the biggest increases in higher education expenditure, the violent crime rate declined in eight of the 10" (ibid.). In a society organized by race, funding for criminal justice rather than education has significant racial consequences.

Furthermore, in 2003, the City University of New York senior colleges were funded at fifty-five percent of SUNY (State University of New York) state-operated colleges when compared on a full-time-equivalent student basis (FTE), down from 81 percent in 1990. In a Professional Staff Congress report to the CUNY Board of Trustees in November 2006, it was revealed that 72 percent of CUNY students were people of color, compared to only 19 percent at SUNY. This difference, taken in the context of the disproportionate population of persons of color within the corrections system makes quite an extraordinary statement about the disparate way that funding is allocated by race, intentionally or not.[15]

That the median income of whites is $55,096 versus $34,001 for Blacks and $40,766 for Hispanics, exposes the true nature of this racial discourse.[16] There is not now, nor has there ever truly been an even playing field on which motivation could ensure success society-wide. Rhetoric calling for personal responsibility in striving for upward mobility serves only to reinforce images of lazy and unmotivated, frequently criminal Blacks and Latinos. As the data demonstrate above, spending money on prisons rather than schools calls into question the integrity of that discourse.

It is this connection between the impact of racially discriminatory policies and practices on the lives and dreams of communities of color *and* the fate of our society as a whole, that motivated this study. The individualist creed that underlies the capitalist ethic and inspires a philosophy of social survival of the fittest has a devastating effect on all people. Whites more frequently than other groups support mainstream explanations often because of the material benefits they receive from the system (however small) and because even if they are poor, there is a stronger belief that they too can one day achieve the "American Dream." To this notion, James Baldwin once said:

> But this cowardice, this necessity of justifying a totally false identity and of justifying what must be called a genocidal history, has placed everyone now living into the hands of the most ignorant and powerful people the world has ever seen. Moreover, how did they get that way? By deciding that they were white; by opting for safety instead of life. (Baldwin 1984, 92)

CONCERN FOR THE COMMON GOOD AND THE FUTURE OF US ALL

By incorporating the language of standards, merit, individual responsibility, and civility, racially coded language provides justification for de-funding of the public sector and maintaining more privileged populations as the main beneficiaries of public higher education. To what extent do whites accept these explanations? How aware are they of the vast economic changes that have occurred since the 1970s both in the United States and globally? Heightened awareness of globalization allows us to become more cognizant of how our past, like our present, is embedded in a history larger than our own and how the institutions, processes, and values that have shaped U.S. history arise out of global processes (Foner 2003, 35).

The increasingly concentrated wealth at the top has resulted in the constriction of social programs and access to resources for all people and certain groups especially. Ideological explanations are drawn upon to justify these changes. During a period when the *rapports de force* have provided the social and political milieu for a move to the right, the successful de-funding of the public sector (Giroux 1997), and the dismantlement of the welfare state, what is on the minds of ordinary people, particularly whites?

This book therefore examines dominance and privilege rather than subordination or underprivilege. Studies about race generally presume that a discussion about race is about the "other." Whiteness is assumed, considered the norm and the center. However I examine ways that whites participate in maintaining status, and access, rather than explanations for social inequality based on the cultural deficits of the poor that have been so widely discussed since the 1960s (Glazer and Moynihan 1963; Lewis 1966; Valentine 1968; Leacock 1971). The findings seek to contribute to the literature on race by providing insight into how whiteness influences day-to-day perceptions about society, ultimately reproducing racialized patterns in everyday living. The current experience of those classified "white" needs to be examined within the context of fundamental historical transformations that include economic pressures, an extended period of conservative ideological onslaught, and increasingly limited opportunities for nearly all people.

The idea that upward mobility and the American Dream can be achieved by anyone who works hard has become less secure. Instead, some communities have been depicted as lazy, unworthy, the cause of everyone's troubles (including their own), and beyond the scope of our concerns. Many people have lost hope in the possibility of liberal reform. Historically whites have been and are currently being seduced to an ideological position that defends the status quo and the polarization of wealth and does not challenge the vast inequalities that have been exacerbated in the global economy. With a belief that, following Eric Wolf, "historical processes are pre-eminently political and economic, reinforced through ideology" (Schneider and Rapp 1995, 3), the research done for this book set out to measure the effectiveness of this campaign in the present context and offers an analysis of the implications for academia, based on the findings.

WHY HERE, WHY NOW?

Schools, and the domain of education, provide groups with different types of knowledge that ultimately function to reproduce a social division of labor. They distribute and legitimate forms of knowledge, values, languages, and style that constitute the dominant culture and its interests and act as part of a state apparatus.[17] Finally, they produce and validate economic and ideological imperatives that underlie the state's political power (Giroux 1983, 258). A vivid example of this process as it is articulated in school achievement can be found in data indicating, "Among youth from the top quartile, 42–44 percent graduated from college, as against only 6–9 percent of youth in the bottom quartile, a gap of more than 35 percentage points."[18] (Haveman and Smeeding 2006, 131). Related to funding, in 2006–2007 differences in total revenues per pupil ranged between the 5th ($7,740) and 95th ($22,653) percentiles of districts with median spending $10,754 (Zhou and Johnson 2009, 4) revealing how structural inequality patterns itself into the educational system. At the same time,

> To understand modern universities and colleges, we need openness to contradiction. For universities both reproduce and subvert the larger society. We must distinguish between the functions universities publicly promise to perform—the social goods they are chartered to produce—and certain of their actual consequences that, while commonly unintended, are no less real: the production of dissent, deviance, and the cultivation of an authority-subverting culture of critical discourse. (Gouldner 1979, 45)

The next four chapters explore these issues through the perspectives of the hundreds of people who participated in this research. Chapter 2 focuses on understandings about identity. How do students see themselves and each other; how is identity conceptualized? What is whiteness or blackness, and what does it mean to be Latino, Asian, or Jewish? What is the process by which people are classified? First recollections of "a thing called race" are explored as well as how identity manifests within campus politics. Chapter 3 summarizes students' thoughts about what it means to be "American," their beliefs about democracy, the flag, the foreign-born experience, national identity, and the relationship of race to these topics. The chapter examines students' beliefs about assimilation and the American Dream.

Chapter 4 explores how students interact with each other. Whom do they associate with on campus, and with whom do they socialize outside of campus? How often have they been in the home of someone of another race? Do they perceive social segregation on campus or racial tension? What are the rules for interaction? These questions are addressed as the chapter examines students' beliefs about colorblindness, human nature, and interracial relationships. Chapter 5 examines how poverty and wealth are theorized in everyday conversation. In what contexts do whites question dominant narratives, and when do they uphold mainstream explanations for why "things are the way they are," such as poverty and inequality? Do students believe whites are discriminated against in today's world? Do they believe everyone has a fair chance, and if not, do they think measures should be taken to equalize opportunity? Do they view education as a right or as a privilege solely for those who merit advancement? Do they think society ought to get "tough on crime"? This chapter analyzes students' views about equality and justice in today's society.

Finally, chapter 6 provides an analysis of what people had to say about these questions, outlined in three sections. I suggest fourteen mechanisms and sites through which patterns of racialized inequality are perpetuated and identify nine "cracks in the wall of whiteness": places, spaces, and times when we can make a difference through an analysis of the meaning of white racial consciousness at this moment in time. In conclusion, the chapter offers recommendations for higher education in particular, education in general, and society at large to increase awareness about the role of race in everyday living and offers possible trajectories for future research.

This book is an attempt to understand and shed light on the everyday thinking of whites in order to demonstrate how common ideas function to reproduce racialized patterns of inequality and render structural causes and outcomes invisible. For example, the issue has been raised that the gap between whites' perceptions of equality and the actual existence of inequality is sustained by misinformation, a lack of accurate information, regulated ideological discourse, and a sense of hopelessness. However, how does it happen, in everyday interaction? What are the mechanisms that produce, reproduce, and reinforce mainstream narratives that defuse and disempower the agency of ordinary people? What can be done to address this dynamic?

This book explores, therefore, the appearance of two nations, separate and unequal (Hacker 1992; Shipler 1997), and asks whether this is a random act of mysterious blindness (you know, "shit happens") or whether multiple processes and mechanisms convey the notion that poverty is "natural," especially the kind patterned along lines of race. Mainstream explanations about why certain people (and groups) are poor tell us it is because "they" are "less smart," "genetically weak," "lazy," "angry," "greedy," "violent," and "unmotivated." Could these justifications actually reflect manipulation? Just because I'm paranoid, it doesn't mean no one's following me. Does it matter whether these depictions are deliberately orchestrated to elicit racial loyalty and maintain the economic order?

In a society founded on power on the one hand, and built upon democracy and equality on the other, it is not just that there are two worldviews. One represents the replication and reproduction of power relations, and the other represents the opportunity for a better, more just and equitable world for all.[19] This book focuses how it happens that, while the majority of whites do not fall within the category of the richest one percent, they take on a worldview that supports that group's interest and frequently contradicts their own material reality.

The goal of this research was to further our understanding of the racial dynamics in the United States and support the development of strategies that challenge the pervasive inequality and injustice that continue to plague the United States and the rest of the world. To what extent have we indeed achieved a "post-racial" society? Where is agency located for whites who observe contradictions in the mainstream narrative? How might we strengthen our efforts toward a more racially and socially just and humane world order? How might we reclaim the ideals that so proudly define the United States as a nation, only this time truly actualize the notion that "all people are created equal"? Howard Winant writes:

> Today, racism must be identified by its consequences. Racism has been largely—although not entirely, to be sure—detached from its perpetrators. In its most advanced forms, indeed, it has no perpetrators; it is a nearly invisible, taken-for-granted, commonsense (Gramsci) feature of everyday life and global social structure. Under these conditions—racial hegemony—racism may be defined as the routinized outcome of practices that create or reproduce hierarchical social structures based on essentialized racial categories. (Winant 2001, 308)

RACE, ETHNICITY, AND WHITENESS

> The discovery of personal whiteness among the world's peoples is a very modern thing—a nineteenth and twentieth century matter, indeed. But what on earth is whiteness that one should so desire it? Then always, somehow, some way, silently but clearly, I am given to understand that whiteness is the ownership of the earth forever and ever, amen.
>
> —W. E. B. Du Bois 1920, 29–30

The concept of whiteness has been recognized over the last several decades as a means to address a significant and missing dimension within discussions of race and ethnicity. However, notions of white racial identity have long been significant in the writings of scholars of color. Among the many examples include, William J. Wilson, who in 1860 wrote "What Shall We Do with the White People?" analyzing presumptions of whiteness in the Declaration of Independence and during the early years of the United States as a nation (Roediger 1998, 58). Similarly, Frederick Douglass critiques the centering of the white experience in his famous speech, "What to the Slave Is Your Fourth of July?" (Douglass 1970, 349). In 1861, Harriet Jacobs describes the annual practice of "muster," a time when armed whites terrorized the enslaved population in anticipation of revolts. She suggests that this institution served to unite whites across class lines (Roediger 1998, 336). In 1891, Anna Julia Cooper examined the naturalization of whiteness in the women's organization Wimodaughsis (Cooper 1998, 88). However, "discounting and suppressing the knowledge of whiteness held by people of color was not just a by-product of white supremacy but an imperative of racial domination" (Roediger 1998, 6).

WHAT IS "WHITENESS"?

The concept of whiteness has powerful utility as a means to critique systemic patterns of racial inequality. It reveals the ways in which whites benefit from a variety of institutional and social arrangements that often appear (to whites) to have nothing to do with race. Being white has generally been associated with ancestry from the European continent and the denial of African blood. The borders of whiteness have shifted during different periods in history to include or exclude various groups. Many immigrants of such ancestry have enjoyed exceptional achievement upon their integration into U.S. society (Brodkin 1998). However, the claim to European heritage is often less significant than whether one is identified as white in everyday interactions (Alba 1990, 3). By enlisting in this pan-ethnic "club," whites "became party to strategies of social closure that maintained others' exclusion. . . . That the once swarthy immigrants from southern, eastern, and even northern Europe eventually became white, is another way of saying that 'race' is an achieved, not an ascribed status" (Waldinger 2001, 20).

Many controversies have emerged about the concept of whiteness. These relate to terminology, the origins of racialization, and levels of individual, institutional, social, and collective responsibility for racial inequality. A key debate is whether whiteness should be reformed as an identity or abolished as an assumption of privilege (Roediger 1994; Ignatiev and Garvey 1996; Kincheloe et al. 1998). Many scholars have called for interdisciplinary studies of this concept, which has shown significant contemporary saliency as a topic for investigation.[20] This is particularly so as the boundaries of racial classification shift, precipitated by twentieth-century population migrations as well as political and economic transformations within the global world system.

Race and Ethnicity Theory

Theories about race and ethnicity provide the framework within which the study of whiteness has emerged. This section reviews the history of the concepts of race and ethnicity and summarizes how this idea of "whiteness" developed over time.

The initial emergence of the notion of pan-European racial superiority and the system of racial hierarchy, exploitation, and oppression has been pinpointed to over six hundred years ago with the appearance of capitalism (Cox 1948, 322). It is true that "civilizations were recognized as distinct constellations of socio-cultural formations for thousands of years prior to the rise of the modern, colonial, capitalist, Eurocentric world-system" (Bush 2009, 5). Anibal Quijano suggests that globalization is the "culmination of a process that began with the constitution of the Americas and colonial-modern Eurocentric capitalism as a new global power" for which the social classification of the world's population around the idea of race was fundamental (Bush 2009, 5). While contact and interaction across geographically distinct populations occurred during earlier times, there is no evidence of race prejudice even in the Hellenistic empire, which had extended further into Africa than any other European empire (Cox 1948, 322). St. Clair Drake describes the sixteenth century as "a historic watershed in global relations between Black and white people," and states that neither racial slavery nor systemic white racism existed prior to this, although color prejudice was present in some places (Drake 1987, xxiii).

While interethnic interactions have a long history, they did not necessarily reflect inevitable conflict, competition, or struggle (Smedley 1998, 690). Identities were constructed by a wide range of characteristics including, but not limited to, place of birth, language, kinship, religion, or occupation. They were generally context-specific and malleable up to the seventeenth century (Smedley 1998, 691, 692). Furthermore, Drake found that, up to the seventeenth century, blackness was not a stigma, nor was race essentialized in the way that it later came to be (Harrison 1998, 620, 621).

With the emergence of capitalism, the colonial exploration of the globe, and the beginning of the slave trade between Africa and parts of the "new" world, racial notions began to take hold as an expression of pan-European hegemony. They were used to justify the subordination and exploitation of large numbers of people who formed a labor pool for building settlements and cultivating the land. During the earliest period in the development of capitalism, "the white man had no conception of himself as being capable of developing the superior culture of the world—the concept 'white man' had not yet its significant social definition—the Anglo-Saxon, the modern master race, was then not even in the picture" (Cox 1948, 327).

Racial dynamics, however, quickly developed within the context of the expansion of capitalism and colonial settlements. This process initially took the form of a European center with Euro-dominated colonies. Ultimately, the British settler colony of North America evolved into the United States, which then became the new center (Drake 1987). A vivid example of this process of racial development was the fateful Bacon's Rebellion in 1676 in Virginia, which established boundaries distinguishing between Africans, Europeans, and native peoples (Zinn 1995, 37–59). This event is generally portrayed solely as a response to common exploitation and oppression, as African and European bond-laborers rebelled to demand an end to servitude. However, another key component of this struggle was an orchestrated attempt by the dominant elites to drive a wedge between these groups and the native population. Any combination of these forces was a tremendous threat to the white planters, whose wealth was great compared to that of the general white population. Poor Europeans had much more in common with enslaved Africans, and a potential alliance could have been disastrous for those in power. "In the early years of slavery, especially, before racism as a way of thinking was firmly ingrained, while white indentured servants were often treated as badly as Black slaves, there was a possibility of cooperation" (Zinn 1995, 37).

The plantation bourgeoisie responded to the threat of coalition by offering European laborers a variety of previously denied benefits, such as amnesty for those who rebelled, corn, cash, and muskets for those finishing their servitude, the right to bear arms, and the opportunity to join slave patrol militias and receive monetary awards. "They constituted the police patrol who could ride with planters, and now and then exercise unlimited force upon recalcitrant or runaway slaves; and then, too there was always a chance that they themselves might also become planters by saving money, by investment, by the power of good luck; the only heaven that attracted them was the life of the great Southern planter" (Du Bois 1979, 27).

This may be viewed as the nation's first "affirmative action" policy (Harrison 1998, 621). These actions were taken to quell this potentially dangerous alliance and as a means for control. Racism on the part of poor whites became a practical matter (Zinn 1995, 56). The explicit use of race and white supremacy was implemented as a tool to divide and conquer. Prior to this period, there was little advantage and therefore little motivation for poor whites to ally themselves with the ruling powers. At this time, though, they were accorded "social, psychological and political advantages" calculated to alienate them from their fellow African bondsmen (Morgan 1975, 331–33, 344; Du Bois 1979, 700). In other words, racism was implemented as a means of control to establish and maintain intact the structure of social organization.

Racial domination became encoded in the process of nation-state building for the United States as "Blacks were sold out to encourage white unity and nationalist loyalty to the state" (Marx 1998, 267). Slavery, therefore, played a critical role in providing a justification for the unification of whites racially as a nation (Marx 1998, 267), a pattern that continues to impact national identity, notions of whiteness, and formulations of race in society today.

Whites were told that their whiteness rendered them "superior," and to maintain this status they needed to place their allegiances with those in power who had the resources and could divvy up benefits. While particularly applied as a black–white polarization, this ideological formulation of race was also flexible. A stigma of racial inferiority could be invoked as needed to maintain divisions and enforce a social hierarchy. For example, during the mid-nineteenth century, Chinese workers were used as the primary labor force in building California's railroads. They were brought to the Americas as replacement workers for enslaved Africans, sometimes using the same ships that bought people from Africa (Zia 2000). Their subsequent brutalization, subjugation, and exclusion were framed overwhelmingly in racial terms (Smedley 1993, 268). This stigma was similarly applied to native and Mexican peoples who were characterized as savages, unfit to own and govern their land "coincidentally" at the time that those lands were desired by the wealthy elite. The "Trail of Tears" and the annexation of one-third of Mexican land are brutal testaments to this history of internal colonization, land appropriation, and genocide.

Throughout the eighteenth and the early nineteenth centuries the formation and consolidation of working-class whiteness (Roediger 1999, 14) was founded not just on economic exploitation but also on racial folklore (Du Bois 1970). Du Bois describes this dynamic eloquently:

> It must be remembered that the white group of laborers, while they received a low wage, were compensated in part by a sort of public and psychological wage. They were given public deference and titles of courtesy because they were white. They were admitted freely with all classes of white people to public functions, public parks, and the best schools. The police were drawn from their ranks, and the courts, dependent upon their votes, treated them with such leniency as to encourage lawlessness. Their vote selected public officials and while this had small effect upon the economic situation, it had great effect upon their personal treatment and the deference shown them. (Du Bois 1979, 700, 701)

Throughout the eighteenth and nineteenth centuries, various theoretical trends emerged in the social and biological sciences to further justify the ordering of the world. These included Linnaeus's classification by descent (The Great Chain of Being), Cuvier's racial categorization that sorted humans into three subspecies (Caucasian, Mongolian, and Ethiopian) with differing permanent abilities, and a series of other typologies that attributed various characteristics to the classifications they named. "These models created a new form of social identity as the concept of 'race' developed as a way to rationalize the conquest and brutal treatment of native populations and the institution of slavery" (Smedley 1998, 697). During the following period the issue of origins (polygenist versus monogenist) was debated, providing the context for Charles Darwin's *On the Origin of Species* (1859), which demonstrated there were no permanent forms in nature (Banton 2000, 57).

By the mid-nineteenth century, virtually all whites in the United States had been conditioned to this arbitrary ranking of peoples, and racial ideology had diffused around much of the world, including to the colonized peoples of the Third World and among Europeans themselves (Smedley 1998, 695).

The Twentieth Century

The end of the nineteenth century and first half of the twentieth were marked by two significant U.S. Supreme Court decisions concerning the Fourteenth Amendment that[21] signified important shifts in the racial order within the United States (Baker 1998, 2). In 1896, *Plessey v. Ferguson* codified the practice of "separate but equal," and in 1954, the *Brown v. Board of Education* ruling overturned it. Dominant theories of social Darwinism and later writings on cultural relativism paralleled these events (Baker 1998, 3), even as these events contributed to shaping the direction of social science concepts. "The social context from which turn-of-the-century constructs of race emerged—industrialization, poll taxes, public lynching, unsafe working conditions, and Jim Crow segregation—at the same time gave rise to a professional anthropology that espoused racial inferiority and, as a consequence, supported and validated the status quo" (Baker 1998, 3).

The turn of the century marked a period of contestation about who was to be included in the category designated "white," as a huge influx of immigrants from Europe and other parts of the globe tested the boundaries of citizenry and racial identity. Paralleling the pace of immigration at the end of the nineteenth century, the first decade of the twentieth century witnessed the largest number of immigrants (8.8 million) admitted into the United States (Kraly and Miyares 2001, 47). The vast majority (92 percent) of these people originated from Europe.[22]At issue was the question of how they would be integrated and racially designated in U.S. society. The nation's expanding industries needed labor; mass immigration made cheap labor easily available. Immigrants were exploited but also "used as an instrument for more effective exploitation of others, whether native or immigrant. For this reason, immigrant workers were sometimes compelled to put aside their ethnic loyalties" (Steinberg 2001, 38). African, Asian, and Mexican workers were used as a low-paid labor source for the least skilled jobs and sectors and established the infrastructure for industrialization and modernization. European immigrants worked primarily within the modern industrial sector that strategically provided them with opportunities for upward mobility (Blauner 1972, 62). This reality challenges the popular notion that all Americans "start at the bottom" and work their way up the ladder. The racial labor principle designated a different bottom for different groups (Blauner 1972, 62, 63). At the same time, up to nearly the mid-twentieth century, white ethnics, particularly Jews, Italians, and Irish, were not fully accepted as whites, but neither were they designated Black.

In social theory, the first half of the twentieth century brought further developments in the understanding of race and ethnicity. Franz Boas's study of immigrant head shape called into question the presumption of the immutability of race and laid the groundwork for the later writings of Ruth Benedict, Margaret Mead, and Melville Herskovits (Smedley 1993, 278). While justifications for anti-immigration legislation were articulated in language about the inferiority of immigrant stock as demonstrated by their physical frailty, Boas asserted that physical differences between immigrants and native-born populations disappear after these groups live in the same environment. During this period, Du Bois significantly contributed to the paradigm shift in the social sciences toward recognition of the connection between race and the concept of culture, united in an understanding of economics and politics (Baker 1998, 107–10). He described race as a social relationship, integral to capitalism, and the ultimate paradox of democracy constructed to reinforce and reproduce patterns of systemic inequality (Du Bois 1986, 372). "Back of the problem of race and color, lies a greater problem which both obscures and implements it: and that is the fact that so many civilized persons are willing to live in comfort even if the price of this is poverty, ignorance and disease of the majority of their fellowmen: That to maintain this privilege men have waged war until today" (Du Bois 1953, xiv).

From Biological to Social Scientific Explanations of Race

During the first half of the twentieth century the usage of an ethnicity-based paradigm to understand social relations in the United States emerged as an extension of challenges made to biologistic and social Darwinist conceptions of race (Omi and Winant 1994, 12). Ethnicity was offered as a way to describe the process of group formation using a focus on culture and descent rather than biology and on the process of migration and the adaptation of immigrants in the United States. In 1913, Robert Park of the University of Chicago, a leading theorist within this group, asserted that by their second generation, Poles, Lithuanians, and Norwegians were indistinguishable from native-born Americans (Schaefer 1995, 111). Park projected that ethnicity would dissolve as immigrants integrated into society and that there was a pattern of integration into U.S. society, which he labeled the "race relations cycle." This involved stages of contact, accommodation, assimilation, and amalgamation achieved through intermarriage (Steinberg 2001, 47). Park considered all modern nationalities to be a mixture of several groups.

According to this idea, ethnicity was expected to disappear into a new "American" culture. This period marked a new stage in the consolidation of whiteness as a racialized category such that European Americans were transformed into a pan-ethnicity that represented the distancing of individuals from their national origin, heritage, and language, and being grouped as "white" (Alba 1990, 312). Two books in particular drew attention to the primacy of race within the social relations of U.S. society and signaled a paradigm shift from the belief in biological to cultural explanations of racial difference.

In 1945, *Man's Most Dangerous Myth: The Fallacy of Race*, by M. F. Ashley Montagu, a physical anthropologist, asserted: "The idea of 'race' was not so much the deliberate creation of a caste seeking to defend its privileges against what was regarded as an inferior social caste as it was the strategic elaboration of erroneous notions, which had long been held by many slaveholders. What was once a social difference was now turned into a biological difference, which would serve, it was hoped, to justify and maintain the social difference" (1945, 20). Gunnar Myrdal's *American Dilemma* (1944) put forth a call for racial democratization, emphasizing the need for the assimilation of African Americans. Myrdal wrote, "If America in actual practice could show the world a progressive trend by which the Negro finally became integrated into modern democracy, all mankind would be given faith again—it would have reason to believe that peace, progress and order are feasible. America is free to choose whether the Negro shall remain her liability or become her opportunity" (Myrdal 1964, 1021–22).[23]

Myrdal's study became "the blueprint for state-based racial reform in the post-war era, strongly influencing debates about segregation and the runner-up to the *Brown* decision" (Winant 2001, 158). His suggestion that racism revealed a contradiction between American ideals and practice was considered a major advance at the time it was written. It later became apparent that this work marked a shift in emphasis from a biological focus to the social scientific notions of cultural inferiority still evident today (Steinberg 2001, 265).

SOCIAL SCIENTIFIC THEORIES OF POVERTY

The next phase of race and ethnicity theory was marked by Glazer and Moynihan's publication of *Beyond the Melting Pot* (1963). The authors asserted that immigrant groups do not "melt" into U.S. society but are transformed into new social forms based on political interests rather than on culture or heritage (Omi and Winant 1994, 18). New communities were unlike each other and unlike those from where they migrated. Moynihan and Glazer argued that the United States had developed a pluralist model that acknowledged differences but emphasized cooperation. By the 1970s, they spoke of ethnicity as a social category that allowed contemporary forms of group expression based on distinctiveness and, in turn, provided an opening to demand rights based on the group's character and self-perceived needs (Glazer and Moynihan 1975, 3).

Beyond the Melting Pot examined five ethnic groups in New York City and implied (sometimes explicitly) that the American commitment to progress and achievement was justly and equally apportioned. The book asserted that inherent cultural norms, ideology, and values led to the success and progress of one group but not another. Structural relations of the social system were neither considered nor deemed significant in their analysis (Mullings 1978, 11). In this way, Moynihan and Glazer equated the histories and rationalized the social inequities experienced by Jewish, Italian, and Irish immigrants ("ethnics"), Puerto Ricans, and African Americans.

While the concept of the "undeserving poor" had long been established, deriving from the period of early capitalism when pauperism was the fate of large numbers of people who forfeited their land and were displaced to the city, it was during the 1960s that the phrase "culture of poverty" emerged. In formulating this framework, Oscar Lewis compares groups of people who are poor, and whom he characterizes as having negative traits, values, and norms, to those who were poor but do not appear to have such negative attributes. He writes, "The culture or subculture of poverty comes into being in a variety of historical contexts. Most commonly it develops when a stratified social and economic system is breaking down or is being replaced by another, as in the case of the transition from feudalism to capitalism or during the industrial revolution" (Lewis 1961, xxv).

Lewis states elsewhere that the causes and consequences of poverty are a direct result of the total social system, in particular, industrial capitalism (Lewis 1969, 190–91). He asserts that the structure of society is the most important factor in the perpetuation of poverty. Lewis's description of the characteristics of what he called the "culture of poverty" included a high degree of family disintegration, disorganization, resignation, and fatalism. Unfortunately, his work was used as a justification to blame individuals and groups exhibiting these characteristics and to justify inequality through an explanation of the inherent cultural weakness of the poor (Lewis 1969, 191) rather than as a means to critique the system within which these character-istics appear. This (mis)interpretation of Lewis's work parallels the underly-ing assumptions, particularly about the weakness of the African American culture, in Moynihan and Glazer's writings (1963) as indicated above and in Moynihan's later writings (1965) about a "tangle of pathology" character-izing Black families with negative, self-perpetuating values. These theories functioned to bolster mainstream discourse that continued to emphasize the superiority of whites and white (ethnic) culture and the inferiority of African Americans and Latinos in particular. Eleanor Leacock's critique of this theo-retical trend emphasizes that groups have different histories. Adaptive acts are institutionalized as internalized values appropriate for living in a given position in the socioeconomic system. She writes, "Poverty, as a structural feature of our society, cannot be changed by a change of attitudes only" (Leacock 1971, 34).

The dynamics shaping mainstream discourse from the late 1960s to the mid-1970s were complex. Liberal public officials had long used "damage imagery" that conveyed negative portraits to argue for policies and programs to help the poor (Scott 1997, xvi–xvii). Simultaneously, many groups and individuals were calling for a new vision of society based on social equality and justice for all and concern for the common good. This led to the characterization of this period as a "Second Reconstruction." The prevalence of the culture-of-poverty framework reflected a conservative influence that sought to command the parameters of thinking about the poor in an attempt to limit the power of a vision of society concerned with the common good, so well articulated by many popular movements of this period (DiLeonardo 1999, 59; Steinberg 1999, 222). The ruling elite was clear about what was at stake should structural factors responsible for the unequal organization of society be revealed.[24]

Theoretical notions of the culture of poverty have remained a central part of public discourse. In the 1990s, this concept was utilized in attacks on the public sector and debates about welfare and higher education. Issues of standards and merit have been raised without the language of race, yet imply cultural deficits of Black and Latino communities and implicitly presume white superiority.

Another explanation for group differences that reemerged during the 1970s is the concept of ethnicity. While previously employed in discussions about the process of assimilation, this notion had not been consolidated as an explanation for differences in social position between "white ethnics," "model minorities," and other communities of color. This marked the emergence of oblique cod-ing of race in literature, media, and discourse, allowing racialized policies and practices to function without the bluntness of explicit language. After all, who would argue against upholding "standards" for education or measures to make our communities "safe," or disagree with the need for "family values"?

During the late 1960s, "momentum built within white ethnic neighborhoods to the extent that their concerns and grievances demanded the attention of the society at large" (Ryan 1973, 1). "Partly it [was] a consequence of the growing discontent among white ethnics with their socio-economic position in America, partly it was one facet of the broader movement toward self-definition on behalf of many groups within American society. . . . It is in part a reaction to the social and political upheavals of the 1960s compounded by the inflationary economic spirals which followed" (Ryan 1973, 1). The white ethnic position accepted the civil rights demand for outlawing discrimination, but not if it called for proactive or affirmative measures (Glazer and Moynihan 1963, 17; Omi and Winant 1994, 19). This perspective asserted that, "through hard work, patience and delayed gratification, etc. blacks could carve out their own rightful place in American society" (Omi and Winant 1994, 19) and thereby echoed the culture-of-poverty argument from the perspective of white pan-ethnicity. During this period, ethnicity theory arose as a dominant paradigm. Ethnic identification by whites was constituted in a form of "white backlash" against the social programs that were set up as part of or as a result of the Civil Rights Act (1964), Voters Rights Act (1965), Immigration Act (1965), War on Poverty, and the Welfare Rights and nationalist movements of the 1960s. White ethnics (partially funded by the government as Heritage Societies) asserted that they too, suffered, and should be the recipients of social programs to address inequality in the United States. Rather than the disappearance of ethnicity, there was resurgence and a demand for the recognition and acceptance of white ethnic groups as a political force.

It is ironic that, although the antipoverty and civil rights programs and policies were portrayed as benefiting Blacks and Latinos exclusively, in fact, many white ethnics (particularly women) also benefited. For example, 75 percent of students initially admitted through the Open Admission Policy in the City University of New York were white ethnics who were the first in their family to attend college (Ryan 1973, 164; Lavin, Alba, and Silberstein 1979, 69). Information such as this was muted in the public discourse as the "new ethnicity" movement took strong stands against such programs and demanded resources for their own groups. Emphasis was placed on ethnicity as the primary classification for discussing groups as carriers of culture. These ideas then influenced the discourse about rights, equality, democracy, community self-definition, and resistance.

By the mid-1970s, Moynihan and Glazer had reevaluated some of their own earlier thinking and put forth what is known as a "bootstraps model"

(Omi and Winant 1994, 21). While this model recognized the injustice of slavery and racism, it articulated the idea that successes and failures of specific groups are a result of different norms that they brought to bear in dealing with circumstances they faced. Little else is deemed relevant, including the economic climate, the reigning ideological stance of benign neglect, or the existing social structures within which all groups exist (Omi and Winant 1994, 22). Black, Latino, and Asian ethnic or national categories are not viewed as notable (e.g., whether someone's family is from Haiti or Ethiopia; Peru or the Dominican Republic; China or India), whereas a white ethnic classification is considered significant (Omi and Winant 1994, 22). Ethnicity generally asserts an upward distinction in status, whereas race signifies a downward distinction since whiteness is assumed to be "natural," and not "raced."

In *Ethnic Dilemma, 1964–1982*, Nathan Glazer writes that while the 1960s legislation intended to lead us to a colorblind society, it actually increased color consciousness in the United States and forced institutions to pay an increasingly high level of attention to race and ethnicity (Glazer 1983, 3). He argues that this legislation led to more discrimination and division, not less. This perspective has been a central and underlying presumption of the anti-affirmative action argument that has gained steam over the past twenty years and to the emergence of calls for "colorblindness." Glazer asserted that the laws of the 1960s were the wrong solutions to the problem of discrimination and that the expenditures of the early 1970s were ineffective. His writings signaled another political shift to the right and a further attack on measures intended to equalize resources such as school integration, affirmative action, and various social welfare programs. This trend has continued throughout the past two decades, with continuing consolidation of the conservative agenda articulated, for example, by the Project for a New American Century and parallel polarization of wealth worldwide.

CRITICAL RACE THEORY

In the late 1970s, along with critiques that examined the intersection of race, class, and gender, and power and dominance in general, a body of work developed among legal scholars of color, including Kimberle Crenshaw, Mari Matsuda, Richard Delgado, Charles Lawrence, and Derrick Bell. This "1980s generation of liberation scholarship [that] came to be known as 'Critical Race Theory'" (Matsuda et al. 1993, 5) asserts that new discussions about race are needed to address racism as endemic to life in the United States and globally. Collectively, their work is "pragmatic and utopian," seeks to "respond to the immediate needs of the subordinated and oppressed," and involves "both action and reflection" (Matsuda et al. 1993, 3). Critical Race Theorists believe in the privileging of contextual and historical descriptions and attempt to "confront and oppose dominant societal and institutional forces that maintained the structures of racism while professing the goal of dismantling racial discrimination" (Matsuda et al. 1993, 3). This tradition expresses skepticism toward dominant claims of neutrality, colorblindness, and objectivity, insists on context, and is interdisciplinary and eclectic. The basis for their theoretical assertions is the recognition of experiential knowledge: "Critical Race Theory works toward the end of eliminating racial oppression as part of the broader goal of ending all forms of oppression . . . [and] measures progress by a yardstick that looks to fundamental social transformation . . . not just adjustments within the established hierarchies, but a challenge to hierarchy itself" (Matsuda et al. 1993, 6–7).

Over the past decade, these scholars have contributed broadly to the study of social stratification as shaped by inequality based on race. An important aspect of this intellectual movement is an emphasis on race in order to eradicate injustice, not solely as identity politics concerned with the recognition of difference (Ford 1999, 105). This perspective analyzes race and racism through a critique of power and thereby contributed to the formal emergence of whiteness studies because the focus became the system itself and not solely the consequence of systemic patterns. This work is framed in this tradition.

WHITENESS SCHOLARSHIP AND STUDIES

Discussions of the "souls" and "ways" of white folk (Du Bois 1991; Ellison 1970; Hughes 1990) have long been part of the intellectual tradition interrogating the role of race in U.S. and global society. David Roediger's *Black on White: Black Writers on What It Means to Be White* (1998) documents this rich history. Implicit in these works is the importance of understanding not just how whites view "others" but the very meaning of being "white," as racialized attitudes presume representation of one's self (hooks 1995, 31–50). "Sincere fictions" and ideological constructions lead to self-characterization as a "good person" or "non-racist" or "colorblind," all the while individuals hold beliefs and support positions that presume an assumption of white superiority (Feagin, Vera, and Batur 2001, 186). Racist sentiments are not solely articulated as prejudice; they are also expressed as culturally sanctioned beliefs. A system of self-deception and denial holds these contradictions in place (Wellman 1993, xi, 29) such that "the obsessive denial that race matter(s) was obviously a white creation" (Lazarre 1996, 25).

During the last several decades another body of literature has emerged with whiteness as the central theme. This includes a number of works that shed light on the dynamics of white supremacy and racialization; although they may not have "whiteness" as their focus, they significantly help us theoretically understand the processes that historically and currently underlie white racial construction. Such works provide the framework within which this book is situated.

While much of the scholarship does question and challenge the naturalization of whiteness and the corresponding assumption of privilege, dominance, and hegemony, not all of the literature is directed toward this end. There is no agreement, for example, about whether white racial identity should be deconstructed, reconstructed, or eliminated, or about how changes might take place. Furthermore, much of the literature focuses on identity rather than structural change. The next section of this chapter notes various trends and emphases in current analyses addressing such questions.

LABOR HISTORY AND POLITICAL ECONOMY

Writings about labor history and political economy are among the most significant and substantive contributions to our understanding of whiteness. The works of Theodore Allen and David R. Roediger are especially notable. Allen traces the origin and nature of the "white race" and how this concept was utilized as a means of social control, in *The Invention of the White Race: Racial Oppression and Social Control* (vol. 1, 1994) and *The Origin of Racial Oppression in Anglo-America* (vol. 2, 1997). He documents the context within which Bacon's Rebellion occurred, and discusses prior and subsequent periods when ruling-class policies created and reinforced racial oppression, drawing upon analogies from the history of British rule in Ireland. Roediger, on the other hand, provides a framework for understanding the relationship between the economic benefits and social construction of whiteness.

In *Wages of Whiteness: Race and the Making of the American Working Class*, he traces how, when, and why "being white" became so important to workers included in this designation (Roediger 1999, 5). Ultimately, he argues that whiteness "was a way in which white workers responded to a fear of dependency on wage labor and to the necessities of capitalist work discipline" (Roediger 1999, 13). In other words, "the pleasures of whiteness could function as a 'wage' for white workers . . . status and privileges conferred by race could be used to make up for alienating and exploitative class relationships . . . fashioning identities as 'not slaves' and as 'not blacks'" (Roediger 1999,

13). His analysis provides the historical background for understanding present-day formulations of white identity by showing how racial hierarchy was established and implemented throughout the course of capitalism's development as a world system. He shows how the patterns of social organization discussed here were structured from the very beginning periods of European expansion and then U.S. nation building.

The history of European immigrants as they underwent the process of racialization between the late eighteenth and twentieth centuries is summarized in another notable work, *Whiteness of a Different Color* (1998) by Matthew Frye Jacobson. He particularly focuses on the ambiguity and shifting nature of racial categorization and how it serves divergent political purposes at different times. The book also provides critical background for understanding the current racial order as he documents how the development of pan-ethnic whiteness shifts with the need for labor and/or the political necessities of the elite, to allow the flexibility to incorporate or exclude different groups. Historians provide insight into the complex and sometimes contested development of "pan-ethnic" whiteness in the twentieth century (Roediger 2005) and a nuanced understanding of the emergence of "white" people as an expression of power in the course of history (Painter 2010).

WHITENESS AS IDENTITY

Several works analyze whiteness from the perspective of individual experience, generally exploring how race shapes the lives of a particular group of whites, often counterpoising race and class or race and gender. In *The Social Construction of Whiteness: White Women, Race Matters* (1993) and *Displacing Whiteness: Essays in Social and Cultural Criticism* (1997), Ruth Frankenberg draws on life history interviews of women to analyze "the daily experience of racial structuring and the ways race privilege might be crosscut by other axes of difference and inequality" (1993, 1). She concludes that, in order to displace the colonial construction of whiteness as an empty cultural space, we need to analyze the position of whiteness in the social order.

Lorraine Delia Kenny's *Daughters of Suburbia: Growing Up White, Middle Class and Female* (2000) examines the intersection of race, gender, and class, combining "auto-ethnography" with an analysis of high-profile media images of white teenage girls such as Amy Fisher.[25] Kenny focuses on the process of racial identity formation among middle-school girls in a white suburban setting, and how they come to see themselves as the cultural norm. She suggests that whiteness requires silences in order to function, although she primarily focuses on the individual experiences of this particular group of white teenage girls. She alludes to a "mechanism" that perpetuates racialized patterns, although she doesn't describe it as such.

Racial Situations: Class Predicaments of Whiteness in Detroit (1999) by John Hartigan Jr., and White Trash: Race and Class in America (1997) by Matt Wray and Annalee Newitz present ethnographies that articulate the relational functioning of dominance and subordination along these two axes. These authors focus on experiences of individuals, particularly poor whites, rather than on structural aspects of relationships; they advocate a positive reconstruction of white identity, rather than a society-wide transformation. They promote the "White Trash Girl" persona—implying that whites, too, can and should be proud of their cultural identity.

Cultural Representations of Whiteness

The most widely recognized critique of whiteness as displayed in popular culture, media, and public representations forms appears in works such as Toni Morrison's Playing in the Dark: Whiteness and the Literary Imagination (1992) and bell hooks's "Representations of Whiteness in the Black Imagination" (1995). These groundbreaking writings provide incisive depictions of the meaning of whiteness and its "hidden" centrality within all aspects of modern life. Morrison describes her project as "an effort to avert the critical gaze from the racial object to the racial subject; from the described and imagined to the describers and imaginers; from the serving to the served" (Stowe 1996, 71). In her article hooks describes the amazement of her white students as they discover that "Black people watch white people with a critical 'ethnographic' gaze" (1995, 34). These works follow the long-standing tradition of scholars of color who assert the importance of understanding whiteness.

In Yurugu: An African-centered Critique of European Cultural Thought and Behavior (1994), Marimba Ani explores the cultural influences of European-dominated societies on institutions and structures. She describes key elements of European experience and expression that have historically provided the means for imperialistic success, not based on military might but through colonization of people's cultures, religions, aesthetics, notions of identity, and ideology. Ani writes, "European culture is unique in the assertion of political interest" (Ani 1994, 7). She explains this, saying that European thought presumes its own logic, superiority, universalism, and natural state, thereby describing the cultural origins of consciousness and worldview under capitalism that set the stage for global white supremacy. Ani provides a critical analysis of the underlying tenets of mainstream ideology.

Various works explore relationships between white, Asian, and Latino identities, locations, and borders in a racialized society and help interpret the perspectives of research participants. These include, for example, *De Colores Means All of Us: Latina Views for a Multi-Colored Century* (1998), by Elizabeth Martinez, who deconstructs the origin myths of the United States, and *Forever Foreigners or Honorary Whites? The Asian Ethnic Experience Today* (1998), by Mia Tuan, who points to the subtle and not so subtle ways that Asians are excluded in U.S. society except when they are needed as "model minorities" (Tuan 1998, 161).

Constructions of Whiteness

Documenting legal, economic, and political processes related to the negotiation of whiteness are books such as *White by Law: The Legal Construction of Race* (1996) by Ian F. Haney Lopez, *White by Definition: Social Classification in Creole Louisiana* (1994) by Virginia R. Dominguez, and *Making Race and Nation* (1998) by Anthony Marx. These works argue that the judicial system functions as a powerful mechanism for the regulation of society and plays a central role in the social construction of race (Lopez 1996, 9). Lopez illustrates the contingent, fluid, and transient nature of whiteness by analyzing immigration cases where people from Hawaii, China, or Burma were excluded, those from Mexico and Armenia were included, and those from Syria, India, and Arabia were sometimes included and sometimes excluded. Dominguez documents how the parameters of white identity are constructed through historical processes of legal classification of white, Black, and Creole identity. Marx compares the histories of South Africa, Brazil, and the United States, explores the significance of racial encoding in state actions, and recognizes the influence that social movements have had historically in challenging established patterns (Marx 1998, 269–81).

Karen Brodkin's *How Jews Became White Folks & What That Says about Race in America* (1998) and Noel Ignatiev's *How the Irish Became White* (1995) examine the transformation of particular European immigrant communities that were not initially accepted into white, Anglo-Saxon society. These books document the particularities, opportunities, and trade-offs that specifically Jewish and Irish communities experienced and negotiated as they accepted the status of white pan-ethnicity. Ultimately, however, they articulate different visions: Ignatiev calls for the abolition of whiteness, whereas Brodkin seeks for us to build a multiracial democracy. These are important differences, although both works contribute substantively to our understanding about how whiteness has been produced and reproduced in U.S. society.

In an interesting edited volume of essays from the 30th Annual American Italian Historical Association (AIHA) Conference (1997), the essay that most clearly analyzes Italian American ethnicity through a critique about racialization and whiteness states: "What makes contemporary American society interesting, but not unique, is the simultaneous operation of contradictory myths. These cultural and structural paradoxes emerge from the ongoing dialectical social discourse as each myth calls forth its anti-myth" (Krase 1999, 103).

Whiteness in Pedagogy and Discourse

Interrogating whiteness within pedagogy and discourse are Henry Giroux's "Rewriting the Discourse of Racial Identity: Towards a Pedagogy and Politics of Whiteness" (1997), Lisa Delpit's *Other People's Children: Cultural Conflict in the Classroom* (1995), and Alice McIntyre's *Making Meaning of Whiteness: Exploring Racial Identity with White Teachers* (1997). The authors rightfully target the educational system as a locus where racialized images, beliefs, and ideology are produced and reproduced. They recognize the potential that exists within academia to disrupt patterns of learning that order and rank groups and individuals in a racialized society. Delpit in particular illustrates the dynamics of power in this domain and articulates ways in which positionality determines outlook and success.

Several edited volumes provide interdisciplinary, multilayered analyses about whiteness in local and global settings and allow for multi-vocality. Some emphasize the need to reform whiteness into something positive (*White Reign: Deploying Whiteness in America*, Kincheloe et al. 1998), while others more clearly seek to dismantle structures of inequality through a deepened understanding of power and privilege (*The Making and Unmaking of Whiteness*, Rasmussen et al. 2001). Most include essays that express a range of perspectives such as in *Off White: Readings on Race, Power and Society* (1997), by Fine, Weis, Powell, and Wong. These works analyze racial domination and the consequent formation of white identity; less apparent are the authors' beliefs about how to use whiteness as a theoretical tool to impact structures of institutionalized power.

DECONSTRUCTIONS—WHITE ANTIRACIST STRATEGIES AND CRITIQUES

Providing a framework for my exploration of "cracks in the wall of whiteness" (chapter 6) are several important works that have an explicitly antiracist focus. Well known to whiteness theorists, Peggy McIntosh's "Unpacking the Invisible Knapsack: White Privilege" (1992) has been reprinted extensively because it provides a way to understand how advantages of being white are structured into everyday living. McIntosh identifies "conditions of daily experience that [she] once took for granted, as neutral, normal and universally available" (1998, 100). She says that some of these privileges convey a sense of belonging (from "flesh" colored bandages and "nude" stockings to the dominance of white images in positions of power); other privileges convey protection (such as the presumption of white innocence as opposed to a presumption of Black guilt); still others confer permission to dominate or to not listen to people in less powerful positions. She draws these conclusions through an analysis of gender and heterosexual privilege and dominance and emphasizes the need for a thorough understanding of systems of dominance, in order to reconstruct power on a broader base. In this way, McIntosh makes assumptions of whiteness explicit.

Stephanie M. Wildman takes this notion a step further in *Privilege Revealed: How Invisible Preference Undermines America* (1996) by analyzing the intersection of privilege based on race, gender, sexual orientation, economic wealth, physical ability, and religion, in order to deepen our understanding of systems of privilege that perpetuate the status quo (1996, 5). She asserts that invisible privileges function to maintain hierarchies of oppression and suggests that they should be exposed and challenged.

First published in 1977, David T. Wellman's *Portraits of White Racism* (1993) is based on five case histories and allows us to understand both the personal and the structural bases for racism. Wellman asserts that "racist beliefs are culturally sanctioned, rational responses to struggles over scarce resources" invoked to defend white advantages (1993, 29). While chapters within *White Racism* (2001), by Joe R. Feagin, Hernan Vera, and Pinar Batur, focus on the description of particular racist events that have occurred in the recent history of the United States, the chapter entitled "Sincere Fictions of the White Self" is devoted to an analysis of "personal ideological constructions that reproduce societal mythologies at the individual level" (2001, 186). The authors describe white attitudes about welfare, crime, and affirmative action, analyze the racialized components of these beliefs, and conclude with recommendations for antiracist engagement. Their book is a useful reference to understand everyday thinking.

In the literature interrogating white supremacy and racism are three explicitly activist-oriented antiracist works. Both *Whites Confront Racism: Antiracists and Their Paths to Action* (2001) by Eileen O'Brien and *A Promise and a Way of Life: White Antiracist Activism* (2001) by Becky Thompson document the history of antiracist activists in the United States. O'Brien asserts that while the stories of white activists are generally not well known, the knowledge of their existence and practices is integral to an understanding of participatory possibilities for challenging racism (O'Brien 2001, 2, 3). Thompson traces the relationships of these activists to broad social movements led by people of color, nationally and globally. Both articulate their belief that these individuals and movements represent significant possibilities for future challenges to white supremacy.

The New Abolitionists, known for their journal *Race Traitor*, explicitly call for the abolition of "whiteness" defined as a biological and cultural fiction, a club into which certain people are enrolled at birth. They assert that to consider reforming whiteness as a legitimate identity is dangerous because it provides the basis for right-wing, ultraconservative white supremacists to validate a white-power position as a corollary to national and ethnic pride movements, shifting the focus to personal relationships and "getting along" rather than to political struggle. "It is fortunate that in the nineteenth century they had abolitionists instead of diversity consultants; if not, slavery would still exist, and representatives of slaves and slaveholders would be meeting together—to promote mutual understanding and good feeling" (Ignatiev 1998, 4).

EXAMINATIONS OF WHITENESS AROUND THE GLOBE

Inquiries into the meanings of whiteness around the globe have been especially located within media studies, the humanities and social sciences, and the field of education. More recent work has taken place in performative and communications studies and in the examination of nationhood. Discussions do not necessarily link whiteness to systemic and historical patterns of white supremacy nor to capitalism. These works are particularly multidisciplinary and engage a broader critique of European dominance in the global order, either on the local level or the international sphere.

Some draw on broader critiques of globalization from cultural, economic, and political perspectives (e.g. Allen 2001; Bhattacharyya, Gargi, and Small 2002; Gordon 2003; Levine-Rasky 2002; Leonardo 2002). Others reflect how the examination of whiteness and its post-colonial legacies is particularly apparent in recent work by scholars in South Africa (Kinloch 2002; Steyn 2001), Australia, New Zealand (Anderson 2002; Cowlishaw 1999 and 2004; Hage 1997; Moreton-Robinson 2003), Mexico, Latin America, South American and the Caribbean (Davila 2003; Harris 2006; Langfur 2006), and the United Kingdom (Ware and Back 2002; Bonnett 2000; Gillborn 2006). Joost Cote makes the point that "European imperialism spawned settlements of invasive white communities throughout Asia and Africa . . . the discourse of whiteness transforming a national discourse into a discourse on civilization" (2009, 1). This body of work raises new questions about the relationship of the world capitalist empire as it originated in Europe and developed in the United States, as well as its current manifestations within Asia, Latin and South America, and Africa.

The literature increasingly explores the intersectionality of pan-European supremacy, male supremacy, and the economic order, as well as Christian and heterosexual dominance. These writings examine whiteness as revealed in social patterns and through material evidence. They explore the meaning, implications, and significance of whiteness for the daily lives of ordinary people. Most of the discussions recognize the fluidity of categories and of continuous racial formations and reformulations along with the critical interconnections with other forms of social identity.

These provocative writings provide a better understanding of the "what" and "how" of white supremacy, though perhaps less of the "who" and "how not," spaces of resistance and opposition that represent hope for the future. There is, however, some promise that future work will thread together disparate global analyses of whitenesses past and present, helping to chart possible trajectories for the future.

CONCLUSION

Building upon existing literature and recognizing intellectual debts and forbearers linking everyday white racial consciousness and the mechanisms that reproduce structures of racial inequality, I aim to show the interconnection between economic and political analyses and the lived experiences of ordinary people.

Ethnography Framed in Political, Economic, and Social Theory

Writings about whiteness tend to be either narrative and ethnographic or formally theoretical, addressing issues of legal, political, and social construction of race. Works that examine the experience of "being white" often read as "stories" with weak structural analysis. While engaging, they generally leave the reader with an uncertain sense of the implications of these narratives. This book interweaves the everyday thinking and theoretical context of current events and political transformations during the last three decades within U.S. and global society, although it is framed within the historical social system that spans the last six hundred years.

Emphasis on Economic Explanations for Inequality and Racism

Literature about whiteness does not often discuss the lack of awareness of white people about the factors at work that shape their employment, education, housing, and healthcare opportunities. For example, how did Long Island get to be so segregated? Why are positions of power dictated by whites? Attitudes and beliefs are primarily explained as a consequence of the bombardment of racialized imagery and discourse, particularly from the media. This book explores the implications of this lack of understanding, as expressed through the misperceptions and narratives drawn upon to explain systemic inequality.

While the significant contributions of curricular and co-curricular multiculturalism are not to be negated, they have unfortunately functioned largely to divert our attention from issues of power and subordination that are integrally embedded as forces that shape the possibilities for all people in the United States and globally. Identifying the need to expose and analyze economic and political processes as connected to discourse and consequent beliefs about race is central to my argument about the role of mechanisms in the perpetuation of structural patterns of inequality.

"Mechanisms" for the Reproduction of Patterns of Racial Inequality

Explicitly, how does it happen that many "well-meaning" whites accept mainstream discourse about whether we have achieved racial equality, whether or not individual and collective efforts for change actually can make a difference, and what is the true character of human nature? I emphasize the notion of agency, that is, if people do not believe that they can make a difference and they do not understand the factors shaping their own possibilities, they will be hard-pressed to resist economic, political, and social pressures and more easily succumb to accepting hegemonic arguments for racial and other forms of inequality and injustice. If people believe that it is human nature to stick with "one's own" and to care only for one's immediate circle, the parameters within which they are able to examine, analyze, and determine whether to submit or dissent are structured narrowly and rigidly. The true possibilities for humanity are rendered invisible, and certainly impossible. Yet the inverse can also be true.

Linking Agency and Structure, Everyday Thinking and Institutions, Identifying "Cracks"

At the heart of this book is a firm belief that the everyday thinking of ordinary people integrally relates to the perpetuation of patterns of systemic racial inequality. Therein lies the implicit potential for challenging those patterns and for constructing a more egalitarian and just world. Linking hegemonic discourse and ideology (as practiced primarily though not exclusively by poor, working-, and middle-class white populations) to the safeguarding of the status quo (as shaped and dictated by the most powerful and dominant sector of global society) provides us with critical knowledge of how an unfair and inhumane system can persist. By understanding the beliefs that underlie support for institutionalized policies and programs and the mechanisms that allow these patterns to be replicated and reproduced, we can take action. This book has explicitly sought "cracks in the wall of whiteness" in order to identify where weaknesses exist within the current racial order. This knowledge strengthens our strategic ability to dismantle the formulations of race that have shaped U.S. and global history over the last six hundred years. Without linking agency to structure, we discuss only chickens or only eggs without ever understanding the inherent relationship between the two.

Understanding everyday thinking and recognizing that social and racial consciousness has a direct relationship to the perpetuation and reproduction of patterns of inequality means that we can intervene to alter the dominant narratives about poverty, privilege, race, gender, and almost all relationships of dominance and subordination. The emphasis here is on agency, for if race has been socially constructed, it can also be socially deconstructed.

> The point of historical studies of racial identities in the working class . . . has never been to mount a facile indictment of white workers as simply racist. Rather it has been and is now to understand how historicized racial identities dramatically shaped what workers could do and dream in their lifetimes and how better deeds and dreams can be made possible in ours. (Roediger 1994, 77)

With this grounding in mind, we turn next to a discussion of the ethnographic study conducted to seek answers to the questions raised above.

THE PLACE AND PEOPLE

This section briefly describes the primary location for the ethnographic research and connects the overall political, social, and economic framework with the findings. For the second edition of this book, Brooklyn College was revisited for a mini-study and research was also conducted at a private liberal arts college in the metropolitan New York area to provide insight about similarities and differences within diverse environments. Where included, data from the "revisit" study are specifically noted.

The student population of Brooklyn College (BC) resembles many multicultural urban centers that have emerged throughout the United States over the last several decades. This heterogeneous community roughly mirrors the population of the borough and comprises nearly seventeen thousand students from over one hundred nations, speaking over ninety-five languages.[26] The BC campus thus provided opportunities for generalization, access, and comparison. While the research was conducted at this site, the study is not "about BC." These findings could have been generated similarly in any urban area within the United States. I integrated the findings of other studies into the text so that comparisons could be made. The overall dynamics and relationships between individuals and groups are patterned through dominant structures and narratives throughout the nation.

Brooklyn, the Borough

> It may not be generally known that our city is getting to have quite a worldwide reputation.
>
> —Walt Whitman 1862 (Snyder-Grenier 1996, 1)

In Unity, There is Strength (Motto on the 1898 Borough Seal of Brooklyn)[27]

Bedford-Stuyvesant, Canarsie, Bushwick, Bensonhurst, East New York, Flatbush, and Borough Park—these neighborhoods are diverse when viewed together, homogenous when viewed alone. They are culturally rich, yet many of their residents are poor. Brooklyn is often thought to be violent and full of conflict, yet Brooklynites are reputably proud and cooperative, with a strong sense of history and community.[28] Discrepant images are simultaneously conjured up when talking about the borough. While overall demographics depict a multicultural milieu, most areas reflect a concentration of one group. Neighborhood populations vary so greatly that one (Crown Heights) is 2.2 percent white, yet another (Dyker Heights) is 81.8 percent white.[29] In fact, one-third of all neighborhoods have an 80 percent or greater white concentration and another one-third have a 20 percent or less concentration of whites (BC OIR 1999b).

These images of Brooklyn, the place, reflect the incongruity in notions of whiteness and allude to a disjuncture between the idea of a harmonious multicultural setting and a divided reality.[30] It became clear while doing this research that for some whites whose connection to European ancestry may be one or two steps removed, "Brooklyn" also functions as an ethnic identity, as more than one participant self-described as a "Brooklyn-American."

Writings about Brooklyn reflect this fragmentation by generally focusing on one community or another and tend to describe relationships between them as either peaceful and integrated or hostile and separate. Analyses are characterized by an ethnic rather than racial focus and generally depict isolated communities, rather than diverse peoples who interact in public spaces and then retreat to homogenous "homelands." Much of the literature speaks to a history of tension and conflict between groups but generally does not assess the experiences of commonality or difference in the ways they perceive each other or function on a day-to-day basis. In contrast, the works of Roger Sanjek (1998) and Steven Gregory (1998) examine the dynamic history of racial politics in New York City, drawing on ethnographic work conducted in Queens.

Literature about Brooklyn portrays the contradictory images of the borough's identity. Some works focus on the public sphere and patterns of settlement rather than on the particular experiences of the city's people. New York City, as a whole, is characterized as multiethnic and multiracial, and authors speak repeatedly of the city's reputation for tolerance, diversity, and adaptability. One example is *All the Nations Under Heaven: An Ethnic and Racial History of New York City* (Binder and Reimers 1995), which presents a detailed examination of the many migrations to New York City since 1524—though little attention was given to the role of New York City as an early port for slave ships, or to the pressures placed upon the native populations once Europeans arrived. Recent discoveries at the Lott House in Brooklyn provide further evidence of the complicity and involvement of Europeans in this area with the slave trade, in contrast to popular notions.[31] By focusing on how diversity works rather than on points of contestation, New York City is analyzed through a "white gaze."

As mentioned earlier in this chapter, Brooklyn neighborhood boundaries are defined by race and ethnicity such that a dominant group (or groups) generally characterizes each area. This segregation and corresponding disparities in resources have been a source of historical tension documented by several important works, such as *Canarsie* (Rieder 1985) and *The Closest of Strangers* (Sleeper 1990). Written from a liberal perspective during and after the school decentralization struggle in the late 1960s, both explore the grievances of whites in their relationship with the African American communities. They generally portray racial inequality as if it were due to a mysterious force of history and social tension as a consequence of Black anger.

While the story told here could have taken place in any number of urban institutions in the United States, for purposes of context, I now briefly summarize the recent history of the place where the bulk of this research was conducted.

Brooklyn College, Institutional History

After the Open Admissions Policy was instituted, a relatively large number of faculty was hired to teach the increased number of students. During the budget crisis of the mid-1970s, however, many faculty lines were lost, with few replacement hires until the late 1990s. The impact on the numbers of faculty was so dramatic that, with retirements, deaths, and people leaving for other jobs, the number of faculty of color is estimated to have dropped approximately 50 percent.[32] Another consequence was that by the 1990s the faculty included mostly those whose first years at the college were during the 1960s and 1970s, an era with a social environment very different from that of the students whose thoughts are represented in this book.

Many Brooklyn College students, along with some faculty and staff, played an active role in struggles both on and off campus. Support for Open Admissions was not, however, necessarily universal, as a professor in the English Department, Tucker Farley, describes: "I remember being shocked because I came to Brooklyn College and CUNY since there was Open Admissions. It was 1971. I was shocked to hear people talking about the 'ineducables.' To me, that translated very much in terms of race."[33]

Professor Farley indicated that, while this was not everyone's perspective, she felt it was a common view among faculty. The struggle for Africana and Puerto Rican Studies was also highly contested. While the activism of students resulted initially in the founding of two institutes that subsequently became departments, substantial and continuous struggles occurred, some that persist to this day. At Brooklyn College, "during the struggle for Black and Puerto Rican Studies, students were physically assaulted by racist whites in the cafeteria because these Black and Puerto Rican students had chosen the Studies program as their major" (Jennings 1985, 10).

Of this period, a faculty member of the department of modern languages, William Sherzer, said: "They were rough years, because the campus had to re-define itself—was it a Jewish college like it always used to be? My white, non-Jewish students were as upset often at the politics of the conservative Jews as the blacks were. . . . [They thought] that Open Admissions was going to change this Jewish part of Brooklyn College that we've always had. And I'm not mentioning this as being anti-Semitic—first of all, I'm Jewish."[34]

Professor Paul Montagna of the sociology department described what he felt was the "moderate, liberal, left" nature of the faculty in their support of ethnic studies: "I am supportive, and I was supportive. My department, we have continued our support whenever there seems to be an issue—we can always be counted upon to sign protest statements or whatever."[35]

Professor Farley went on to speak about a later incident: "I remember sitting in the faculty lounge. There was a man in my department who was reading the newspaper the day the cops had shot a young Black boy in Brooklyn mistaking him for, they said, a man who had committed a crime in the neighborhood. I was just grief-stricken, and shocked and he was too. Then I realized that he was taking the point of view of the policeman, thinking how horrible it was to have been the policeman and I was taking the point of view of the parent, thinking how horrible it was to have a child killed. That just blew my mind."

She asserts that while BC has an institutional image of progressiveness, this type of incident was not unusual throughout the course of her thirty years of teaching. She describes an environment that is outwardly, or by public acclamation, open and liberal in the best sense of the word but also one with many tensions residing beneath the surface.

The political environment and concern for diversity at the college has ranged from very to minimally active, from moderate to progressive, and has fluctuated over time. The assessment of institutional commitment and whether the campus is a friendly environment for all students differs depending on who is asked. Historically, significant frustration has been expressed by various constituencies about the lack of attention to this issue.

A FEW COMMENTS ABOUT THE STUDY

In citing participants' comments, I use descriptions given by the individual. Some people spoke of themselves solely as white; others talked specifically about being foreign-born and others described themselves ethnically or in religious terms but not racially. In a few instances students described themselves as "human" or used an identifier different from what they had used in a previous point in the discussion. The criteria I use are rooted in their self-description. A national or ethnic tag, class origin, or age is included only if the individual presented himself or herself that way. While I recognize that there is tremendous political significance in the terms of identity, for the purposes of this book I rely upon what I saw as the most standard formats.

Where particularly relevant, I note whether a focus group was mixed, all white, or consisted of students, all of color. All statements are from students, unless explicitly stated as a faculty or staff respondent. Participants were told that research was being conducted about the experiences and views of students on the role that race plays in their lives, in the lives of people around them. They were informed that the focus was particularly on developing an understanding of white students' experiences. All names are pseudonyms except where individuals granted explicit and written permission.

Many students remarked that they have rarely, if ever, engaged in discussion about these topics. If they had, they said it was with people from their own racial or ethnic group. Several students commented that they felt uncomfortable and awkward because the questions often made them reflect on assumptions of which they were not conscious but decidedly incorporated into everyday thinking and living. Repeatedly, the experience of the focus groups was described as one in which they could hear the perspectives and experiences of students from different backgrounds about sensitive and controversial issues and without concern for penalization from faculty members who might judge what they said. Most students indicated that they had never been in any environment in which they felt they could interact, speak, and listen openly about these issues.

Participant observation of campus activities provided insight into the meaning and tone of interactions between students. These included, for example, community events, such as the taping of a radio program on immigration with several student panelists. In other cases these were campus meetings. I also conducted interviews with seven faculty members who had been at the college for the last thirty years, and I researched archival materials about movements for access, diversity, and self-determination at the college. This material provided background for understanding the college environment, its students, and the ways that various issues have been addressed on campus over time.

SUMMARY

As noted earlier in this chapter, despite a public emphasis on multiculturalism and diversity, the on-campus social and political lives of students are generally segregated. Students enter college with assumptions about racial and ethnic identities, having commonly attended high schools within their own communities.[36] These assumptions are sometimes challenged by the experience of working together in community service projects, classes, or student activities, but they often form invisible lenses that shape interaction.

Conversations often dissipate when differences of opinion emerge. Tensions run deep beneath the surface, as frequently perceived realities diverge between whites and people of color. Whites may try to understand these differences but often blame nationalist leanings of people of color, culture, or even human nature for the tension. This study aimed to document these beliefs and provide an analysis of the implications of general patterns in everyday interactions.

There are several issues that I would like to clarify about the material in this book: the use of a black–white paradigm, the meaning I ascribe to the phrases "ordinary people," "whites," and "everyday thinking," the implicit potential for misconstruing intent or reading things into what someone says, the use of categories (including racial categories) to describe patterns of thinking, and the role that my own identity, racial and otherwise, played as I conducted the research.

Du Bois states, "the concept of race is a group of contradictory forces, facts and tendencies" (1970, 133). Categories shift and populations redefine themselves; census classification is highly contested territory. This project primarily involved reflection upon the everyday perceptions and thinking of those people in the United States defined as white. Because of the particular history of this nation, and because often, although not always, Black and white appear most starkly as poles, there are times when I do not explicitly discuss beliefs and perceptions related to Latino, Asian, native, and mixed populations. Chapter 2 briefly summarizes some of the particularly significant findings related to these groups. However, as whites' attitudes and beliefs are frequently most glaring in relationship to Blacks, the frame of reference is often set in black/white terms (Martinez 1999, 127–29). "In this country as well as in many others, unfortunately, blackness has come to symbolize the social bottom" (Basch, Schiller, and Blanc 1994) and a host of related characteristics (as quoted in Harrison 1998, 612). The legacy of slavery in the United States played a critical role in shaping the notion of race and in its ongoing impact on relationships between groups, therefore providing additional rationale for utilizing a dichotomous framework. While generalizing about patterns found in the beliefs expressed by whites provides useful points for reflection, it is not to convey that all whites share the same beliefs. This terminology refers to the patterning of thinking, beliefs, or experience of whites as a group.

This stands as an acknowledged oversimplification, for there are many relationships of power and dominance that complicate the consequences of a racialized organization of society and are, in and of themselves, critical sites for study. These include but are not limited to immigration status, language, gender, and class, national, and religious affiliation. By analyzing white people's understanding of the everyday experience of race in U.S. society, I hope to provide insight that may be used in theorizing about other forms of inequality. Where possible, I note ways that I believe these other factors influence the perspectives described; however, the focus of this book is on the way that racialized thinking affects beliefs.

The phrase "ordinary people" is used throughout this book to refer broadly to the millions of people who live and work in the United States but who are not in political positions, and/or members of the powerful elite who legislate, determine, and influence policies that structure society. The use of "everyday" thinking, experiences, perceptions, and "forms of whiteness" refers to interactions, beliefs, and actions that occur routinely in daily life.[37]

There is of course in any project the potential for misconstruing the meaning of someone's statements. I have attempted to withhold comment and analysis until after the reader first has the opportunity to reflect upon them. However, "as racism is organized through discursive patterns of signification and representation, it must be investigated through the analysis of discourse" (Wetherell and Potter 1992, 4). "Racism can be the unintended consequence of everyday discourses and practices that perpetuate and reinforce an oppressive structure of power" although this is "not to argue that racism is a simple matter of linguistic practice" (Harrison 1998, 611). For the purpose of this book, I analyze discourse as it "institutes, solidifies, changes, creates and reproduces social formation" (Harrison 1998, 611). In this light, it becomes apparent that racialized thinking occurs not just among whites, but also throughout the society at large.

As language conveys meaning, discussions about race are contested because the very notion itself is one born of struggles about power, privilege, and profit (Baker 2001). I selected the categories for race and ethnicity on the survey because these appeared to be most frequently used in other recent survey materials. In retrospect, I would have separated U.S. and foreign-born for Latinos and Asians, although I chose not to do so because of the smaller percentages of the overall BC population that they represent. I regret this, however, as it limits the comparisons that can be drawn between foreign- and native-born participants.

The term "racialization" is increasingly being used as a means to describe a process in contrast to essentialized categories (Darder and Torres 1998). I also use this term to articulate social meanings of race as opposed to biological and immutable notions, a means to deconstruct relationships of power. While I certainly recognize the multiplicity and the simultaneity of other factors,[38] this project particularly examines the way whites racialize both themselves and everyone else, and how this translates into everyday practice.

A final issue is that of my own identity. At the time of the original study I had been employed at BC for ten years. Despite my specific formal duties, my reputation on campus, I believe, was one of student advocate, counselor, and educator. Throughout this time I actively participated in campus life. All of this, I suggest, functioned in my favor to provide a setting where students felt "safe" to speak. I was conscious of the dynamics of power in my relationships with students and made an explicit effort to acknowledge and elicit concerns so that they might be addressed. I believe my whiteness allowed white students to speak more freely than they might have with a person of color, presuming perhaps that I shared their worldview. My age allowed enough distance to avoid feelings of peer competition.

It is my deepest hope that, by listening closely to the voices of our young people, we might discover opportunities for reconstructing a public understanding of the role of race, today. Organized by issue, the next four chapters provide ethnographic material upon which to reflect. It is my belief that institutional structures are reinforced and can be challenged by the everyday thinking of ordinary folks. I hope this material provides insight about their attitudes and about the possibilities for improving our effectiveness in educating our youth about civic responsibility and the importance of socially conscious leadership, broadly understood to be the millennial goals for academia.

2

White, Black, and Places "In Between"

I'll talk to you, but I don't want another lecture. I know I'm not a racist, so why should I be labeled with something you think defines what I am? I would be happy to take on racists, and I do.

—Joey, white male

What are the definers, parameters, and categories of race? Who gets to choose their identity; who does not? What mechanisms determine and shape how people navigate the racial landscape of everyday experiences? This chapter explores various meanings and implications of racial identification. The first section, "What is Race, Anyway?" examines the experience of "being white" in diverse settings and challenges the presumption that whites who have regular contact with people of color are necessarily more open-minded, aware of racism and the everyday experiences of Blacks, Latinos, and Asians. I suggest that this interaction often actually discourages engagement and reflection, which are deemed unnecessary because there is a belief that one "knows." In what is sometimes called a "post-racial" era, this paradox is of particular importance.

Ambivalences and ambiguities emerge repeatedly in discussions about these issues, as students allude to their awareness of multiple realities. Several conversations provide insight into a tentative voice quality that is sometimes evident when whites speak about race, a mechanism that allows the retraction of one's comments if they are not well received. It also becomes quite apparent that discourse(s) of whiteness are neither "unified nor monolithic" (Kincheloe et al. 1998, 9). Individuals are complex; not all whites hold the exact same set of beliefs. One individual can hold quite divergent beliefs simultaneously. However, the process of generalization provides the means to understand patterns of thinking that influence how people act. While research about race has traditionally centered on analysis of people of color, this book focuses on patterns of thinking among whites, a critical process for anyone interested in understanding and addressing current evidence of racial inequality. Finally, it is also true that while whites as a group more commonly adhere to an ideology of white superiority (both because they have a greater self-interest and lesser exposure to experiences that run counter to it), they do not do so exclusively. The ideas can be and are espoused by anyone subscribing to the notion that the social structure is what it is because of something inherent in groups themselves.

Furthermore, we need to analyze data about dominant and subordinated groups in different ways. In a racialized and hierarchical society where presumptions about values, standards, and how people should think and act are viewed from the dominant perspective, subordinated groups are perceived as visitors (sometimes welcome, sometimes not). As such, interpretations of their experiences and actions are filtered through an environment where rules, expectations, and interpretations presume the experience of the racial norm. Studies about whiteness often uncover these unspoken social mechanisms that position whites with greater status, structurally higher incomes, and positions of power regardless of individual intentions, beliefs or perspectives. Eduardo Bonilla Silva speaks extensively of this in his book, *Racism Without Racists*. It is therefore critical to analyze how patterns in the everyday thinking of whites reinforce the status quo. Contradictions, incongruencies, and inconsistencies, create fissures that provide opportunities to challenge patterns of racial inequality. These openings create opportunities for ordinary people to make choices at the polls and in their workplaces, neighborhoods, and schools that can counter the status quo.

Within this chapter, the section "Everyday Experiences" explores students' recollections of their first experience of "a thing called race," thoughts about interracial friendship and campus politics. What happened and why was the event memorable? Students reveal their feelings of confusion and ambivalence about race. "Race's Roles" examines various perspectives on specific group identities and how they are perceived, understood, and negotiated. While one would presume that Brooklyn was a place, site, or backdrop, several people make clear that Brooklyn is their ethnicity. What does this mean in an analysis of race and racialization? We explore students' perceptions about the characteristics and positioning of various groups.

Finally, the section entitled "Race to Identity" summarizes several themes related to identity and discusses the racialization of resistance. This mecha-

nism diverts attention away from critically examining the political and economic context and voicing dissent. Examples are provided where students
resist the construction of whiteness and share their awareness of white supremacist ideology, white privilege, and the consequences of racism but are
afraid to speak out.

The identifiers used with quotes are those the speakers themselves provided, and relay the individual's self-description.

WHAT IS RACE ANYWAY?

> My first recollection of a thing called race was when they stole our bikes.
> They thought we wouldn't miss them. I'm tired of hearing we're wrapped up
> in money. Whatever I have I pay for with allowance; I work for what I get.
>
> —Nancy, white female

In the opening quote of this chapter, Joey expresses concern that he will be
lectured to and presumed to have a certain worldview. While he describes
himself as antiracist, Joey does not indicate that he wants to hear different
perspectives or that he has anything to learn. Nancy appears certain of what
was in the minds of the people who stole her bike, and that "they" were Black.
What assumptions is she making about allowance or working for what she
gets; what might she be suggesting about how "they" obtain these things? In
discussions about race, assertions are frequently made about other people's
motives, beliefs, and experience.

Tables 2.1a and 2.1b provide data about students' attitudes toward the
inclusion of the historical and current experiences of people of color in the
curriculum. These statistics are particularly significant given this type of self-
confidence. Might the process of talking about race reveal vulnerabilities they
would prefer to avoid?

White students (both U.S. and foreign-born) believe significantly less that
these efforts raise academic standards and significantly more that these efforts lower academic standards than do Latinos and Blacks. Asian students
believe significantly less than Black students do (both U.S. and foreign-born)
that curricular inclusion raises academic standards.

These data can be compared to polls taken at other universities. For example, a survey conducted in Florida by the Central and South Florida Higher
Education Diversity Coalition and administered for the Ford Foundation
Campus Diversity Initiative indicated that nearly nine of every ten students
(88 percent) reported that courses and campus activities emphasizing diversity and diverse perspectives have a positive effect on education. More than

Table 2.1a How Much Do Efforts to Include More about the Historical and Current Experiences of People of Color in the Curriculum Change Academic Standards?: Data from the First Edition

	Raises	Doesn't Change	Lowers
Overall	38.0%	51.4%	10.6%
Latinos	47.9%	50.0%	0.0%
Asians	33.3%	56.4%	10.3%
U.S.-born Blacks	41.9%	48.8%	7.0%
Foreign-born Blacks	50.8%	36.5%	1.6%
U.S.-born whites	20.6%	66.9%	11.8%
Foreign-born whites	25.6%	65.9%	4.9%

Table 2.1b (2009) What Impact Do You Feel Incorporating the Experiences of All Groups in the Curriculum Has on Learning?: Data from the Second Edition

	Improves Learning	Good Idea But Doesn't Impact Learning	Irrelevant	Interferes With Learning
Overall	56.3%	30.1%	7.8%	5.8%
Latinos	64.3%	28.6%	7.1%	0.0%
Asians	46.7%	40.0%	6.7%	6.7%
Blacks	64.3%	28.6%	7.1%	0.0%
Whites	54.8%	28.6%	14.3%	2.4%
Indigenous	100.0%	0.0%	0.0%	0.0%
Multi or Biracial	72.7%	9.1%	0.0%	18.2%

half (55 percent) of the participants reported that multicultural courses raise standards, while one-third (33 percent) reported that they have no effect. However, in response to a different question on this survey, 40 percent agreed with the statement "adding material about women and minorities to the college curriculum makes it less rigorous" (Diversity Web 1998). Clearly, the phrasing of questions impacts responses; at the same time, consistent with the Brooklyn College data, more students of color than white students believed these courses raise academic standards (Diversity Web 2001). In 2009, students overall more strongly expressed that incorporating experiences of all groups in the curriculum improves learning. However, this may be a reflection of a change in wording from including more about "persons of color" to incorporating all groups.

In 1999, the Association of American Colleges and Universities (AAC&U) issued a report for the Ford Foundation Campus Diversity Initiative summarizing national research and stating that a key finding indicates, "diversity in the curriculum has a positive impact on attitudes toward racial issues, on opportunities to interact in deeper ways with those who are different and on overall satisfaction with the college or university. These benefits are particularly powerful for white students who have had less opportunity for such engagement" (Humphreys 1998).

Aside from perceptions of the impact of a multicultural curriculum on learning, many studies have found that diversifying the curriculum has an impact on, for example, advancing cognitive development and enhancing civic awareness and the sense of responsibility and social consciousness (Kogler 1999, 12). This assessment suggests that regardless of perceived value, curricular inclusion leads to desirable outcomes, especially in the context of liberal education. However, at the same time, assumptions and stereotypes about the experiences of communities of color are sometimes used to defend the status quo and to negate the need for structural change.

Livin' the White Life

The following passages offer insight into how students understand what it means to be white and to what extent the culture of poverty and individualist frameworks are currently operative.[1] Whites frequently talk about racism as something they rarely experience or observe. This is often attributed to their being "colorblind." Race is something "other people" (undefined) experience or more accurately, something "they" (undefined) use to advance "themselves." Because of the increased diversity of the urban and campus populations, whites reveal that they feel their daily interactions in public spaces provide the basis upon which to feel confident about their understanding of race and the lived experiences of people of color. Interestingly, studies have shown that the election of Barack Obama as the U.S. President similarly appears to provide just the moral credentials needed to increase whites' comfort expressing preferences that favor whites at the expense of Blacks (Kaufman 2009).

However superficial or noninteractive, daily contact provides a space in which whites can assert their own perceptions and interpretations as "truths" to justify broad-sweeping generalizations about Blacks, Latinos, and Asians because they feel "they know." This point, in fact, contradicts the popular integrationist assumptions that contact alone results in greater understanding between groups. It is evident that while exposure can lead to greater awareness, this cannot be assumed.

In this statement, Barbara (white female) acknowledges she has the luxury of not thinking about her racial identity, and explains why:

I don't think of racial identity, it's true. I guess being black, Latino, or Asian, you might think about race because you might not get a job because of race. You would think of it because it would be a hindrance. It's my personal experience, so I think it's true. When you think of discrimination, you don't think of white. The media gives you this idea. It's an issue of blacks, Latinos, and Asians not being allowed in a club. If there were more whites in a place or a neighborhood, they don't fit in.

To be white means being able to assume that race will not interfere with getting a job or taking care of business, so you do not need to think about it.[2] To Barbara, race is not white; it is a disadvantage, never an advantage, even in a white-dominant and white-normative society. This perspective often leads to whites' denial of their own racial identity. One can more easily hold on to advantages (including not having to think about one's race) by denying they exist. This perspective asserts that talking about race is what perpetuates racism, as illustrated by Julie's (white female) comment, "People choose their own fate. If you're white, green, blue, whatever color your eyes are or the texture of your hair, your intelligence and hard work makes or breaks you. Some people nowadays have it easier, but everyone started out in the same position. It is possible for anyone to succeed."

This masking of whiteness frames race as a process that discriminates only negatively, and never positively. Race prevents but never provides admission to the "white club." To recognize enhancement would be to acknowledge privilege and suggests responsibility for addressing inequality. As a popular recording artist coaches his friend to deny cheating even after his girlfriend catches him with another woman, so are whites encouraged to believe in and speak of their good intentions when they become aware that something they say or do can be perceived as racist. "We never really experience discrimination. We don't have to think about it," explains Lori, a white female staff member.

Whites can say that race doesn't play a role in their lives and they hate racists, yet they do little to change the consequences of racism or structures that sustain white dominance. "I'm bigoted against bigots," says Georgiana (white female administrator). However well intentioned, statements such as this implicitly dismiss the need to look further at one's own experiences and privileges. They conceal the structuring of institutionalized racism that provides daily advantages, even the luxury of advocating for a "colorblind" society. Deborah (white female) aptly points out, "I don't think whites recognize that they are the cause of the discrimination, because they are doing it. They are holding other races back and they don't see it."

Race is rarely described as something that imparts a positive identity for whites, or as an idea that historically diminishes as well as bestows group and/or individual power, status, or wealth. This dynamic disguises privileging because it appears as if discrimination takes place only overtly and explicitly rather than through day-to-day interactions. In this way, discrimination is recognized when it disadvantages, but not when it advantages. When whites acknowledge the role of race in their lives, it is often as a claim of reverse discrimination, not when they, for example, are hired, receive a mortgage, or are given the benefit of the doubt. This process of plausible deniability allows whites (particularly those with a lot of contact with people of color) to deflect challenges to their belief that race doesn't matter. Barbara tells us:

> It's always in the media that there is discrimination of blacks, Latinos, and Asians. Racialization is common. It's not an issue of being discriminated against if you're white. Race is automatically associated with discrimination. But there is not as much discrimination as portrayed. I associate race as a barrier. Whites don't experience discrimination but you can be white and discriminated against because of your heritage if you're Italian or Jewish or something.

In this statement, the ambiguity of race emerges is in the questionable whiteness of Italians and Jews. However, race is a negative characteristic that white people do not have, so they generally don't need to understand, deal with, or play an active role in addressing structures that maintain racial inequalities. Whether you should think about or do something is thought to be determined by whether and how it impacts you personally. This mechanism also manifests in the way that issues are framed in mainstream discourse that diverts the public from civic engagement. We are made to believe in the "social survival of the fittest" and that it is unrealistic and unwise to care about more than your own personal concerns. For example, the consequences and reality of violence, terror, and poverty around the world have become slightly more visible in the aftermath of September 11, 2001, yet people have suffered from imperialist and military interventions throughout history.[3] This point was dramatically articulated in the following satirical quote, reflecting on a concert given for the families of victims of 9/11. "According to a study . . . by the United Nations Economic and Social Council, 4.2 billion people—a full 70 percent of the planet's inhabitants—could use an all-star benefit concert" (*The Onion* 2001).[4] As Jim Wallis, editor of *Sojourner*, said in response to someone weeping after hearing about the death of a Black youth from violence, "I understood more clearly than ever before why our society was allowing the deadly carnage to continue. For most Americans who are white and middle class, it isn't a whole generation of 'us' that is being lost. Rather it is 'them.' We tell them what we think of them in clear messages every day: they aren't important, they don't count; they don't exist" (as quoted in Loeb 1999, 88). This is harshly apparent as the number of violent civilian deaths during and since the 2003 invasion of Iraq is estimated at between 94,902 and 103,549.[5] Furthermore, there have been 654,965 (392,979–942,636), estimated excess Iraqi deaths as a consequence of the war as of July 2006, according to the *Lancet* (Burnham et al. 2006, 1421). Where are the lives of these human beings in conversations about U.S. foreign policy?

"We, who have lost very little, who have sacrificed very little, who have paid very little, we 'turn the page,' to use Rich's phrase, and we continue to speak of 'our' war, of 'our' fight against the terrorists, 'our' ideals, 'our' kindness, 'our' courage; things that we value far more than the lives of millions of others, people whose deaths do not hurt us, whose loss does not affect us, and whose sacrifice we do not see bloodying our own hands" (Hamourtziadou 2007). This so-called invisibility of whiteness masks presumptions of white as better, nicer, and more moral and the United States as more democratic and free. Tim Wise, author and antiracism activist, describes the process of denial after the repeated school shootings that occurred around the United States in the late 1990s:

> Two more white children are dead and thirteen are injured. Another "nice" community is scratching its blonde head, utterly perplexed. Once again, we hear the FBI insist there is no "profile" of a school shooter. Come again? White boy after white boy after white boy, with very few exceptions to that rule (and none in the mass shooting category) decide to use their classmates for target practice, and yet there is no profile? What went wrong is that we allowed ourselves to be lulled into a false sense of security by media representations of crime and violence that portray both as the province of those who are anything but white like us. (Wise 2001)

Wise points out how the media described these boys as loners and picked on but never seemed to notice a "certain highly visible melanin deficiency" (Wise 2001). This invisibility and presumption of white innocence has dire consequences. Patterns cannot be identified and remedies cannot be sought. When whites do recognize that race plays a role in everyday living, it is often viewed either as a problem that people of color need to overcome, or as something that now negatively affects whites, such as affirmative action or scholarships and opportunities available to people of color but not to whites. Whites can be benevolent or generous (if they choose) but are not necessarily compelled to acknowledge or expose the system-wide aspects of racial inequalities. These require a radical transformation of society to address and eradicate and would likely eliminate some of the privileges of whiteness and render to others rights to which all had claim.

Many white students appear conflicted by having some understanding of the destructive impact of racism but being resistant to giving up a worldview that positions themselves as the current victims of unfair treatment. That is how they explain why they are at a public rather than private institution or away at school. They attribute their financial difficulties to the benefits they were not privy to because they believe scholarships and awards are disproportionately distributed to Black and Latino students, despite the fact that data do not indicate that this is the case.[6] They often attribute their difficulty in finding jobs to the policy of affirmative action.[7] Two women (both white and born in the United States) articulate this perspective. Beth says, "As unfair as minorities think things are, when a white person tries to get a job, they're overlooked because of quotas. Look at who works for the City." Similarly, Mindy says, "Black people want jobs for being black! What about me? I have bills to pay!"

Students sometimes described affirmative action as unfair, particularly as they argue that full equality has now been achieved. They express their belief that Blacks, Latinos, and Asians now receive more than their fair share of the "pie." However, when asked about how to explain evidence of social and economic disparities, white students generally do acknowledge that they exist. They then either revert to explanations of individual or group weaknesses that lead to impoverishment or reveal that they really don't understand why there are such differences in standards of living, wealth, and resources between groups. They do not go so far as to support affirmative action efforts but are generally willing to recognize that conditions of whites and people of color are not equal. They are unclear about what affirmative action is and how it works but accept what they say they hear, that "affirmative action is anti-white." When race is acknowledged as something that white folks have, the impact of race is inverted. Race then becomes expressed in the belief that it is hard to be white today. A Quinnipiac University poll conducted in 2009 found that "American voters say 55–36 percent that affirmative action should be abolished" though there were important differences in opinion when this question was posed related to issues of race, gender and ability and distinctions between the responses of Democrats and Republicans (Quinnipiac 2009).

Related to this, students sometimes will acknowledge that race plays a role in their lives, yet they aren't sure of its significance. This is evident in the following statement by Sharon (white female) and the subsequent exchange that occurred in an all-white focus group:

> I never grew up around white people, only Turkish, Russian, U.S.-born Jews, Pakistanis, blacks, Spanish, Christians, "crazy" lesbians, Middle Eastern people. I have always been culturally disadvantaged. I know blacks that hate Jews and Jews who hate blacks. The only people I hate are white trash. They burned down the house of a black family who moved in. I witnessed police aggression

against my boyfriend (who is black). They stopped him in Central Park because they said he looked like a rapist. They picked up someone else, too for the same reason but they looked nothing alike—just that they were black.

This intertwining of incongruous beliefs about race was common. Sharon counterpoises people of different religious, national, and ethnic affiliation and sexual orientation with whomever she views as "white." When asked about this, she said she wasn't sure who was white, but they certainly weren't the people she knew. Her association of white with middle class and straight became clearer through the discussion. As Rose Brewer so eloquently states, theorizing about race, class, and gender must be historicized, contextualized, and understood as simultaneous forces (1993, 16). In this case, Sharon racializes religion, sexual orientation, regionalism, and the "crazy" versus the "sane." She articulates an antiracist position for those individuals who engage in overtly racist actions, whether toward "white trash" or police who profile. At the same time, she implies that these incidents are isolated, and the people involved are "bad apples," rather than part of a systemic problem. Her good friend Nancy (white Italian female) responds: "Not for nothing, Sharon, if I saw your boyfriend walking down the street at night, I would cross to the other side. He's scary looking and you have to worry about your safety. Would you walk right up to a wild dog?" Sharon appeared outwardly unfazed, yet it was not clear if she was affected by this comment. She simply laughed. This provides an example of collusion between whites when speaking about race in private discussions. Nancy is her friend and it is more than likely that Sharon might not want to make waves even if she was offended. While Sharon objects to racial profiling, she is quiet about Nancy's comment about her boyfriend. This exchange reflects the complex interconnectedness of race, class, and gender in mainstream social discourse and the ambivalences that function to undermine principled engagement about race.

In the 2000 study, whites reported significantly less often than Blacks that they think about their racial identity and significantly more that they never do. U.S.-born whites reported significantly more than foreign-born Blacks that they believe their racial identity has not affected their life experience at all and reported significantly less that their racial identity has impacted their life experience a lot. In 2009, whites and Asians more frequently report thinking about race daily or weekly, much less than people identifying as Latino, Black, Indigenous, multi- and bi-racial. Whites and Asians more frequently say they never or occasionally do so (see tables 2.2a and 2.2b).

Contradictions abound as whites negotiate their racialized identity in diverse environments. Some humanization occurs with contact with people from different backgrounds, yet this exposure also lends itself to being used as a

Table 2.2a   How Often Do You Think about Your Racial Identity?: Data from the First Edition

	Never	Once a Month	Once a Week	Daily
Overall	40.2%	24.4%	11.2%	24.4%
Latinos	31.3%	31.3%	12.5%	20.8%
Asians	25.6%	41.0%	5.1%	23.1%
U.S.-born Blacks	25.6%	25.6%	2.3%	39.5%
Foreign-born Blacks	22.2%	3.8%	12.7%	39.7%
U.S.-born whites	52.2%	20.6%	8.1%	17.7%
Foreign-born whites	54.9%	18.3%	18.3%	7.3%

Table 2.2b   How Often Do You Think about Your Racial Identity?: Data from the Second Edition

	Never	Occasionally	Once a Month	Once a Week	Daily
Overall	9.5%	49.5%	8.6%	12.4%	20.0%
Latinos	0.0%	50.0%	0.0%	28.6%	21.4%
Asians	6.7%	66.7%	6.7%	13.3%	6.7%
Blacks	7.1%	42.9%	7.1%	17.9%	25.0%
Whites	11.6%	51.2%	11.6%	9.3%	16.3%
Indigenous	0.0%	0.0%	50.0%	50.0%	0.0%
Multi or Biracial	7.7%	38.5%	7.7%	15.4%	30.8%

defense against having to examine one's own beliefs. Race is a problem only for those who raise it. Racism is something that bad people do overtly, not a relationship of power. Structural and systemic patterns are generally ignored.

Paul Rogat Loeb, an affiliate at Seattle's Center for Ethical Leadership, also discovered this pattern when he visited over one hundred campuses: "White students voiced the same ambivalent concern, bought into the same myths that said you could strip away historical contexts and still understand people's lives" (as quoted in Wilson 1995, 182).

Sometimes people use their experiences as a woman, being gay, or growing up poor to think about dynamics of race, racism, and racialization.[8] These openings provide opportunities to raise awareness of the structures of society as Catherine (white female) illustrates:

> Minority—see, that's wild, the word minority. It's not even like race anymore because I was a minority, and I'm not black. You can break minority down by so many things. I know what it feels like to be the minority because I went to school in Bensonhurst. If you weren't Italian, you were minority. I'm not Italian,

plus, I'm always dealing with, "Oh, well she's a girl, she can't do that." I think once you are a minority, then you know how it feels and you could understand what people are going through to a certain point. There are also people who make themselves a minority. They harp on it like, "I can't do it because I'm a girl," or "I'm black." Sometimes people use it as an excuse but I do think once you are a minority, then you start caring about other minorities.

Catherine grapples with her understanding of the complex nature of relationships between groups and suggests that we can position ourselves not only as individuals, but also as part of a broad community (Chang 2000). She alludes to the possibility of coalition. Similarly, in the statements below, Joan acknowledges the role of race and power in stereotypes about crime; Fernando speaks of his awareness of the normalization of whiteness.

> Because the boys in Columbine were white, people thought they wouldn't or they couldn't do such a thing, because they look nice. If they were black, people would most likely assume that they could. We always assume that Spanish and black people commit most of the crimes. It doesn't necessarily happen. It's just what the media and society want you to believe. A lot more bigger crimes are committed by white people on top that have more power and stuff. It's just covered up because they have power and money. (Joan, white female)

> It's been portrayed on you by society itself. If you're not white, you're different. That's how it's laid down on the table. It's always been like that. (Fernando, Latino)

Students often express awareness that when crime is reported in the news, the emphasis is on street crime, particularly when stories reinforce racialized stereotypes. They appear to understand that the magnitude and impact of white-collar crime is often much greater but much less frequently reported and often without explicit notation of its consequences. Several students spoke about how the "war on drugs" was highly publicized and targeted inner-city young people of color, yet corporate crime and violence are rarely portrayed in the media, despite its devastating impact on millions of people's lives.[9] In 2009, some raised questions of the crimes related to government and military policies. This generally reflected a greater awareness of the way these representations are framed to maintain the gaze on poor communities, particularly those of color.

These passages suggest entry points (or "cracks") that can foster understanding about the structuring of society and how patterns of dominance and subordination are reproduced. In fact, survey findings by Mitchell Chang of the University of California, Los Angeles, indicate that learning about one significant difference in U.S. society transfers well to thinking about other differences and subsequently reduces multiple forms of prejudice and misunderstanding. The implications of this are great for academia (Chang 2000). Heightened awareness of the way that whiteness is the assumed norm, could lead to greater awareness of other forms of inequality. This would require, however, that someone believe that it is in their interest to be open to these possibilities. They may be uncertain as to how to identify themselves or how to understand the existence of social problems as traditional explanations become less tenable. Catherine illustrates: "If I am asked, I say I'm Catholic. I really hate saying white, what the hell does that mean?"

The desire for creative self-definition can serve multiple functions. Whites can deny their whiteness yet still receive the protection that status provides, whether they choose to or not. This starkly contrasts with the situation of people of color, few of whom can say that they don't think about their identity, that they do not know what it means, or that they do not think race has impacted their lives.[10] On the other hand, the desire for self-identification can also represent resistance toward the perpetuation of racial categories and a racialized world that structures realities. This becomes clear when Catherine questions the status quo: "I think blacks think that if whites are into hip hop they're trying to be black. Or anyone who's not black who tries to rap. What are you trying to be?"

In charge of the college radio station, Catherine is particularly sensitive to the racialized nature of music. She explains how she struggled to incorporate a variety of programs to be responsive to the whole community. She says that she was met with much suspicion. It appears that some of her resistance toward describing herself as white is her desire to take a position as a "race traitor." While she is not ideologically identified as a "New Abolitionist," her comments reflect a desire for a radically new perspective on race that acknowledges structural racism and creates something new.[11] The New Abolitionists speak of the tremendous power of crossover culture to undermine both white solidarity and male authority (Ignatiev and Garvey 1996).

The idea that whites involved in hip hop are expressing appreciation and respect for "Black culture and history" and resistance to mainstream "white culture" can also be countered by the question of whether this is yet another form of appropriation and exploitation of Black history and contributions. Georgiana, a white administrator, held the perspective that "there's good whites and good Blacks; there's bad whites and bad Blacks. We're all the same. What I hate is wannabes with their pants hanging down. I want to slap them in the face."[12] Salim Muwakill, senior editor of *In These Times* and op-ed columnist for the *Chicago Tribune* states, "By condescending to appreciate Black culture, Wiggahs may be making a humanitarian gesture, but this role of cultural adventurer seeking novelty among the exotics is what so incenses many blacks" (1999, 67).[13] Muwakill later suggests that "Wiggahs" may represent "'lead scouts' in our multicultural future" (1999, 67). This contradictory description provides evidence of both existing challenges and possibilities.

Sometimes, race is acknowledged as playing a significant role in everyday experiences. For example:

> I'm not going to speak for everyone but for me sometimes it's an advantage to be white. I can't really pick a specific time, but sometimes, you could just feel something, like people treat you differently sometimes. I can't really pick a specific example, but I know that it happens. Like if you're sitting on the bus, and there's a black person sitting over there, and then you're sitting here and an old white woman comes over, and she'll look, and then she'll sit next to me. I'm like—are you sitting next to me because I'm white or are you just sitting next to me because you like that seat? (John, white male)

> Every night when I get off real late from work, at the bus, this neighborhood is very black. I'm like a minority as a white person in this neighborhood and there's a whole bunch of black guys that get off the bus with me and there's a few taxis just waiting on the street. All these black guys, we're all walking in the same direction and the taxi drivers are like, just to me, as a white woman, "Taxi?" and they just ignore all the other black guys and black women. I'm the one who's being solicited for a taxi ride exclusively, so it's an illustration right there. (Marsha, white female)

These comments reveal an awareness of the way that whiteness affects daily interactions. John and Marsha speak of a silent nod and being given the benefit of the doubt in situations where they are perceived to be safer, more reliable, and friendlier than someone of color. These interactions allude to another misperception, as more than 80 percent of violent crime occurs among people of the same race: A white person is much more likely to be murdered or robbed by someone white than by someone Black (Steinhorn and Diggs-Brown 1999, 123). This continues to be true as the Bureau of Justice Statistics reports that 86 percent of white victims were murdered by whites and 94 percent of Black victims were murdered by Blacks.[14]

Their willingness to share observations about ways they have been treated and their consideration that this has to do with their whiteness indicates a level of social consciousness that is not commonplace. This openness reveals an opportunity to discuss systemic patterns and structural causes. If whites are able to acknowledge experiences such as these without ambivalence or defensiveness, it is possible to analyze what happened, and why, in a broader social context. When John talks about his family, he says,

My parents were brought up Italian. My mom was Italian Catholic and she was really, really hard to live with. She used to tell me, "Don't go outside of your race, whatever you do." She blew a fit about the last two girls that I went out with. One was Puerto Rican and the other was a Russian Jew. She'd get all mad and say, "I don't want you with those—." I would mess with her and tell her, "I'm going to go out with a black chick." But from an early age, they tell you, "Don't you ever date, or ever marry a black girl." My mom said she'd write me out of the will if I did. I'm a real Italian guy.

Herein lies another mechanism: Being white means having an understanding, keeping discussions "in the family"; John knows what would bother his mom and taunts her. He doesn't engage her about the way she thinks; he resists in a personal way without taking an active stance in challenging her attitudes. (Chapter 4 explores beliefs about interracial relationships in more depth.)

Fernando (Latino), on the other hand, reveals his awareness of the psychology of white denial about race and how it reinforces advantage and privilege. "I don't think that whites want to let go of the advantages that they do get. It's a really big advantage to have one step ahead of your competition. Who wouldn't want that?" He juxtaposes a concern for the collective good with the self-centeredness that is encouraged by our society. The very admission of privilege might threaten the security of the advantages received; however, acknowledgment alone does not make social change. Fernando also suggests that privilege may be incremental, discrete, and not necessarily dramatic but any advantage bolsters one's chances of success and of well-being. Many scholars such as Beverly Daniel Tatum have spoken about the significant and measurable costs that racism imposes on all of society (1997, 14).

When You Say It, I Don't Have To

As mentioned in chapter 1, in a racially organized society, language about race is often coded and implicitly conveys underlying assumptions and values. Discussions about the impact of race on daily living can be challenging because there is greater concern about whether one will be labeled a "racist" than with deepening one's understanding of the lived experiences of people of color or why people react the way they do. This section explores several discursive mechanisms that help whites mediate that concern. Here, Mara and Diane (white females) explain their thoughts about "black English."

I'm not racist. I get along with everyone. But there's always underlying things we don't understand, like black English vernacular. A lot of white people feel it's an ignorant version of English, a less sophisticated sublanguage. It sets people aside as an isolating device, like a defense mechanism, "This is our culture, our language." I don't know how black people feel, but it's one of those things that separates people because it's seen as different. You can say it's not as good as standard American English but it's a separating device. (Mara)

> A lot of black people, when they're in their home or community, they speak with the black English vernacular. But if they work with white people, they switch over to the way I'm speaking. It's a device to affiliate yourself. (Diane)

These students attempt to understand the use of "Black English," yet they feel left out and waver about whether to say that outright. They are unsure of their support of the Black English vernacular. Jenna (white female) tells us "a lot of white people feel this is an ignorant dialect and reflects ignorance." Phrases such as "a lot of people think" can be a way to "test the waters" to see whether it is acceptable to say what one really thinks. The speaker can observe how people react before making a statement. Diane responds by taking a stand supporting Black vernacular. "It's just a simple difference, which doesn't carry any value. It's not better or worse, it's just a simple difference. But it's hard to get past that, and it's easy to judge." The dynamic, where someone has distinguished himself or herself from a previous speaker or someone else, appears to be used as a way of asserting moral authority by "outing" others. This was similar to what John was doing in relation to his mother's opposition to interracial relationships. By talking about her racial attitudes, he appears less culpable. Students often discuss their parents' attitudes, describing the older generation as "backward." In 2009, students readily spoke of their generation being post-racial, while their grandparents were entrenched in racial ideology. Suzie, a white female says, "If you pick any younger person off the street and ask if there's a problem with race, it wouldn't be. There wouldn't be as if as a problem as if you pull like a seventy-five year old. If you grew up in a time where you're used to something, people are resistant to change." Volker, (white male) suggests his idea about how to overcome racism: "Let all the old people die. I'm serious. I mean let them go. I mean look we have a black president right now."

However, personal ambivalence is revealed when people explain their own points of view. Marsha (white female) explains, "I don't categorize people, I just feel more comfortable with people of my same personality and attitude. I was brought up trying to categorize people in groups, trying to hang out with a lot of Jews because of my parents, especially my mom—she's a secret racist you know. She doesn't want to know anybody."

Marsha doesn't explain what she means about her mother, yet suggests that they hold different views without saying so explicitly. Her statement is somewhat ambiguous in that she says she identifies and associates with people based on personality and attitude. If they happen all to be white, she implies it happens by chance. It appears she believes that she herself is oblivious to race and exposes her mother as a racist, which perhaps may underscore her own lack of culpability. She distances herself from her mom and in turn expresses a desire to separate herself from racist attitudes. Jenna continues:

> Whites are perceived unfairly because everybody sees them as racist all the time. I see a lot of white people trying to struggle not to be, but in turn, they end up even worse because they try to be extra nice, which a lot of races don't like. I think they're perceived very unfairly; they are always abused. I don't think you can see them as racist or privileged until you get to know them a little better.

The perception that the accusation of racism occurs unpredictably articulates a sense of victimization. Jenna explains that whites are judged unfairly when people of color convey that they feel patronized by "extra niceness." She determines that whites are "always abused" and concludes that you can label someone as a racist or as privileged only when you get to know them personally. She does not explain her criteria for passing such a judgment. Her statement places bias and advantage in an individual context. This approach is often engaged in the media where racism is portrayed in personal and interpersonal terms, with larger questions about structure and responsibility lost in the background (Cutting 2000, 9). Scholar Emily Noelle Ignacio argues that this frame of individual racism only works because we are socialized toward it, rather than systemic patterns. She argues that we must isolate the rhetorical patterns that guide us toward this frame, and then challenge them (2008, 169).

The issue occasionally arose about whether dominance is just an expression of demographic majority. Jenna asks, "Isn't the percentage of white people in America about 80 percent? That's a huge majority. Most politicians are white; most people in power and big businesses are white; and economically most rich people are white." While whites comprise approximately 75 percent of the population, however, white men, who are 33 percent of the population, are 100 percent of U.S. presidents, 90 percent of the U.S. Senate, 95 percent of the Fortune 500 CEOs, and 85 percent of partners in major law firms (Hahnel and Pai 2001).[15] The idea that the reason there are more whites in positions of power, and wealth, is because representatively they are a statistically larger population is often raised in conjunction with the sometimes explicitly stated belief that people of color want more than their "fair share." However, Dari (Black female) challenged Jenna's dismissal of racism as a function of majority rule: "Population doesn't really matter. In North Africa there's a huge Black population and not many whites. They still discriminate against blacks."

An important opportunity emerges when unequal treatment is acknowledged as this provides an opening to explore other situations where the role of race can be identified. Similarly, when one individual articulates conservative views, they are sometimes freed to acknowledge racist dynamics. However, tension continuously arises and dissipates as the boundaries of explicit recognition of whiteness constantly shift. This dynamic was particularly apparent in the focus groups that included both whites and students of color. Dari's comment above resulted in Marsha's defense of white innocence. Struggles over the terms of plausible deniability are evident:

> I don't really think whites are advantaged. It seems like it's always been, like going back to the South and black people and all that—I know that's changing and it's changed a lot. It's changed to a great, great extent, but I think it's still there to a certain extent. It hasn't really gone away completely. But people are working on it.

Arguing that race matters, Dari and Diane respond:

> Dari: I was in a class where the professor would hand papers to the white students but put down on the desk, papers for the students of color.

> Diane: My daughter goes to a Catholic high school, all girls. There's a Rite Aid nearby and they're not supposed to let students in before three o'clock. They got out of school early and the guy at first wouldn't let them in. They were all white. But then he did. About ten minutes later a whole group of black girls came and he wouldn't let them in. My daughter came home and related the story to me. She felt bad for the girls that didn't get in. I said, "Well, I don't know what you could have done. The only thing you possibly could have done was say something to the guy, and then get all your friends and leave"—you know, like a protest or something.

Diane and her daughter recognize the different treatment but take the position that there really isn't much one can do. She dramatizes an act that might appear natural, as in speaking up or taking action, by describing it as a "protest." Images of activists are often racialized as dominant ideology portrays whites as "nice," "accommodating," "quiet," and "peaceful," while Blacks are considered to be "aggressive," "violent," "noisy," and "troublemakers."[16] It can't be assumed that, if someone acknowledges a racist act, that person believes racism is a systemic and structural problem. The tendency to view explicitly racist actions as isolated incidents is prevalent, masking systemic patterns within an individual-centered framework.

Racism: A Problem or an Excuse?

People use prejudice as a huge excuse for everything in everyday life. This happened to me—I got a grade I didn't deserve. If they didn't study, people are quick to say, "He's prejudiced, or she's prejudiced." It's sick, it's really a disgrace, everybody is quick to say it's prejudice. (Andrew, white male)

Everyone should be individually responsible, but people are always complaining about the system, or racism, or being poor. You can get around that. If you live somewhere else, your chances of overcoming these problems wouldn't be as good as they are if you're in this country. Everyone just takes things for granted in general. (Gerda, Russian female)

In the oscillating nature of most discussions in groups that included both whites and students of color, Marsha defends the possibility of misunderstanding, rather than intentional racism:

I'm pretty sure that every one of us has been misunderstood. I've been misunderstood. If somebody just walked past and you heard something about your race, you'd get offended by it automatically.

Andrew's explicit statement above about opportunism provided space for Marsha to defend the actions of people of color and to provide explanation for why things happen. In many of the focus groups, whites indicated some understanding of the dynamics of racism but then concluded with a rejoinder that dismisses broad social consequences. Several comments on the survey relate to this issue:

Minorities hold themselves back because it is easier to claim responsibility on someone else rather than look at yourself and say what can I contribute. They blame it on history. "I believe all are equal and that everyone should be treated fairly. No exceptions should be made just because someone is a minority. We should all just be treated the same." "We are all equal. Blaming race or anything else is not fair. It's easier to blame others for your own mishaps." "Stop these quotas. People should get jobs by their qualifications, not the color of their skin."

The fear of being labeled racist sometimes results in ambiguous statements made with a tentative quality of voice or diction that suggests ambivalence. It may mediate the possibility that someone could take issue with something one said. Jenna's statement below is almost undecipherable but provides an example of this speech pattern:

People assume that if you're white, most of the time and most people and well, white people, a white person usually, obviously not speaking for everyone, there's those people that are, they do not discriminate, they are not racist, but a lot of people are. I think the majority of people are racist to some degree. A white person, it's like that thing we were talking about. You stick more with

your own group, so a white person would more likely see a white person as being, like nice, not necessarily nice in character but less likely to do something
to you. If someone's hiring someone for work, they would most likely hire
someone of their own racial background.

While initially Jenna says she thinks most white people are racist, she ultimately dismisses this, saying that discrimination occurs not as a consequence
of racism but because people are more comfortable with people they perceive
to be like them. Even if this is the case, what are the implications of this,
given that power and resources have been concentrated in one sector of the
population? What happened to the idea of meritocracy, equal opportunity, or
the American Dream being accessible to all? Just as the assumption that one
would be closer to family members than to any friend, the notion that whites
stick together because they are more familiar provides a rationale for limited
interaction between whites and people of color. This rationale reinforces
defenses against the very socialization that can help to break down barriers.
Jenna's reasoning also appears to stem from the perception that if you are
white, you are less likely to be hurt by someone white.[17] As noted above,
crime rates do not bear out this perception statistically; whites are more likely
to be victimized by someone who is white. Nevertheless, the perception is
that whites are safe with whites.

Discussing dynamics of everyday racial profiling on their jobs, Angelique
explains, "It happened on my own job, they assumed I was nice. If you look
like them, and they think they're nice, they consider [you] nice," while Barry's
experience as a Black male is quite a contrast: "It happens to me all the time. I
enter the elevator in the building where I work wearing a suit and a tie and you
can just feel everyone check their bags, especially the older women."

Angelique alludes to profiling that presupposes the "niceness of whiteness," but by speaking in ambiguous terms she does not make it clear whether
she believes there is a racial undertone on the part of the people at her job.
Barry, on the other hand, is clear about how people perceive him and that
there are racial implications to the incidents he describes.

EVERYDAY EXPERIENCES

Through the Eyes of Children (First Recollections)

One of the questions that drew the most interesting responses was about
students' first recollections of a thing called race. Don (white male) tells us,
"I remember at first not knowing exactly what it was. Like certain words or
whatever, but then you hear the words again so you start making some connec-

tions, you know that's the way it is." Nancy protests, explaining that race has always been part of her consciousness, "Since there's different kinds of people around, it's not like you grew up only seeing white people and all of a sudden you see a Black person in the street, and you say, 'Oh, what's wrong with that guy.' There were always different kinds of people around you. I think it's like 'retarded,' like when did you learn that word. You always knew it."

These students, growing up in an urban area, describe how on some level they were always aware of race. Don acknowledges that he attached meaning to the term by observing how race was handled and discussed by the people around him. For Nancy, it appears that race was an assumed part of her world. Gerda, on the other hand, having lived mostly in Russia and Australia, does not hide her surprise upon her first interaction with a Black person. She cautiously describes her experience, though it clearly left a deep impression on her:

> If you're a little kid living in New York, it's a regular thing, it's your routine, you go to school, you have little black kids, you have this and that. You go to private school; you see all different kinds of things. I was born in Russia; I don't think there are black people in Russia. I had never seen one before. I was six years old, and also lived in Australia. When I came here, I saw the first black person in my life. I said, "Oh my God, Ma" . . . She said, "Yeah, you know, they have them. . . ." Then I thought it was just that one person, and then my mother was like, "Oh, you know, there are people who are colored and there are Puerto Rican people." I hadn't seen this as every other little kid that sees this on a daily basis, so it is different I think.

This points to one of many significant differences between the experiences of U.S.-born and foreign-born whites explored in chapter 3. In this example, Joanne recollects an incident that marked what she describes as the first time she experienced "race difference" and how overwhelmed and shocked she was by what she witnessed.

> When I was in junior high school something happened where I think a black kid had gotten killed or something. I don't know. There was this big thing in Ben-sonhurst,[18] something happened. I don't remember what it was, yeah he got beat up or something, oh, he got killed. I had been walking on 86th Street and it was late. All of a sudden I see this older man and he's running and he's heavy-set and he's running and running around the corner. I see these big black kids running after him. I don't know what happened with the verdict, but whatever happened, it caused them to do this. The guy tripped and fell, and the black kids, teenagers, started kicking him. I was like, wow, that was just way too much for me. That was the first time I really experienced race difference. It was to the extreme. I had never experienced it before, and then that's what I had to experience.

Why does Gerda refer to "little black kids" and why does Joanne speak of "big black kids"? Joanne says, "It is way too much for me. . . . I had never experienced it before, and then that's what I had to experience," while clearly knowing Yusuf Hawkins was shot. It appears that she distinguishes between the two incidents. What do these recollections signify? Does this reflect a belief by whites that race is something that only affects "them"? John DeSantis, journalist, suggests that the presence of white hecklers at protest marches after the murder of Hawkins evoked the following reflection: "Many blacks reasoned, if so many people were unashamed to show this evil side of themselves, then how many whites, people they worked with every day and said hello to, harbored such hatred as well" (DeSantis 1991, 118). The implication of these questions is great, yet rarely discussed.

As mentioned in chapter 1, 70 percent of whites hold at least one misperception related to the achievement of equality of all races, 56 percent hold two or more, and 31 percent held them all (Morin 2001, A1). Furthermore, studies show that the election of Obama in fact increases the misperceptions about equality, with whites increasingly holding the belief "that racism is less of a problem in the United States today than in times past. They also expressed less support for policies designed to address racial inequality. Given the continued prevalence of racial disparities in virtually all aspects of American society, these results raise important implications for the status of policies aimed at eliminating racial injustice" (Kaiser et al. 2009, 556). "Nationally, representative U.S. samples show that prior to the election (January 2008), 63 percent of Americans reported that racial discrimination against Blacks was a serious or very serious problem (CNN, 2008a). In the week after the 4 November 2008 election, only 54 percent of respondents in another independent sample agreed with this sentiment (CNN, 2008b)" (in Kaiser et al. 2009, 559). Breaking this down by race however, tells a somewhat different story. In the week after the election, 49 percent of whites and 86 percent of Blacks said that racial discrimination is a serious or very serious problem.[19] This dynamic reinforces the notion that opportunities exist and Blacks and other communities of color exaggerate the existence of discrimination.

Another aspect of this is that despite the hype, only 43 percent of whites actually voted for Obama. That did not include the majority of whites in any category (such as income, age, education) except those 18–29 years old, 54 percent of whom voted for him. Analyzing white votes by religion, the majority of those who indicated Jewish, "other religion" or "no religion" supported Obama.[20]

The next section summarizes students' thoughts about identity in everyday interactions.

But Some of My Best Friends Are . . .

I have a problem when you ask who I identify with. Ninety percent of my friends are Spanish. They are who I enjoy being with. I don't much like Italian people even though I'm Italian. I used to believe in the "American Dream" and the melting pot. Everyone expected us to melt together but it was too hot. Now there is no American culture, only combinations. People refused to melt so it destroyed American culture and created difficulties. (Angelo)

National and ethnic identities are viewed as destroying American culture. It is implied that people who self-identify as anything other than American create tension: "We" were willing to get along but "they" insist on flying their flag, speaking their language, identifying by their homeland, coming and going, eating their foods, including their histories in the history books, etc. . . . This attitude implies that we can't be American and multicultural at the same time. This issue is explored in more depth in chapter 3.

Susan, a white student, responds to Angelo's comment above, saying, "New York is not a melting pot. Look at the segregation of communities." She acknowledges the complexity of diversity in an urban setting and expresses some ambivalence about its significance. She seems to want to understand neighborhood segregation and whether it is just the "way things are." Is New York a multicultural haven, is Brooklyn a model of diversity, or is it a constellation of separate communities? As previously noted, Brooklyn neighborhoods vary from 1.9 percent white in Bedford-Stuyvesant to 92.3 percent white in Dyker Heights (Brooklyn College Office of Institutional Research [BC OIR] 1999). While some demographic shifts have occurred in the past decade, the level of racial concentration has not dramatically changed.

Choice of identity is a sensitive topic, as Ricky (Italian male) illustrates:

This is a touchy issue. Some people take pride in being Italian, but their loyalty is to the U.S.A. I understand that the color of someone's skin matters, but it is really about how the person is inside, what kind of person they are. One incident with someone of a race and the whole race gets a bad name. Stereotypes cause societies problems but some people just hate, like the KKK.

Is the same dynamic true about stereotypes of Blacks, Latinos, or Asians? Is he particularly thinking of situations involving Italians and/or whites? Perhaps he thinks all whites are labeled as racists after one highly publicized incident. What is the climate within which these incidents arise? By saying that some people just hate, rather than exploring possible causes of racial hatred or the consequences to those who are the objects of hate, there is no discussion of the context nor of structural causes.[21] Angelo describes his perceptions of how relationships between groups play out:

The perception among minorities is that white people get more. In class one time, we had half Jewish Orthodox, and half students of color. I was the only white, non-Jew. A Jewish student got a copy of the test ahead of time and the blacks wanted it. A brawl broke out. I didn't fit anywhere.

It is not clear whether the test was obtained through legitimate means or whether the whole situation raises issues of academic integrity, just that the Jewish students got the test and the Blacks wanted it. By doing so, Angelo emphasizes the racial component. He does not identify himself with the students who felt wronged; rather he frames himself as a bystander, victimized by both groups. He implies that he is "neutral," neither allying with the Black students nor asking the Jewish students to share with the whole class. He concludes that minorities perceive that whites get more, and then uses an example when whites did. His complaint appears to be that he does not always receive privileges, as he does not appear to ally himself with those who challenge unequal circumstances. The racial difference between him and the students who wanted the test appears to have prevented him from joining forces with them. Angelo continues, revealing that he feels he is the victim of reverse discrimination:

My parents worked sixteen hours a day all their life and I work, too. I have had black friends and black girlfriends. Now everyone's pissed and feeling screwed. Everyone generalizes. The only trouble I have ever had in New York City has been from Italians. This is even more reason to hate Italians more than anyone! But again, I help everyone on my job but one black guy didn't like what I did, so I was reported. He said he was going to write articles about the racism in this school.

While somewhat ambivalent about the role of race versus class and his own personal sense of victimization, Angelo again concludes with a story that illustrates his feelings that whites are treated unfairly. He describes an incident where someone accuses him of discrimination. Rather than considering the student's perspective or overall experience, or whether he may have erred himself, Angelo dismisses the grievance. By criticizing Italians and describing his relationships with Blacks and Latinos, but then concluding with a story about a situation where he feels unfairly accused of racism, Angelo illustrates another dynamic that disallows engagement about the role of race. This mechanism of defense, consideration, and return to the defense of whites as victims is commonplace, as if the very process of consideration clears one's name.

Campus Politics

Student organizations on campus reflect both the diversity and the complexity of the student population. More than 125 clubs and organizations are arranged as academic or fraternal or fall into a general category that includes cultural, activist, and religious groups. Each of the three divisions (day, evening, and graduate) is represented by its own student government structure.[22] The Greek-letter organizations fall under their own council. This current structure has functioned for the last thirty-five years. During this time, the day-student government has been generally the domain of two parties. The Working Together Always (WTA) student government organization's constituency is primarily students of color. The Liberal Party (TLP) consists predominantly of Jewish students, although it includes Italian and various other white ethnic students. Both organizations have included a few people who do not fit this description, but the general demographics have historically prevailed. In this exchange, the students discuss whether actions of the two parties are racialized or coincidental:

Cora (Black female):

> I pass in front of Boylan [Hall] like a million times a day and no one from The Liberal Party asked me to vote. Everyone from Working Together Always came up and asked me. I was walking with her and said, "Hold on! How come you didn't ask me if I voted already or anything?"

Randy (white female):

> You don't always know what's going on, you don't always know for a fact that it's racial. You might think it is, but it doesn't necessarily have to be.

These students are clear that one is viewed as the party of color, the other as the party of whites. Nancy reflects, "Racial and religious segregation of our campus is an incredibly important issue. White students don't participate because they are afraid of being labeled a racist. They think students of color will argue with us and whisper. We have to be able to disagree yet still talk. There are strong issues; we all have opinions. It helps to see different views."

She appears to hold students of color responsible for the lack of understanding and communication and feels that white students feel intimidated by them. Her comments suggest that she believes students of color are to blame for the tension that white students experience and for the segregation. She also conveys that white students believe that if they don't talk about race, they can ignore its impact. This may be partially true. Living in a white-dominant world, as W. E. B. Du Bois described in his analysis of a double consciousness, Blacks have to become bicultural just to survive. Whites do not have that burden, as their experience is normalized and presumed. Peggy McIntosh, in her essay "Unpacking the Invisible Knapsack: White Privilege," lists forty-six everyday assumptions that a white person can make but a person of color generally cannot (1992). Assumption number 32 states, "My culture gives me little fear about ignoring the perspectives and powers of people of other races." Similarly, number 34 states, "I can worry about racism without being seen as self-interested or self-seeking."

> People always assume that because we are white we are privileged, but it is not always true. There are a lot of white students who want the hatred to end. We want to stop having only other whites as our only input. I want the segregation to end. We may share problems, but I guess what happens (like poverty) to students of color happens in greater numbers. But there is more help for students of color such as scholarships and internships. (Nancy, white Italian female)

This dynamic of a defense of white innocence, consideration of responsibility, and then a reversion back to a defense ("but [they get] more . . . scholarships and internships") is often evident. The perception that students of color receive a disproportionate amount of scholarships is raised once again.

Is privilege solely an intentional, explicit, and obvious process, or can it also include the ability to collude, collaborate, enforce, ignore, defend, and protect a worldview that elevates one group and subordinates another? The concept of being privileged is essentialized, as is the notion of being racist. In other words, you either are or you are not privileged or racist, and the moral implications of either designation are so weighty that you ought to make sure you are not and have ready explanations and justifications. Otherwise, you are unpredictably vulnerable.

When the possibility of an uneven playing field is acknowledged, a disclaimer often follows about how things are unfair for whites. This is where the possibility of dialogue, increased awareness, and agency lies. However, without exposure to explanations about inequality that do not reside in individual weakness, both poverty and wealth appear to just mysteriously exist. Historically rooted hierarchies are not recognized for their lasting legacies. "To be poor in America is bad, but to be Black and poor is worse" (Jennings 1999). The mechanisms through which long-standing patterns are attributed to individual failings allow people to dismiss the possibility that we have responsibility for the perpetuation of social and racial inequality. Recognizing the mechanisms establishes that we could all take responsibility for its elimination.

Some willingness to acknowledge structural relationships is evident; however, whites often resist the idea that our society is not as it is portrayed to be: the "land of the free," "home of the brave," "champion of democracy," or a glorified "salad bowl." Phrases such as "I guess what happens" make it appear as if the forces that structure society are beyond our control, disconnected from what we do in daily life. Poverty "just happens" (because you're lazy?); wealth "just happens" (because you work hard?). Questions are posed ambiguously, holding no one and nothing responsible for current and historical patterns, nor for changing them. The institutional structures and daily actions that maintain and enforce injustice and inequality are masked and ultimately reproduce relationships and dynamics of power. As Nancy states, "Black kids at my high school fell asleep and refuse to work but the Asian students worked hard. What's the difference? It's the work ethic." Her perceptions, analysis, and conclusions are asserted as truths, although within the field of education this is a hotly contested topic. In education, the effects of differing historical and current patterns, resources, and conditions on various groups' academic achievement are well recognized.[23]

Nancy cites her opinion as fact and generalizes as if she is qualified and entitled to pass judgment on the performance of these groups. When asked, she objected vigorously to the idea that her statements may be biased or racist; for her, they are truth. Work ethics, like standards and merit, constitute a coding that is implicitly racial. This exemplifies the continuing influence of the "culture of poverty" framework. She continues, "I went to another school and our campus is much more segregated. You have to be here to believe it. It is disgusting the things which are said by Let's Celebrate Commonalities (LCC).[24] Well, it was to deal with this but they don't invite me or my sisters to the events anymore. I try to be fair. WTA, they just vote Black and do not pay attention to the issues." John appears to agree, "WTA's main purpose is to serve minority students, which I don't like. The group they forget about is white males. We're discriminated against. They are for minorities but they're not for white males. When you are in student government, you should encompass all groups."

Nancy and John convey their belief that whites are fair but minorities are prejudiced. They comment on WTA but not on TLP and appear to believe that whites are inclusive while minorities are exclusive.[25] Nancy asserts that WTA votes based on race and alludes to the idea that TLP votes on issues. Whites commonly believe this—that whites vote issue, but people of color vote race.[26] However, research has shown that whites more frequently vote along racial lines than do people of color. Nationally, whites were the only racial group that did not cast a majority of their votes for President Obama, and in Alabama, Mississippi, and Louisiana, only 10, 11, and 14 percent of whites did so respectively, all these being states covered by Section 5 in the Voting Rights Act (NAACP Legal Defense and Educational Fund, Inc. 2009, 1). This was a distinctively racial pattern as it was a significant decrease in votes by white Democrats from 2004 to 2008 (ibid 12–13).[27]

Nancy continues talking about student government voting patterns and allegiances:

We don't communicate. Most of us in TLP have to spend time correcting the spelling errors in the minutes that WTA typed. If someone is white it gets voted down, if [he or she is] black, the item gets voted up. Like with the debates which TLP won. What does police brutality and daycare have to do with us? It is an issue, but you can't eliminate workfare. How can WTA deal with the big issues if they can't even deal with their own budget? TLP wanted to set the standard, to do realistic things, not deal with police brutality, childcare. They won and there is no activity.

Who is held accountable for this lack of understanding and communication? Does communication necessarily mean seeing the world the same way? Nancy indicates that she believes that white students are more literate than students of color, by saying that they are burdened with teaching students of color how to spell. She implies that whites are fair and evenhanded and Blacks are self-interested, voting only for "their own." Her statements about WTA's concerns about police brutality and childcare indicate a lack of awareness of and sensitivity to the everyday lives of many students. She also reflects the belief that we should be involved with issues that personally affect us and that caring for everyone or fighting injustice is something only "they" do. She suggests that "they" complain rather than do the hard work of running society. This reiterates an ideological emphasis on individualism and that the belief in caring for the common good is at best unrealistic and at worst threatens one's own quality of life. The discussion alludes to their feeling that whites set high standards while people of color drag them down, as society has a "zero-sum" capacity (i.e., if conditions of one group improve they will necessarily worsen for another). The implication of these comments is that whites are realistic, whereas people of color are too idealistic, and that results in nothing getting done. Nancy further articulates this point by saying that "WTA is racial. It's black and Hispanic, but [in] TLP we're white, all different kinds. Chinese, black, we have everything. WTA is involved only with several groups. Every person of color is multiply involved."

Whites are portrayed as just, inclusive, multicultural, and fair, regardless of the actual demography of either organization. The comment that every person of color is involved with more than one group is stated as an indictment. She implies that these students are trying to represent themselves as involving more people than they actually do. She does not attempt either to understand why this might be the case or respect what it takes to be involved in several organizations at the same time. Nancy continues: "WTA are imbeciles who can't be spoken to. Everybody just sticks together."

She pursues the position that TLP members (does she implicitly mean whites?) are intelligent and open-minded, while WTA members (does she implicitly mean students of color?) are incompetent, unreasonable, and closed-minded. Nancy asserts that followers of her party interact with all kinds of people; followers of their party stick to themselves. She implies that her members are easy to get along with, friendly, and welcoming, while theirs are hostile and exclusive. She states,

> We are all divided by racial clubs. It is emphasized and radical. The Latino group marches all the time with their flag. It makes us mad. Chanting, but by now, we should all be American. Why do they have to march every semester? Even at baseball games, they brought their flag to demand recognition for their country.[28]

Nancy suggests that assimilation is an assumed and desirable status. She questions, "Hasn't everyone been given time to assimilate?" implying that this club ought to stop clinging to separatist, self-centered notions of community. Why can't "they" be more like "us," who dropped our national origins to identify as pan-ethnic whites?[29] At another point in the discussion, Nancy asks why there was an African students' club, and how she "just knew" they would not let her in. When asked if she had tried to join, she responded, "no." She said, she just "knew" how "they" were. When asked about their policy in welcoming non-African students into their group, the president of the African Student Club said,

> This is quite an interesting question. I would be honest with my response. If a white Italian woman (or anyone) approached me when I was the president and said she wanted to join, I would have said to her, "Great! Our next meeting date is. . . . What is your email address and/or phone number so that I can remind you about the meeting and tell you about upcoming events?" I would have received her without any hesitation. During my term as president, I invited and included non-Africans and non-club members into our club meetings and events. Take African Week, for example; of the eight dancers that performed, only three were club members. I would have welcomed her.[30]

Nancy concludes, "I have pondered the separations and believe it has to do with all these ethnic clubs. We need to come together and celebrate our common heritage and history. But the problem is being separated." Again the question can be raised as to who is held responsible for the separation between groups. It appears that Nancy feels "they" are because "they" always want to talk about their own heritage.[31] There is a relationship between this belief and the relatively moderate support for diversifying the curriculum (see tables 2.1a and 2.1b).

Who benefits from the separation, and in what ways? The answer depends on who is posing the question and why, and it is inevitably complex. Many studies have shown that diversity and integration can have a particularly beneficial impact on whites, whose experiences with people of color tend to be more isolated and limited. Also, racial, national, or ethnic affiliations can have very positive effects for people of subordinated groups, as they can affirm identities that may be rendered negative or invisible within dominant white culture. Recognition of the different starting points of whites and people of color needs to be part of discussions attempting to sort out "problems" and "solutions," including segregation and/or reasons for group identification.

This "naturalizing" of the white experience also makes social conditions appear to have mysteriously developed as opposed to there being scientific and structural explanations for how they came to be. For example, in discussions, segregation, prejudice, poverty, and privilege are often described as human nature or in ways that imply intransigence—that is, "things just happen" or "this is the way it's always been and always will be." Affirmative action is viewed as providing unfair advantage based on "skin color" because no other factors are relevant or evident.

Notions of individual responsibility, structural patterns, and the idea that positive change can really occur and that ordinary people can make a difference are rarely part of discussions. Herein lies both a mechanism (the mystification of poverty and privilege and the denial of the possibility for social change) but also a "crack," because, once interrogated, students were clearly troubled by the difficulty they had in explaining these issues. This void provides an opening to discuss economic and political causality and in turn can present an opportunity to explore the socioeconomic context of everyday experiences of ordinary people. That context offers explanations for social inequality that could invalidate racist justifications for blaming individuals and groups for their situations (e.g., the "culture of poverty").

Nancy goes on to further discuss the differences between the two student government parties: "In my sorority, most of us work two jobs. I want the segregation to end. Talk to me. Someone needs to hold WTA more responsible. There were no whites on the slate. I know the inside workings. People are putting up a face. I might have joined WTA if asked. But they screw us over a lot. TLP tried to work with WTA; we don't care who wins, only what matters for students."

Here, she asserts that whites work hard, and may be suggesting that they are not privileged. By insisting that she wants the segregation to end but that WTA should be held accountable, she again appears to blame them for the separation. She does not reveal that both the sorority and student government organization with which she is affiliated are overwhelmingly white.[32] She says WTA needs to be held more responsible for not having whites on their slate, but she does not hold TLP responsible for not having students of color.

Additionally, Nancy's comment reflects her beliefs that students of color are out of control and whites (TLP) care for students, while students of color (WTA) only care about power. She continues to explain her position:

> Up to last semester the fraternity and sorority council was all white. The first to try [to get in] was Alpha Zeta. At first we didn't want a Latino fraternity. It was against the idea of being all together. Isn't that racist, why is that okay? Will they make us look bad by not living up to our standards? There are serious requirements. We have probation when you first come in. Then Alan came up with his fraternity. We were skeptical. Our nationals make us work on a philanthropy like child abuse.

While Nancy herself acknowledges that the council had been all white, this statement reflects a lack of awareness of the whiteness of Greek-letter organizations. No issue was raised about their exclusivity when the council was all white. It was only when the Latino fraternity wanted to join that the issue of racism was raised and the concept of "we are one" asserted. She explicitly questions whether the Latino brothers can live up to the "serious" requirements of the council. She implies that the council is concerned that this new organization may diminish the Council's reputation, and she assumes that these new organizations may ask to waive standards. She suggests that this new fraternity might not be serious.[33]

> The Latino fraternity wanted to be in charge of approving all ethnic fraternities and we said "No." We wondered "Were there going to be rallies, mob scenes?" We wondered if they were activists. We asked, "What is your philanthropy?" They said they were multiethnic but they all look black. We needed to know what they were going to do. If they were to bring Al Sharpton, no, not okay. That is spreading hatred. We are not pleased with the Latino fraternity. They are business-based and separate and they don't support events. They only come when they want money.

There appears to be a presumption of the potential for violence when students of color are involved and an accusation of opportunism. Philanthropy is considered acceptable as a form of patronage but activism goes too far. Is it okay to help individuals but not to address structural patterns? Furthermore, Nancy questions the fraternity's multiethnicity, thereby challenging their authenticity. Ironically, most Greek-letter organizations on campus are often ethnically identified (e.g., as the Jewish fraternity, the Italian sorority, the mixed [Jewish and Italian] fraternity and so forth). Nancy wonders whether this is really a diverse group and implies that a mixed group would be more acceptable. In contrast, Catherine, also a sorority member, makes observations but does not pass judgment or place blame on students of color. She suggests that something should be done, but she's not sure what or how to make a sustainable impact on the intergroup dynamics on the campus:

> On campus there are many cultures. I've learned a lot because I came to the Student Center but there are a lot of times where it's like all minorities and no white people. I'm used to it now, so it's all right. But there's a lot of, not segregation but everybody's split off from each other. Fraternities and sororities hang out in this part of the cafeteria and the Jewish people hang out in another part. The blacks and Hispanics don't mix with each other. WTA is minority; TLP is white. Rarely do they cross over.
>
> The radio station, it's basically white. Black people come in but they stick together. A couple of years ago, our music format was alternative and basically white deejays, specialty shows, urban or whatever. Then we had a major urban format (R&B, hip hop) so we had alternative and urban formats. So we have white music and black music if you think about it. That's the way it is. You can make people meet and hang out, but that's going to be one time, and then, they're going to go back to their own groups.

Given that whites less frequently think about their racial identity, feel race has impacted their life, or think that something should be done, they are presumably less likely to take a stand to address segregation. Awareness of these dynamics and mechanisms provides opportunities to engage in discussion about structure, causality, and possibilities for change.

RACE'S ROLES

Students articulate various perspectives about how race, and particularly whiteness, functions and is reproduced. Each provides insight into how relationships are formed through a racialized lens. Here are three such examples:

> Race gives you a kind of bondage, like a protection group. Everyone pushed the immigrants away, you know. (Nonna, white female)

> Being white has given me a different perspective, being on the outside of a lot of the racism. It's given me a perspective, to see it for what it really is. If you want to be really honest, when I walk into a store, and someone else walks in behind me who is black, of course I notice who's being watched and who's not. It's completely clear how ridiculous and truly racist our society is no matter how many laws or whatever is said. You can see it every day. It's very obvious because they don't try and hide it from a white person. (Leon, white male)

I have friends of different races. The Italian kids when they're chillin' they make fun of the Chinese people, the Jewish kids make fun of the Italians, and I have this Chinese friend, you'd think he's black! (Vera, white female)

In this exchange students express awareness of the roles that racialization performs, but they also seem to suggest some level of ambivalence about the process and its significance. Nonna speaks about the protection of association based on race. Her comments presume a white experience where race provides protection and privilege. For people of color, racial identification is often more complicated and may implicate one negatively, such as through racial profiling that assumes negative attributes. For people of color, racial classification frequently functions to reduce status or weaken one's position in a society that places such high value on being white. In this way, "racialized narratives of invidious distinction" bestow positive and superior status (benefits of the doubt) on whites and confer negative and inferior status (presumed guilt) to Blacks, Latinos, and Asians (another mechanism). Implicit in these comments is the recognition that racial norms establish rules of acceptable conduct and structure relationships between individuals and groups based on racial classifications.

Leon reveals that he is conscious of the everyday discrimination that takes place between whites and people of color. He acknowledges that there is a presumed consent to these practices among many whites, almost like a "wink." He does not indicate whether he challenges offenders when he notices discriminatory practices; it appears that he simply observes. Leon's awareness, however, raises questions as to whether he finds these actions offensive.

Vera, on the other hand, reveals her understanding that race and ethnicity are often used as means to exert one group's superiority over another. She suggests that the process repeats itself between groups, as a flexible hierarchy. This awareness provides an opportunity (a "crack") to discuss how difference is used as a means to dominate, subordinate, and divide. Difference is not the problem, it's the value and meaning brought to those differences. She describes the fluidity of race as she speaks of someone who takes on an identity that falls outside the boundaries of where that individual would typically be classified. She explains that her friend is Chinese but that the way he acts (or possibly how he looks) complicates the notion of what race signifies. She seems willing to accept categories even when they may be confusing or complex.

In these passages, students describe "race's roles" as simultaneously flexible and rigid and tangible, yet elusive. Racialization performs distinct functions; yet can also be challenged. Awareness and sensitivity to this fluidity provide "cracks in the wall of whiteness" that can be engaged to develop a deeper understanding of how race has been used historically and presently to justify dominance, subordination, and exploitation. Attentiveness to the construction and reproduction of racialized patterns can thereby interrupt the process of formation of institutionalized, systemic, and recurring relationships and structures.

Overall responses indicating never or occasional decreased slightly from 2000 to 2009 (from 62.1 percent to 60.2 percent) and daily interaction increased (from 7.1 percent to 12.6 percent) (table 2.3). As in 2000, Latinos indicate greater levels of interaction between "races"; this is further discussed in the section below. In this survey, 85.7 percent of Blacks indicate that they are never or occasionally in the home of someone of another race; 100 percent of those identifying as indigenous do so. Of Asians, 71.5 percent report they never or occasionally are in the home of someone of another race; however, 21.4 percent indicate they do so daily. What might this signify about who is welcome, where?

Table 2.3a   How Often Are You in the Home of Someone of Another Race?: Data from the First Edition

	Never	Once a Month	Once a Week	Daily
Overall	62.1%	19.1%	11.8%	7.1%
Latinos	37.5%	22.9%	22.9%	14.6%
Asians	56.4%	25.6%	2.6%	15.4%
U.S.-born Blacks	72.1%	14.0%	7.0%	4.7%
Foreign-born Blacks	71.4%	17.5%	7.9%	3.2%
U.S.-born whites	61.8%	19.1%	15.4%	3.7%
Foreign-born whites	76.8%	15.9%	4.9%	2.4%

Table 2.3b   (2009) How Often Are You in the Home of Someone of Another Race?: Data from the Second Edition

	Never	Occasionally	Once a Month	Once a Week	Daily
Overall	30.1%	30.1%	17.5%	9.7%	12.6%
Latinos	14.3%	28.6%	14.3%	14.3%	28.6%
Asians	28.6%	42.9%	0.0%	7.1%	21.4%
Blacks	50.0%	35.7%	3.6%	3.6%	7.1%
Whites	23.3%	30.2%	27.9%	9.3%	9.3%
Indigenous	8.3%	16.7%	33.3%	25.0%	16.7%
Multi or Biracial	50.0%	50.0%	0.0%	0.0%	0.0%

Brooklyn Americans and Human Beings

Living in a racially diverse city bestows pride among its white inhabitants, as it lets them claim to be colorblind, multiculturally oriented, and nonracist. George, for example, says, "I call myself a Brooklyn American, partly to be funny but in reality it is a strong core of who I am. It is my sensitivity. A kernel of me knows that I am Jewish and white, but being from Brooklyn means having sensitivity . . . being liberal, accepting of all people. I live in a white Italian and Jewish environment."

Taking this comment at face value, one might conclude that George's chosen Brooklyn American identity breaks down racial barriers and allows him to align himself with the majority minority population of Brooklyn. In some ways, his gesture is similar to the self-identification as a "world citizen," or when people describe themselves as "human" without the constraints of a national, religious, or racial identification. This can provide an opportunity to recognize our interconnectedness.

However, I would also suggest that this type of identification also allows whites to deny how they are perceived while still receiving the privileges of that perception. Although mitigated by many other factors that can alter the terms of privilege (class, immigrant status, language, sexual orientation, ethnicity, gender, religion, etc.), denying one's race is a luxury rarely afforded people of color. George can use his Brooklyn American identity when he wants to, yet live as a white male as he conducts his daily activities. Whites can choose where to live (as long as they can afford to), be secure of personal safety, select schools, watch movies or television, or attend classes and generally expect to see people in positions of power who look like them. As long as they have the money, race will not hinder their options.[34] Likewise to self-describe as "human" or "colorblind" can protect similar privileges.

Several students spoke of trying to understand the meaning of white identity within a diverse environment; they found it different from being in a homogenous, overwhelmingly white, setting. Terry (white female) explains;

> It has to do with New York's diverse population. I'm not originally from here. Where I'm from there's not a whole bunch of different people. Here there are Jewish people, a lot of Italians, a lot of this, a lot of that. It's the first time I've ever experienced this. Where I used to live, it was just like I wouldn't know what you were and I wouldn't ever think of it.
>
> When I first moved here people could tell the race of someone like this, "Oh he's definitely Russian" or "He's definitely Jewish." How can you tell? What is it that points this out? I would never have known, I could never guess your race, still now. It's because of how I was brought up. Race just wasn't an issue.

I didn't see it. Even if there were diverse people, there definitely were, but it was not to the extreme. I didn't see it.

Terry's experiences leave her confused by the diversity in New York City. However, by explaining that she could never guess the race of her classmates, she dismisses the reality that racial images are prevalent in history books, media, and the arts. She suggests that race is only an issue in diverse environments; otherwise whites don't need to think about it at all.

Regardless of the extent to which an individual explicitly or implicitly supports or challenges patterns of racial inequality (e.g., in schools, the criminal justice system, etc.), whites can think of themselves as open-minded and dissociate themselves from people they consider "racist." They can define the parameters of their association yet also distance themselves from the groups and individuals who they feel do not embody the qualities they value. A common image of Brooklyn, for example, is as violent, crime-infested, and impoverished, as Randy illustrates: "Talk to people who live in Connecticut or Rhode Island, wherever it'd be more predominantly white in the area. Tell them you're from Brooklyn. They look at you like, 'Oh my God, there must be guns and killing all over the streets.'"

Is it possible to imagine someone of Haitian descent describing him or herself as a "Brooklyn American"? The chameleon quality to this designation—such that whites can be connected to, yet distanced from, negatively racialized images—bestows a freedom not frequently granted to people of color. Similarly, the repeated references to being Jewish or Italian raise the question of whether these identities are white plus something, minus something, or just plain "different."

Images that portray New York City as the diverse and multicultural capital of the world mask racialized patterns, segregation, and economic and political disparities. Unspoken rules that govern interaction are ignored. Urban images provide a narrative that says "race doesn't matter." This paradox blocks analysis of the very different experiences of various groups. A glaring example of this is a sign seen posted in several restaurants: "Misbehaving children will be sold." For someone whose ancestors and their children were in fact sold, this sign holds a meaning very different from its meaning for someone who does not have that history.

Two contrasting views of life in Brooklyn portray on the one hand, tolerance, peaceful coexistence, and diversity, and on the other, conflict, tension, and violence. Might one view express racialization from a dominant white perspective and the other intensely negative images of blackness? Mara asserts that living in urban areas provides exposure to different people, which in turn leads to increased open-mindedness:

The reason people act that way in the south is because they're not so open-minded to different cultures and different races as people in the north. When people come from other places in the world they usually come right to New York or Florida. Most immigration comes here. People in the south are not used to different races. Whatever you don't know, you are usually afraid of. They're not so open to different people. Not that they're narrow-minded, but because of the experiences they probably have.

Sam (white Italian male) doesn't appear to fully agree with Mara's description of Brooklyn:

Brooklyn is very diverse but when you go inside the neighborhoods, East Flatbush, you step inside Bensonhurst, it's another nationality there, so it is diverse, meaning that there's a lot of different cultures. People just feel safe when they're around their own. You shouldn't be scared of other races but that's how people are, you can't change the way they are.

These passages articulate the role that fear plays in reinforcing patterns of interaction. Individual incidents of hate crime leave whites feeling afraid of losing what they have but also uncertain about what they have been taught about different groups. If, in fact, racialized violence or poverty can't be blamed on individuals, one might have a social obligation to do something about inequality and/or bias. If, in fact, police are discriminatorily brutal, then claims of racial injustice may have merit. One would then have to consider whether whites are better off socioeconomically as a group because of a superior culture (an implicit assumption in white-dominated society) or if there are social dynamics that discriminate, positively, to place whites in more advantaged positions. Questioning the underlying causes for the current organization of society challenges the notion that whites are better off because they are better. Traditional beliefs about why some people (and groups) have greater success than others can then be questioned.

The following sections briefly describe findings that convey whites' understandings of the identities of Latino, Asian, Jewish, and Black populations.

Latinos "In the Middle"?[35]

While the meaning of being "Latino" is shifting in today's world, this identity is frequently described as ambiguous and in-between, and often associated with intermarriage. Comments such as "Latinos mix more because they're not really white but not really Black; it's really somewhere in the middle. The Latino kids hang out with the white kids or the Black kids, it goes both ways," "Latinos are comfortable with either Black or white, from my perspective," and "Latinos are kind of like, in the middle between Black and white" were extremely common.

Intragroup diversity is rarely mentioned, and, when it is, it's often in the context of tensions such as between Dominicans and Puerto Ricans, reinforcing a stereotype of Latinos as argumentative and combative.[36] Participants attribute the heightened visibility of Latinos in the United States to global migration and the increased political power of Latin American countries. Jenna (white female) reflects these issues: "They fit in with black and white and anything else but do have discrimination among themselves. I have friends from the Dominican Republic and from Mexico and they wouldn't get along, just because they weren't from the same place but they were still Latino. Other races, they would get along with them just fine. That bothered me to think they couldn't get along among themselves."

These statements indicate several assumptions about Latinos. They presume a common Latino life experience and that the categories of Black, white, and Latino are distinct. They convey prevalent stereotypes such as that Latinos don't get along with one another, yet relate well to other groups. They imply that "Latino" is an invisible category—what are they "in between"? It is also notable that this paradigm is not applied in the same way to Asians.

In the survey for this study, Latinos reported more than any group that they had been in the home of someone of another race and significantly more than any other group that they socialize daily outside of campus with someone of a different group. Latinos additionally reported more frequently than U.S.-born white students that they believe BC should diversify course material (52.1 percent versus 27.9 percent) and believe significantly more than all whites that efforts to include the historical and current experiences and contributions of people of color in the curriculum raise academic standards (Latinos, 47.9 percent; U.S.-born whites, 20.6 percent; foreign-born whites 25.6 percent). Joan (white female) offers this explanation: "Latino people are friends with white people, Latins, Italians, and Blacks. Because, they're between—they're not really Black and they're not really white so they can communicate. It's easier for them to get used to both."

Students' ideas about Latino identity assume rigid and exclusive classifications and by doing so, they delegitimize the particular experiences of this group. They also tend to reinforce the fallacy that race is a biological reality.[37] Recently, because of increased migration from the Latin diaspora and the shifting population demography of the United States, more interest has been generated about the history, culture, nations, and language incorporated under the umbrella considered "Latino." A large body of literature examines race and Latino identity, addressing a range of critical issues. These include the role of phenotype and critiques of a black/white paradigm (Martinez

1999, 129), labor force and political integration (Cordero-Guzman, Smith, and Grosfoguel 2001; Darder and Torres 1998; Moore and Pinderhughes 1993), transmigration (Basch, Schiller, and Blanc 1994), and racial identity (Martinez 1998; Rodriguez 2000; Rodriguez et al. 1991). This topic is complex—"The experience of Latinos in the United States demonstrates that ethnicity involves both internal and external components, which are culturally, politically and subjectively influenced and multi-leveled" (Rodriguez 2000, x)—and increasingly important as we grapple with the meaning of race in today's world. In fact, "Latino" is not considered a race at all, but an ethnicity within which there are people of African, Indigenous, European and Asian heritage.

Asians: At the Top? In the Middle? Entirely Invisible?

This section briefly describes students' perceptions about what it means to be Asian in the United States today. Numerous books (Zia 2000; Chou and Feagin 2008) explore the particularity of the experiences of Asians and Asian Americans (Tuan 1998; Ancheta 1998; Espiritu 1992; Yun 1989; Takagi 1992). However, Mia Tuan suggests there is a relative absence of literature exploring the experience of racialized ethnics whereby both race and ethnicity are salient features that shape how they are included, excluded, or marginalized. She asserts that this is particularly true for Asian Americans, because the perception is that they have been accepted into the mainstream and have achieved exceptional success academically, economically, and socially (1998, 21–23).

Within this study, there were some striking statistics that raise questions about the particularity of experience of Asians, especially in relation to this racialized identity. For example, they report significantly more (12.8 percent) than foreign-born white students (6.1 percent) that they witness racial tension among classmates and friends. Might this be because of a particularly heightened sense of awareness, given the way they are treated in U.S. society—as either "Forever Foreigners or Honorary Whites" (Tuan 1998)? Or perhaps, might this represent "hidden injuries of race" (Osajima 1993), consequences that accompany perhaps "subtler and yet oftentimes more frequent experiences with racial marginalization" (Tuan 1998, 3)? Some of the responses by Asian students articulate this feeling of invisibility. Sandy (Korean female) explains, for example, "My first recollection was in high school and the kids tried to set me up with this guy who was Chinese. They said you guys should get along really well because you look alike. That was the first time I distinctly remember that I felt racism in that way, saying that I should be with my own kind. I wasn't able to be with someone else because I didn't look like him or her. That's the first time I felt bad."

Ambivalence about assimilation as an attainable goal appears also to be expressed in that, in the survey conducted for this research, Asian students believe significantly more (46.2 percent) than U.S.-born white (26.5 percent) and foreign-born white students (25.6 percent) that historic inequality contributes to the average lower incomes and poorer housing of Blacks yet simultaneously believe significantly less (53.9 percent) than U.S.-born Black (86.1 percent) and foreign-born Black students (87.3 percent) that if people don't have equal access to resources, measures should be taken to equalize opportunity. This may well reflect uncertainty about assimilation as a positive goal, as well as their own experiences of being portrayed as a "model minority." They may recognize the role of historic discrimination but also believe that success is based on merit.

In relation to whether Brooklyn College should increase multicultural programming and hire staff and faculty of color, Asian students believe significantly more that they should (51.3 percent/30.8 percent) than U.S.-born white (19.1 percent/11 percent) and foreign-born white students (19.5 percent/12.2 percent). Asian students appear negatively impacted by social racialization, yet other factors also affect their everyday experiences, thereby influencing their perceptions and beliefs.[38] Many spoke about generational pressures against interacting with people from other backgrounds.

> Sometimes it just has to do with your parents—if a Chinese ever brought a black person home, the parents would say something about it. I'll tell you that much, my parents would. I mean, they're not racist, they're not trying to teach me to be racist, and it's just the way they feel. The same thing is with their parents, so sometimes it's genetic. (Leah, Asian female)

The data above provide information that might, with further research, lead to analyses, for example, of why Asian students believe less frequently than Blacks that measures should be taken to equalize opportunities if people don't have equal access to resources. In a very interesting summary article comparing the experiences of Asian Americans with those of African Americans and analyzing whether they have a greater number of options available to them, Miri Song, lecturer of sociology at the University of Kent, suggests that we need to "rethink and broaden the conceptualization of ethnicity and the need to re-examine our understanding of the images and labels applied to various ethnic minority groups" (2001, 57). Song particularly argues against the theorizing of ethnic minority groups as homogenous, because she asserts this intensely misrepresents the vast diversity—cultural, economic, and political—that is contained within the group classified as "Asian" and perpetrates the "model minority" image that does not uniformly apply (Song 2001, 57–82).

Being Jewish in Brooklyn

Religious and ethnic identities often take on particular importance. For example, in response to the "Everyday Understandings" survey question "What is your racial, ethnic, or national group?" nineteen of the 497 respondents wrote in "Jewish." The next largest write-in response to this question was "none," indicated by four students. Several comments were made by students who did not consider themselves to be white, as they self-identify as Jewish. They felt that religion, not race, was what separated them from their classmates and from other communities. Furthermore, "some Jews argue that because anti-Semitism prevents them from full participation in society, Jews, as a group, should not be considered white" (Hyde 1995, 93). Given the large numbers of Brooklyn College students who define themselves as Jewish (25.1 percent) and that the meaning of being Jewish was discussed regularly within the focus groups, it seemed important to include this summary of beliefs. It is also important to note that the Jewish population is diverse so the presumption that all Jews are of European descent is inaccurate. What it means to be Jewish is also dependent on one's particular affiliation, as the experience of Orthodox commitment is quite different from that of individuals who have a more secular identification. Socioeconomics plays a role, too, as the experience of a working-class Jew may be quite different than that of someone with wealth. Each of these factors demonstrates the complexity of the interconnections between racial, religious, and class experiences.

Both the college and borough communities have tremendous intragroup diversity, but students pointed to several important dimensions of the racialized experience of Jewish identity in today's world. For example, Sonya (Black female) points out, "If you're Jewish it doesn't stand out, it doesn't jump out if you're Russian, but there's no hiding it being Black. It's out there in the open. If you're Jewish you don't have to speak Hebrew or observe the Sabbath." At the same time, several students spoke to the way that their own Jewish identity had been challenged because of the particularity of their experience. Leon (white male) explains:

> I remember someone once asked me "What are you?" I said, "A lot of nationalities, and my religion is Jewish." They wanted to know why I didn't have the little curls and the hat, did I ever try ham. It was shocking. You live in Brooklyn, how do you not know that there are different kinds of Jews? Do you think that only those people who look like that are Jewish and everyone else is Italian or Russian, or whatever? I'm white but I'm Jewish. You'd be surprised at the ignorance that you're faced with. People just don't understand at all. They're so in the dark about people around them that they don't understand what their cousins

are like. You'd think that if you live so close to different kinds of people you'd have some idea, but the questions I get asked are ridiculous.

Nonna (white female) speaks of a similar experience, "I'm Jewish and I'm Russian. When I came here, the Borough Park people they had an attitude. 'Don't even say you're Jewish, because you are not.' They don't believe that if you don't wear the hat, you can still be Jewish." Jerry (white male) recognizes how what it means to be Jewish is different depending on one's geographic location:

> I'm of Jewish background. It's very common to see a Jewish person in Brooklyn but I've been to Missouri and I wouldn't even tell people that I'm Jewish. You see highways sponsored by the KKK and stuff out in the open. I would be an alien to them. They wouldn't know, they would be like, 'What does a Jewish person look like?' It's a very strange concept to them.

While whiteness in Brooklyn is generally considered to include the Jewish community, in other areas of the country Jews are considered not quite white.[39] Distinctions are sometimes made about who is considered "sufficiently" Jewish. The community itself is internally stratified, and there is a lack of general understanding about what it means to be a Jew in this context. Both Leon and Nonna are concerned that their Jewishness has been called into question. They perceive a lack of understanding about their identity both within and outside of the Jewish community. It was Sonya who summed up these complexities by recognizing the role of race and skin color in shaping experience. In a public forum in 1999, entitled "Multiculturalism and Jews," David expresses some resentment that emerges from this ambiguity: "I am Jewish not white and Jews are a minority; why isn't the multiculturalism movement about me?"

In *How Jews Became White Folks: What That Says about Race in America*, Karen Brodkin explores this issue as it relates to twentieth-century political, social, and economic developments. She examines in depth the transformations that have taken place within the Jewish community from a time during the early part of the twentieth century, when they were considered nonwhite immigrants, to a current status incorporated in a pan-ethnic whiteness. In a National Opinion Research Center (NORC) survey on attitudes about different racial and ethnic groups, Jews were the only group viewed positively compared to whites in general (NORC 1998b, Question 266). Brodkin extensively discusses the history of Jews as model immigrants and traces the federal programs that assisted their upward mobility in a form of affirmative action (Brodkin 1994, 78–102).

While issues related to the positionality of Jews and Italians arose within the discussions, the particularities of these identities within the panethnicity of whiteness deserve their own investigation. Overall, even in the cases where students did not want to identify as white, they generally recognize that they are perceived as such by other people and were willing to pursue the discussion.

Black Students' Perceptions, Experiences, and Beliefs

Throughout this book there are references to attitudes toward people of African descent, both implicit and explicit, in the analysis of whiteness. This section specifically summarizes some of the responses of Black students about the issues explored. This material deserves full examination of its own, as it was not the focus of this study.

Reflecting personal awareness and experience, Black students' beliefs about racial inequality are reflected in that they (48.8 percent of U.S.-born; 71.4 percent of foreign-born) believe significantly more than U.S.-born white students (29.4 percent) that discrimination contributes to the lower incomes and poorer housing of Blacks. They believe significantly more (55.8 percent of U.S.-born and 55.6 percent of foreign-born) than white students (U.S.-born, 26.5 percent; foreign-born, 25.6 percent) that historic inequality contributes to the lower incomes and poorer housing of Blacks. Furthermore, their experience with the police harshly demonstrated their feelings of vulnerability. Max describes how this has impacted his everyday life. He says, "When I started hanging out by myself, my father was always protective. I realized it's because I am a Black male. I would be stereotyped, picked up by police and put in a detention center. I was in the fifth grade."

The acute awareness that anything could occur regardless of one's own actions was expressed clearly in the survey: Black students (55.8 percent of U.S.-born and 58.7 percent of foreign-born) believe significantly more than white students (26.5 percent of U.S.-born; 25.6 percent of foreign-born) and Asians (28.2 percent) that the NYC Police Department uses excessive force. This continues to be true in 2009. In the recent survey, 39.2 percent of Black students agreed or strongly agreed that "my chances of finding a job are harder because of my race, as compared to 11.6 percent of whites. Similarly, 17.9 percent of Blacks agreed or strongly agreed that "People of color are treated the same as whites when applying for jobs" compared to 27.9 percent of whites.

Challenging the common grievance of whites that Blacks receive special privileges, a columnist for the *Nashville City Paper* suggests Blacks do receive preferential treatment. Blacks and other people of color are preferred targets of law enforcement officers. People of color are recipients of preferential treatment in our criminal justice system; they receive longer sentences than whites for the same crimes committed. It is certainly preferable to deny a home loan to a person of color in particular neighborhoods where whites are the majority, if you are a white-owned institution (Secours 2001c).

Another important issue raised by these data is whether the beliefs and experiences of native and foreign-born Blacks are similar. While there are many differences in perspectives, there are also similarities. In this study, for example, as these two groups perceive the possibility of achieving the American Dream, the overall influence of race in determining attitude is apparent:[40] U.S.-born Black students (48.8 percent) believe significantly less than foreign-born whites (76.8 percent) that the American Dream can be achieved by anyone who works hard. Foreign-born Black students (44.4 percent) believe significantly less than foreign-born (76.8 percent) and U.S.-born whites (64 percent) that the American Dream can be achieved by anyone who works hard.

A number of foreign-born Black students expressed that they did not think about being Black until they arrived in the United States and were repeatedly reminded. They expressed sentiments like Jean Paul's, which implicitly communicate the subjugation and negative stereotyping of Blacks in the United States: "Even as a Black person from another country, a lot of times you're scared of black Americans because back in your country, you hear these negative things about blacks."

On several occasions whites noted that they feel confused about why, when they bring up race, they are not always met with a positive reception by students of color. For example, at an open forum entitled "Who's Black, Who's White," Rona, a white professor, asked: "I just don't understand. Blacks get angry when I say race matters. Is it denial, or just too harsh, too overwhelming, too long a wait? Why do they acknowledge it themselves and resent when I raise it?"

Evan (Black male), responded, "How can they trust where you are coming from? They sense you have a preconceived notion of who they are; you are emphasizing their difference and not your own. They presume a lack of identification, a fronting 'See, I'm not a racist.'"

In another example, Louis, a white professor, says: "I notice that, consistently, when asked how they identify themselves, Blacks and Asians say 'human being.' I think they are conflicted because they know that people see them as colored or not white."

While both faculty members express a desire to understand the apparently contradictory responses of people of color, they tried to generalize and simplify the reasons why people identify themselves in one way or another. Evan's response indicates his acute recognition of perceived stereotypes and presumptions about how people of color are assumed to identify themselves.[41] His comment also notes the posturing that sometimes takes place when whites want to be seen in a positive light and certainly not as racist. This desire can, in fact, prevent individuals from increasing their understanding of themselves; by trying to seem aware, they shield themselves from seeing what is really going on.

These quotes and data illustrate the experience of discrimination and the heightened desire to take action to make a difference, on the part of Blacks versus whites. It is interesting, however, that both foreign- (15.9 percent) and U.S.-born Blacks (18.6 percent), U.S.-born whites (32.4 percent), and Latinos (20.8 percent) believe significantly less than foreign-born white students (48.8 percent) that the United States is a land of opportunity for all people. This points out that the category "white" is not monolithic. The recent experience of Eastern European immigrants appears to lead them to believe that the United States is indeed full of promise in a way that U.S.-born whites, especially those experiencing downward economic pressures, do not feel. This theme is explored in detail in chapter 3 in the section on "Race and the Foreign-Born Experience."

THE RACE TO IDENTITY

Many people, particularly though not exclusively "white" people, negotiate their recognition that race matters with their denial that race exists. Individuals pull in and out of a parking spot as if realizing there is a broken bottle in the way. They acknowledge racialized characterizations, such as "it was black people who stole our bikes," but then state "it's not that I'm racist," or "it's not that I think all black people. . . ," as if to legitimate their initial comment. This chapter examined how race is often conceived as a barrier for people of color but rarely as a status enhancer for whites.

The resistance that most whites express toward talking about race and recognizing ways that everyday experiences are infused with racialized notions masks structural inequality. In turn, this process allows for the reproduction of institutional patterns that perpetuate the status quo and prevent the understanding how group experiences differ. Studies of white racial thinking have emerged within academia relatively recently. When presumptions of whiteness as natural and superior (in hegemonic discourse) are exposed, the link between how people think and the persistence of institutional inequalities becomes increasingly clear. This provides opportunities to challenge long-standing patterns of power and subordination.

Put another way, once white privilege is acknowledged, cultural explanations for the positioning of different groups in the structure become less convincing. Common practice is to do what one can to deny white privilege rather than figure out how to reconcile contradictions. In fact, it is one's responsibility to uphold dominant explanations about the positioning of

individuals and groups, or anarchy and chaos might rule! Structural explanations for inequality can be considered. However, students' conclusions
almost uniformly dismiss their ambivalence and confusion as if it were too
overwhelming to consider any possibility other than that poverty is the fault
and responsibility of individuals or their group affiliation. It's as if they say,
"I cannot acknowledge that there may be structural causes because who then
could be blamed for 'those people's problems'?"

This chapter examined racial identity and mechanisms of racialization that
reinforce, reproduce, and expand upon a culture-of-poverty framework. An
underlying implication is the way that resistance is racialized and implicitly perceived as an outgrowth of Black radicalism—the notion that indeed
Blacks want more than their share of resources and of power. Interestingly,
Obama's health care proposal is seen as reparations and he himself has been
portrayed as a socialist, calling for the redistribution of wealth. These ideas
are conveyed as tyrannical and seditious at the same time that levels of wealth
inequality and economic challenge for most people are at their highest in
almost one hundred years. When challenging the status quo, one is viewed
with disdain, as if the very idea and act of dissent is something that only subordinate and inferior peoples engage in as a means to blame the system for
their own personal deficiencies.

This racialization of resistance is to me a cornerstone in the reproduction
of whiteness. The social stigma against raising questions, being critical, voicing opposition to the status quo, is viewed as "a Black thing" and something
very negative, to be engaged in only by someone in a subordinate status. The
white radical tradition is rich within the labor, communist, and abolitionist
movements throughout history, yet activists have been marginalized, stigmatized, and dismissed as lunatics. Meanwhile, the widespread development of
white supremacist groups and thinking is not viewed as a significant threat
to society (or at least not to whites).[42] Cathy Cohen thoughtfully explores the
question of what constitutes agency or political resistance in queer, Black,
and feminist experiences: "it may be that through the repetition of deviant
practices by multiple individuals new identities, communities, and politics are
created and a space emerges where seemingly deviant, unconnected behavior
might evolve into conscious acts of resistance that serve as the basis for a
mobilized politics of deviance" (2004, 43).

There has been virtually no public discussion of the lack of racial profiling of people such as Dylan Klebold and Timothy McVeigh, of skinheads in
general. Their radicalism (right-wing and white) has not been viewed within
an overall context as part of the rise of white supremacist groups throughout
the United States over the last twenty years.[43] They are not recognized for
the threat and connections that they represent as players of far-right ideology

that is counter to "American values"; that would not be possible, because they are white males who by definition exemplify those values as well-meaning, upstanding citizens, and anyway, "that kind of stuff doesn't happen here." White students running wild on spring break in Daytona Beach are either presumed to be "all talk, no action," good-intentioned teenagers "feeling their oats," or simply as "boys who will be boys."[44]

Their whiteness shields them from public scrutiny, and their radicalism was not perceived as a threat in the same way that the words and actions of Al Sharpton or of protesters against police brutality, the death penalty, and the bombing of Vieques are portrayed. Post-Katrina, two photos were differently captioned: Blacks were described as having looted and whites as having found food. This evident distinction brought media scrutiny.[45] Even Jenna Bush, daughter of the former president, provided a vivid example of positive white racial profiling in everyday practice as she was reprimanded for under-age drinking, not once but twice. Had this been Colin Powell's son, would the reaction have been the same?

The framing of opposition politics as an ideology of people of color has resulted in the dramatic reformulation of the meaning of liberalism. At another stage in history to be a liberal was something to be proud of, as it represented an image of someone caring, generous, and willing to stand for what's right. Today this concept has been vilified. In a recent presidential election, when Michael Dukakis confessed his previous liberal affiliations, he was practically out of the running for office. George Bush Sr., in fact, to demonstrate Dukakis's radicalism, argued that Dukakis was a card-carrying member of the American Civil Liberties Union. Notions of "bleeding heart liberals" and Democrats as people who patronizingly support social services illustrate the extent to which the political tenor of our society has moved to the right over the last thirty years (contrary to a popular belief that society is becoming more open-minded, liberal, and equal). This shift articulates a disdain for communities of color and the incorporation of the culture-of-poverty framework into dominant discourse. However, in the first decade of the twenty-first century it appears that there is yet another shift underway with at least two-thirds of Americans agreeing with many core progressive ideas (Halpin and Agne 2009). Some of that shift is evident in everyday interactions between people but much less apparent in data related to inequalities in housing, education, income, access to health care, and so on. The question is whether that shift makes social change easier or harder. Does it translate to greater dissatisfaction with the system? Where is blame placed?

When social patterns bend in your favor, you need not pay attention. However, as evidenced in this chapter, openings do exist to increase awareness, as many students revealed significant understanding of the processes and mechanisms of racialization and how they might be overcome.[46]

3

"American" Identity, Democracy, the Flag, and the Foreign-Born Experience

What images are conjured up by the concepts of democracy, nation, and patriotism? What does the flag mean to people in the United States; what function does it serve? Does this national symbol represent something different for foreign-born versus U.S.-born individuals, or to people of different races? In what ways has U.S. natural identity been racialized throughout history? Is it still? As discussed in chapter 1, Euro-dominance emerged as an intrinsic component of global capitalism and the development of the United States so it is important to analyze the racial character of the nation.

In light of the tragic events of September 11, 2001, and the years since, the concept of national identity and characteristics ascribed to "the American people" have become more present in public discourse. With a growing foreign-born population, the question has been raised as to whether the United States can be a truly multicultural union. Does claiming national allegiance provide a vantage point from which to stand for peace, justice, and equality (Nussbaum 1996, 136) or does it divide us from each other and people of other nations? What functions do nationalism, patriotism, and citizenship serve in today's interconnected world?[1]

ON BEING "AMERICAN," DEMOCRACY, THE DREAM, AND THE FLAG

Congresswoman Barbara Lee articulated her thoughts about being American eloquently when she voiced the only "no" vote on the Senate floor to the question of giving President Bush full powers to go to war with Afghanistan in the fall of 2001. She spoke of her definitions of patriotism and democracy and challenged the mainstream equation of loyalty and military might. She asserted that as a citizen, one has the right and freedom to represent one's point of view and to dissent—central tenets of democracy. She said,

> If I am going to be patriotic, and I am, and if I am going to be a good American, which I know I am, I am going to make sure that our democracy works and I'm going to hold it accountable and make sure that it works not only for my constituents but for the whole country. . . . Being patriotic at this moment in our history means participating in decisions about the future of our world. It means participating in decisions that will hopefully bring us to peace. . . . (Davey D. 2001)

Similarly, as said by a focus group participant in 2009,

> After 9/11 it was a different sector of Americans who, you know, who felt more American. I'm not saying that they were crazy Americans after that but I think that because a lot of black people feel like, more like an American but how much are you American because you're not afforded the same rights. I think that they felt like okay it was them against us and for a minute we were part of the us so it was more like a kind of reinvestment thing kind of in America. It didn't stay that; it was really strong after September 11th for a little while. It faded away but I think that's still relevant. It kind of perked up people for a little bit and then it went away and then it was easier to call back upon it during the elections because it was a greater investment in America because it was like, it was us against them and we were part of the us. (Josh, Black male)

While many people reveal that they feel disconnected from what it means to be an American, waving a flag, referring to oneself as "American," and the expression "God Bless America" instills a sense of superiority in relationship to the rest of the world. This identity has conferred elevated standing to those who hold it. However, a recent survey found that the global image of the United States was significantly less favorable than it was a decade ago (Pew Global Research Project 2007). At the same time, distinctions are made between images of "true Americans" and people of status made questionable by the ambiguous borders and margins at which they are positioned. Native-born Blacks, Latinos, and Asians hold tentative status as Americans, depending on circumstance. Additionally, different experiences appear along lines of generation, race, and language, and between immigrant and native-born populations.

U.S. national identity is one of many dimensions through which the social hierarchies of U.S. society operate, at times to contradict and at others to enhance the status of its holder. This chapter reviews and analyzes perceptions and views about these issues.

On Being "American"

> What is a "good" American in a country where an estimated 60 million [people] were either born in a foreign country or have foreign-born parents?
>
> —G. Pascal Zachary (2002, 23)

Ambiguity about what it means to be "American" and how you become "American" and/or a citizen allows race to both reinforce structured inequality and challenge it. Most U.S.-born white students said that they do not think about what it means to be "American"; they just "are." Similar to being white, being "American" and a U.S. citizen is an assumed state of being from which all "others" depart. This status can be bestowed by birth, through inheritance or naturalization, by association, or through a belief system, but it can also be retracted, especially for people of color. Discrimination against the Arab American population post 9/11, many of whom were born in the United States, testifies to their vulnerability, regardless of their place of birth or citizenship. A political cartoon that circulated soon after the events of September 11 showed one man, who appeared to be white, angrily shaking his finger at a man who appeared to be Arab and saying, "Go back to where you were born." To this, the man asks, "Chicago?"

Assumptions about race thereby define who belongs and their corresponding entitlements. During the fall of 2001, this issue became acutely visible when, for example, the Federal Bureau of Investigation summoned hundreds of men with Arab surnames for interviews about terrorism. The government justified this blatant racial profiling in the name of "homeland security." However, one might wonder why the government did not round up microbiologists, given significant evidence that multiple envelopes of anthrax were sent to various individuals by an American microbiologist (Blackhurst 2001). If the reasoning is that perpetrators of mass murder should be swiftly and summarily executed, why not call upon tobacco industry executives along with abortion doctor murders? (Williams 2001, 11) In fact, rounding up populations based on preconceived notions about their character has occurred throughout U.S. history.

The following exchange demonstrates the ambiguities of American identity:

> Don't you get a certificate for being an American? You do. Yes, you do. You become an American by going for a special test and they give you your certificate. It's by law. (Sonya, Black female)

> No, that's when you become a citizen, not an American. Being an American is a belief system; it's the way you act and think toward other people. It's not where you're from or where you're born. (Keri, Black female)

If you are a citizen you get a lot of benefits that you don't get if you are not. But you are still an Irish person who just became an American citizen. (Bella, white female).

> America started off as immigrants you know, so it's not like somebody's actually American. Ancestors came here from different countries so if you were born here you are automatically an American. (Leon, white male)

The struggle to understand the meaning of being American shifts between something tangible (naturalization and citizenship), something unambiguous (bestowed by birth), something ambiguous (a belief system), and something transitory and continuously shifting (a combination of any of these).[2] It was apparent that even white students who said they never thought about being American expected a range of privileges as part and parcel of their birthright, including the "psychological wage" of a belief that "we are the 'best'" and the material goods that accompany being located in the homeland of the world elite. "[The United States] has no collective identity except as the best, the greatest country, superior to all others and the acknowledged model for the world" (Hobsbawm 2003, B8).

Does being American mean giving up other national identifications? Assimilation and pluralism are compared by Louis (white male faculty member):

> People in the U.S. are not as nationalistic. Americans are open to embracing anyone as an American. It's interesting that people who are born here and lived here their whole life still don't think about being an American. To have an American identity draws out notions of assimilation and maintenance of a cultural identity. Do we have assimilation or pluralism? Pluralism is when many different cultures are living together. Assimilation is more complicated. Many people hold a negative connotation with it because it assumes that people should change. People do not just want to be American; they want to keep their own identity.

Certain questions about national identity continuously arose in discussions. To identify oneself as American, for whites, is often linked to the choice between giving up association with one's heritage, being pan-ethnic white, or not being completely American. Many students were ambivalent about whether an immigrant can ever really be "American." Kim (Black female) asserts that "just because you're an American citizen, it doesn't mean you have to forget where you come from or the culture you had, or start changing anything." Mia (Latina) agrees, articulating a slightly different multicultural perspective: "American culture is a combination of everything. It is the big melting pot. There's no one set standard to what American is. There is no such thing."

Table 3.1   The United States Can Be Multicultural and American at the Same Time

Disagree	Moderately Agree	Agree
57.9%	20.6%	21.4%

The survey data in table 3.1 provide insight into beliefs about this issue. Foreign-born whites (68.3 percent) agree significantly more than foreign-born Blacks (42.9 percent) that the United States can be multicultural and American. These statistics appear to reflect the racialized experience of foreign-born Black students of being seen first and foremost as Black while the foreign-born white students feel that their ability to assimilate is not hampered by how they are racially identified.

Does loyalty preclude dissent;[3] is there only one way to be patriotic? Is patriotism important? Why? The concept of being American has held distinctive meanings for different people at various times in history, just as patriotism has been evoked simultaneously to make the case for inclusion and exclusion, unity and dissent, and both military service and conscientious objection. In this way, the United States has two contradictory traditions (Scott 2003, 1). Benedictine Sister Joan Chittister, OSB, writes in her weekly column in the National Catholic Reporter, "The world wants to know who we really are—international menace or mighty hero?" (2003).

Similarly, the idea of the United States as a benevolent global keeper of peace projects the image of its citizens as nice (white) guys. This imagery was exemplified in a comment made by a firefighter, as reported in November 2001, on CNN. He said, "We in the United States take care of everyone all over the world and this is what we get?"[4]

Another important issue is that the common equation of the label "American" with someone from the United States, rather than the continent, intrinsically racializes the image of who is and who is not included. Elizabeth Martinez points out that the concept of "Las Americas," the entire interrelated hemisphere, has been rendered irrelevant and nonexistent, as the United States has defined these terms solely in relation to itself.[5] In fact, there are many who might support a moratorium on equating "being American" with "being of the United States" and call for the national identity to be redefined as United Statesian, U.S. American, or some other phrase! It would just be right.

The important question of whether being American can mean something more than residing in the United States rarely arose in discussions. In an article entitled "Don't Call This Country 'America': How the Name Was Hijacked and Why It Matters Today," Martinez discusses the relationship between the appropriation of this label and the U.S. history and worldview. She argues that, while there are more than twenty countries within the continents of North and South America, it is the policy of manifest destiny to deny their existence. . . . In unthinking self-defense, we unite with a name that reflects a worldview both imperialist and racist" (2003, 70). This articulates a presumption of U.S. dominance such that there is no consideration of a broader "American" world. Furthermore, the mystification of the term "American" and its equation with someone from the United States, specifically of European descent, function to reinforce patterns of structured inequality by naturalizing these two concepts as one and the same. Toni Morrison explains that the conflation of national and racial identity is particular to the United States. She says, "Deep within the word 'American' is its association with race. To identify someone as a South African is to say very little; we need the adjective 'white' or 'Black' or 'colored' to make our meaning clear. In this country it is quite the reverse. American means white" (1992, 47). Only Jean Paul raised this issue:

> Growing up, I always thought of myself as an American even though I wasn't born here. I was born in Haiti in the Caribbean and part of the continent of America. When I was six years old we kids were discussing, we live here in America; doesn't that make us automatically Americans? If somebody's from the continent of Africa, they're African, no matter what country they're from. Until I came here, I realized no, I'm not American; I'm just an immigrant. I'm Haitian and I've been living here for six years. I have to be a citizen to be a quote unquote American. It's controversial to me, that you can't be an American just because you weren't born here, and there are fifty states on the flag.

This testimony points to the uncertainty in people's minds about the racial and national nature of American identity. Jean Paul raises issues of homogeneity, assimilation, Eurocentrism, and incorporation into mainstream society. The equation of being American with being from the United States speaks to the centering and naturalization of whiteness, for this question is less a concern for foreign-born whites. National pride was frequently presumed, regardless of an individual's awareness of his or her identity, as Mara (white female) articulates:

> I consider myself to be an American. I was born in America; my parents were born in America. I think my grandparents were born in America, but I have Irish, German, and Dutch heritage. I love this country and that means a lot to me. Sometimes I'm amazed at myself when I hear, like, "God Bless America" or "The Star Spangled Banner." I get emotional, and I think, wow, God blessed this country.

What does it means to say "God blessed this country" when there are as many gods as there are religions, and when most of the world's people do not subscribe to a religion that believes in a Judeo-Christian "God"?[6] Why bless our country (5 percent of the global population) and not someone else's? Immanuel Wallerstein discusses God's unequal blessings and how the United States has always defined itself, measured by the yardstick of the world: "We are better; we were better; we shall be better" (2001).This notion reinforces national pride and presumes superiority, as illustrated by Karen, who said, "Being an American is being born here, and having your parents from here. Having a sense of pride, but I don't get all sappy. I don't know why not." However, Diane (white female) points out that patriotism is complicated:

> A lot of foreigners appreciate America more than people born here because people who are born here don't realize the history of America. They don't really see the revolution or anything. They just say I was born here so I'm American. But people who actually come from different governments have more a sense and appreciation of the different freedoms that Americans take for granted. I never really thought if I was really an American or not. I just assumed I was born here, my parents were born here, my grandparents were born here, and I don't speak another language at home. I associate [being American] with people that were born here. In retrospect, people that come here, they come here for a reason. I think they're more American than people who are actually born here.

These passages portray conflicting images of whether, in order to be a "real American," you must uphold a certain ideology or feel a national pride, or whether it's enough to be born here or immigrate to the United States. Students explained their sentiments but were not sure what is "true." They think out loud and seem to presume that, in order to claim American identity, you need to pledge allegiance to the flag and be patriotic in very specific ways. They tend to view citizenship as the most definitive criterion for being truly American but clearly believe that this identity involves loyalty to symbols but sometimes articulate their confusion about how this is decided:

> With that 9/11 thing okay we got threats from like the Middle East and then you know we're all like oh my god, okay, he's Middle Eastern be careful but remember when we had like that Russian threat also? We never went like oh Russian people be careful. (Lily, Asian female)

In light of changing demographics in the United States, it was interesting that Diane raised the issue of the language spoken at home. In 1996, 35 percent of public school students in New York City spoke a language other than English at home (Tell 1999). In 2008, nearly 42 percent do so.[7]

Students grapple with understanding what determines someone's identity and status, both self-determined and those set by state or legal systems. Race plays a role for example as to whether one has the luxury of defining this position. Whites generally have the option to be patriotic and nationalistic or not, and to choose the terms by which one's identities are negotiated. You can decide to think about being American, or not. You can identify one way one day, and another on a different day. A person of color, however, as Jean Paul described, does not have that privilege. One's identity is selected for you, like an arranged marriage with legal mandate. Consider (white female) Jenna's statement:

> Being an American means freedom: freedom of religion, freedom to be whoever you want, to say whatever you want, political freedom. That's why so many people come here, because other countries don't have that freedom, you can't practice whatever religion you want, you can't speak out politically. There's so much more opportunity in America. There is an American Dream, but people have to work for it.

Jenna suggests that if one doesn't achieve the American Dream it is because one did not work hard enough. Some of the contradictions implicit in this perspective came to light in the aftermath of September 11, 2001, as media coverage noted concerns about the unequal distribution of funds raised for families of the deceased (Barstow and Henriques 2001, A1) and about differentials in the severance packages of people who lost jobs.[8] While rarely explicit, these long-standing economic disparities have become increasingly difficult to explain and justify; they thereby provide an opening for broader discussion about how one actually achieves the American Dream, why some people do and others don't. Tables 3.2a, 3.2b, and 3.2c document whether students consider themselves to be American—most significantly, U.S.-born white students do so significantly more than any other group, and foreign-born Black students do so significantly less than any other group.

These data suggest evidence of the racialization of the foreign-born experience such that foreign-born whites are more easily assimilated into U.S. society than foreign-born Blacks. Another contrast is the difference in response between U.S.-born whites and U.S.-born Blacks. One explanation sums it up: "Though I was and am an American, I [don't] have what most Americans feel—that unique sense of belonging" (Gilmore 2002, 27). In 2009, it was interesting that many Latino and Asian students expressed substantively more uncertainty than any other group about whether they consider themselves American. Another striking finding in response to this question was that female respondents (24.5 percent) disagreed with the statement that they consider themselves American significantly more frequently than men (13.6 percent) did.

An interesting finding of a survey by Columbia University's Center on African American Politics and society and ABC News Polling Unit found

Table 3.2a   I Consider Myself to Be an American: Data from the First Edition

	Disagree	Moderately Agree	Agree
Overall	21.8%	28.4%	49.9%
Latinos	33.3%	29.2%	37.5%
Asians	30.8%	38.5%	30.9%
U.S.-born Blacks	4.7%	34.9%	58.1%
Foreign-born Blacks	47.6%	38.1%	12.7%
U.S.-born whites	2.9%	12.5%	83.8%
Foreign-born whites	32.9%	37.8%	29.3%

Table 3.2b   I Consider Myself to Be an American: Data from the Second Edition

	Strongly Disagree	Disagree	Agree	Strongly Agree	Don't Know
Overall	4.8%	14.3%	53.3%	20.0%	7.6%
Latinos	0.0%	14.3%	57.1%	14.3%	14.3%
Asians	0.0%	20.0%	40.0%	13.3%	26.7%
U.S.-born Blacks	3.6%	21.4%	50.0%	17.9%	7.1%
Foreign-born Blacks	7.0%	9.3%	58.1%	18.6%	7.0%
U.S.-born whites	0.0%	50.0%	50.0%	0.0%	0.0%
Foreign-born whites	0.0%	15.4%	38.5%	46.2%	0.0%

Table 3.2c   How Often Do You Think about Your National Identity?: Data from the Second Edition

	Never	Occasionally	Once a Month	Once a Week	Daily
Overall	8.6%	47.6%	11.4%	17.1%	15.2%
Latinos	7.1%	50.0%	14.3%	21.4%	7.1%
Asians	13.3%	53.3%	13.3%	6.7%	13.3%
Blacks	3.6%	57.1%	3.6%	17.9%	17.9%
Whites	7.0%	48.8%	11.6%	20.9%	11.6%
Indigenous	0.0%	50.0%	0.0%	50.0%	0.0%
Multi or Biracial	7.7%	46.2%	7.7%	23.1%	15.4%

that the election of Barack Obama as president led to an increase in Blacks reporting that their national identity was more important than race, leading to about equal numbers saying that race was more important. They found stark differences between income levels such that Blacks who make less than

$20,000 a year are more likely to identify as American first, as compared to those earning $100,000 or more. Furthermore, 60 percent of Blacks said they have more in common with people of the same social class than racial group (Harris 2008).

In 2002, the national organization Public Agenda conducted an extensive survey of immigrants in the United States. They found that 42 percent chose "I have become an American" and 41 percent took a middle position: "I act like an American outside, but at home I keep my own culture and traditions" (Farkas, Duffett, and Johnson 2003, 30). While a follow-up survey was conducted in 2009, this question was not included. Of available data however, the Pew Hispanic Center found that among Latino youth the percent identifying as American ranges from 3 percent (first generation immigrants), to 33 percent (second generation), to 50 percent (third generation and higher). Two-thirds of Latinos aged 16–25 are U.S. born.[9] In another survey, of foreign-born Muslims, 25 percent said they identify first as American, 46 percent as Muslim, and 23 percent as both (Kohut 2007a 37).

Discourse of the United States as the "land of opportunity" and leading model of democracy at work makes it difficult to discuss social stratification and structural inequality. Especially after the World Trade Center tragedy, any questioning of U.S. foreign policy has come to be viewed as an attack on "America." Mainstream discourse presumes a white middle-class experience. The justification for random interrogation of Arab Americans is framed as "I have nothing to hide, why should they?" However, this perspective epitomizes the experience of individuals who have never been "the persistent object of suspect profiling, never been harassed, never been stigmatized just for the way they look" (Williams 2001, 11).

Democracy Is . . .

Deeply rooted in the idea of American identity is that of democratic values, including idealized principles of freedom, justice, and individualism.[10] This section explores students' beliefs about these ideals and how they are actualized in everyday living. It focuses on implicit and underlying assumptions common in popular discourse. These complex notions sometimes contradict one another; tensions are considered acceptable in discussion of ideals. Students were asked, "What does democracy mean to you?"

Jacob responds, "[It means] being able to say what you want to say, when you want to say it." Spoken in one of the focus groups, this comment was followed by a discussion about how the United States is different from other countries in the world. Jacob asserts a principle that he believes has been true for all people in the United States. Freedom of speech has been central to the self-definition of the United States as a nation, founded as it was by people fleeing religious and political persecution. The Bill of Rights explicitly stands for freedom of speech, including the right to dissent. Meanwhile such rights have been parceled out to those considered "deserving," in contrast to those who are not, throughout U.S. history. "'Us versus Them' thinking easily becomes a general call for American supremacy, the humiliation of 'the other'" (Nussbaum 2001, 11).

In *An American Dilemma*, Gunnar Myrdal articulated the moral contradiction whereby the United States professes an allegiance to democratic and egalitarian ideals while allowing the reality of racial discrimination to exist within its boundaries (1964 [1944]). Other observations of the difference between the ideal and the practice of democracy in the United States appear in the works of, for example, Frederick Douglass, Anna Julia Cooper, and David Walker (Blassingame 1982; Wiltse 1965; Lemert and Bhan 1998) and more recent discussions of the use of torture, the funding priorities, and bailout of the very rich point to this incongruency.

The United States is viewed as the epitome of democracy as it incorporates the principle of egalitarianism. However, what do these comments imply? John (white male) thinks out loud:

> It's a lot different than the founders thought it would be. I don't think there's as much democracy as there was, because of big business. They control so many aspects of our lives. It's not so much a democracy anymore. We don't really have much to say about it. It's kind of biased because it's not what I think, you think, he thinks, but just what they think. Anyway, there are so many races now. Then the white male was in charge. Now women are in charge, blacks in charge. Hispanics and Asians come here. It's totally different. It was founded as a democracy but changed.

John questions the degree of big business's control in today's world and asserts that global corporatization has stolen the democratic process from everyday people. He also raises concerns about whether diverse groups can share power. John alludes to feeling that things are out of control but seems ambivalent about whether it is corporate elite or women or people of color who are now in charge.[11] In contrast, others feel that democracy in the United States does serve the interests of the people. Penny (white female) explains:

> [Democracy is] the people ruling the country. We are represented in the government, our views and our thoughts and what we want. We are given equality, but the government, of course, is there to instruct and to provide and to guide us. If they disagree with what we say, what we want, of course, they're the ones to have the final say.

Jeanne furthers this idea by expressing how she believes the United States is unique:

> People sneak in here, so people who are already here don't realize how fortunate we are to be free. We have a president; the difference between a president and a dictatorship, the president is president and he doesn't have all the power. I don't know about everybody, but certainly we have it better than in other countries.

These comments portray a benevolent image of the United States: The government directs, the police protect, the schools educate, and individuals are responsible for the course of their lives. They imply that if one does not "make it," it is due to lack of motivation or hard work. This is reminiscent of the culture-of-poverty framework discussed in chapter 1. At the same time there is ambivalence about whether everyone has an equal chance or people of color face discrimination as expressed by Sam (white male):

> A lot of us immigrants do very well because we do have the chance to go to school. You go to public school, you don't need to pay money for that. If you have the brains, you're able to put your mind to something. You're able to achieve a goal, or ambition that you want to succeed to become someone and you get that education. But I don't think it's a land of opportunity for all people. There's so much racism in this country and prejudice against minorities and black people. It's not fair but a lot of organizations or institutions, or even work places, discriminate against people.

Leon (white male) believes people are different and should be treated accordingly. He says, "Not everybody is created equal. You can't ask everybody on the street what they think about something, and then implement that idea. Not everybody is as smart as everybody else. Not everybody has the same opportunities. Everybody feels equal, but not everybody is."

These comments raise many questions. Are those in power there because they're smarter (or better educated) than the rest of us? Why can't we involve everyone in the important decisions—isn't that the definition of democracy? Connections are drawn between economic, social, and political power, but explanations of the evolution of various patterns remain individualized. Are "they" in positions of power for the benefit of society as a whole or for themselves? How did they get to be in a position of power? Is it because, in fact, they are truly better and smarter? Students express significant ambivalence about this narrative, in particular as they talk about the origin of the nation and the ideals associated with U.S. exceptionalism:

> The idea of America had good intentions, but it left a lot of people out who were not WASPs. The founding fathers thought they were doing something

revolutionary and good but they were not. Their intentions were good, like the Constitution and the formation of democracy. Opportunity is there but everybody can't achieve it. A lot of people work really hard but they won't achieve their actual dreams. Yet there is that potential. (Shalom, white male)

I don't think it was at all a democracy. Not one bit, when you think about it, what was the first thing they did when they came here? They killed all the natives and abused the slaves! What was the country built on? It was built on slavery, and that's not democratic at all. You don't have slaves now, or if you do, they're called below-minimum-wage workers. It's more democratic now; you don't have slaves. (Catherine, white female)

The people who made the Declaration of Independence, they were upper-class rich people, right? They made it. These weren't middle-class regular working people. Now you have the right to vote, back then it was a democracy for the elite only. (John, white male)

Interestingly, during the years between 1970 and 2000 the number of eighteen- to twenty-nine-year-olds who voted in presidential elections dropped from about one-half to one-third, and from one-third to less than one-fifth for congressional elections (Galston 2001, B16). In the 2004 and 2008 elections this trend was reversed, with roughly 47 percent and 52–53 percent turnout respectively.[12] The United States ranks 139th internationally in voter turnout in national elections since 1945. In the 2000 presidential election, 49.27 percent of the voting-age population voted (International Institute for Democracy and Electoral Assistance 2003a, b). Of these, "38 percent of U.S. voting age citizens who had not completed high school voted in 2000, compared to 77 percent of those with a bachelor's degree or higher (Livingston et al. 2003, vi). In 2008, 58.23 percent of the voting age population voted, with 23.4 percent of those with less than a ninth grade education and versus 76.2 percent of those with an advanced degree.[13]

It is also significant that nearly a third of the members of the House and Senate, but only one percent of the population they represent, are millionaires (Sklar 2003a, 58). By 2008, 44 percent of Congress were millionaires.[14] Additionally, about "one in fifty adults has currently or permanently lost the ability to vote because of a felony conviction. . . . The racial impact of ex-felon disenfranchisement . . . is truly astonishing. In Alabama and Florida 31 percent of all Black men are permanently disenfranchised. In five other states—Iowa, Mississippi, New Mexico, Virginia, and Wyoming—the number is one in four" (Marable 2002).). Of the African American population 8.25 percent, and 13 percent of Black men—are disenfranchised, a rate *three* times the national average (Manza and Uggen 2006, 253). Marable argues that "in effect, the Voting Rights Act of 1965 which guaranteed millions of African Americans the right to the electoral franchise is gradually being repealed by state restrictions on ex-felons' voting rights. A people who are imprisoned in disproportionately higher numbers, and then systematically denied the right to vote, can in no way claim to live under a democracy" (2002). How does this affect whose interests are most represented in the government and who more frequently ends up in political office? The cost of running a campaign creates a further challenge that prevents most people from even considering the possibility.

Much confusion exists about whether the narratives are faulty, or whether things have changed. In 2009, lively discussions engaged the question of whether there is actually a proportional number of persons of color in positions of political leadership. The overriding thinking was that there is, but the media misportrays this as if there continues to be a lack of diversity. There is a strong belief in the ideals upon which the nation was founded (such as democracy), but as quickly as people defend the values, they also articulate their recognition of evident contradictions. There is significant discomfort in conversations about whether the United States is really the special nation that it has been portrayed as being. The ambivalence and confusion about whether the ideals of the U.S. nation are myth or reality forms both a mechanism in maintaining the illusion of superiority and an opening to discuss the complex history from a perspective that acknowledge the experiences of ordinary people. The story of "America" is most often told through a lens presuming exceptionalism and superiority, but can simultaneously reveal incongruencies. Furthermore, the contradictory history of the U.S. nation has consequences for nation identity. Critical discussions provide opportunities to discuss the historical construction of origin narratives[15] and the nature and positioning of "Americans" in relationship to people around the globe.

The American Dream

The ideal of the American Dream has been depicted routinely in many forms of media throughout the second half of the twentieth century. Stories about "Dick and Jane," family shows such as "Father Knows Best," and folk tales about making it big in "America" provide the imagery for what life is like in "this great country." Everyday discourse is saturated with stories of immigrants who arrive penniless and get rich through hard work. This idea is a central pillar of the ideology of U.S. society—that all Americans have the chance to pursue their dreams. If they work hard enough, they can achieve success (Hochschild 1995). For many, this was the case. The post-World War II era of rapid industrial growth and U.S. hegemony around the globe brought much to many. However, for many African Americans, Latinos, and

Native Americans, this dream was never a reality. After immigration laws changed in 1965, increasing numbers of people came to the United States, just when deindustrialization began to occur. The most prominent explanations for why these groups were not upwardly mobile drew increasingly from a culture-of-poverty framework.

So what is this dream? Central tenets revolve around the achievement of success in the forms of high income, a prestigious job, and economic security (Hochschild 1995, 15). The idea that this is an achievable goal for all has been built into what it means to be an American. Consider President Bill Clinton's speech in 1993 to the Democratic Leadership Council: "The American Dream that we were all raised on is a simple but powerful one—if you work hard and play by the rules, you should be given a chance to go as far as your God-given abilities will take you" (Hochschild 1995, 18).

This statement expresses the implicit criteria for achievement and what one can expect in return. It is a fundamental presumption underlying an impressive ideology that has lured people to this country and kept them working against the odds (Hochschild 1995, 25). The assumption is that if they are not succeeding, it is because of their own weaknesses and not the fallacy of the American Dream. Clinton spoke at a time when people's expectations had greatly increased regarding what qualifies as achieving the American Dream.

Meanwhile, the median income per year needed to fulfill these dreams jumped from $50,000 in 1987 to $102,000 in 1994 and continued to grow during the following decade. Meanwhile, a study by Metlife in 2009 indicates that the "insatiable consumerism is clearly on the wane . . . at least in the short-run. . . . the definition of the dream has shifted significantly over the past 12 months—and that the public is in the midst of redefining what success and meaning look like in America" (2009, 4). However, they found that "roughly one-third of Americans (34 percent) believe that they have already achieved the dream—down only slightly from 37 percent one year ago—and 72 percent believe they can achieve the American dream in their lifetime" (2009, 5). Significantly, "38 percent of Caucasians . . . believe that they have achieved the dream, [but] the percentage falls to 30 percent for Asians, 29 percent of Hispanics and just 19 percent for African Americans" (Metlife 2009, 35). Despite this, more than half (56 percent) of those surveyed expressed concern about losing their job in the next year and "50 percent say they could only meet their financial obligations for one month if they were to lose their job" (2009, 5). The very definition of the "dream" is in flux with notably more people indicating family, children, and marriage as significant components (Metlife 2009, 10). These contradictory findings point to the power of the ideology of the American Dream.[16]

In a study by the Brookings Institute Economic Mobility Project, more than half of those surveyed said they think the American Dream is no longer attainable for the majority of U.S. citizens. There is much uncertainty about what lies ahead. The United States stands out as having relatively less mobility from one generation to the next with roughly 50 percent of the differences in parental income being transmitted to their children (d'Addio 2007, 31). Decreased economic mobility does not equally impact different groups: "almost half of Black children whose parents were solidly middle class in the late 1960s end up falling to the bottom of the income distribution, compared to 16 percent of white children" (Isaacs, Sawhill, and Haskins, 2008, 10).

Furthermore, "income inequality, by many measures, is now greater than it has been since the 1920s . . . the incomes of earners at the 99.99th percentile of the income distribution—those making more than 9,999 out of every 10,000 other earners—have soared over the last three decades, from less than $2 million in the late 1970s to about $10 million in 2009" (Leonhardt 2009). This means that in 2007, the share of income of families of the top 10 percent was 49.7 percent; the top 1 percent earned 23.5 percent of all income (Saez 2009, 3).

Another component of the Dream is the connection to a community of like-minded individuals with similar values, all working to protect and maintain the image of middle-class Americans who do not mind paying taxes to help the "poor and unfortunate" but not so much that their own quality of life might be diminished. With media coverage of a "war on terrorism," we have been faced with the reality of poverty rampant throughout the world, yet the realities of the stratification within the United States are blurred. The "united we stand" slogan and "we are in this together against a common enemy" rhetoric obviates internal tensions and differences and further promotes the notion that America is the "greatest country in the world," with more modernity, more technology, more efficiency, more liberty, more culture, and more democracy than anywhere else.

> The United States is still a petri dish. This is the only country in the world where you have this many people coming together and trying to get along. Before that you had just people killing each other. Like you had the Crusades. Everyone is trying to work with each other still and that's why I'm very positive and optimistic about the country and where it's going to turn. (Aquilas, Asian male)

This notion, deeply ingrained in the American psyche, signals that:

> We are more civilized than the rest of the world. . . . We represent the highest aspirations of everyone. . . . We are the leader of the free world, because we are the freest country in the world, and others look to us for leadership, for holding

high the banner of freedom, of civilization. . . . The Twin Towers are a perfect metaphor. They signaled unlimited aspirations; they signaled technological achievement; they signaled a beacon to the world. (Wallerstein 2001)

This issue is of supreme importance as we analyze students' perceptions about the American Dream, for we find ourselves at a time when the United States' decline as a hegemonic power looms large on the horizon. We need as a nation to reconsider the belief in our solitary greatness, engage our "closest friends and allies," and accept that they, too, have ideals and interests (Wallerstein 2001). The substance of the American Dream, as even a far-fetched ideal, has been shaken, even among those patriots who most vigorously defend its possibility. The events of 2001 and after have propelled a coming to terms with the realities experienced by the everyday American. Increasing lines at the unemployment offices and greater numbers at soup kitchens and homeless shelters are just the beginning. Such trends are compounded by the expanded privatization of all aspects of social services, to such an extent that schools, medical facilities, and policing, for example, have increasingly become domains for profit-bearing as opposed to being services delivered for the public good.

As Jennifer Hochschild, professor of politics and public affairs at Princeton University, states, "The political culture of the United States is largely shaped by a set of views in which the American Dream is prominent, and by a set of institutions that make it even more prominent than views alone could do" (Hochschild 1995, 37). It is therefore important to assess how this central pillar (the notion of the American Dream) is understood in order to understand everyday thinking about race. Table 3.3 reflects beliefs about the accessibility of the "Dream."

Foreign-born white students (76.8 percent) indicated that they agree significantly more than all Black students (foreign-born, 44.4 percent, and U.S.-born, 48.8 percent) that the American Dream can be achieved by anyone who works hard, but U.S.-born whites (64.0 percent) agree significantly more than just the foreign-born Black students (44.4 percent). Discussing their thoughts about the "Dream," John (white male) says, "The American Dream is who you know. People who have money are definitely going to be successful. They've already got the luck, money, and confidence. All they need is willpower. Otherwise

Table 3.3   The American Dream Can Be Achieved by Anyone Who Works Hard

Disagree	Moderately Agree	Agree
11.4%	30.3%	58.2%

to succeed is a lot of work. Success is having money." Joanne (white female) agrees but offers a different explanation for the unequal distribution of the Dream as a reality: "The American Dream is a reality for some people, but not everyone gets a good job and education. People get here and see a white picket fence, they see all kinds of people and think the society is culturally mixed but they find out about redlining. People don't know how to accomplish the dream and get discouraged. You just have to keep fighting."

Kevin (white male) says that he would have thought more than 60 percent would agree with the idea that everyone can achieve the American Dream, but suggests that people don't know what it is. He notes that there is a contrast between people who say "the American Dream can be achieved by all" and those who say "everyone can be assimilated," and he asserts that this is because the American Dream is in the future whereas assimilation is in the present.

In recent years, most studies indicate that despite the troubling economic times, about two-thirds of respondents still indicate a belief that they can achieve the American Dream.[17] However, there is also clearly a trend that redefines the "dream" away from solely focusing on economic mobility and toward family, friends, and good health.[18]

In studies by the *Washington Post* and the National Opinion Research Center related to perceptions of the current status of equality in society, whites consistently state that they believe discrimination is lessening, and Blacks report the persistent reality of racial inequality in their lives. In the survey conducted for the second edition of *Breaking the Code of Good Intentions,* there were several interesting findings. In response to the statement "People of color are treated the same as whites when applying for jobs," 85.7 percent of Latinos, 78.6 percent of Blacks, 65.1 percent of whites, and 53.4 percent of Asians indicated they disagreed. In response to the statement "People of color tend to exaggerate the degree of discrimination they face," 28.6 percent

Table 3.4   The United States Is a Land of Equal Opportunity for All People

	Disagree	Moderately Agree	Agree
Overall	28.0%	43.0%	29.0%
Latinos	27.1%	52.1%	20.8%
Asians	23.1%	48.7%	28.2%
U.S.-born Blacks	41.9%	39.5%	18.6%
Foreign-born Blacks	36.5%	46.0%	15.9%
U.S.-born whites	25.0%	42.7%	32.4%
Foreign-born whites	15.9%	35.4%	48.8%

of Latinos, 66.7 of Asians, 32.2 percent of Blacks, and 46.5 percent of whites indicated they disagreed or agreed strongly.

Paul Street, Research Director of the Chicago Urban League, describes the divergence of views as the "White Fairness Understanding Gap," more fully discussed in chapter 4 (2001, 9–11). These data are critical to an understanding of the viability of the American Dream, in the way that different populations perceive the dream as a myth or a reality. If, as a nation, all people cannot count on freedom, justice, equality, and opportunity, then the ideology that says these are the reasons the United States is special is undermined. For many whites, race usefully explains why the dream is no longer attainable. Hochschild explains the connection this way:

> Something is wrong with the American Dream, and the problem is associated with blacks (and immigrants) in some way. Identifying what is wrong and how blacks are implicated in it is a difficult and thankless task for which they receive almost no institutional support. It is far easier to cling to the Dream, insist that it really works, and find someone to blame for the lacunae. (Hochschild 1995, 69)

The divergence in perception between all whites and foreign-born Blacks, and foreign-born whites and all Blacks, affirms the role of race in everyday living. Otherwise, why would one group perceive the dream as reachable yet others perceive it as unattainable? U.S.-born whites have experienced some of the downward economic trends of the last decade, young whites today may not see themselves as upwardly mobile. They may feel lucky to attain even the same socioeconomic status as their parents. Various trends point to this tension, such as young people not leaving home until their late twenties, expanded patterns of part-time, temporary employment without benefits, and increasing numbers of middle-class white college students attending public institutions. Jenna (white female) suggests that this economic instability is the result of individual unwillingness to work hard.

> People from other countries come here and work harder for the American Dream, than people who live here. I've seen people come into my neighborhood from other countries and open stores, work the stores like eighteen, twenty hours a day. A lot of American people don't do that, people work for a paycheck and, that's it. You get comfortable, but I think people in America have in common no matter what race you are, no matter what religion you are, the freedom that America has for everyone.

Many students were unsure of whether they believed that the American Dream is a reality today. Others said that they had never heard of this concept. Among people who had an idea what it meant, white students strongly believed the dream was attainable by anyone who worked hard enough. In discussions, whites often resisted the notion that success is more easily achieved for whites. One such interaction evidenced this dynamic. Nancy begins by asserting, "You don't know our experience; you assume we're all middle-class and privileged."

Irma replies, "But our problems are intensified because of our color, our hair; our language is made to seem like a handicap. I know you are not trouble-free but you have to understand our troubles are constantly compounded because of language or the neighborhood we live in."

Nancy attempts to negotiate the two positions: "We may share problems, but I guess it happens to you in greater numbers. Poverty is talked about as if caused by race only. It seems more typical among you. But there is more help for you, internships, scholarships, I can't get. You can get minority scholarships that I can't. At my job this guy was being paid twice what I was and he was doing half as much.[19] People think 'middle America' is fine and dandy but it is not true. Look at their kids like in Columbine. Where do these kids get their ideas?"

To which, Irma replies, "But why when it happens there, we have to pull the country together. Why not pull together for all the daily violence? People don't understand the struggle of everyday for people of color."

One might assume that Nancy's awareness of racial inequality reflects a willingness to support measures to take action to level the field or to be part of a collective struggle for justice, compensation, and reparation, but this is not necessarily the case. Perhaps she is willing to acknowledge differential treatment when she speaks with a Puerto Rican woman whose life experience she cannot deny, at least to her face. Table 3.4 illustrates students' beliefs about the United States as the land of equal opportunity.

Foreign-born white students believe significantly more than any other group that the United States is a land of equal opportunity for all people, a consequence of their racialized experience. Similar to previous European immigrants, they have been provided opportunities to improve their standard of living (e.g., access to various social services under the policies that assist political refugees), more than communities of color of the U.S.-born. U.S.-born white students are experiencing the economic pressures of the recent decades and feel less certain about their own futures. Between 1962 and 2001, a Gallup poll survey has intermittently asked, "Do you think Blacks have as good a chance as white people in your community to get any kind of job for which they are qualified?" Among whites, the response of "not as good a chance" has grown from 4 percent in 1962 to 13 percent in 2001 in relation to educational opportunities, and the response "as good as" dropped from 94 percent in 1962 to 87 percent in 2001 (Krysan 2002).

A 2007 Gallup poll found that 80 percent of whites believe Black children have as good a chance as white children to get a good education; 16 percent indicated not as good a chance. Of Blacks, 49 percent said they believe they have as good a chance and 51 percent said they do not (Saad 2007). A survey conducted by Columbia University's Center on African American Politics and Society and ABC News Polling Unit in 2008 found that 52 percent of Blacks believe that Blacks have already or will soon achieve racial equality, compared to 44 percent who believe they will not in their lifetime. Of whites, three-quarters think that Blacks have achieved or will soon achieve racial equality compared to 20 percent of whites who believe that racial equality for Blacks will not happen in their lifetimes or ever happen"(Harris, 2008, 17).

In the following passage, Michael (white male) speaks explicitly about the intersecting roles of class and race in determining social status.

> We live in a biased hypocrisy. There are a lot of glass ceilings to keep certain groups down just by definition. In corporate environments, you see more people of Caucasian ancestry in higher positions. Some people and groups can break through, mostly Caucasian. You have to work real hard. If you are born poor, there are 200 percent odds against you that you can achieve the same thing as someone with money. . . .
>
> You have to break through class. Racial and class lines meet. The economy is segregated and this adds to class stratification. It's deeper than just race and culture, it's class and money, but mostly money. If you're born into a trailer park, you can work very hard and become a CEO of a major corporation. However, you have 200 percent more odds as the son of a CEO who is going to work less hard than you to achieve the same thing. It's a ladder you have to break through. If I'm on the lowest part, and I have eight glass ceilings to break through, it's going to be harder for me to do it than someone who's on the fifth and I'm five floors lower.

The American Dream inspires pride and hopefulness, though when whites experience economic pressures, rather than looking toward structural explanations for their troubles, they primarily blame individuals and groups. For example, when Nancy (white female) describes her difficulty in financing her education, she targets racially designated scholarships as the problem. Rather than viewing minority assistance as a means to address historical inequities, she characterizes them as perpetuating inequality by advantaging students of color over herself.

Contradictory realities and images such as the shootings by white middle-class youth around the country versus the common association of violence with poor and Black people provide opportunities to point out implicit assumptions. For example, Nancy wondered if her thinking was valid that these occurrences were out of the ordinary for white folks. She did not appear to place the actions of the teenagers in Columbine within the context of the historical violence of U.S. society as expressed through enslavement, Jim Crow laws, the disparate use of tax funds to support or deny public services, or the experiences of excessive force used by police described by many students. She was puzzled about where this violence comes from among whites.

A much deeper understanding of history and the current structure of the United States might reveal the racial presumptions that lead one to be surprised by these incidents. Comedian Chris Rock points out the implicitly Eurocentric assumptions that are perpetuated by the media in their attempt to explain what happened in Columbine, Santee, and scattered incidents around the country, where young white males were responsible for shooting incidents at their schools. Rock focuses on the racial dynamics that lead a young person to murder classmates because "they felt mocked" and that "nobody wanted to be their friends." He questions the way the media sought all types of structural explanations in these cases, whereas when those involved are Black the explanation is directed at dysfunctional individuals and cultural failings (Rock 1999).

Tim Wise (author and antiracist activist) questions why there is no profile for these school shootings (2001) and states that, despite common perceptions, whites commit three times more violent crimes each year than Blacks and are five to six times more likely to be attacked by another white person than a Black person (Wise 2002, 40). In 2009, approximately 92 percent of all crimes were intraracial and 8 percent interracial (Thomas 2009, 68). Racialized images reinforce a dispassionate apathy about the violence experienced by many people on an everyday basis, whether physical, political, or social, for they convey the notion that white people need not be concerned; it is not their problem.

This section outlines several mechanisms that create, reinforce, and reproduce mainstream discourse and structures about race and nation. These include the ideas that hard work is the primary factor determining whether one achieves the "American Dream," and lack of effort is the cause of failure. U.S. national character is unique and superior. Real Americans are of European descent. The process of racialization and its consequent negative impact (racial subordination) and positive impact (privileging) are illusive—implicit but unspoken in notions of identity, opportunity, and equality. Resistance is viewed as anti-American and ungrateful. It's preferable to ignore (or deny) historical and global factors that have led to the betterment of living conditions in the United States in contrast to those of people around the world. Acknowledging the history of colonial and imperial legacies and their current manifestations raises questions of who is responsible for addressing their consequences.

Simultaneously, popular notions of democracy, the U.S. ideals, and the "Dream" of a wholesome life where human needs are met provide openings for engaging a deeper understanding of the racialized structure and ideology of U.S. society. The profound and righteous idealism embodied in notions of freedom, equality, justice, and democracy for all provides ways to envision a better world. Inconsistencies and incongruities in application of these principles, when acknowledged, provide the means to discuss how mainstream discourse about U.S. history and present-day group positioning are strictly regulated to maintain the status quo. Economic downturns put pressure on increased whites, who either can turn to the common explanations about who's to blame or become more open to a deeper social analysis from the perspective of the majority rather than the elite.

The Meaning of the Flag

Like the American Dream and democracy, the U.S. flag has come to symbolize the elevated status of the United States in the global order. In *To Die For:The Paradox of American Patriotism*, Cecilia Elizabeth O'Leary, assistant professor of history at California State University, Monterey Bay, traces the development of the flag's symbolic meaning to the period after the First Reconstruction and through World War I (O'Leary 1999, 7–9). She documents the legal and political struggles over the definitions of loyal or disloyal citizens. She says that during this period (1870–1920) there was disagreement and conflict over which icons, heroes, events, and identities would constitute the national memory and the historical narrative.

Many of the symbols and rituals of patriotism that we now assume as having always existed actually came into being within the last century. The "Pledge of Allegiance" was written in 1891; the "Star-Spangled Banner" was taken as the national anthem in 1931. O'Leary traces the points of contestation, contradiction, and ambivalence about American ideals and their everyday manifestations. She ultimately speaks of the contradictions of U.S. nationalism, as did Immanuel Wallerstein when he insisted that we reckon with national traditions of both patriotism and resistance (Wallerstein 2001). It is a challenge that many have recently faced—that is, how to understand contradictory patterns without essentializing either trend. In some ways, this is at the heart of seeking to understand everyday thinking and the process of looking for "cracks" in the system. For if we grant agency to participants and recognize contradictions, it would appear we have the ability to make a difference. This is the context within which to analyze students' perceptions and

beliefs today about identity and allegiance, particularly at a moment in time
when such notions are fragile.

Students discuss their awareness of how flags often come to symbolize political expression. The presence of other national flags signifies for some a disrespect for the American flag, which is to be respected, assumed to be a natural
part of routine living that should not be tampered with. Helen (white female)
expressed a commonly held sentiment: "You're living in this country; you
should respect the flag, that's all. If you don't like it, go somewhere else." They
feel, as Allen (white male) says, that the flag symbolizes American pride. He
expresses the emotional component of this association: "I was in Israel for a year
and a half, and whenever you see an American soldier or an American flag, you
just go nuts. I think it's just because we were in a different country. It was in the
background the whole time. It's more of like a third-world type of country, and
when you say, America, you think of the land of opportunity, it's everything."

Don (white male) agrees that feelings about the flag appear to differ depending on the situation: "In a different country I saw the American flag and
felt all patriotic. But we're here and we see it all the time, we don't appreciate
it. The American flag, it's not something I think about." At the same time,
some students objected to the use of flags as expressions of pride by people of
other national origins. "WTA[20] is supposed to be a student government group,
but they had a national flag on their backs!" explains Gerda (white female).
"You can't mix the two at this time of elections when you hold up a national
flag and say vote WTA, holding up your flag and waving it. You can be proud
of your country and what you are and everything."

For other students, the omnipresence of the U.S. flag in public spaces seems
to feel oppressive. A degree of uneasiness was evident in the connection
drawn between the symbol and the reality of the ideals that the flag supposedly
represents. Jeff (white male) explains, "In the Marines it's ridiculous, we were
in the gas station and they sell like 100,000 Confederate flags. I thought, it's
not just the flag, it's the fact that they're selling them at gas stations; it's all
over the place." Similarly, Marsha (white female) appears concerned about the
over-use of the flag as a symbol that should not be questioned:

> I always considered myself very American, and now, thinking about it, I re-
> ally don't know if I consider myself that much American. Having other people
> say how they feel about being viewed as an American, as [opposed] to being
> from another country. I don't really agree with a lot. I look at the flag on houses
> and I really don't agree with a lot of the things that go on within America, I
> don't think they're very American.

Yet for other students, the flag is not something they are conscious of
and they are ambivalent about its meaning. "I want to think more about the

American flag thing," Jeff continues. "I never really gave it much thought, I mean, my father has them plastered all over the house and he has one tattooed on his arm, but I never really gave it much thought." Tania (white female) also expresses feelings of detachment about the meaning of the flag. "I was born and raised in America. When I see the American flag, I just see a piece of material. I remember when we used to have to stand up and say our 'Pledge of Allegiance' to the flag. That's about it, personally."[21]

Comments either reflect a strong belief in the symbolic power of the flag in representing the nation and its ideals or articulate an absence of association, an assumption that the flag is a symbol devoid of meaning. Not all students were willing to defend the representational meaning of the flag, yet those who were seem willing to fight to have it recognized.

The objection to waving any flag other than that of the United States appears to signify a belief that all people should assimilate and stand under one banner. Other expressions of individual or group identity are viewed as divisive. The students who described an emotional involvement with the symbol articulated its meaning as being equated with all that is good.

While for some people the flag is a symbol of the dominant assertion of the U.S. Empire, for others it is a symbol of the Abolitionists, the Suffragists, the Populists, and the Wobblies, representing a more radical tradition; for still others it appears to lack meaning. Who gets to claim the flag as their own? (Hightower 2001) Particularly after September 11, it became apparent that one cannot assume to know the political beliefs of someone wearing or carrying the flag. Perhaps this is a positive development in that its meaning has become less rigid. While some people cringed at the flourishing of flags everywhere, the expanded public debates about patriotism, loyalty, symbols, and dissent provided visibility to otherwise hidden assumptions. Discussions such as those on the *AlterNet*, *Common Dreams*, *Rethinking Schools*, and *Teaching for Change* websites, as well as in the *New York Times*, *Boston Globe*, and *Newsday*, emerged on campuses throughout the country and in national media. This debate increased awareness of the history and costs of blind acceptance and the incorporation of these symbols into everyday living. Bill Moyers eloquently outlines these issues:

> The flag's been hijacked and turned into a logo—the trademark of a monopoly on patriotism. On those Sunday morning talk shows, official chests appear adorned with the flag as if it is the good housekeeping seal of approval . . . more galling than anything are all those moralistic ideologues in Washington sporting the flag in their lapels while writing books and running Web sites and publishing magazines attacking dissenters as un-American. They are people whose ardor for war grows disproportionately to their distance from the fighting. They're

in the same league as those swarms of corporate lobbyists wearing flags and prowling Capitol Hill for tax breaks even as they call for more spending on war. . . . The flag belongs to the country, not to the government. And it reminds me that it's not un-American to think that war—except in self-defense—is a failure of moral imagination, political nerve, and diplomacy. Come to think of it, standing up to your government can mean standing up for your country. What do you think?[22]

While the fragility of our times heightens the challenges faced by the most vulnerable populations, it can also foster awareness of inequalities and injustices that have long existed. Engagement is critical, as "if patriotism were defined, not as blind obedience to government, not as submissive worship to flags and anthems, but rather as love of one's country, one's fellow citizens (all over the world), as loyalty to the principles of justice and democracy, then patriotism would require us to disobey our government when it violated those principles" (Zinn 1990, 118).

The next section specifically examines the differential in experiences of U.S.-born versus foreign-born students that emerged from the original study.

RACE AND THE FOREIGN-BORN EXPERIENCE

The ideals of American democracy, which have influenced liberal democracies around the world, rely crucially on the notion of consent as the basis of citizenship. What makes someone an American is that he or she agrees to be one. . . . By raising their hands and taking the pledge of citizenship, immigrants formally enact the consent upon which our political system depends; yet which native-born citizens only tacitly affirm.

—Danny Postel (2001, A12)

As articulated above, ideas about what it means to be American are deeply implicated in the foundation of our society. People came to the United States for a multitude of reasons and circumstances, and their experiences, once arrived, also varied. These are important considerations within an analysis of the role of race in everyday living. The concept "the United States, a nation of immigrants" disguises the unequal status of various groups in how they arrived, what they experienced when they arrived, or how their lands and peoples were "incorporated" as part of the U.S. nation. "A nation of immigrants" presumes a white and European experience, where choice is the primary factor in migration. Furthermore, this perspective entirely disregards the reality of the many native people and Mexicans whose land these "immigrants" occupy.

Bonnie Honig, author of *Democracy and the Foreigner* (2001), argues that while democracies need immigrants, "[we're] nervous about what they are going to do to our democracy. We criminalize alien populations, bar them from political activity; marginalize them in terms of the labor force. We practice xenophobia and xenophilia at the same time" (quoted in Postel 2001, A12). While what Honig asserts is certainly true, she does not account for the differential in experiences of immigrants upon their arrival to the United States. Why is it that a boat of refugees from one country is allowed entry, while another is turned away? Additionally, "Malcolm X argued that in the process of Americanizing, European immigrants acquire a sense of whiteness and [an understanding of] white supremacy" (Roediger 1994, 187). Furthermore, providing commentary about the racialized nature of the Americanization process, he asserted that the first English word immigrants learn upon arrival to the U.S. is "nigger,"[23] as the racialized nature of U.S. society bears down upon them. In the 2009 survey, several distinctions point to this racializing process (see table 3.5).

Table 3.5   Experiences and Attidues about Race (Second Edition)

	Born in U.S.	Born outside U.S.
Think about their racial identity on a daily/weekly basis	35.7%	25.0%
In the home of someone of another race		
Weekly/Daily	27.8%	9.7%
Occasionally/never	55.5%	71.0%
Witness racial tension on a daily/weekly basis	27.4%	16.6%
Incorporating the experiences of all groups in the curriculum		
Improves learning	66.7%	32.3%
Good idea but doesn't change learning	19.4%	54.8%
Racial inequality is a thing of the past (Agree/strongly agree)	8.2%	34.4%
People of color tend to exaggerate the degree of discrimination they face.		
(Agree/strongly agree)	36.1%	56.3%
Some people talk too much about race	71.2%	81.3%

New York City has experienced tremendous growth in its immigrant population, paralleling similar increases nationally. Between 1970 and 1998, the city's foreign-born population grew from 18 percent to almost 35 percent, approaching a level comparable to that existing at the turn of the twentieth century (41 percent in 1910) (Foner 2001b, 1–31).[24] As mentioned in chapter 1, the major trends include a sharp decline in the native white population (although partly offset by increased East European immigration) and sharp increases in the West Indian, Latino, and Asian populations, impacting the suburbs as well as the city (Mollenkopf 2001b).

The foreign-born white students who participated in this research predominantly come from families who originated in the Ukraine, Russia, Uzbekistan, and Belarus. Their characteristics are somewhat different from those of immigrants who arrived prior to 1990. They generally had professional backgrounds and were often neither explicitly Jewish nor religious. Most important, over 85 percent were granted full refugee status, with federal subsidies easing their transition with housing, job training, and education. Simultaneously, this group arrived during a period when many social programs were being cut, resulting in benefit reductions. This led to decreasing beliefs in the idealism of capitalism and a shift from predominantly Republican to Democratic political orientation. In New York City, where approximately half of all Eastern European immigrants to the United States settle and where they form the second largest group of foreign-born students in the public schools, this group has retained advantages of status and resources relative to other immigrant communities (Orleck 2001). This relatively privileged position and corresponding political allegiances appear to be reflected in the data as discussed in this section.

Most of the literature about immigration to the United States and urban areas focuses on immigrants from African, Latin, or Asian countries or separately addresses the recent influx of Eastern Europeans, particularly from the former Soviet bloc. Minimal scholarship has attended to a comparison of the racialized experience of different groups of European descent (native to the U.S. and foreign-born). Yet, as delineated here, there are divergent beliefs that often reflect distinct experiences. This section explores some differences and possible explanations.

Foreign-Born Whites versus All Other Groups

Foreign-born whites often view the United States as the land of opportunity, an idea likely shaped before they arrived, as part of Cold War ideology. They tend toward a perspective in direct opposition to what they were told by their governments (Soviet and post-Soviet). Upon arrival, the treatment they receive reinforces their beliefs as they absorb a "Horatio Alger" narrative that inverted communist ideology in relationship to a capitalist perspective. That is, everything that was bad about their prior lives would now be good, in "America." As Barbara frames it, "They hear everything is good, even before they get here."

They arrive with a worldview that established freedom as a U.S. phenomenon and, as both the narrative and the statistics below indicate, they defend this image. Their experience as white immigrants has meant they have generally fared well, for example, in educational achievement, with slightly fewer high school diplomas but higher levels of college accomplished.[25] However, as they come to feel the impact of the increasing polarization of wealth and power under the reign of global capitalism, they may find themselves in more dire circumstances and seek explanations for the difficulties they face.[26]

In contrast to the highly transnational and transmigrant nature of immigrants from the African, Latin, and Asian groups, the experience of Eastern European immigrants tends to root them in their new surroundings, where they feel welcome. Annelise Orleck, associate professor of history at Dartmouth College, reports that among the Soviet Jews she studied, most do not return home for visits. They say that everyone they know is in the United States. Orleck quotes one woman as saying, "America is my country, not Russia. I have no one left there to worry about" (2001, 135).

However, there is a lack of scholarship analyzing the particular racialized experiences of the European immigrants of the last two decades, how they align and diverge in attitude and beliefs from U.S.-born whites, and how their experiences align or diverge from immigrants of African, Latin, or Asian descent. As the percentage of individuals who emigrated from European countries in 1999 was approximately 22.5 percent of all immigrants (Kraly and Miyares 2001, 49), these questions would likely shed light on the racialized experience of different groups of immigrants.[27]

While the ethnographic data included here provide insight into the daily lives and beliefs of this population, comparisons between different group experiences could easily form the basis of a future study. David Roediger's *Working Toward Whiteness: How America's Immigrants Became White, the Strange Journey from Ellis Island to the Suburb* is excellent for historical background. In *Whiteness of a Different Color*, Matthew Frye Jacobson alludes to the challenge of examining the racial component of the immigrant saga (1998, 275), yet this is not his focus. Nancy Foner (2001) briefly discusses this issue, and several chapters of her book specifically analyze employment patterns. The impact of pan-ethnic and racial experiences on the ideological stance of various populations is not addressed, though Foner does articulate the significance of race within the immigrant experience:

Immigrants' race has crucial consequences for their experiences and reactions to New York life. Whereas whiteness is an asset for newcomers of European ancestry, dark skin brings disadvantages. Because of their skin color—and because American society's generalized negative view of blacks is so different from racial conceptions in the home countries—black immigrants develop new attitudes and new perceptions of themselves in New York. (Foner 2001b, 14–15)

Some of the statistically significant differences that emerged between the perceptions of foreign-born white students and all other students include:

- Fewer foreign-born white students (18.3 percent) than any other group (Latinos, 45.8 percent; Asian, 43.6 percent; U.S.-born Blacks, 48.8 percent; foreign-born Blacks, 71.4 percent; U.S.-born whites, 29.4 percent) believed that discrimination contributes to the average lower incomes and poorer housing of Blacks; and,
- Fewer foreign-born white students (25.6 percent) than Asian (46.2 percent), U.S.-born Black (55.8 percent), or foreign-born Black (55.6 percent) students believed that historic inequality contributes to these circumstances.

One faculty member, Louis, offered the explanation that "foreign-born whites come into U.S. society believing less in discrimination because they don't have the history of Jim Crow. They don't know what U.S. apartheid was. The Russians don't get it. They are fresh from being discriminated against as Jews, and feel there is so much freedom here." This analysis is further borne out by the following data:

- More foreign-born white students (19.5 percent) than any other group (Latinos, 8.3 percent; Asian, 10.3 percent; U.S.-born Blacks, 2.3 percent; foreign-born Blacks, 1.6 percent; U.S.-born whites, 9.6 percent) believed that people of color are treated equal to whites when applying for jobs, housing, and when approached by police;
- More foreign-born white students (23.2 percent) than any other group (Latinos, 2.1 percent; Asian, 7.7 percent; U.S.-born Blacks, 11.6 percent; foreign-born Blacks, 4.8 percent; U.S.-born whites, 7.4 percent) believed that there is equal and fair treatment of all people in the media; and,
- More foreign-born white students (48.8 percent) than any other group (Latinos, 20.8 percent; Asian, 28.2 percent; U.S.-born Blacks, 18.6 percent; foreign-born Blacks, 15.9 percent; U.S.-born whites, 32.4 percent) believed that the United States is a land of opportunity for all people.

These statistics reflect the racialized experience of immigrants who are treated as whites regardless of their foreign-born status, and also their adherence to mainstream explanations about the causes of poverty. Their defense of the structure as fair and equitable denies discrimination expressed in racialized patterns of assimilation or rejection. This process is evident as social services and the ever-present and useful "benefit of the doubt" are available to white immigrants but not to those from the African, Asian, or Latino immigrant groups. The case of Amadou Diallo is a recently publicized example of this distinction. The racialized image of this individual, in the eyes of the four police officers and the jury, led to his murder and the officers' acquittals. A wallet in the hands of a young Black man became a gun. Had Diallo been Russian, would this image transformation have occurred?[28]

There is an irony to the perceptions of foreign-born whites, as the civil rights movement laid the foundation for the liberalization of immigration policy in the 1960s. These statistics indicate, however, that foreign-born whites are unlikely to support measures to eradicate structural causes for racial inequality. In other words, once arrived, foreign-born whites assume the dominant position, rather than recognizing where support came from to increase their opportunities and, in turn, supporting opportunities for better conditions and access for other groups.[29]

Foreign-born Whites and Specific Groups

Foreign-born Whites versus Foreign-born Blacks

Several significant differences emerged in the data between beliefs held by foreign-born whites and foreign-born Blacks. For example, more foreign-born white students (54.9 percent) than foreign-born Black students (34.9 percent) believed that all people, regardless of color can be assimilated into U.S. society; and fewer foreign-born white students (15.9 percent) than foreign-born Black students (30.2 percent) believed that the United States cannot be multicultural and have an American identity at the same time.

Reflecting on these data, Kevin (white male) suggested, "It is interesting that foreign-born Blacks and whites disagree that the United States can be multicultural. Blacks want to keep their heritage and to hold onto it. Whites want to distance themselves from their past. They have something to gain. They want their families to be raised as Americans."

The race and immigrant status of foreign-born whites does not cause as much difficulty for them as for foreign-born Blacks in a racialized society. They more easily assimilate into a white-dominated society, so perhaps they do not see the challenge in integrating their ethnic or national background into their identity as Americans. Several foreign-born Black students noted that their racial identity became an issue only after they arrived in the United States. "Black immigrants face a unique set of social circumstances upon entering our borders. . . . The term 'cross-pressures' [names] the contradictory circumstances that mark the West Indian experience in the United States" (Bashi 1999, 890). One factor is that they come from societies in which they form majorities and which urge them to downplay race, and their experience in the United States provides opportunities for upward mobility but simultaneously immerses them in a society in which race is a key structuring principle (Bashi 1999, 891).

An interesting difference in responses in the 2009 survey included levels of agreement with the statement "Immigrants contribute more to society than they receive in return." Seventy-one percent of Latinos agreed or strongly agreed, 21.4 percent disagreed or strongly disagreed. Among Asians 80 percent agreed or strongly agreed versus 13.3 percent who disagreed or strongly disagreed. Blacks reported 85.7 percent versus 14.3 percent, and 43.2 percent of whites agreed/strongly agreed versus 46.5 percent disagreed/strongly disagreed. Whereas Latinos, Asians, and Blacks clearly value the contributions of immigrants, whites are much more divided.

Foreign-Born Whites versus U.S.-Born Whites

Several important differences also emerged between the responses of foreign-born and U.S.-born whites: More foreign-born white students (43.9 percent) than U.S.-born white students (27.9 percent) believed that the recent emphasis on eliminating remediation affects all students equally; and more foreign-born white students (11.0 percent) than U.S.-born whites (2.9 percent) believed that someone who takes more than four to five years to get a bachelor's degree is not serious about his or her education.

Various social services and supports, generally available to foreign-born white students because of their status as political refuges, are less often available to foreign-born Blacks, Latinos, or Asians who come to the United States more often for economic reasons. This reality reinforces white immigrants' adherence to a dominant narrative about lazy students (of color) who just want their degree without working for it. These statistics place blame for a person's circumstances firmly on the individual or the group. This attitude undermined the efforts to fight the anti-remediation policies. Foreign-born white students tended to ally themselves with those in a dominant position who withdrew support for the policy of open admissions and for public higher education in general, implicitly assuming racialized positions. This provides an example of how attitudes and beliefs have an impact on public policy. The lack of broad support by the entire student body allowed the policy changes to take place and, in turn, reproduced and exacerbated the pattern of inequality in CUNY.

The data also indicate that students may not recognize what they have to lose, whether in relation to their own education or to the principle of support for public education. By not understanding this, they implicitly colluded with a structural devaluation of public education rather than participating in efforts to shed light on the real reasons for students taking longer than four years to graduate. These factors include reductions in financial, academic, and student support services as a result of the funneling of public funds away from schools and into the building of prisons (Professional Staff Congress 2001a).

In the process of identifying with the narrative that renders them superior, foreign-born whites tend to buy into the American Dream rather than ally with those who understand that this struggle for access to education expresses a pattern of subordination and domination that constricts possibilities for all but the most wealthy and powerful. Foreign-born white students who accept this position may not recognize how supporting the dominant view might hurt them, too.

A roundtable discussion reviewing survey results with students and staff produced the following observations:

> Foreign-born blacks are on the other end of the spectrum from foreign-born whites as to whether there is police brutality, or discrimination. I thought they would be more similar but I guess foreign-born whites are still white. What catches people's eyes is race. Foreign-born whites believe that everything is okay, more than foreign-born blacks. Foreign-born whites wouldn't see discrimination as clearly because they say "What are you complaining about? You are making excuses. Look where we came from." (Lori, white female)

> Foreign-born whites are not singled out in society. It's the color, not their accent or what country they came from. But it's contradictory, too, because foreign-born whites can fit into the mainstream. (Deborah, white female)

These comments were made by U.S.-born whites who, when faced with evidence of the role of race in everyday living, acknowledge its impact in relation to European immigrants. While all of them had initially said that they rarely think about race and, in fact, did not feel their lives were affected by their own racial identity, they clearly observed the role of race in white immigrants' lives in the United States. They were able to suggest some of the reasons why the perspective of foreign-born whites might differ from foreign-born blacks, Latinos, and Asians. At the same time, they acknowledged that the process of assimilation can be contradictory, as most immigrants have to struggle, but some have to struggle more than others because of racialization. Not everyone starts out at the same place, as is clearly indicated by the way that different immigrant groups have been integrated into different employ-ment sectors of U.S. society. Where a group enters can make all the differ-ence in their capacity for upward mobility (Feagin and Feagin 2003).

Transnational Identity

Much has been written during the last five years about the transmigrant na-ture of recent immigrants.[30] This experience is particularly characteristic of individuals from the African, Latin, and Asian immigrant groups who often come to the United States seeking relief from the severe poverty in other parts of the world, often where the United States has had a role economically or politically destabilizing their homeland. Scholars argue that "In today's global economy, changes in the technologies of transportation and com-munication (jet air travel, faxes, electronic mail, the internet, videos) have changed the qualitative experience of immigration. . . . Immigrants today are there not just in their memories and imaginations, but vicariously, in that very moment; they are able to participate—economically, politically, socially, emotionally—in a regular, constant way, often creating two "homes" that rest on the pillar of an identity (or identities) that incorporate two or more nations, social worlds, at the same time" (Pedraza 2005, 423).

While the issue of economic migration is vast and deserves full explora-tion, within this study of identity as framed in the political and economic context, reflections about transnational identity arose repeatedly. This brief section summarizes some of them.

> If I go to Haiti now, people would not consider me Haitian. Even though I'm going to try real hard to act like the way they would act and speak without an accent, but they would still find differences. They'd be like "Okay, I don't un-derstand your Creole." It's very Americanized now, my attitude. They wouldn't really relate to me anymore. They would probably call me an American, but when you come here in America, like they don't want you here either. You have a French accent and it's like, you don't belong on either side. When you go back, they find something American about you, but when you come to America, they find something Haitian about you. So it's more like, you're none of them, as opposed to, you're both. (Jean Paul, Black male)

> When I go back to my home country, they see you as from the other country, too. You're not Chinese anymore; you're just from a different country. When you come back to America, they see you as Chinese because the way you talk, the language you speak and the skin color. I feel like I was in the middle—part of me is Chinese; part of me is American. (Edward, Asian male)

Mara (white female) tries to understand Edward's and Jean Paul's experiences, saying, "I guess it's really difficult to get both nationalities, but it's more like you are none of them, because you don't belong anywhere." She continues, "I found it enlightening that people that aren't from this country, kind of feel in the middle of this country and their country. It kind of made me feel like they feel left out, not part of America and not part of their own country and I never really thought about that before, it was a little sad."

Further exploring this notion, Diane expresses her opinion about this predicament, albeit through her eyes as a white woman.

> I really don't think that choosing a nationality is fair. It's really limiting yourself to different things that you could experience. I don't believe my future is as an American. I always desired to travel all over the world and somehow get a piece of every culture and language to put in me, to make me like whole, like an international person or something because I'm the kind of person who likes to go and experience new things and just to settle for one nationality would be limiting.

Differences are generally used to separate, not unite, but the respondents also appear to perceive an alternative, more pluralistic perspective. It is evident that many people have the experience of being excluded, and this has societal implications for the overall sense of community. While students express different opinions, they all seem to struggle with the impact of transmigration. They assert their own meanings about identity, regardless of how they are defined by society.

For whites, this lack of a sense of belonging is less of an issue, as they can more easily define their identity. Race does not interfere with their option to choose how they describe themselves. However, self-ascribed identity is a luxury for people of color. Transmigrant experiences appear to be perceived as somewhat irritating, because they do not easily conform to strict categorization. Some students felt pressured to choose between the identity of their origin or heritage and being American. At the same time, Diane's comment presumes a freedom of choice that she experiences and assumes others do also. There is an assumption that you can be Italian and American or Polish and American but being Chinese or Haitian does not as easily leave you that option.

NATIONAL IDENTITY AND SYMBOLS: SUMMARY

This chapter explored beliefs about national identity, patriotic symbols, and values such as democracy. A good deal of idealism persists, with most people continuing to assert that anyone who works hard can achieve the American

Dream (58.2 percent, table 3.3), that public higher education is a right to which all people should have access (83.3 percent) though foreign-born Black students (92.1 percent) agree significantly more than U.S.-born white students (72.8 percent), and that all people should be given a fair chance to succeed (92.9 percent).

Clear contradictions were also evident. Only 29 percent of all students believed that the United States is a land of opportunity for all people, with an additional 43 percent "moderately" believing so (table 3.4). More foreign-born white students (48.8 percent) than any other group (Latinos, 20.8 percent; Asians, 28.2 percent; U.S.-born Blacks, 18.6 percent; foreign-born Blacks, 15.9 percent; U.S.-born whites, 32.4 percent) believed in the opportunities in the United States.

Regarding democracy, most students felt that freedom of speech most exemplified this ideal. They believed that in the United States one may say anything at any time. There was little awareness of political prisoners and activist movements that have been censored throughout U.S. history. There was little understanding of the daily experience of many young people in public schools who resist authoritarianism and end up in detention or special education classes or are expelled.[31] It is important to explore ways to increase awareness about events such as the tear-gassing and beating of protesters against the International Monetary Fund (IMF) in Seattle, Quebec City, Washington, D.C., Rome, and in Sweden and Copenhagen. What is the significance of *New York Post* headlines like "CCNY Bashes America," and "Once-Proud Campus a Breeding Ground for Idiots" (Clarion Staff 2001, 5) in response to teach-ins about imperialism and terrorism and the meaning and reality of democracy in U.S. society?

The dynamic whereby resistance is racialized posits that freedom of speech exists in the United States; however, whether something is considered unpatriotic depends on who says what. Seditious, critical, and oppositional discourse is aggressively marginalized and implied to be criminal, crazy, disloyal, and/or ungrateful. This is evident in the suppression of facts about the role of the United States in global affairs, especially in the many instances of U.S. military intervention throughout the twentieth century.[32]

These apparent contradictions sometimes lead whites to act "politically correct" in public while they are more open in private settings. A line is drawn between talking and taking action to equalize opportunity where they perceive they may lose something. Whites appear to say one thing yet do another; embrace diversity but "not in my backyard."

The perspectives of foreign-born whites are often distinct from those of whites born in the United States. Foreign-born whites appear to defend the system, whereas U.S.-born whites appear to defend the symbols and more readily have justifications for why racial inequality exists. Whether this is the result of having had a U.S. education or of being influenced by mass media is not clear. However, both positions articulate a willingness to identify with ideals yet hesitancy about committing to action and/or structural explanations. This chapter provided material for reflection on white racial identity and consciousness to the extent that they frame people's rationales for taking various positions, whether in the voting booth or in everyday interaction.

The media present us with images that craft a narrative projecting a common experience, the implicitly "white" experience. Even when diverse images are presented, they generally either portray Blacks who assimilated (such as on *The Cosby Show*, *The Jeffersons*, or *The Fresh Prince of Bel-Air*) or interracial friendships in a way that camouflages or denies racial inequality and undermines our ability to analyze significant and dramatic structural and systemic patterns. Images of people "getting along" lead one to conclude that there must no longer be a "race problem" (*The Hughleys*, *White Men Can't Jump*, *Regarding Henry*) (DeMott 1998, Chito Childs 2009). While a deeper exploration of the role of media is conducted in chapter 5, these images deserve mention here because they convey messages about who is considered "American." There are positive aspects to these shows, which offer a hopeful vision and a less stereotyped view of different groups of people, though they significantly defuse the idea that something needs to be done. Portraits of sameness imply that race is a set of interpersonal relations, focusing attention on individuals and away from institutional inequality.[33] When structural patterns are rendered invisible, symbolic representations of what being American means dominate. Demands for patriotism and nationalism, with implicitly racialized ideological underpinnings, can be beckoned at specific times such as after September 11, to draw lines between who is and who is not a trustworthy, loyal, and "true" American.

Narratives about the melting pot, presumed assimilation, and upward mobility avert attention from the economic and social forces that structure the everyday experiences of people worldwide. They present "normal," using criteria that even few white Americans can achieve. Individual circumstances are decontextualized; the responsibility for being poor is placed firmly on the shoulders of those viewed as "too lazy" to work hard enough to get ahead. Misrepresentations and lies are perpetrated outright. Media images, whether about gender, sexuality, class, or race, tell us who we are and who we want to be.

In the context of the issues discussed in this chapter, the message most clearly voiced was that there are few spaces in the academic setting where assumptions about critical issues related to national identity and the ideals can be examined. Students expressed a desire to learn about different points of view in order to intellectually develop their own perspective and appeared to support a recent trend in higher education that has identified civic development as a core value.

The Association of American Colleges and Universities released a statement on the role of higher education in the wake of the tragedy of September 11, 2001, from which the following excerpt is drawn:

> The academy both embodies and imparts democracy's finest principles of intellectual freedom, reasoned inquiry, civil liberties, openness to a full range of views and experiences and the determination to comprehend issues in all their complexity. (AAC&U 2001b)

While I do not feel certain that the outcome will be a national realignment of institutional strategic outcome objectives for universities, and I might question the direction that this type of thinking will take (e.g., another National Dialogue but this time on terrorism and combating the "enemy"), surely there are openings from which to expose contradictions contained within U.S. foreign, and domestic policies as they relate to the American Dream and the nation's image as the champion of freedom, justice, and democracy worldwide. These notions form the core of U.S. national identity; this is an important endeavor. That articles raising questions such as "Has the American Dream Become Our Nightmare?"[34] or even The Onion's satiric "New Poll Finds 86 Percent of Americans Don't Want to Have a Country Anymore"[35] are not so uncommon certainly indicates that there are opportunities for engaging questions about democracy, nation, materialism, and the American Dream.

4

Making Sense, Nonsense, and No Sense of Race and Rules

> Men often hate each other because they fear each other; they fear each other because they do not know each other; they do not know each other because they cannot communicate; they cannot communicate because they are separated.
>
> —A. Philip Randolph (Mazel 1998, 136)

This chapter explores the dynamics of relationships between groups and how they are understood and mediated. What are the rules of interaction? In what contexts do people question mainstream thought and when do they uphold it? Attitudes toward interracial relationships are discussed and beliefs about human nature and colorblindness as a goal for society are examined. Does intergroup contact influence attitudes and beliefs? Do close relationships (versus casual associations) change how people think, and in what way? What factors influence adherence to stereotypes and which contribute to an individual's identification as an anti-racist?

CONTACT MATTERS

> I don't want people to jump on me, but I don't think it's bad if you don't necessarily socialize with people other than your race just as long as you don't make fun of them or make racial remarks about them. If you want to stick to your own race and you want to socialize with them, and that's who you've been brought up with, then I think that's okay, just as long as you don't have an attitude toward someone else. (Gerda, Russian female)

Many students feel that the diversity of an area (e.g. whether at a school or in a city) does not reflect substantive interconnection between people's lives, although casual contact does occur in classrooms and public spaces. Several expressed a belief that implicit rules structure their relationships with people from different groups and question why "things are the way they are" and whether they can or should change.

The statistics on casual interaction reflected in table 4.1 parallel data from the 2001 and 2008 College Student Survey (CSS) designed by the Higher Education Research Institute (HERI) at the University of California and administered to Brooklyn College students.[1] Participants commented on the data.

> The neighborhood is why you hang out with the people around you. If you are white, you get looked at weird if you go to a Black neighborhood. Like why are you here? The same applies in reverse. Maybe they would be scared of white people. In school, you sort of have no other choice. I think whites are scared of blacks because of the movies and how they portray African Americans as criminals. It's the media. (Vera, white)

In the 2009 revisit survey for this project 62.9 percent of all students said that they socialize outside of class either daily or weekly with someone of another race. However, there were differences between groups: 46.4 percent of blacks indicated they do, compared to 62.8 percent of whites, 71.4 percent of Latinos, and 60 percent of Asians. Of all students 29.5 percent said that

Table 4.1 Intergroup Contact

(a) How Often Do You Socialize outside of Campus with Someone of Another Race?

	Never	Once a Month	Once a Week	Daily
25.5%	20.6%	16.5%	37.5%	
(2nd ed. 2009) Never	Occasionally	Roughly once/month	Roughly once/week	Daily
9.5%	20.0%	7.6%	16.2%	46.7%

(b) How Often Are You in the Home of Someone of Another Race?

	Never	Once a Month	Once a Week	Daily
62.1%	19.1%	11.8%	7.1%	
(2nd ed. 2009) Never	Occasionally	Roughly 1x/month	Roughly 1x/week	Daily
30.1%	30.1%	17.5%	9.7%	12.6%

they never or occasionally socialize outside of class with someone of another race. Of Blacks, 46.4 percent indicated this, compared to 25.6 percent of whites, 28.5 percent of Latinos, and 40 percent of Asians. As to how often they are in the home of someone of another race, overall 22.3 percent of students indicated daily or weekly whereas 60.2 percent said occasionally or never. See table 2.3b for the breakdown by race that again evidences differences between groups.

> I am surprised because NYC is so diverse. You live right next door to somebody of another ethnicity or background. You'd think that you would go and say "Hi" to your neighbor. (Fernando, Latino)

> It's not that we don't socialize, because socializing really doesn't mean that you have a friendship with a person. Like me, I socialize with everybody. Most of the people I socialize with at college are people of different races, different cultures, but when it comes to friendships I usually have friends that share the same basic, common ground, like common goals. . . . Not that I'm racist in any way or like I play favoritism but it's just that we have more in common, we have more to talk about. I know in school, you socialize and learn about different cultures. But when you need a friendship, a friendship really means a lot. Because there's a difference between friends and people you talk to. You can have acquaintances, people you're socializing with, but friendship, you really have to have a lot in common with a person to be friends with them. (Jenna, white female)

Results from the pilot survey indicate a number of statistically significant differences between students within various groups in their patterns of socializing. For example, juniors and seniors indicate more frequently than graduate students that they socialize outside of campus with someone of another race. Students who are thirty years of age or younger indicate that they have been in the home of and socialize outside of campus with someone of another race more frequently than students over age thirty. Students who are involved in campus activities indicate that they socialize with someone of another race more frequently than students who are not involved.

Several participants expressed the sentiment that intergroup socializing occurs less on a commuter campus, because they don't spend time "hanging out." They felt that students stay with friends that they established in high schools, or with friends they made from their neighborhood. The segregation of neighborhoods and schools compounds what occurs on a commuter campus, where students draw from many neighborhoods. Allen (white male) says, "I could pretty much go back to my own neighborhood, after school. I don't have to talk to one person here."

Students also explained why they think so few report having been in the home of someone of another race (tables 4.1, 2.3b):

When you think of a neighborhood you can visualize who lives there. (Natalya, white)

Sixty-three percent of students have never been in somebody of another race's home? They wouldn't say it outright but if you do it like that, it's faceless. Everybody's anonymous, so you can see it's an unwritten rule. (Allen, white male)

Historical segregation is a factor, too. Jews don't talk to non-Jews. We might say "hi," that's all. A stigma is passed on by generations. Probably it is good to increase diversity programming. The world will be different in fifty years. People just have to see that there are no differences among people. (Andrew, white male)

Shelley (white female) comments, "I don't think about who I socialize with. I try to keep an open mind, but I do feel a great resentment and tension toward me from other groups." In the following discussions, students considered other factors that may contribute to the comparatively lower levels of off-campus socializing between groups.

If you live in a white neighborhood or a black neighborhood, then you might meet somebody at school that is of an opposite culture or something. It might be harder to be friends with them because they don't live near you. Especially when you are younger and in elementary school, you can't drive over to them. Your parents can drive you but it's easier to be friends with somebody on your block or two blocks away, than a mile away or three miles away. Some neighborhoods are mixed, but not all of them. The ones that are not, it's harder to be friends with ones from other neighborhoods. (Edward, Asian male)

Other generations may not want or allow you to have other races in your house. You can't even bring people into the neighborhood. Such as Mill Basin, Bensonhurst, Howard Beach. The tone has been set for who interacts with each other. It happens on both ends. People are afraid to go into neighborhoods, and people are not wanted. People are afraid of retribution. Look at what happens again and again. If you have friends, and bring them over, your neighbors might burn your house down. Or, you have to worry that your friend will be hurt. Look at what happened with Yusuf Hawkins, Michael Stewart, and so on and on and on. (Lori, white female staff)

People get killed just for being in another neighborhood. I remember when the black kid was killed in Bensonhurst. The tone has been set. We're in the U.S., we should be allowed, but our neighbors might say something. Other races feel they might get lynched just for being another race. It's the fear of the unknown. (Kevin, white staff)

Kevin alludes to the idea that there are contradictions between the notion of the United States as the "land of the free" and everyday realities. These individuals articulate how intergroup contact outside the boundaries of a space perceived as safe, such as the campus, could be "dangerous." Unwritten rules are understood, forming an unspoken agreement about who, when, where, and under what terms socializing and contact between groups may occur. This interpersonal dynamic forms another mechanism by which the segregation of daily living is enforced and whites, in particular, remain less exposed and aware of the everyday experiences of people of color. While contact does not necessarily correlate with consciousness, empathy, or understanding, most studies recognize that "you need people to interact with each other to realize that the 'other' isn't that different."[2]

Another important issue is that, while the perception is that Blacks, Latinos, and Asians self-segregate more than whites, in fact this is not the case. One of the most significant findings of the Association of American Colleges and Universities survey about the impact of diversity on students in higher education was that "contrary to widespread reports of self-segregation among students of color on campuses, the research finds this pattern more typical of white students. Students of color interact more with dominant students than the reverse" (Smith et al. 1997, vi). This continues to be true as "When black friends eat together at tables in the dining hall, or hang out together in groups, whites take notice. Yet no one comments on the tables of whites eating together in the dining hall or on whites hanging out together on campus. The students showing the greatest degree of self-segregation are white. White students reported on average that two-thirds of their close friends were white, but only a third of black students' close friends were black. In addition, many whites saw black students on campus as a homogeneous group, and were relatively unaware of the divides between black students" (Jaschick interview with *Race and Class Matters at an Elite College* author, Elizabeth Aries 2008).

Even if one feels inclined toward developing relationships with people from different groups, it appears that various factors are calculated into the decision to engage or not that may not emanate from an individual's personal opinions but from an assessment of possible risks. These might entail consequences from one's family or one's community, as noted above. Participants repeatedly calculated the risk of negative outcomes that could occur if they challenged unwritten rules about intergroup socialization, as is evident in the following comments.

> To me it's racist, but they feel different, you just don't feel comfortable with it. They don't say they're gonna kick the person out or they don't want the person in their house, it's just that they'd feel uncomfortable and you as their

daughter would not want them to, so naturally, you just don't bring people of other races home, you just keep them outside. It automatically builds a barrier between you and other races; we've all done that. (Jeanne, white female)

People who were born here, like children of immigrants, become very Americanized—they associate with and socialize with different cultures because at school and work, you're always seeing a mixture of different races, and different nationalities communicating with each other. . . . But the parents, the immigrants themselves, were raised under different conditions of their own countries and they're not used to seeing other races. They grew up with their kind of people and when they come here, they're a little maybe hostile, a little, maybe hesitant to accept other people. I don't think its intentional racism—it's because of lack of understanding and lack of communication. (Leah, Asian female)

As the risks of engagement are calculated and unwritten rules are sorted out, people appear to think aloud about the parameters of who can do what, where, and when. For example, Deborah (white female staff) says that "buying a house in a neighborhood is different than visiting," and others explain:

Segregation in New York depends: sometimes it is because of racism, some people do prefer to live in neighborhoods with their own kind of people but it's because they just share the same interests maybe, because they came from the same country. It has to do with fear of rejection, that you may not be accepted. You might say a joke and somebody in your group, from your background, they will understand it, and somebody from another country, they won't understand, they'll think you're weird. (Jeff, white male)

A black friend came over and my neighbor asked whether she was coming to clean. The rules have been set, the tone; you don't cross the line. (Barbara, white staff)

Other participants feel that the patterns of interaction whereby people stay with their "own" group are "natural," to be expected and not necessarily problematic. Nonna (white female) expresses that people want to be with a group that "better and easily understands you," while Leon (white male) says, "It depends on where you grew up, your parents and their beliefs." Other ideas included the following:

It's basically who you are friends with because that's whose house you go to. If you're friends with somebody who's not within your race, of course you're going to go to their house. (Jan, Native American female)

Certain classes encourage getting to know people, like Core 3[3] where I worked with a lot of people but I did not maintain contact or make "friends friends."

Socializing involves deliberate choice. My friends' friends[4] are people who I grew up with, gone to school and shul with. We live in the same community; my parents are friends with theirs. It all makes sense. (Andrew, white male)

But you can't force people to talk to each other. What are you going to do, stand on a podium? They won't listen. (Mia, Latina)

While these comments indicate that some students believe that increased intergroup socializing can be positive, others thought nothing needed to be changed in current patterns of interaction. They felt they should be allowed to relate to whomever they please. There was a sense that to encourage intergroup interaction is to interfere in ways that are irrelevant, inappropriate, and unnatural. Among the students quoted below, one claims that intergroup interaction just doesn't work.

If you want to interact, it's right there in front of you. There's so many people here, you can interact with anybody you want to. . . . When it comes down to it, it depends on the person, if they want to, they'll do it. (Don, white male)

Segregation on campus is the people's choice. (Vera, white female)

Sometimes when you try to do things, it gets worse, so you don't touch it. If you leave a group the way it is, it might not have any contact but if you touch the group it might turn into something worse. It's like orange juice and apple juice, you don't mix it and it's okay. But, when you mix it, it tastes nasty. (Jeanne, white female)

We pay to come to BC and should pretty much do what we want as long as we're not interrupting anybody's learning process. (Leon, white male)

Another dimension of intergroup relations is the degree of tension experienced on campus. Table 4.2 indicates that while almost one half of the student body report they never witness tension, the other half does, with almost 9 percent saying they do so daily.

Foreign-born whites (61 percent), more frequently than Asian students (30.8 percent), said that they never witness racial tension, and foreign-born white students (6.1 percent), significantly less frequently than Asian

Table 4.2   How Often Do You Witness Racial Tension among Classmates/Friends?

Never	Once a Month	Once a Week	Daily
49.2%	29.1%	12.9%	8.8%

students (12.8 percent), said that they witness racial tension daily. Women more often say they witness racial tension daily (11.0 percent) than men (4.3 percent).

Beliefs about whether racial tensions exist and whether segregation is a problem impact white students' level of participation in events about intergroup relations. If they don't sense a problem or have something to gain, students would have no reason to attend such events. Accordingly, if they do feel that tensions exist, they may be concerned that attention will be drawn to them as individuals, so they might stay away for fear of being called racist, as Nancy suggests. Some suggest that in fact it will only be through focusing on a new vision that whites will join the efforts to challenge racism. Until then, they experience discussions about multi-culturalism as a threat and will resist taking part in the process (Tanaka 2009, 92).

During the spring of 1998, efforts were underway to engage intergroup dialogue on campus. On three occasions, attempts were made to initiate discussions with community members about the state of intergroup relations on campus. These efforts included a student leadership luncheon, a forum on whiteness, and a community-building retreat. In all three cases only faculty, staff, and students of color attended. Personal invitations were extended to cultural clubs and departments with a majority of white members; deliberate outreach was conducted. What accounts for the lack of response? Might this reflect differing perceptions about the need for such discussions?

Table 4.3 reflects the disparity between the percentages of students who socialize on campus versus off campus with people from their own group. This difference is generally explained by saying that on campus it is "easier," "safer," and more convenient to socialize with other groups. One does not have to go out of one's way to make it happen. Concerns were voiced that minimal intergroup contact contributes to the perpetuation of stereotypes because it does not afford people the opportunity to get to know one another as individuals. In the 2009 revisit survey, 48.1 percent of students indicated they

Table 4.3   Socializing versus Working with Classmates from Own Group

Do You Usually Work with Classmates from Your Own Racial/Ethnic Group?	
No	Yes
62.4%	37.6%
Do You Usually Socialize with People from Your Own Racial/Ethnic Group?	
No	Yes
37.1%	62.7%

never or occasionally worked with classmates of another race; 35.6 percent said they do so daily or weekly.

The following passages illustrate the concerns about lack of interaction.

You have to look into high schools. As a matter of fact, in junior high school, because that is where it's developed. Little by little they just start falling out. A lot of white folks expect to see me in front of a bodega buying a six-pack for my friends and smoking a blunt. It gets me upset. You don't know what I've been through and what my parents have been through so I can come to school. There's an assumption from a certain race, ethnicity, background about what you're gonna wind up doing. With a kid at seventeen, dropping out of school, getting your GED when you're twenty-one and just bumming your life working in a grocery store or a deli. Then they say, "I'm not talking about you, I'm talking about the rest of them." A white woman once said to me, "They have such bad attitudes . . . Oh, no, not you." But people cross the street when I walk with my friends. (Fernando, Latino)

I definitely think that's a big problem that people have not been in the home of another race because I think in life you'll judge people until you get to learn about their culture. There are so many different cultures out there, and once you get to know the person and you get to learn them, you see so much more, you just understand so much more about them when you get to know them, get the chance. It does not surprise me because look at the cafeteria.[5] But it is surprising. I think it is due to comfort. It is natural but I do think it is a problem. If I am a CEO and I am more comfortable with people who are like me it skews my hiring decision. Maybe it is not really the best person. But there is a time factor. Brown versus Board of Ed and the Montgomery Bus Boycott were not that long ago. Being in class with different people encourages contact. But it hasn't been that long ago since segregation was made illegal. (Andrew, white male)

It's a problem that people haven't been in the home of someone of another race and it could also be an environmental issue, like where you're brought up. There are also a lot of stereotypes. People who don't associate with people of other races—they don't understand; they stick to the stereotype; this is how they are. Then they rationalize why they don't hang out with these people. (Joanne, Latina)

If you hang out with predominantly white kids you are going to be more into yourself, into your race. These are the only people you know, the only ones you are around. So if they are being taught that black people are a certain way, they're gonna believe it. (Nancy, white female)

Many people agree that contact does matter, particularly when it helps to dismantle stereotypes. However, some articulate a belief that bias will automatically vanish over time, so no action is needed. Others feel strongly that there are positive reasons to increase the levels of interaction. Carl (Black male) explains, "Relationships break stereotypes and let you see people for who they are. You don't feel barriers; it makes people more approachable, more open. It changes people's body language." Marian agrees—"It is more difficult to negate stereotypes if individuals are isolated from each other"— as does Deborah (white female staff): "Without exposure, there is no change. With exposure, barriers drop and there is more understanding of commonality. When people mix they find out we're all the same. But, even with exposure, open-mindedness is still slow."

> I disagree with leaving it alone. Sometimes it's not even planned—like the people who you hang out with. A lot of times when you see people hanging together with their own, it's not because they say, "Okay, we're all white" or "We're all black," it just happens that way. It's a natural clique. I don't know if it's because of similar experiences, but that's just how it happens. I don't think people get up and say, or maybe some do, but I don't think people just get up and say "Let's just hang with each other today because we're all white." (Sam, white male)

As Sam's statement makes clear, recognizing or desiring increased intergroup contact still leaves open the question of how to accomplish such a change. This consideration implicitly raises the question about which factors make a difference in changing patterns. Several participants felt that simply living in New York City gave them a different perspective on intergroup relations and contact. Frequent exposure means that people are accustomed to interacting and it is assumed that the "problem" of "race relations" was to be found in other regions of the country, but not in New York. Some students attribute residential segregation to the ease and logic of associating with people whom one perceives to be "like" oneself. Here students reflect upon experiences they had outside the NYC metropolitan area.

> From my perspective as a white person, if you go down South as a New Yorker and you try to deal with people down there, there's a lot of tension. That's a local thing. It's different cultures that you're dealing with. I went to a very small rural Texas town for a year and it was very conservative, very agricultural and there was just not a lot of basis for communication. There's not a whole lot to relate to people on. I got along with people okay; it was just there were differences. There was always like this division, of well, I'm a New Yorker and you know, it's like I can't really relate to people talking about cows and stuff. (Allen, white male)

When I went to Idaho, Brooklyn seemed like another country. The people there were very, very nice, a little too nice and it scared me a little, it was just weird. They didn't have any racial aggression towards me, but the way they acted around me was different. Like, I wanted to go horseback riding and this guy was talking to me like I was illiterate. He was like, "Would . . . you . . . like . . . a . . . horse?" He helped the next guy and it pissed me off a little bit. You know I'm not illiterate, just because I'm not exactly white. . . . He thought I was Latino but really I'm Jewish. (Alex, white male)

The problem is not so much here, but other places. Here we are used to being around lots of different people. (Deborah, white female staff)

Contrasting these ideas about how diverse groups mix well in Brooklyn and New York City, some students attempted to explain neighborhood segregation.

It's a Brooklyn thing, because right when someone immigrates they go into their own neighborhood, like, their own culture right away, everything's grouped right off the bat, they just go into their own area. (Zena, white female)

You have a Jewish group, you have a Jamaican group, Haitian group, and Chinese group, and so everything is evenly divided. It is done so people are able to communicate; it makes it easier. (Nicky, white female)

Many issues in these discussions were left without general agreement. Students expressed a desire to talk and ask each other questions in order to better understand different perspectives. A range of mechanisms for the reinforcement of racialized patterns emerged. For example, "human nature" was frequently invoked to explain why neighborhoods and socialization occur in a segregated fashion. Similarly, silences, fear, notions of what constitutes comfortable and familiar interaction versus awkward or unfamiliar interaction all help to reproduce the patterns of intergroup relations that we are told are "natural." Each of these mechanisms is simultaneously matched with possibilities where presumptions can be explored. For example, raising the questions, Who are one's "own" people? Who is viewed as like oneself? Who is viewed as different? provides an opportunity to explore notions of community. The willingness to talk about these issues and to listen is a very important and critical tool that can be used to confront traditional patterns.

Questions that arose included: Why are people most comfortable within their "own" circle? How do they define own? Is there significance to the evidence that suggests students associate on campus with people from different groups but off campus with their "own group"? Do these issues warrant serious consideration or should they just be accepted as the "norm," and not problematic? In the 2009 survey, 82.5 percent agreed or strongly agreed that most people prefer to live in neighborhoods of their own ethnicity; 86.1 percent of whites agreed/strongly agreed, 78.5 percent of Latinos, 73.3 percent of Asians, and 71.5 percent of Blacks. Students struggled with what they thought and appeared to listen closely, not only to what other people were saying but also to hear themselves, as if they were uncertain of their own opinions.

> It's more difficult for people to break through barriers like language, culture, and religion to interact with someone from a different country, than it is for somebody to find someone from their own culture who already speaks the same language, has the same religion and then just says, "Hey, let's hang out." But it really has nothing to do with comfort because you could be comfortable with a person of a different culture also but you have to be willing to go through the breaking of these barriers. (Diane, white female)

> Well, you know, I can be friends with anybody, but I think it's how I grew up. My parents are white, when I was a kid I went to an all-white grammar school. I lived in an all-white neighborhood, all-white high school. I didn't practically see people of another race until I was older. I think it's what people are used to. I don't consider myself racist or that I'm prejudiced. I can be friends with anybody, people that I work with, I'm close with a couple of them, black women and I love them. We don't socialize outside of the office. Not that we wouldn't, we just don't. Everybody has their own little life that they go home to. (Helen, white female)

Another concern raised several times was whether higher educational and income status or "maturity" lead to a greater degree of interaction with people from different backgrounds. The general assumption was that these factors do lead to increased interracial interaction, resulting in greater numbers of friendships, both platonic and intimate. However, this notion was repeatedly challenged, and there was no agreement about whether they make a difference.

> I do think our campus is segregated. Not very, but it is. Look in the cafeteria. It has to do with the maturity level. As you mature you get a little bit more open-minded. (Terry, white female)

> Look at Brooklyn Heights versus Seagate. Education plays a strong role because in the Heights you see lots of beautiful mixed children and interracial couples. Education makes you open-minded. (Sabrina, white female)

> But that's not true. Look how white Harvard, Oxford, and Yale are as well as the corporate world. That's a myth. (Jared, Egyptian and Italian male)

It was apparent that students understood the importance of learning diverse perspectives, especially as they pursue careers in particular professions. They generally felt that racialized perceptions do affect how doctors form opinions about the health of their patients, lawyers about their clients, the potential that teachers see in their students, and the impressions that police officers form in the communities they serve. Students are clear that race plays a role but are less sure whether it is positive or negative and how racialized images should be handled.

> If you teach in a public school they expect you not to be racist when they assign you to a school, they're already racist. One of my dad's friends is a teacher who was assigned to Chinatown because he was Chinese. On the other hand, his friend who graduated with him is white and is assigned near his house because those were mainly white people so they already have some racist idea that they should assign you to different schools. (Leah, Asian female)

> Perhaps you have a job where you have to appeal to the customer, I mean, if you don't know the customer's needs or what they're fond of, you're going to sound like a moron and embarrass yourself, like you could say the wrong thing in front of them, or something, you know. (Jeff, white male)

Would a white teacher who was placed within a white district protest? Why or why not? Who benefits from being racialized, and who does not?

> In the medical profession and teaching, segregation has negative effects. If a teacher is racist, he or she will mistreat the student based on stereotypes. Whether he or she abused the student to be mean or not, if he treats the student poorly and the student feels discouraged, then maybe he or she wouldn't want to study more. I heard a lot of cases like this where because they were discouraged and they feel that they are, I don't know, hated, or misrepresented by the teacher, they don't want to do well anymore. They don't want to study. I think like for sure, racism has negative effects. (Jeanne, white female)

> It's very important for doctors to get to know other ethnic groups because when you're a doctor and you're in a region that cannot communicate with you, and if you can understand a couple of words, that can make a difference between life and death. If they're telling you something in Spanish and you don't understand, but you know a couple of words here and there, you can pretty much understand them by what they're telling you in speech and their motions, what they're describing to you, can be very significant or you can call your friends and ask them to translate. (Helen, white female)

While it is clear that knowledge of different cultures and languages is considered useful in the work world, it is instructive to look back at how these situations are framed—who "cannot communicate" with whom, who is

discouraged versus who discourages. Even when responsibility is acknowledged, relationships are constructed in a dominant/subordinate manner that
leaves positioning of people from different groups intact on an unequal basis,
reproducing patterns of presumed power relationships. This dynamic is also
evident in the ideas that students have about how class and social status impact everyday living.

> Sometimes it just depends on status, because I have friends who are white
> and regular people, but you are not always at an advantage if you're white. For
> example, with the president, everybody knows, it's an unwritten code that to be
> the president of the United States, you have to be a white male. It's not written
> in the Constitution but look at the history of how many women presidents there
> have been or how many black presidents were there—none. So you can have an
> advantage if you are white, depending on your status in society in general. But
> like a friend of mine, a regular old Joe who is white, just gets by daily like I do,
> just a regular person. (Beverly, Black female)

On several occasions, students spoke about periods in their lives when
they interacted with people from a variety of backgrounds more frequently
than at others. They referred to after-school programs and community
centers that existed in their neighborhoods up through the mid-1990s. Students strongly expressed that these were spaces where they could interact
with young people from different neighborhoods. They remember having
had very positive experiences and learning to get along well. They felt
comfortable and found they had a lot in common with young people who
were not from their own racial or ethnic background. These students repeatedly articulated their concern and confusion about why these projects
were eliminated when they contributed so much to the community's well-
being. They also universally expressed, however, that group boundaries
and segregation solidify in high school. The following comments reflect
these discussions.

> When I was a kid, at the youth center, I was good friends with all different
> kinds of people. We realized we were just as poor as each other. None of us
> were working; we discussed social issues that affected us all. We never had
> racial fights. Now we are not in touch at all. The center was closed down. Now
> we wouldn't be friends. We are older. Blacks are at black colleges. Maybe we
> realized that we were equally poor, now they are more advantaged because they
> get full financial aid.[6] The divide is so large. (Nancy, white female)

> In my old neighborhood there was a community house for kids to do their
> homework. All kinds of kids. The teachers ran it and high school kids worked
> there. They were trying to close it down. It stayed open until 1 A.M. on Friday

nights. Your mother and father knew where you were, playing basketball, and board games; there were tournaments. Me and my friends knocked on doors to keep it from closing; we went into buildings for people to sign our petition. But a lot of people were not interested. They didn't think it did anything for us. I'd say "We're the youth of America, you have to help us." One lady cracked me up. She said, "I don't give two shhh . . . who you are. You're not paying my bills. Get off my doorstep." We kept it open by throwing parties, better than most house parties. That's how we kept it open. They're still trying, and now they are not even getting help from the city. (Fernando, Latino)

I went to one of the most diverse high schools in Brooklyn. Every single section was a color. On the fourth floor, by the locker rooms were the Chinese kids. On the first floor, in the middle was the black kids; outside, the white kids. The teachers didn't make us be like that. I remember that the second floor was Dominican. It just was. (Nancy, white female)

The above testimonies lead one to consider the factors that play a role in the shift in young people's affiliations from mixed groupings to segregated ones. Studies about this shift in friendship groups note generally that junior high school is often a transition period (Lewin 2001, A1). Economic and social pressures foster division between young people. It appears this occurs when teenagers themselves begin to compete for specialized high school and college programs, scholarships, jobs (on their own, without parental help) and when they start thinking about their careers. This is also the time in their lives when they may begin to date. The focus of their relationships as a result becomes much more directed toward how they will navigate as adults within a racialized society. This issue is important to consider, as diversity education and programs and curricula in higher education need to be extended throughout young people's academic experience or must be, as has been stated, a "cradle to grave" project, in order to be effective.[7]

Students' reflections about their experience of having more friends from different groups when they were younger raise the question of how race is used to deflect attention from a broader analysis of global economics, to explain why they feel tremendous pressure about their futures. (These explanations may be irrelevant at earlier ages.) In the context of the increasingly scarce resources as the economy constricts, real wages decrease, and poor and middle-income people compete in an increasingly tight labor market, their uncertainty about their job futures is justified. However, "the majority of white men who are not in the top one percent of the population owning 48 percent of society's net wealth, have reason to be angry—but not at Black people. Their grievance is deliberately steered toward those who are not responsible for their problem" (Mullings 1995, 31–34).

Community centers helped build a sense of commonality and interconnectedness and fostered goodwill between people from different groups. Neighborhood interactions drew together young people from various schools and cultivated friendships, understanding, and connections. Without interaction in positive settings such as this, Jack Levin of Northeastern University observes, academic and economic pressures frequently add fuel to a potentially volatile mixing of diverse communities. "We see very high levels of competition, for grades, for campus resources and for jobs. . . . At elite schools, the combination of hyper-competitiveness and diverse student populations may ironically give them the highest volume of hate crimes" (Tolerance.org 2001b).

Most hate crimes nationwide are committed by youths under the age of twenty-two (Tolerance.org 2001b) as the pressures felt by young people in the process of becoming independent adults heightens intergroup tensions. At the same time, some students pointed out the positive impact of interactions and ways to foster intergroup relationships on campus. Beverly explains, "We need to be more assertive with friendships. Before I started coming here, I never had a Jewish friend, and now I have two, and they're cool, just like anybody else. If people took initiative to just say 'Hi,' and not assume because this person might be different from me racially or culturally, you know, just forget about it." Other students describe their experiences and what works in forging cross-group relationships:

> As an incoming freshman, we were blocked together so I'm in three classes with the same people. We developed a very nice friendship in a family-like

Table 4.4a   I Consider Myself to Be Colorblind When It Comes to Race: Data from the First Edition

Disagree	Moderately Agree	Agree
17.6%	43.3%	39.2%

Table 4.4b   I Consider Myself to Be Colorblind When It Comes to Race: Data from the Second Edition

	Strongly Disagree	Disagree	Agree	Strongly Agree
Overall	5.7%	26.7%	36.2%	21.0%
Latinos	0.0%	14.3%	21.4%	42.9%
Asians	0.0%	13.3%	40.0%	33.3%
Blacks	10.7%	25.0%	42.9%	7.1%
Whites	4.7%	30.2%	34.9%	14.0%

atmosphere. It was a really great help. We studied together. A lot of the kids in my class graduated high school in January, so they're like young, seventeen, because we started in February and it was a great help for them. For freshmen to be blocked with other students makes a lot of this happen, friendships, working with others. It's great, there's about twenty of us. (Randy, white female)

The opportunity was provided . . . now I have friends from Poland, I have Jewish friends, friends from basically everywhere and if the opportunity wasn't provided in college . . . chances are at work I would never have met them. This was about the only opportunity that I had and now I have a few friends from basically other races, so the opportunity arose. (Joan, white female)

It's important to be somewhat worldly and have some knowledge of other races and cultures so you just don't sound stupid in a normal conversation. But it is important to feel comfortable and be able to help other people [from] different backgrounds. [Yet] I also don't think you need to run around with a checklist to make sure that I have a Columbian friend. (Jeff, white male)

In these passages, students articulate their beliefs that interaction between groups is positive and that they have benefited from experiences in which they have gotten to know people from different backgrounds. Another key finding in national research on diversity initiatives has been that virtually all students desired opportunities for interaction because they recognized that it prepares them for the world they live in. Additionally, as mentioned in chapter 2, exposure to diversity positively impacts academic success, cognitive development, and overall institutional satisfaction (Smith et al. 1997, vi). This seems to be recognized now in the corporate world, too, where increased diversity and multiculturalism are embraced because they are "good for business." Furthermore, the presence of racial diversity increases students' capacity for integrative complexity, a cognitive outcome (Antonio et al. 2004, 509).

This section explored reasons given for the relatively minimal intergroup interaction among students outside campus that included parental and neighborhood pressures, and both implicit and explicit stigmas. Participants spoke about the effect that stereotypes have and their belief that people develop closer relationships with those who share similar backgrounds, live in close proximity, and therefore perceive to be better able to understand each other. Such beliefs directly relate to mechanisms that reinforce racialized patterns such as the segregation of everyday living, unwritten rules of interaction, and the social pressures supporting both individualism and competition. Openings exist in the recognition of the benefits of diversity, as well as in idealism and experiences that provide a vision of a more equal and just world. The ability of students to identify times in their lives when there was more interaction and shared experience provides an opportunity to construct those spaces through social and structural changes that serve the common good.

Several people express irritation that their usual pattern of interaction is being questioned and feel that to discuss this is intrusive. Others feel that the cycle of segregation is reproduced through lack of contact, knowledge, and experience. They raise the practical issue of how to become acquainted with people from other groups. Finally, participants noted numerous unwritten rules that undergird interaction. They feel that children learn the boundaries and consequences of stepping out of line. Kevin (white male staff) illustrates the seriousness with which these rules are regarded: "People get killed for being in another neighborhood!"

Participants allude to a concern that such restrictions on their mobility constitute a lack of freedom. They assume, then question whether education and income correlate to tolerance and higher levels of intergroup relationships.

COLORBLINDNESS

As many of those who participated in this research are in their twenties, they accept the notions that we now live in a "colorblind" or "color-neutral" society and that, to the extent we do not, we should strive to have been part of the dominant discourse for most of our lives. In the third edition of *Racism without Racists: Color-Blind Racism and the Persistence of Racial Inequality in the United States* Eduardo Bonilla Silva changes his conclusion from "The (Color-Blind) Emperor Has No Clothes" to "The (Color-Blind) Emperor Has New Clothes," signifying the development of three new "racial spaces" (white, honorary white, and collective Black) (2009, 269–270).

In this study, there was a significant range of opinion about "colorblindness" issues. Female respondents were much more likely to say they consider themselves colorblind (44 percent) than males (32.7 percent) while in 2009, 50 percent of females said they consider themselves colorblind when it comes to race whereas 72.8 percent of males said so. Students were asked about their thoughts regarding colorblindness as an ideal and whether they thought U.S. society has achieved this "state of being." Michael (Latino, white) was clear about his thoughts: "I don't agree with colorblindness, I want to learn about different cultures." But Joanne (Latina) had questions: "Do you want people to see you as you are, or as a stereotype? I was brought up, that you see someone; you take them for whom they are. The way they present themselves, the way they speak, and the way they act, not just physically." Michael continued,

Being colorblind is the wrong thing to do. It's like when they had the feminist movement. Someone said enough is enough, why are we all trying to be men when there's something about us that's unique and different. Differences are beautiful. I am not going to treat you like someone who just sits and hangs out. I want to know, man, I want to pick your brain, I want to see what your culture's like, I want to see what's down over here. I don't want to just put my blinders on and ignore the culture—I, like, observe it, suck it in, it's beautiful, our differences.

Etienne (Haitian male) articulated his perspective, formulated from his own experiences in this society where the actions of some are generalized as the actions of all. As mentioned earlier on, whites are seldom taken as representatives of their race, whereas people of color frequently are.

We can't be 100 percent colorblind. It is good to see people for who they are. Would you want somebody to see you and your culture and see most of the people who haven't done something to tear it apart to have them view only one person who did wrong as everybody from that culture? That's how I see colorblindness, to not stereotype people. I don't see it as ignoring that person's culture, just that you know people discriminate on that basis.

These students describe their racialized experience in very different ways. One is able to enjoy difference in its richness as a cultural voyager, while another articulates racialization as being stereotyped by the negative views with which society has portrayed Blacks. In a dialogue examining the meaning of race in daily living, Professor Madison described how his neighbors were dead-set against allowing Blacks to rent apartments in his building. He expressed that colorblindness does not exist because people of color mostly cannot "hide," although white ethnics, such as Jews, can change their names. Assimilation is therefore more of a possibility for them.[8] In this discussion, not all students were convinced, as Karen reveals: "But you can't just blame race. A French person applying for a mortgage faces more discrimination than a U.S. black." She argues that immigrants have a harder time regardless of race.

The notion that colorblindness confers "invisibility" for subordinated groups was raised from several perspectives.

Colorblinding undermines the point that social inequality exists. We should strive for the idea that people are different; we should preserve and appreciate that, and not just make homogenous cultureless beings. What's interesting is that when you are a token or in the subordinated group you end up representing your whole group. People watch me closely. Rabbis are only publicized when they molest a kid. People feel obligated to say "Orthodox" Jew. We are exoticized. (Shalom, white male, Jewish)

> I was the first black person to move into my building. I was invisible until I broke my leg and walked on crutches. All of a sudden people became friendly. Someone said that I was no longer scary. However, when I got better, I was invisible again. (Antoine, Black male)

Antoine was approachable to his neighbors only when he was vulnerable. Is it possible that he was being observed the whole time—that his humanity was invisible when his neighbors perhaps perceived him as dangerous? When he was on crutches, he appeared to have been humanized, but once healed he was stereotyped again. Rather than his neighbors being colorblind at all, it appears they might have been starkly aware of his blackness.

It is this awareness of the normalizing of whiteness that led to the following student's realization that his own perspective about the school curriculum might be culturally defined. At first, he expressed surprise that anyone would think that including the experiences and accomplishments of people of color in the curriculum would raise standards. "What does that have to do with academic quality?" Andrew asks. But then, after consideration, he quickly retracts his initial response.

> Oh, now I understand. They probably feel that the history course or the art course is too Eurocentric. I can see that. I just never thought about it. I assumed that we are studying the right things. I think a lot of the responses by whites reflect that we don't really think about race as playing a role. We assume that everyone should be, and is, being treated equally.

Andrew's initial statement alludes to a common belief that indeed we do live in a colorblind society. However, his willingness to examine his thinking points to the possibility of engaging people in expanding their awareness about the everyday realities of people of color that they may not have considered. This important "crack" is useful only with exposure to alternative ways of viewing everyday situations and a recognition that there are real consequences to holding the perception (i.e., that the "right" things are being studied) expressed above. Beverly Daniel Tatum, renowned psychologist, speaks of this: "Stereotypes, omissions, and distortions all contribute to the development of prejudice" (1997, 5–6). She discusses the significant consequences of Eurocentric curricula reflected in the remark of one of her white male students, to wit, "It's not my fault that blacks don't write books" (1997, 5). She wonders whether any of his teachers had actually told him that there were no Black writers, or whether, given the omission, he had drawn his own conclusion (1997, 5).

Discourse about how "we are all human" and "we are all the same" emerged infrequently in the focus groups. However, Benjamin DeMott makes the case that in the 1990s what he calls an "'aegis of friendship' orthodoxy" shifted the discourse to sameness and "they're just like us," in place of prior constructions of the subhuman character of Black identity (DeMott 1995, 187). This resulted in reinforcing the misperception that Blacks, Latinos, and Asians are doing as well as or better than whites and translated into support for frontal assaults on affirmative action, welfare, and housing programs.

The argument for colorblindness is also framed in the notion that the problem of racism is that we keep talking about it. If we could just focus on being human and stop talking about race, we would overcome racism. This was explicitly articulated in an article that appeared in the *Chronicle of Higher Education*: "The opposite of being pro-diversity is not being anti-diversity. It's being diversity-indifferent, and that's me. My T-shirt would not say 'Diversity Sucks.' It would say, 'Diversity—Who Cares?' Why am I sick of all the praise for diversity? Because it cloaks an agenda that is anti-merit, pro-preference, and anti-assimilationist" (Clegg 2000, B8). Various assumptions underlying this statement will be further investigated in chapter 5.

In examining the notion of colorblindness—whether people believe we now live in a colorblind society or that it is an attainable goal—one observes that there is recognition of the value of diversity, of understanding different ways of living and perspectives. However, concerns were raised that allowing the space for differences also provides space for prejudice and bias. Several people stated that they wanted to be dealt with as an individual, rather than as part of a group. Others voiced concern that, by striving for colorblindness, one undermines the struggle for equality. They felt that since not all people are (or have been) treated equally, one couldn't simply say that we all start now from the same place. A colorblind perspective allows whites to distance themselves from the realities of historical and current inequalities while continuing to provide "public and psychological" wages of white status and privilege.[9] Similar to anxieties experienced by whites during Reconstruction, "'The white man's burden' has been resurrected for the turn of the twentieth century, only now it is whites claiming the status of victim" (Gallagher 1995, 179–80). History plays a significant role in people's everyday lives and will continue to do so unless inequities and historical prejudices are addressed.

HUMAN NATURE

Everyone just takes things for granted in general. It's part of human nature; we always want more.

—Gerda, Russian female

Common within discussions were strong opinions about the types of interaction between groups that people feel are natural and what they believe are not. Underlying this issue is the question of whether we can or should intervene in current patterns of relationships. We may believe that interaction between groups is positive but feel, for example, that people naturally gravitate to those they consider to be like themselves or from their own group. In that case our attack on the problem of racism would be different from that of people who feel that circumstances structure relationships in segregated patterns and that there is no "natural" predisposition toward associating with one's own group.

The first set of comments below represent the position that people are naturally greedy, impatient, and self-centered. Certainly, a concern for the common good requires some willingness to put the interests of the group as a whole ahead of one's own self-interest, though it is possible to view the well-being of an individual as linked to the well-being of the group. Patience, one might argue, is essential if one determines that action is required to improve the quality of lives of all people. In the context of this discussion about race and racial inequality, white students allude to feeling that the expectations of people of color about the elimination of inequality are unreasonably high and imply that they feel that Blacks and Latinos expect too much, too quickly.

> People are way too impatient. I just don't understand, people want everything, like, right now; right now [bangs the table]. I don't understand, like, patience is a big thing for me and a lot of people don't have it. (Don, white male)

> By definition we have desire. When we come out of the mother's womb we're already crying, "Get me this." We live with that our entire life. Out of desire grows greed, greed for money and power. As long as there are things to satisfy our desire, there will be power. As long as there's power there will be inequality because somebody will have more and that makes us unequal, or somebody will have less and that makes us unequal. (Shalom, white male, Jewish)

One might question, however, whether views about what is too much or too quick might in fact depend on who is the one facing challenges.

Another set of beliefs about what constitutes human nature is illustrated by the view that people prefer to "stick to their own" and that they fear difference and change. There appears to be general agreement on these points, as they were never contested in any of the groups where they were discussed.

> People are standoffish unless you're involved in something together. (Joanne, Latina)

Michael explains that he believed that it is our natural propensity to classify that propels stereotyping. He describes his disappointment when he discovered that, despite the apparent neutrality of cyber-communications, these too have been constructed to identify individuals according to pre-designated categories:[10]

> It's idealistic to believe we would not stereotype. It's our nature, permanent, conditioned. I thought you could go online and expected this beautiful experience not being judged by how I look, or my skin color. I am a blinking cursor. The first question is age, sex, location, and nationality, within the first sentence! We can't exist without knowing. What is it about us? I can't talk to you if I don't know what you are. Is it because we're social beings that we live by these rules? It's idealistic to think that if we exist as a human being with no identity, just our minds being judged. We'd all go batty in two minutes because we need something to ground us or we feel out of place.

In the 2009 focus groups, ideas about human nature continued to emerge. Here are a few of the comments:

> It's human nature to have someone who is inferior to you and I think . . . blacks are the ones who are inferior now but I'm pretty sure that will move onto another race and after that it's going to keep going because there's always going to be somebody who feels that another race is inferior to them. (Ravon, Black Latino)

> There's a fear of the unknown. Like when they went to Africa like oh my gosh who are these people. It's just fear of the unknown, so you just build up your defenses and immediately just say okay this person is inferior to me. (Carol, white female)

Commonly articulated narratives reinforce how we think about one another. Competition is ingrained in a mainstream worldview, so it is difficult to consider options. Our ability to change established patterns of intergroup relationships is hindered by a belief in the selfish, individualistic, and competitive nature of human beings. This discourse reinforces the status quo, rather than allowing people to believe that caring, cooperation, and generosity might be our natural predisposition. Just imagine the possibilities!

INTERRACIAL MARRIAGE AND RELATIONSHIPS

> I wouldn't care if you married an animal. Personally it's a different story. Lots of things come into play like your parents might be of a different religion, and culture comes into play. If you can't get along in your own race, how can you get along with others?
>
> —Don, white male

This section explores students' views on interracial relationships and testimony about related conflicts with parents or friends, in one case, as early as fourth grade. They speak of how they developed awareness of societal attitudes and the techniques that they use to negotiate what they perceive to be contradictions (see table 4.5).

U.S.-born whites approve of interracial marriage significantly less than all other groups except for foreign-born whites. U.S.-born whites disapprove of interracial marriage significantly more than all other groups except for foreign-born whites. Whites consider marrying someone of another race significantly less than all other groups. The inverse is also true: whites would not consider marrying someone of another race significantly more than all other groups.

This has shifted however, in the last decade. A recent Pew Research survey found that roughly 83 percent agree that, "I think it's all right for blacks and whites to date each other" (Doherty and Michael Dimock 2007, 43). In the 2009 revisit survey, 82.8 percent of respondents indicated that they approve of interracial marriage and 70.4 percent said they would marry someone of another race. This change is also evident as 14.6 percent of all new marriages in 2008 were between people of different races or ethnicity (9 percent of whites, 16 percent of Blacks, 26 percent of Hispanics, and 31 percent of Asians) which is double what it was in 1980. Of all marriages, 8 percent are interracial or interethnic, 13 percent of those ages 25 or under, but only 3 percent of those 75 or older.[11]

However, explicitly segregated proms are still considered a tradition in areas of the South. The film *Prom Night in Mississippi* covers the first integrated prom in Charleston, Mississippi, prompted by Morgan Freeman's offer to cover expenses.[12] His first offer in 1997 was rejected. While in 2007 a Gallup poll found that 77 percent approve of interracial marriage, up from 4 percent when the question was first asked in 1958,[13] as a couple in Louisiana discovered in October 2009 when a Justice of Peace refused to marry them, that increase certainly does not represent full acceptance.[14]

Interracial relationships appear more acceptable as an idea but not as a lived reality, as the following narratives indicate. These stories provide much

Table 4.5   Interracial Marriage

	Disagree	Moderately Agree	Agree
I Approve of Interracial Marriage			
	14.9%	22.7%	62.4%
I Would Consider Marrying Someone of Another Race			
	36.7%	25.2%	38.1%

material to reflect upon. Why, for example, is the father's friendship accept-able but his daughter's is not? Why is there is so much concern about what boxes will be checked on the census form (especially when there is a move-ment to eliminate racial and ethnic categories from the census entirely)? Why is it presumed that someone of multiple lineages would be "confused"? These questions highlight the rigid nature of the racial hierarchy in U.S. society and illuminate the contradictions of the social reality of race without a biological basis, and they also illuminate boundaries for interaction.

> In Queens there were mostly white kids, now that I think of it. There was one Indian kid, one Hispanic kid. I don't remember any black kids. In fourth grade there were a couple of black kids. Summer camp was mixed; there were a lot of black kids there. I didn't know it was called race. I just knew people were different. I was this little blue-eyed blonde girl and I didn't look at people like, "Oh she's Puerto Rican" or "He's Asian." I'm not like that, I never was. But a lot of people were and I remember this kid that I was friends with. I found out he liked me; I was okay, that's so cute. Then my parents found out and they flipped, flipped, flipped. First of all, I was eight years old. Then the whole race thing came out. Oh, God it was bad. . . .
>
> My father was just like crazy. And it's weird 'cause my father's got a friend who's black. But this is his daughter now. He got really crazy. He said, "Don't bring any niggers in this house." And I was like, what? It wasn't so much a big deal that he was black; it was just that this boy called my house. But then, it wasn't even this boy, it was this black boy, you know! He was like, "No black boys, only white boys for you." As I grew up, they realized I like Hispanic, Asian, white, black, it didn't matter to me. . . .
>
> Where I live it's very mixed. . . . Later on it was like I'm not even talking about getting married, and it's "All right, when you get married and if you have kids," I'm like, "What are you talking about?" "If you have kids, they're not going to know what they are." They're not going to know what they are? "You know, they're not going to know if they're black or white and when they have to check off the thing, they're going to check 'other.' They're going to feel like a freak." I was trying not to laugh, because they were being real serious. I'm like, "C'mon, you know like, sometimes I feel like checking 'other' because I'm like six nation-alities, you know." But I mean, I'm white, so that was big. The whole thing was the kids. It was like, "I don't want your kids to be confused." "I don't want your kids to be picked on." But when I was a kid, I was picked on, because they called me a geek, so they're going to pick on my kids anyway, you know. (Catherine)

What causes the reaction by a white father of an eight-year-old daughter when a Black classmate calls her?

> The first time it really affected me in my soul? My daughter was dating a black boy, and I liked him, but I wouldn't have been happy if she decided to

marry him. Because I just didn't think it would be—I don't know, I totally didn't want it. He was an intelligent boy, he was polite, nice—I didn't think she'd have an easy life being married to a black person. . . .

Yeah, I thought she was having problems, I didn't think she realized how prejudiced the world still was, and what it would mean for her, if she chose to go that way. I felt she was asking for problems by being in a relationship. Externally I was supportive, whatever she wanted was fine. We never talked about it in any kind of real depth. I saw the difference, even in family, and so did she, as time went on, she saw the difference in cultural things, and stuff like that. He was a black-Chinese person, so there was a lot of culture in it. . . .

I mean, I'm Jewish, my husband's Italian, and I see there's a difference—I think black, white, Chinese, is too much of a dramatic difference. For me and my husband, I see the difference in a lot of ways. And his mother is Jewish, and he had a very dominant Italian father, and there just are differences, a lot. (Doreen, white female staff)

Why is race an issue when a mother determines whether she approves of a daughter's boyfriend? What are the underlying assumptions and messages inherent in these incidents and why do they exist? How are "rules" communicated from one generation to another?

My sister married a black man, and there were people in my side of the family who did not come to the wedding, simply because of that fact, and that's what her life would be now. Which I don't really understand, because, if it's not really affecting you? My grandfather didn't show up. My father was there. . . .

My father got much more accepting, simply because my father is just always right away negative, very negative towards any differences, but, yeah, with my father, he did come around. But you see it still in little ways, as how he treats their children, but then again, it could be just how he treats all children, so I don't know . . .

I try to understand my own family, which I thought was very maybe, open, especially since my mother had so many children, and they weren't necessarily so orthodox, or you know, we grew up Catholic, so you're supposed to, if someone hurts you, turn the other cheek and not judge someone, let God judge them, and things were very contrary to what we were going to do in church every Sunday. That conflict was very confusing. (Barbara, white female staff)

Barbara struggles to understand what she perceived as contradictions in religious notions toward humanity and acceptance of all peoples. She appears to feel there is evidence of hypocrisy. She continued:

I grew up in Crown Heights and moved to Coney Island, I didn't see a difference because there was a majority of black, and they didn't see a difference with me, because I grew up there—I don't think it was a matter of black and white in that time, I think it was a matter of your wealth—money—yeah, you were all in the same boat, nobody really thought about who was black and who was white, and that was kind of, you know, an equal thing, and then, I went to Coney Island, and the block that I lived on were a lot of Italians, but there was one family of black people that had moved in, and there was a kid that was there, and, like, I never thought about black and white issues, really, before that, and there was a light-skinned black kid that had moved in there, and he was nice looking, I thought, and I had, like, a crush on him, kind of, and I mentioned it to one of my friends, one of the people I met there, and they were kind of, like, "Oh, you like him?" And then, it kind of made me feel like, "Oh, I'm not supposed to like him?" . . .

   That's when it really hit me, like, okay, I guess I'm not supposed to do that, and then it kind of made me hold back from ever saying anything. I felt like I knew my place. You're not supposed to be thinking about a black guy in that way, like as a boyfriend kind of thing, you know? That's what made me feel I'm supposed to only stay with the whites, because in this neighborhood, this is where I belong, I felt very uncomfortable, because I wasn't sure of what, my thoughts were anymore—I wasn't really sure of what I had been feeling, you know, was that right, or is this right?

These women struggled to think through what appeared to be, as Barbara described, "contrary" circumstances These participants raised issues that included generational and peer pressures and articulated their own ambivalence about how they resolved the tensions they experienced. Each seems to have relinquished some of her beliefs in order to coexist with her family, friends and neighbors. Of the three, Catherine was the only one to express herself directly by confronting her father about his attitudes. At the time of this study, she was in her early twenties, whereas Barbara and Doreen were older. Their responses support the findings of the *Washington Post* survey that indicated greater support for interracial relationships among young people under age twenty-five (Morin 2001, A1).

   At the same time, their awareness of the rules—of the segregation and the contradictory nature of the circumstances—provides opportunities for engagement, discussion, and analysis. By 2009, 93 percent of the Millennial Generation (age 18–29) said it was okay for Blacks and whites to date though 68 percent of those 65 and over said so (Pew Research Center 2010b, 78). Additionally, 85 percent of Millennials indicated that they approved of interracial marriage compared to 38 percent of those 65 and older (Pew Research Center 2010a). At the same time, both neighborhood segregation and longstanding practice continue to result in patterns such as segregated schools (Corbett 2009).

   The following comments were provided as students in the focus groups sought to explain differences in the data between the percentage of people who approved of interracial marriage and the percentage of people who themselves would consider marrying someone of another race. Angela (Russian female) explains, "People say they don't mind but they wouldn't do it themselves; it's not for them. They feel that they can get on with their own ethnic group better." Allen (white male) seems to agree, "It's like more of a commitment to say I would do it." Meanwhile, the following students express different perspectives:

> I would marry someone of a different religion if I don't have to change mine. But then there comes the question of how you raise your kids. You're going to lose something. You're gaining something too, that's true. It could be you raise your kid as an American but what is it to raise a kid as an American? (Tania, white female)

> It comes down to how people think. I know a lot of people who would probably date somebody of another race or another religion but as she said, parents, or your friends or as I've said before, I date somebody from another race and I've been questioned a lot of times from my family and friends, you know. I've got friends who say, "Can't you find somebody from your own race?" So, people still don't accept it. But that's their problem. (Jeff, white male)

Interracial marriage and relationships raise many underlying issues. A multitude of assumptions underlie the thinking that leads a father of an eight-year-old to be distraught over his daughter's friendship and justify his disapproval by framing his concern with questions about the "children." "What will they call themselves?" "How will they know who they are?" "What will they check off on a form?" "They are going to get picked on." This perspective supports the notion that interracial couples ask for a hard life because "the world" is still prejudiced ("but not me"). "There are just too many cultural differences."

Parents can believe that if they are externally supportive their real thoughts would not be communicated, "because we never talked about it." These assumptions are misleading. As Barbara asks, "Why oppose others if they are not hurting you?" When family members choose to "cross the line" the powers of boycott and stigmatization are evident. The capacity of human beings to change their way of thinking, as she describes her father's transition, is also apparent. But she also raises the question, "How can one be religious and taught not to judge people and yet turn around and judge them?"

Barbara explains that when she lived in a Black neighborhood, she was accepted because of her similar economic status; however, when she moved to a white neighborhood, she quickly learned the rules of interaction between Blacks and whites, such as that it was not acceptable to "like a Black guy in that way, as a boyfriend." Barbara describes how that message was communicated to her, even without an explicit statement of race, and then appears to question whether she agrees with these rules. The fact that the parameters for interaction were communicated discretely yet explicitly seems to have had a destabilizing impact on her initial open-mindedness. Her statement that "there was a light-skinned Black kid and he was nice looking" also seems significant. What is the relationship between his complexion, the judgment about his looks, and the message she is communicating to us about why she liked him?

Finally, the idea that people in interracial relationships must have had difficulty finding someone of their own race communicates implicit assumptions that interracial relationships are deviant, of last resort, and they raise questions about what might be wrong with the involved individuals. Once again this assumes many things, such as the notions of who is someone's "own kind" and that racial and ethnic identification necessarily determines "likeness and commonality," and that determines whether people get along. These presumptions are racialized and express underlying rules for social interaction between groups.

WHO'S RESPONSIBLE FOR DIVERSITY AND EQUALITY?

This section discusses respondents' beliefs about who should be concerned with issues of diversity. There was significant evidence of ambivalence about whether diversity is important to our society as a whole, such that everyone should be involved, or whether it is a marginal concern and should be left to those for whom it is an issue.

If we compare these questions, the data appear contradictory. While only 24.5 percent of students say they feel personally responsible, 80 percent believed everyone should be involved (table 4.6). Females (79.5 percent) more often than males (69.1 percent) indicate that they believed everyone should be involved and that they themselves feel responsible to participate in the diversity process (female, 25.3 percent; male, 18.5 percent). Some of the explanations for these differences include the comment of Kevin (white male staff) that he was surprised so many people said they do not feel responsible. "I think that 30 percent is all the white people who are less interested in diversifying because they feel everyone should come to us, not that we need to change." Lori (white staff) agrees with him, saying, "Right, if I don't see a problem, nothing is wrong, so why should I change."

These comments demonstrate awareness that if whites do not feel negatively impacted by race, they would not see a reason to do anything about

Table 4.6   The Diversity Process

Who Should Be Involved in the Diversity Process?

	Yes	No
Everyone	80.5%	18.8%
People who experience discrimination	86.0%	13.8%
People who want to be involved	96.3%	3.1%

Do You Feel Responsible to Participate in the Diversity Process?

Yes	Somewhat	No
24.5%	46.0%	29.6%

racial inequality. These comments presume a white perspective but also provide an opening for dialogue. There is an understanding of why whites might not be concerned; yet the comments seem to reflect why they should be. White students, less than all other students, believed that emphasis should be placed on hiring staff and faculty of color; fewer male respondents did so than female. White students' responses also reveal they believe less than all other students that emphasis should be placed on multicultural programming, as did more males than females. White students believe significantly less than Black and Latino students that great emphasis should be placed on diversifying course material.

In response to these findings, Andrew says:

> I was surprised that blacks think more emphasis should be placed on diversifying course material but then realized why they would think that way. The significant differences between groups meant that whites just never thought about this, so they answered no. They just assume that the books are accurate, and don't read critically, whereas blacks may have thought a lot about it. Now that I think of it, my history book is all about European history, and so is my art course. It's not something you think about but, how would you feel if you were left out of history?

Two specific significant differences between groups include: Whites believed significantly more than U.S.-born Black students that emphasis should be placed on letting things happen on their own. U.S.-born white students believed significantly more than foreign-born Black students that emphasis should be placed on letting things happen on their own. U.S.-born white students believed significantly less than foreign-born Black students that emphasis should be placed on sensitivity training.

In the 2009 survey, females, more so than males, indicated these activities improve learning: Incorporating the experiences of all groups in the curriculum (62.0 percent vs. 43.8 percent); Having a diverse faculty (52.1 percent vs. 36.4 percent); Having a diverse student body (69.0 percent vs. 33.3 percent).

Responses also differed by racial group; the percentages of each group that indicated these activities improve learning are reflected in table 4.7.

The differences in perspectives between white students and all other students about the need to take action complicate the possibilities for engaging whites in dialogue and action related to racialized dynamics of power that structure institutions of higher education. "One of the biggest obstacles to progress in race relations today is white people's denial of the continuing need for significant changes and the existence of biased policies and procedures" (Challenger 2000, 10). However, the awareness of poverty and racial inequality, especially when whites are experiencing increased economic pressures themselves, can provide opportunities to initiate discussions of ways that racism is structured in systemic patterns. One study about the impact of dialogue on white people's general denial of the need for changes found that "interestingly enough, this was achieved not by trying to insist that we are all alike and share the same set of beliefs. Instead we were able to move toward greater understanding and unity by allowing for the expression of different experiences and perspectives." (Challenger 2000, 10).

In this way, academia can engage in open discussions about divergent everyday experiences and support critical analysis about global dynamics of power. These can take place on and off campus through initiatives that establish and reinforce the connection of the campus to the broader community.

These results have been found in other studies as well and clearly indicate:

> Opportunities for interaction between and among student groups . . . produce clear increases in understanding and decreases in prejudicial attitudes. Such

Table 4.7   To What Degree Do These Activities Improve Learning? (2009)

Latino/a	Asian	Black	White	Multi or Biracial
*Incorporating the experiences of all groups in the curriculum:				
64.3%	46.7%	64.3%	54.8%	72.7%
*Having a diverse faculty				
50.0%	40.0%	71.4%	28.6%	58.3%
*Having a diverse student body				
64.3%	40.0%	78.6%	45.2%	58.3%

opportunities also positively affect academic success. Serious engagement of issues of diversity in the curriculum and in the classroom has a positive impact on attitudes toward racial issues, on opportunities to interact in deeper ways with those who are different, on cognitive development and on overall satisfaction and involvement with the institution. (Smith et al. 1997, v–vii)

Another issue in the discussion about diversifying the curricula is that doing so acknowledges the contributions that Africans and other peoples have made to the creation of "Western Civilization" and that Europeans are "both indebted to and descendants of the very folk they enslaved. They don't want to see the world as 'One'—a tiny globe where people and cultures are always on the move . . ." (Podur 2003). The problem is that humanizes the very people they want to exploit. However, by raising awareness of the ways divisions and/or lack of divisions impact all people, changes can be implemented. With an understanding of the mechanisms that reproduce the pattern whereby whites do not recognize the need for personal and institutional commitment to diversity, we can intervene to heighten understanding of dominance and subordination on a broad scale.

OF RACE'S RULES

In discussions about interracial interaction and colorblindness, students express an acute awareness of implicit rules governing their relationships that are often framed as "human nature" and communicated as something intransigent. Participants indicate that they learned the rules by observing and listening to their parents, through community responses to various events, and in discussions with friends. They were taught whom they could associate with and under what circumstances.

Most white respondents say that they did not talk about these lessons as they learned them and articulate ambivalence about what was "right." They are aware of stereotypes but feel that they don't allow them to inform their own thinking. They articulate definite opinions about what they think is possible in relationships between groups and do not seem to think "outside of the box."

They recognize that demographic diversity does not necessarily reflect a deep intertwining of people's lives. For the most part, they seem willing to accept this pattern either as natural or "just the way things are." They articulate an awareness of divergent opinions between groups but do not seem troubled enough to seek an understanding of the differences.

While contact itself does not appear to do harm or intensify the divergence of opinions or perspectives, it does not de facto erode the separation of views and lack of understanding about why people have different perspectives and the experiences that underlie various points of view. Prejudices do not necessarily shift even with awareness that they may be stereotypes. Students conduct business with each other, just as people do within the work world or within public interactions. Just as one learns not to discuss politics or religion, one learns the boundaries in discussions about justice, poverty, or inequality. (If these parameters were not set, we would have to reckon with race and class in the context of our nation's democratic ideals.)

Relationships are established and maintained instrumentally. People interact with each other to get things done. However, limits are evident as an undertone as people get to know one another. Associations are generally of a pragmatic nature, so by necessity people conduct themselves with propriety and good manners.[15] As Joan points out: "It's kind of like, unconscious, the way you act."

Students seem to believe they socialize with people from their own group because the group is what they feel most "comfortable" with and where they feel understood. They say it is easier to communicate, more familiar, and more natural. You don't have to spend time trying to understand each other, you simply do. In business, one has less of a choice about whom you interact with. You can socialize with people at work, but not be friends. For whites, the fear of rejection exists, as does the concern that a comment or a joke would be viewed as racist (and both are greater than their interest in self-reflection). This way, one does not have to worry about "misunderstandings."

It appears that people stay within the friendship circles in which they grew up. One is raised "to keep to one's own." At the same time, participants emphasized the importance of socializing, learning about cultures other than one's own, appealing to customers, knowing how to relate to different people. Several students wanted opportunities for interaction to decrease perceived tensions, such as block programs that put students of different backgrounds together.

The lack of substantive contact appears to reinforce blinders and supports the dominant narratives about human nature that justify why people stick to their "own kind." Children are taught the rules and the consequences of interaction with different people as they grow into adults. One does not bring home people of another race; your parents won't like it or will not allow it. Recall the incidents with Michael Stewart and Yusuf Hawkins. We don't want "that" to happen here. There is an underlying fear of being involved with something so horrendous, so one never crosses the line, or not much, at least. The "rules" emphasize that one can interact with anyone on campus, but you should go home to socialize with your own group. That's "the rules."

Scholars such as Lee Anne Bell, director of the Education Program at Barnard College, have also studied these "unwritten rules." She interviewed white teachers, asking about implicit assumptions indicating knowledge of racism and racial hierarchy. Bell found that unspoken agreements designate "narrow latitude for acceptable behavior" of people of color, as well as who defines terms of interaction, and who has to fit in. She asserts that this knowledge contrasts "markedly with assertions of color blindness and social progress" (Bell 2002, 240–41).

Moments of heightened awareness are generally maintained as simply moments rather than chances to develop a full understanding of the social dynamics that keep people separated. It is acceptable to acknowledge injustice and inequality, but without the everyday negative experiences of race, and with the bombardment of media shaping the discourse, whites tend to consider structural arguments but act individually. For them, their personal experiences teach them that if they play their cards right, if they don't question the status quo, at least they can make it. They may feel a little guilty but they don't usually as they have been told time and time again, that "things are not going to change." In the end they conclude, "What can I do and anyway, for now this works for me."

5

Poverty, Wealth, Discrimination, and Privilege

> The agony of the poor impoverishes the rich; the betterment of the poor enriches the rich. We are inevitably our brother's keeper because we are our brother's brother. Whatever affects one directly affects all indirectly.
>
> —Martin Luther King Jr. 1967 (as quoted in Mazel 1998, 114)

This chapter examines attitudes about poverty, equality, and opportunity in the United States and underlying beliefs about race. The first section, "Theorizing Poverty," explores support for the belief that all people have an equal chance for success, explanations for why poverty exists, and why some people are poor and others are not. "Caring for the Common Good or Only for Oneself?" documents participants' perspectives on the role of media, about education as a right, and attitudes toward the criminal justice system. These three arenas provide points of reference for discussions of individual and social rights, privileges, and responsibilities. The concluding section, "Opportunity, Equality, and Fairness," examines beliefs about whether society has a responsibility to take measures to equalize opportunity. As a whole, the chapter reflects upon how inequality is understood and whether the theoretical framework of the culture of poverty is still dominant.

THEORIZING POVERTY

> There is poverty because there is complacency.
>
> —Allen, white male

167

Why does poverty exist and how can it be eradicated? How much wealth is acceptable and what criteria should be used to compensate labor or determine how wealth is accumulated? Do we have collective responsibility for the well-being of all members of society, or solely individual responsibility for our own quality of life? Is inequality racially organized in our society? In 2000, responses to these questions were not monolithic; discussions were animated as students struggled to articulate their thoughts. While most believe that acceptable and significant progress has been made to address racial inequality but that the process is not complete, others believe that the United States has achieved full equality.

"In the past definitely whites were privileged, but things have evened out greatly over time. I don't think it's 100 percent yet, but it's very close, if anything, 51 or 49 percent even." "It's pretty much even, if not close nowadays. Maybe twenty years ago I would say differently, but there are a lot of new programs that have come out, just to help out, like affirmative action" (Allen and Helen, both white). These comments parallel findings of the study discussed in chapter 1 that found that 40 to 60 percent of all whites say that the average Black American fares equally or better in terms of jobs, incomes, schooling, and healthcare than the average white person, despite the reality that Blacks continue to lag behind significantly in many or most categories. Such perceptions by whites are indeed misperceptions (Morin 2001, A1; Freeman 2001, C3).

A decade later these misperceptions persist and appear to be even more common. In 2010, 71 percent of whites polled believe Blacks have achieved or will soon achieve racial equality, as compared to 49 percent of Blacks.[1] This contradicts the reality that "the wealth gap between white and African-American families increased more than four times between 1984–2007. . . . The fourfold increase in the wealth gap, it said, reflects public policies, such as tax cuts on investment income and inheritances, which benefit the wealthiest and persistent discrimination in housing, credit and labor markets."[2]

These mistaken beliefs are consequential as they underlie political positions that oppose measures to equalize opportunity. If one does not believe that inequality exists, why support actions aimed at making things more fair?

This same gap in perception versus reality and degrees of misperception between Blacks and whites is evident in a CNN/Opinion Research Corporation Poll conducted December 16–20, 2009. When asked whether Blacks have as good as a chance as whites to get any job for which they are qualified, 76 percent of whites responded yes, whereas 45 percent of Blacks did so.[3] However, in a recent study whites just released from prison fared better than Black job applicants without a criminal record.[4] College-educated Black men are nearly twice as likely to be unemployed as their white counterparts.[5]

A 2004 study showed that resumes with recognizably African American names were twice as likely to be ignored as other resumes.[6] Circumstances are so dire that a report has been filed with the United Nations Human Rights Council to push for action on discrimination and structural inequality.[7] A well-researched report by the Applied Research Center documents the disparate impact of the recession on communities of color. This includes rates of unemployment, wealth, income, and housing foreclosure (2010).

Paul Street's analysis of the "White Fairness Understanding Gap" cites six factors that contribute to these misunderstandings. These include an American educational curriculum notoriously conservative on questions of social, racial, and economic justice; the lack of exposure of whites to the everyday realities of African Americans; media distortions that exaggerate affluence among Blacks; neighborhood and school segregation; pragmatic reasons for denying structural causes for inequality; and the general weakness of the political left such that progressive politics is viewed as a zero-sum game (2001, 9).

Most people are convinced that poverty will always exist, despite feeling that progress has been made. Some find it difficult to explain and express what we might do about it; others do not. In reading the following passages, consider what assumptions are being made and where emphasis is given to individual versus societal responsibility. What explanations are provided? What assumptions are being made about how social change occurs? Consider, for example, the implications of saying that "It's all about choice, both self-control and the ability to make decisions" (Daniel, white male) or "People become content in poverty. You know, a person puts himself in that position if you don't have control" (Gerda, Russian female). Daniel elaborates his thinking, firmly asserting that there's little society can or should do:

> There's always going to be poor people. It's not possible for everybody to have everything. It's a proven fact. So many people are lazy. They don't want to work and say, "Oooh, welfare will pay for us" or "Let's have another kid so we can get more money." It's very frustrating to me. They're just lazy.

What is the "proven fact" and why is it not possible for "everybody to have everything?" Where was this information obtained? Perhaps some of the answers lie in the definition of "everything."

> Poverty is not new. It's always been around. There's been poor, middle-, and upper-middle-class. It's just a cycle of society. We have poor people and rich people. If people move a class up, the rich move another up and they're still back in the same situation. The middle class moves another middle up. (Michelle, white female)

Interestingly, a report by the Economic Mobility Project shows that 68 percent of children of white middle-income parents tend to exceed their parents' income whereas only 31 percent of Black children of middle-income parents do so, with a majority of Black children falling below their parents in economic status and income. Furthermore, median family income of Blacks aged 30–39 was 58 percent that of white families of the same age group. In addition, contrary to the popular discourse about the United States, in fact, "Compared with countries like Canada, Finland, Norway and Denmark that have high mobility, the United States has low mobility, as does the United Kingdom."[8]

While many students cited laziness as the cause of poverty, it is evident that some felt uncomfortable blaming people for being poor. They question society's responsibility to ensure a basic standard of living. Several suggest that more people are a step away from being poor than we, as a society, might like to acknowledge. They are cautious about placing blame on people for life circumstances. Janice, for example, explains that she did not think it was right to judge and generalize that "if you're on welfare, you're lazy." John argues that there is no fairness in having to be in the right place at the right time: "How can you control luck?" Other students defend their position.

> I wasn't targeting the people who are poor. There's a difference between poverty and being poor. Somebody who is poor is living in their circumstances, but the example used regarding the poverty person as the person who just sits there for twenty years; they get comforted with a welfare check, because they don't care about anything. (Angela, white female, Russian)

> Sometimes people are irresponsible about their lives and that's how things happen. Some people being poor is not their fault, but other people, like if you spend all your money on drugs, you have no money left, you're bankrupt and then you're homeless, then it was your fault. Society isn't responsible. You can't change it; it's just luck. You have to work as hard as you can. (Catherine, white female)

In 2010 this discourse continues to dominate and is often supported not only by white participants but those of color as well. At issue is the ideology, not just who is speaking. However, interwoven in the explanations for persistent racialized inequality are questions about structure, and why these patterns exist. Keisha, a Black female, had the following to say about why Blacks don't have large amounts of wealth.

> African Americans are not as smart with budgeting our money. Like me personally I'll get money and I'll go to the mall but like, because I wasn't taught about money early on. African Americans they go to check cashing places. We

don't even have bank accounts. White people invest their money and plan college funds. My family we just have enough to get by most of the time. We don't have enough to like really like sit down and be like mom why don't we invest in this or mom why didn't you start a college fund for me? Because we didn't have the money. My parents are not CEOs, my parents don't have like jobs where they make like fifty thousand dollars a year.

Some placed the discussion of poverty within a global and historical context and expressed an awareness of their structural privileges without explicitly framing it in these terms. In 2009, students often raised issues of institutionalized patterns even as they recognized the role of individual responsibility. Here are some examples:

In this country it predominantly, you know, tends to be white holding that, you know, cultural power and economic power so it just continues to benefit. I think, you know, to varying levels of, varying levels it exists all over the world. I don't think there are any like post-racial societies on the planet. (Liam, white male)

When it comes to inequalities, it is structurally based. When you see a school that's in some opulent suburban neighborhood that has all of the amenities that you could ever imagine and then you see an inner school, an inner city school that's falling apart literally, covered in mold, the paint is peeling there is a sense I think from those children in that school I'm not worth it. You can't bother to paint my school and so this is already what you think of me and I think that that is reciprocal and that that helps to perpetuate the problem.

I've also been to a few other countries and you can see that the pattern, the pattern is definitely there and having spent a while in Argentina you could see this way the wealthier side of town, this was the poor side of town and the people on the poor side of town were definitely the darker people. (Karen, white female)

This awareness sometimes led to discussions of how to address inequality, by whom, and whether we, as a society, are responsible for the well-being of all people. Some felt that nothing will happen because no one wants to do it, as Joanne (Latina) expresses in her comments below.

Poverty is here and always will be here because so few people want to deal with it. Many people are willing to judge, "Oh, you're poor, you're a lazy bum, you take welfare." A lot of people will much easier judge poor people instead of trying to see what the problems are, where it stems from, and everything. There's very few people who have made differences. I don't think there are a lot of people out there who are willing to actually take a lot of time out.

Joanne continues by saying something should be done and that we have responsibility for each other:

There's so little done about poverty. Some people just don't care, and say "Okay, those people are poor and on welfare." But I totally disagree. I think it's good to have job fairs to get them jobs. You have to educate the poor, otherwise they really don't know how to change. Don't just give me food stamps, but tell me how I can change who I am. How can I change the cycle that's been happening from generation to generation? My father did the same thing so I'm going to do the same thing. You have to educate. It's not a matter of them being lazy, it's the matter that they're poor and they can't move up in the world unless someone helps them. (Joanne)

The issue of financial management and the use of credit cards frequently arose in discussions about why some people are poor and others are not. Students appeared ambivalent about whether they thought individual weaknesses or the system should be blamed. They often alternated between holding individuals responsible for their own fate and acknowledging structural factors that make upward mobility difficult. This ambivalence is reflected as follows:

People are put out in the world and never taught how to manage money. There's no guidebook to get out of your situation. A lot of people, especially the young generation, when they get out there, first thing they get credit that automatically puts their life in debt. Half of them don't even have a job. How do you expect to pay the bills? How do you expect to get out of your situation and these companies are giving you the Visa card? (Terry, white female)

Once you're in a poverty level, the working poor, it's very difficult to improve your lifestyle. You're working, and your spouse is working, and you're both working at minimum wage. You have rent to pay and if you have children you have to pay childcare. Especially single working women, single parents because their jobs are considered women's work, they don't get paid comparable to a man. Like 62 percent of people living at poverty level are single mothers. There's a statistic that says if they were paid comparable to what men were paid, half of them would no longer be in poverty level. When you're at that level, you don't have proper healthcare, and your expenses are so high, it's very difficult to get a better lifestyle. (Joan, white female)

These comments reflect awareness of systemic barriers to upward mobility but confusion about how people accumulate wealth (or not). The mystification of this process maintains the class structure intact. If there were a greater understanding of the factors that lead some individuals and groups to accrue and/or maintain their levels of wealth and others not to, the systemic inequalities of opportunity would be evident. For example, the fact that academic legacies lend a significant advantage in a person's being admitted to a private elite university (and not just because of his or her ability to pay), or that one of three senators and congressmen is a millionaire, helps to demonstrate how upward mobility is achieved and wealth maintained at the upper strata of the economic and political structure (Sklar 2003a).

Another aspect of this discussion is the way that support for the common good is associated with everyone having a harder time. There is a lack of awareness about the concentration of wealth at the top as well as any sense that a more just and equal world is possible. While concerns are expressed about poverty and inequality society-wide, students also speak about how they themselves were struggling to survive.

> I try and take care of myself, but there are always these issues. I wish somebody would do something about it. People sit here and say, "Why don't YOU do something about it" and nothing gets done. Everyone does have their own life and you only have so much time and energy that you could put into helping everyone else. If you try to help everyone out, and no one helps you, and it's like you're supposed to have this feeling like, "Oh, I helped all these people out, I feel good." Meanwhile, you're lying there homeless. That's not right. So I'm saying, I definitely look out for myself first. And then, I'll look out for everyone else. (John, white male)

The above comment illustrates a sense of personal vulnerability that supersedes a concern for the well-being of all. Several students express the notion that by caring for others one's own quality of life declines. The belief in a zero-sum balance of resources, where the gains of one group are viewed as having to come from the loss of another group, is apparent. This concept was usually evoked in contrasting two groups of relatively similar circumstances rather than in referring to corporate profits or considering alternative ways to approach both the generation and distribution of resources. Simultaneously, these comments reflect awareness that we are all affected by social inequality.

With few exceptions, poverty is described in abstract terms and naturalized as something that "just is" rather than something that exists as a result of structural priorities of those who have (and have had) power in society, and something that we participate in maintaining by not objecting to those priorities through the polls, in schools, on the job, or in daily interactions. This naturalization and mystification of poverty and wealth and the corresponding perspective that nothing can or will change contribute to the inertia that surrounds solving vast national and global inequalities. The belief that caring about someone else will deteriorate one's own conditions similarly serves to deter civic engagement. At the same time, the respondents' awareness and genuine concerns about form a "crack," a means of engagement about what might be done to address this very serious situation.

In 2009, Addy (white female) says:

> I'm just having a hard time coming up with any explanation, any rational reason why this is so. I can identify it as unequal but why does that exist? Why is education so, such a commodity for these minorities? I don't understand that. Why isn't this country throwing the same amount of money to all children? I don't know. Is that racial? It can't be blatantly racial or they would lose their seats in the Senate and various positions in government. I don't understand but people are disadvantaged from the moment, I mean before they're born. I purely and honestly don't understand how anybody could consider themselves better based on the color of their skin.

Barbara (white staff member) explains the way she sees the intersection of class and race. Her knowledge and willingness to speak openly about the commonalities and differences in the experiences of various communities were not uncommon. Such openness provides an opening for discussion about how race is used to divide people and how relatively small degrees of privilege drive a wedge between groups that could potentially ally to address common grievances.

> It also has to do with your financial status. My mother lives in Coney Island which is Latin, black, and pretty much more. I feel very safe with her there, because they, as a community, look out for her. She's a little old white lady, but they look out for each other, and that has to do with financial status. The community, they're in an all-in-the-same-boat kind of thing. They're sharing a common experience. It has to do more with now you're an upper-class white or whatever, a middle-class white as opposed to being in the poverty line— everybody's poor together. When you're financially better off, it becomes an issue of, how do I get ahead. . . .
>
> This research is trying to see whether people can get to that point of understanding. All of us folks together here, in whichever segment, have a lot more in common, but because the way that we've been trained, is number one, not to see the whole context, to see all the individual interactions as injustice is being caused upon us, and not see some of even, the economics. Blacks may be more willing to accept a job at $8.47—I know among the white staff, people realize that working here, you're taking a lower pay than if you go to Manhattan. Constantly, white students will say, "Oh, you're only paying whatever, $5.15? Forget it! I'm not going to work there; I can easily get $8, $9, $10, $12 an hour." Whereas for the black or Latino they say, "Well, at least it's a job."

Such comments identify the way that people are pitted against each other in the labor market. Average wages for whites are higher than for Blacks. This implies that white labor is more valuable. The numbers tell the story: while 29 percent of white households survive below the poverty line, 39 percent of Black households do so (Shapiro 1998, 298). This has real consequences for not only the individual but also the generations that follow. This discrepancy affects access to education and wealth accumulation.

The causes of inequality seem mysterious and disconnected from historical structural patterns; however, it was apparent that students understood the class dynamics that contribute to unequal circumstances. "Historically, race and racial divisions have been fomented in order to keep people from realizing the political or class nature of persistent poverty in the United States" (Kushnick and Jennings 1999, 6).[9] The impact of "the racialization of poverty has historically been to politically delegitimize and pacify the grievances of the poor" (Kushnick and Jennings 1999, 6). "One way of illustrating the complex political and economic factors in relation to poverty and race is to examine poverty in the international arena. If the behavior of poor people is the major cause of their impoverishment, then we can reasonably expect poverty in the United States to be unique" (Kushnick and Jennings 1999, 7). (Either that, or we have a global crisis in motivation). The next section discusses this issue in detail.

Racial Inequality

The question of how to explain poverty is addressed differently when students discuss racial patterns.

Survey responses in 2000 indicated that foreign-born whites believe significantly less often than any other group that discrimination contributes to racial inequality; foreign-born Blacks believe more so than any other group. U.S.-born whites believe less often than all Blacks do that discrimination contributes. All whites believed less often than Asians and Blacks that historic inequality contributes to racial inequality. As with the *Washington Post* survey, these results suggest an overwhelming sense among most whites that society could not possibly still be saddled with segregation and discrimination. Things cannot possibly be as bad as Black Americans say they are (Keith Reeves of Swarthmore College, as quoted in Morin 2001, A1).[10]

Almost a decade later, while most whites continue to believe that the standard of living gap between whites and Blacks has narrowed, Blacks increasingly believe this is the case, despite significant evidence to the contrary.

> Blacks and whites continue to have very different views about the pervasiveness of discrimination against African Americans. Some 43 percent of blacks now say there is a lot of anti-black discrimination, about the same as in 2001. Among

whites, just 13 percent see a lot of anti-black bias now, down from 20 percent in 2001. . . . a majority of blacks (52 percent) now say that blacks who cannot get ahead in this country are mainly responsible for their own situation, whereas only about a third (34 percent) say that racial discrimination is the main reason.

Fifteen years ago, most blacks held the opposite view. Multiple surveys taken since 1994 show that this shift in blacks' perceptions has occurred in fits and starts over time, and that the change pre-dates the election of Obama.[11]

In the same survey, when asked whether enough has been done to address inequality, 36 percent of whites and 82 percent of Blacks said more needs to be done.[12] This suggests that the dominant framework of the culture of poverty has been increasingly rooted not only within the thinking of whites, but also communities of color. However, when asked specifically about the structure of society, the perceptions of Blacks are more accurate.

Students reflected on the prevailing lack of outrage about current levels of inequality. Donna (Black female) suggests that "People are not aware of what is going on; they haven't experienced it." However, Angelo, a white male, takes a different point of view:

> My parents worked two jobs, so do I, and so do my friends. Everyone is pissed and feeling screwed and everyone is blaming everyone else. It's the individual. You can have somebody that lives next door to somebody else and they're both black and they're both on the same level. They're both poor and both in the same school but this one has that, like, drive. He's going to become whatever he wants. The other one's going to be like, "Well, I'm black so there's not much I can do."

It is true that nearly all people increasingly face difficult times, though communities of color experience this in particularly harsh ways; for example they face higher rates of poverty and unemployment, have health care less frequently, have a smaller safety net, if any, and face disproportionate rates of predatory lending and foreclosure (Wessler 2009). Attitudes toward contributing factors to these realities are examined in table 5.1, which compares the 2000 and 2009 survey results.

In 2009, survey respondents were asked, "In your view, how much do these factors contribute to the higher incomes and wealth of whites as a group in the U.S." In response, 25.9 percent indicated that whites are more motivated; 14.4 percent believe whites are more intelligent; 53.8 percent believe whites have institutional advantages and 55.8 percent indicated that the higher income and wealth is due to preferencing by individuals. Many students readily expressed that, although there isn't equality, there should be. They agree that everyone should be given a fair chance but agree less that measures should

Table 5.1   How Much Do You Think the Following Factors Contribute to the Average Lower Incomes and Poorer Housing of Blacks? (2000/2009 responses)

	Not at all	A little/Somewhat	Quite a bit/A lot
Low IQ/(Less intelligent)	48.8%/63.5%	33.7%/27.9%	17.5%/8.7%
Lack of motivation/ (Less motivated)	21.2%/30.8%	50.9%/50%	32.8%/19.2%
Historic inequality/ (Institutional disadvantages)	20.3%/14.4%	41%/51%	38.7%/34.6%
Discrimination/ (By individuals)	10.5%/5.8%	46.3%/53.8%	43.3%/40.4%

being taken to equalize opportunity. They worry that if something were done, they themselves would be treated unfairly. Having "a hard enough time as it is," they couldn't bear additional pressure, whether economic or social.

While not explicitly stated, this perspective alludes to the role of race in the persistent patterns of inequality and explains why whites often assert a belief in the principles of equality and justice but support to a lesser degree measures to ensure those chances, because of their own feelings of vulnerability. Liz (Asian female staff) explains, "The data is conflicting. It says if you work hard you can make it but discrimination is the main reason why you can't make it." Professor Cameron, a white faculty member, objected to the characterization of this study as a search for the mechanisms that contribute to the perpetuation of racial inequality. He offers this perspective:

> Why do you keep saying perpetuation when you should say persistence of inequality? There is a difference. The difference is the victimization mentality of African Americans. They see racism where nobody else will because they have internalized the notion that they are inferior. The focus should not be only on why whites have these attitudes. There is a gap between whites' and blacks' attitudes. If you want to explain the gap, the attitudes of both sides must be investigated.

The tension about where to place responsibility is prevalent, as is the belief that current patterns of social relations are eternal—yet the question of causality rarely arose. Most emphasis is placed on the individual when it comes to taking responsibility, but on the structure when it comes to taking action. Either it is the fault of "complacent people/groups" or it's "just the way things are," "that's the system." Very rarely is a connection made between the role of ordinary people in supporting the system, or of the system in structuring life possibilities for different groups of people in different ways.

The possibility that we could shape a world where everyone's needs matter was not raised in any of the discussions. This naturalization of poverty and narrow sense of possibilities form two mechanisms that reinforce patterns of inequality and undermine our ability to challenge an unequal system. At the same time, these form "cracks" as the desire to live in a world where everyone matters serves as an impetus to understand why we do not.

Unequal Treatment but an Equal Chance at Success?

Another divergence between the recognition that not everyone is treated equally and the belief that everyone has a fair chance to succeed is reflected in the following data. In 2000, only 8.9 percent of all survey respondents felt that people of color are treated equally to whites when applying for jobs and housing and when approached by the police. However, 42.8 percent believed that all people, regardless of color, can be assimilated into U.S. mainstream society. In 2009, 27.9 percent of whites, 17.9 percent of Blacks, 14.3 percent of Latinos, and 40 percent of Asians agreed or strongly agreed that people of color are treated the same as whites when applying for jobs. What is the significance and implication of this discrepancy?

Louis, a white faculty member, asserted that "lots of people say 'I was discriminated against but I still assimilated into society.' Fundamentally people believe everyone can be assimilated but just not equally." This distinction is important, because it highlights the issue of whether power is shared and equal or whether white dominance is maintained with minor accommodations and concessions.[13]

In discussing whether opportunity exists equally for all people, there was ambivalence and unclarity about the role of structure. Most explanations were framed in relationship to an individual's access to resources, as if one could be held personally responsible for whom one knows. Contacts and resources were viewed as critical. Janice (Latina) explained, "Nowadays, the world is mostly built on who has the money, who has the power, and who you know." Gerda (white female) responded, "But aren't we the world? Aren't we society? I'm not saying anything against you, but I'm saying, we are society. We may sit here and complain but you say society and you're complaining about yourself. Everyone does it."

Assimilation was consistently seen as an assumed virtue and that everyone can "make it" in U.S. society if they try hard enough. The presumption was that opportunities are available, so inequality reflects solely differing levels of effort in achieving upward mobility.

CARING FOR THE COMMON GOOD OR ONLY FOR ONESELF?

The political atmosphere in the 1960s embodied a concern for the common good as exemplified by the heightened activism of many subordinated and underrepresented groups. In contrast, mainstream discourse at the beginning of the twenty-first century emphasizes individualism and competition, thus functioning as another mechanism that serves to reinforce the status quo. Discussions today about healthcare portray those people considered not healthy enough to sustain their own lives as "irresponsible individuals" who society does not have the means to protect. Those in prison are considered "criminals" who are kept there so that "law-abiding" citizens can be safe. People on welfare are "lazy" and unwilling to work for their money. Students who take more than four years to get their undergraduate degree are "unmotivated" or not "college material." People who lose homes because of foreclosure are said to have purchased over their means. The unemployed are obviously without jobs because they are not trying hard enough to find one. People in New Orleans were criticized for not leaving the city though studies show that many had no access to cars or funds for public transportation. Civilians who die from the bombing of Iraq and Afghanistan are considered collateral damage.

Another example is the notion expressed in recent tax reform legislation that taxes should be returned to "the people" so they may decide how to use their money themselves. However, the initial concept of taxation was to create a common fund to benefit society as a whole. We rarely hear that we are experiencing the greatest increase in the polarization of wealth that has ever occurred in U.S. history, yet the wealthiest proportionately pay the least taxes and continue to receive bonuses all the while many workers are getting laid off.[14] "In 1989, the United States had 66 billionaires and 31.5 million people living below the poverty line" (Collins, Hartman, and Sklar 1999). In 2010, the United States has 403 billionaires with a collective net worth of $1.3 trillion while there are estimated 39.1 million people living below the poverty line.[15]

These ideological framings are justified as if they are in all of our interests because they emphasize personal responsibility. However, these narratives distract attention from structural causes for inequality, and the increasing polarization of wealth. This recently became evident as billions of dollars became available to wage war on Iraq and Afghanistan, bail out the airlines, auto, and banking industries, and to help rebuild New York City after September 11, but "no funds" exist for affordable housing, health care, or education. These contrasts have worsened over the decade 2000–2010, with bailout of the banking industry, decreased taxation of the very wealthy, corporate deregulation despite pressure on the large majority of people from the significant increases in unemployment, foreclosures, and accumulation of educational debt. "One recent survey showed that 44 percent of families had experienced a job loss, a reduction in hours, or a pay cut in the past year (2009–10)."[16] In 2007, the top fifty hedge and private equity fund managers earned more than 19,000 times as much as typical U.S. workers (Anderson et al. 2008, 4), creating an unequal wealth structure that rivals the 1920s. Looking at comparisons in the military sector, the average army private makes $25,000 compared with the average defense CEO who makes $7.7 million.[17]

Former House Majority Leader Dick Armey said that helping the unemployed "is not commensurate with the American spirit" (Citizens for Tax Justice 2001) while Sen. Jon Kyl (R-Ariz.) said, "Continuing to pay people unemployment compensation is a disincentive for them to seek new work."[18] That rationale is justified, as "what is good for the company is good for all." Unfortunately, profit margins are rarely revealed. The ground rules are such that neither corporate greed nor the impact of nearly 5.6 million lost jobs between 2000–2010 can easily be questioned. This was not always the case. For example,

> When Abraham Lincoln faced the dissolution of the nation in the early 1860s, he imposed new taxes on the wealthy to help save the Union. When Franklin Roosevelt took America to war against the Nazis, he sharply increased taxes on businesses and the rich to help fund that crusade. Now George W. Bush is leading a new battle against international terrorism, and insists that as part of that effort, we need to cut taxes on corporations and the best-off Americans! (McIntyre, 2001)

These Bush tax cuts of 2001 and 2003 cost $2.5 trillion by the end of 2010, mostly because of breaks provided to the top 5 percent of households.[19] This accounts for more than two and a half times the cost of the health care plan.[20] Thus, the tone is set about whether we should look out for ourselves or care for the common good. Where will money come from for health care? Education? Why are these questions raised only in relation to social benefits, but not in relation to prisons or war? Given that we live in a society where whites enjoy a disproportionate share of wealth, the implications of this perspective are highly racialized. However, "White power is so pervasive that it's never perceived or even considered white power. It's just the way things are" (Hartmann 1998). Disproportionate corporate wealth impacts poor and middle-class whites, too, but explanations for their economic insecurity are often framed as due to the benefits that "others" now have, that whites are no longer privy to.

The question of whether policies and practices related to crime, taxation, education, and social welfare are racially coded is addressed in many ways. Students grappled with their own ideas about what is just and where responsibility lies. Alex (white male) reflects, "It's like that movie, *Bulworth*. He said white people pay more taxes so they can get more benefits. According to the statistics, that's what they are doing because SUNY students have more of a white background, and they'd have to give them more money." Diane (white female) responds, "But it should be the other way around. More money should go to the schools that have the more economically disadvantaged people paying less taxes, because they need it more. If the students at SUNY schools are making, like, X amount of money paying X amount of taxes, they have a lot of money, so they don't need all that funding."

Jenna (white female) explains the logic, "In reality, the guy with all the money wants his money's worth. Simple as that. That's what really ends up happening." Are taxes solely an investment in one's own individual future?[21] The irony is that those in lower and middle tax brackets actually pay disproportionately higher taxes. "America's highest income-earners—the top 400—have seen the share of their income they pay in federal income tax alone plummet from 51.2 percent in 1955 to 16.6 percent in 2007" (Collins et al. 2010, 1).

Property rights have always been bound up in the notion of freedom in the United States. Three issues are at stake here. First, when wording about "pursuit of happiness" in the Declaration of Independence was replaced with "property" in the Constitution, the notion of democracy lost its connotations of community and humanity and became implicitly wealth- and class-oriented. Second, intent on minimizing governmental interference, many of the leaders of the American Revolution considered equality of opportunity to mean rough equality of conditions (at least for white males), given that hereditary privileges and mercantilist monopolies were to be dismantled. The belief then was that the natural workings of society would lead to justice, liberty, and equality. The third issue was how taxation would be viewed.

During this period of attempted democratization, many strategies, such as limiting the amount of property individuals could accumulate, were raised in the name of liberty. To lack economic resources was to lack freedom. Jefferson proposed to award fifty acres to those who did not possess it as a means to enhance the liberty of national subjects (Foner 1990). Significant debate took place during that era. In the end, the "idea that political decisions and economic relationships ought to reflect concern for the common good, rather than private gain long survived the revolutionary era" (Foner 1990, 24) though these discussions took place in the context of a slave-holding nation. This tension has remained throughout U.S. history. In the Fifth and Fourteenth Amendments to the Constitution, the phrasing reverted to "life, liberty, or property" (Foner 1990, 20–22). Jenna's defense of the right to be rich, above, is entirely part of the centering of competition within capitalism. She justifies inequality through a defense of individualism and one's right to privilege.

Another conversation that implicitly grappled with issues of common good versus individualism was one in which students discussed how they would handle issues of principle on the job. Would they speak out on behalf of their beliefs or remain silent to protect their jobs? This debate took place between two white students:

> John: When I'm on a job, the bottom line is I'm going to have a boss no matter where I am. I'm going to have to do what she or he or it wants me to do. If they want to see white people on TV, they'll tell me, put white people on TV. That's what they're going to get because that's what I'm getting paid for. That's the bottom line. I'm not going to argue. I won't let my morals stand in the way. Morals aren't going to feed me or provide for a family, that's the bottom line.
>
> Catherine: I guess I'm more into this. I'm not an activist but I have the attitude of one.
>
> John: It'll change, trust me, I used to do that.

If the threat to job security is that acute, and the insecurity about one's future is so linked to holding on and acquiescing, what hope is there to challenge systemic and institutional patterns? How do we raise awareness of the range of options? These conversations reflect the belief that we do best by striking out alone. Students are ambivalent—aware of implications to their actions yet not feeling they have a choice. Marie (Black female) responds to this notion by asking, "Is that lack of willpower or lack of motivation?" I would add, "or a true lack of options?" This provides an opening for discussion about how change can come about and how to understand and to address personal vulnerability. If, in fact, society is headed for more difficult times, would they see that their fate as more closely linked to those who are not as well situated?

> A true revolution of values will soon look uneasily on the glaring contrast of poverty and wealth. There is nothing but a lack of social vision to prevent us from paying an adequate wage to every American citizen whether a hospital worker, laundry worker, maid or day laborer. There is nothing except shortsightedness to prevent us from guaranteeing an annual minimum and livable income for every American family. (Sklar 1997, 71)

In the same vein, racial dynamics were structured into society by people and can therefore be structured out by people with the willingness to do so.

The Role of Media

This subsection examines perceptions about the role that media play in reinforcing racialized images and ideological narratives (see table 5.2).

Foreign-born whites believe more than any other group that there is equal and fair treatment of all people in the media. Most students feel that the media play a strong role in shaping people's ideas of the characteristics of different groups. They believe that media are highly implicated in shaping and reproducing attitudes about race in society, as expressed clearly by students of color: Sonya (Black female) who says, "Media is one of the prime instigators of racism," and Sarah (Asian female) who says, "That image of American culture includes the dominant white race, not someone with almond-shaped eyes and Black hair." Many understand the relationship that images have to perceptions of group identity but appear less clear on the connection of these notions to the perpetuation of racial inequality and the economic structures.

When students speak of their earliest recollections of race, they frequently describe an elder's reaction to a television program. Perhaps the impression made by the show is not sufficient to instill racialized values, alone. It is the negative reaction by a parent or grandparent that imparts the idea that Blacks are subordinate and inferior. Does this reflect generational distinctions in the experience of race? The following quotes illustrate this dynamic. Jenny (Italian female) explains, "It's not that my family is racist, but as a kid, your grandfather or your great-grandfather, when they're still around, might have made comments. Who knows, it could be anything. Maybe it was Spike Lee's *Do the Right Thing* in 1985."

Movies and television shows communicate relationships between people and how groups are positioned in society. "Truly, it comes from the media;

Table 5.2   There Is Equal and Fair Treatment of All People in the Media

	Disagree	Moderately Agree	Agree
Overall	62.2%	26.5%	9.3%
Latinos	70.8%	27.1%	2.1%
Asians	48.7%	43.6%	7.7%
U.S.-born Blacks	76.7%	9.3%	11.6%
Foreign-born Blacks	76.2%	17.7%	4.8%
U.S.-born whites	63.2%	27.9%	7.4%
Foreign-born whites	30.5%	43.9%	23.2%
Males	63.6%	26.5%	8.0%
Females	59.0%	29.7%	10.6%

they depict minorities as inferior, with less education," Fernando, Latino, told us. "Somebody got gunned down, it must be African American or Latino; or there's a drug bust, right away they're gonna think Latino. If it's cocaine, must be Latino; if it's marijuana, must be Jamaican. It's how the media portrays it 95 percent of the time."

Shalom (white male) speaks of his recollections of Bill Cosby's TV show. "He made me think about whether I considered myself part of the mainstream and I didn't. I was separate even though I have instant whiteness. When I wear a baseball cap, I am white; when I wear a yarmulke, I'm Jewish. I can camouflage my privilege, though to be a professor of cinema studies it doesn't help being a white male. You hear it's easier, but it's not. Though, it is still a white man's land." In 2010, Shalom discusses the progress made by Disney in the creation of the Princess and the Frog and both applauds the "first Black princess" but also wonders about the implications of the racially ambiguous Naveen and the predicaments of our time. "Had Naveen been white, the suggestion would have been that Black men can't be princes. It would have also suggested that white is better. If Naveen had been Black, the suggestion would have been that Black goes with Black and white goes with white; that Tiana needed to find a prince the same color."[22]

Messages are communicated both through what is represented and in what is omitted.[23] Marie (black female) states, "Gate-keeping is powerful. You only get whatever the gatekeeper wants you to." Some students, however, do not agree that there is a racial component. "A lot of time the media goes for reaction," responds Joan (white female). "Whoever they can get the biggest reaction from, that's what they'll follow up with." Jeff (white male) goes further to generalize media as a problem, downplaying the role of race:

> If they can get a story, they'll go ahead and do that. When that man was shot forty-one times, it was a very big issue. Then a couple of weeks later the other guy was shot, but not by a white cop, he was shot by the Spanish cop, for pulling out his beeper or cell phone. It was a big issue, but not half as big as the other, because they couldn't get as much of a reaction. First it was a white thing and then it became a whole police thing in general.

Students of color, however, generally see media coverage in a different light. "The media puts into light the Blacks and Latinos committing the crimes. They don't want to show that white people can do the same amount of damage" (Beverly, Black female). "If it's a black or Hispanic person, it's usually in the headlines. Whenever it's a white committing a crime, it usually gets stuck in the back of the paper; you can read it with a microscope" (Darius, Black male). Marie reflects, "Maybe the story about being shot by the Spanish cop was picked up because the Diallo incident was too 'racial.'"

She suggests that publicizing this second incident made the first one appear less "racial."

These comments recognize the exploitation that is inherent in the media industry's interest in what "sells," yet the white students appear less aware of and sensitive to the consequences of these biases. It appears that the implication is that stereotypes sell.

Education as a Right

This section discusses several issues that have arisen as part of a broad struggle to redefine both the constituency eligible for college and its overall purpose. The City University of New York is used here as a point of reference. As discussed in chapter 1, this project is framed as an exploration of everyday perceptions of ordinary whites at the end of the Second Reconstruction.[24] It was, in fact, during the First Reconstruction that the idea emerged that education (including college) should be made available to all people, not just white elites (Du Bois 1979, 637–69). At that time there was significant opposition to what was considered a "revolutionary, poisonous idea of teaching all children to read and write, even the children of parents who had no money to pay tuition fees" (Franklin 2003, 10). It was considered that education was for those with "leisure time," which would certainly not include poor and working people (Franklin 2003, 10). However, "Free primary schooling was among the first income redistribution programs in the nation."[25]

"The City University had its heritage as the first free public educational ladder [and] began a new experiment in democratic schooling: mass higher education" (Gorelick 1981, 194). Established as the Free Academy in 1847, it gave thousands of poor and working people a chance for a college education, though "African Americans were largely absent from a college that was emblematic of democratic opportunity" (Crain 2003, 46). It was not until the struggle for open admissions in the late 1960s and early 1970s (as part of the Second Reconstruction) that activists "demanded that rather than defining human need in corporate terms, the colleges must serve the needs of working-class minority communities—including their need for fundamental social change" (Gorelick 1981, 194), and the doors of the university were opened to people of color. However, "the open admissions policy also generated heated opposition. In 1971 U.S. vice president Spiro Agnew said that CUNY would give away '100,000 devalued diplomas'" (Crain 2003, 47). Shortly afterward New York State and CUNY imposed tuition, precisely the year (1976) in which the student body majority became students of color (Crain 2003, 5).

Other factors also contribute to the undermining of the initial goals of public higher education. Of the seven million students enrolled as undergraduates in the United States in 2003, 70 percent attend public institutions (as do 60 percent of all graduate students). These universities are dependent on public funds, and because they are classified under the rubric of "discretionary funds," they are especially vulnerable to disproportionate budget cuts at times of fiscal constriction (Uchitelle 2003b). Schools often turn to increasing tuition, reinforcing the challenges faced by students from low-income families in trying to pursue their education. Notably, the impact of this is not only on the individuals who may or may not have access to higher education, but also on society, as it loses contributions that could be made by a public with greater access to institutions of higher learning (Uchitelle 2003b). As for the individual, the Census Bureau estimates that the earning differential means that college graduates earn about $2.5 million over their lifetimes, compared to $1.5 million for high school graduates.[26]

Not very long after demands were made to expand educational opportunities in the 1960s and 70s, a national trend emerged expanding what is known today as the "prison industrial complex," at the expense of higher education.[27] In the recent decade, using California as an example, "higher education receives 7.5 percent of total state funds and prisons receive 11 percent. Ten years ago, universities received closer to 10 percent, compared to the penitentiary system's 3 percent."[28] Government priorities shifted away from the support for economic opportunities for the poorest Americans that were won in the 1960s and toward increased tax breaks for the highest income brackets.

The post-World War II boom and consolidation of a middle class in the United States has been reversed such that the economic structure of the country is more unequal than any time since the 1920s. The irony is that the source of the wealth that is being concentrated in the hands of very few, actually comes from the labor of the past. However, the richest 1 percent of households owns nearly half of all individually owned investment assets while the bottom 90 percent owns less than 15 percent. The bottom half (150 million Americans) owns less than 1 percent (Alperovitz 2008). This translates in real terms to realities such as roughly 50 percent of children in the United States using food stamps at some point in their childhood, about 1 in 5 families without enough money for food, and approximately 50 million U.S. citizens without health care.[29] This also affects access to higher education as more people have less money to put toward tuition, and less job flexibility to meet the demands of pursuing a college degree. Four of five high school graduates from the top quintile enroll in college compared to only two in five from the bottom quintile.

Which school someone attends is also affected by family background as only 3 percent of students from the lowest quarter attend a tier one school versus 74 percent of those from the top quarter.[30] This shift affects all people on the lower end of the economic scale, although people of color are disproportionately impacted because they are relatively more dependent on services such as public schools, health facilities, and so on because of a lack of other resources. Huge wealth and resource differentials between whites and people of color increase the challenges, as does the reality that economic downturns disproportionately impact these communities because of their location within the labor market and other factors (Uchitelle 2003a, A1). While the perception is that we have grown increasingly equal, in fact a typical white family is now five times richer than its African-American counterpart of the same class, as the wealth gap between white and African American families has quadrupled since 1970.[31]

Despite this, poor whites have been rallied to support welfare and health-care reform and tax cuts, as the argument is made that Blacks and Latinos, in particular, receive more than their fair share of city services yet pay a smaller share of taxes. The notion that taxes should be returned to the payer in the form of services that correlate to the amount paid—actually, the inverse of the original intent of taxation—has become incorporated into mainstream thinking. Some have asserted that a more accurate way to understand welfare is to look at the vastly increased subsidies and breaks given to corporations over the last several decades.

Another aspect is the belief that immigrants (particularly the undocumented) come to the United States to get on welfare and get a free ride. In the 2010 survey, 26.7 percent disagreed or strongly disagreed with the statement that "Immigrants contribute more to society than they receive in return"; 44.8 percent agreed, 21.9 percent strongly disagreed, and 6.7 percent said they didn't know. Comparing this perception to the reality, the Congressional Budget Office states that "tax revenues of all types generated by immigrants—both legal and unauthorized—exceed the costs of the services they use" and "Undocumented immigrants contribute $7 billion a year in Social Security taxes even though they cannot claim benefits from this program."[32]

Tuition increases of 30 percent and then another 25 percent have made up for a portion of the lost funding for public education (Choe 1999, 13). This has shifted the cost of running CUNY to New York City and its students, so that the budget share covered by tuition increased from 18 to 47 percent between 1988 and 1998 and has continued to grow significantly.The impact of this is racially disproportionate, as tuition cost as a percentage of median family income is 25 percent for whites and 42 percent for both Blacks and Latinos (Choe 1999, 13). This is particularly challenging as "college tuition and fees increased 439 percent from 1982 to 2007 while median family income rose 147 percent. Among the poorest families—those with incomes in the lowest 20 percent—the net cost of a year at a public university was 55 percent of median income, up from 39 percent in 1999–2000."[33]

The argument has been made that when the open admissions policy was initiated in CUNY in 1970, standards dropped and that in the effort to increase access, excellence was reduced (Harden 1998). Some people feel this attitude emerged because, thirty to forty years ago, CUNY was overwhelmingly white, whereas now the majority is students of color.[34] In 1966, CUNY was 96 percent white, whereas the student population of 2001 is 32 percent white.[35] Furthermore, the CUNY Board of Trustees launched a campaign in the mid-1990s to "increase standards," as they asserted that a CUNY diploma was not valuable in the work world. They put forth that students were being passed because liberal faculty hesitate to challenge immigrants and students of color. An article describing one of the protests against this campaign summarizes this position:

> The attitudes expressed by the state's highest officials and by the press: that CUNY students—many of them poor, immigrants and people of color—are ineducable brutes who don't deserve a first-rate university. . . . The state is building prisons while cutting education. They're saying we belong in jail, not in college. Responses to the demonstration from the mayor and governor, responses that went virtually unchallenged in the press—expressed blatant contempt for CUNY students, for the principle of public higher education and even for the democratic act of protest . . . portrayal of CUNY students [is] as a bunch of semiliterate hoodlums. (Kaplan and Solomon 1995, 11–12)

In other words, higher education is deemed to be approved for those who score high on standardized tests and not to the public at large. Inequalities surrounding SAT scores are well documented and show that they do not necessarily predict eventual academic success. Furthermore, there is a general correlation between family income and scores resulting in twelve points for each income increase of $20,000.[36]

Discussions about testing raise questions about whether standardized exams are racially biased. Many whites appear to believe that this issue illustrates how people of color blame someone or something other than themselves for lower scores.[37] In the following exchange, students grapple with this question:

> Some people even think that the SATs, the way they're written helps white males. I don't know if that is true or not, but I don't think so because it's a standardized test. It never changes its format pretty much. (Allen, white male)

I agree. The test never changes its format, just the questions change moderately. You're open to the same books as I am, the same courses, it's standard, it's math and it's English. (Nicky, white female)

Who writes the SATs? If it is whites, it is rich whites. They might say there is an important distinction to be made in the relationships between two wines and how would we know? Some minorities say there is discrimination, but they need to show statistics. (Nancy, white female)

While Nancy raises inherent biases that can play a role in educational testing, she does so solely in relationship to class bias, and none of the students who discussed this issue acknowledged structural aspects of educational disparities, nor the vast number of studies that have analyzed this issue.[38] Within this section on higher education, many issues emerged relating to the tension between caring for all and looking out for oneself. The tendency was to blame individuals for their lack of achievement. Yet, for Scholastic Achievement Test (SAT) scores, there is a strong correlation with family income, indicating discrimination against women, low-income earners, and minority students (Arenson 1999, B7).[39] Such biases are especially insidious, as they foster educational inequalities by implying that some people are more able than others, and they border on a biological explanation for inequality.

A significant and related side-note is the fact that:

> For more than 40 years, an astounding one-fifth of Harvard's students have received admissions preference because their parents attended the school. Today, these overwhelmingly affluent, white children of alumni—"legacies"—are three times more likely to be accepted to Harvard than high school kids who lack that handsome lineage. (Larew 1991, 10)

> With the exception of the athletic rating, [admitted] non-legacies scored better than legacies in all areas of comparison. Exceptionally high admit rates, lowered academic standards, preferential treatment . . . hmmm. These sound like the cries heard in the growing fury over affirmative action for racial minorities in America's elite universities. Only no one is outraged about legacies. (Larew 1991, 10)

While this practice may not be as prevalent as it once was, it continues, perhaps through a shroud of secrecy. For example, "At 40 percent, Princeton's legacy acceptance rate is more than four times higher than the rate of its general applicant pool. Dartmouth, which offered admission to 13.2 percent of its applicants this year, reported that its legacy acceptance rate was consistently 2 to 2½ times higher than that of its overall acceptance rate."[40] While this data can be viewed as irrelevant to the attack on CUNY, it is central to the issue of how the preferential treatment of whites is hidden within the domain of higher education. Rarely (if ever) have we heard out-cries about how legacies pull down standards at Harvard, Yale, Dartmouth, or elsewhere.[41]

The shifting of funds from the institution of education to the prison sys-tem has occurred simultaneous to an increase in media images that depict "urban youth as dangerous, pathological and violent, [and] in turn, find its counterpart in the growth of a highly visible criminal justice system whose get-tough policies fall disproportionately on poor Black and brown youth" (Giroux 1999). This includes the way that hip hop is portrayed almost entirely as a gangster culture while socially conscious artists are often ignored.

The following data demonstrate the context within which today's struggles for public higher education funding occur.

> From 1977 to 1995, the average state increased its correctional funding by two times more than its funding for public colleges, according to a recent ABC News Study. The most egregious example is Texas, where funding for public colleges has grown by 391 percent over that time span; and prison funding increased by 2,232 percent, nearly six times as much. In fiscal year 1988, New York's public university funding was almost twice that of its prison system. Over the next ten years, New York cut spending on public higher education by 29 percent, while the state's correctional system saw a 76 percent increase in its funding. (Choe 1999, 12)

Attitudes about various issues involved with this funding shift are ex-pressed eloquently in the following quotes:

> CUNY, they say it's the poor man's college. If you take away funding from CUNY and put it to prisons, you are denying somebody of working- or lower-class a chance at higher education. (Marianne, white female)

> That's so sad, because if you're working on a population to be educated, the best thing is to provide it for all. That's one of the great things that I saw with the educational system here is that to get into college, it's not something up there where you have to be of this status or you have to be so bright to get in. If they want to separate Ivy League and private schools, go ahead and be a separation and whatever, cause there's always going to be standards where people are go-ing to say it's better to go to this school, or that school. But when you get into the CUNY system and say the standards are being lowered, it's a way to up the standards so only certain people can be given an opportunity to get it. I think that is so sad. (Gerda, white female)

Several students did convey their concern about the future of higher educa-tion. Leon (white male) reflects on the direction of recent policy shifts, saying, "The government has given up on people, given up on education, so now we pay to punish, not improve people. The lack of education is going to lead to crime and violence. Why is more money going to prisons? Is that because they are giving criminals better food?" Keri (Black female) responds, "The government is promoting the education of the white kids more than the kids who attend CUNY. They have more faith in them. They put more emphasis on educating the white group because that's the majority. The majority wants to keep the majority so they have little loopholes to do it."

Contrary to popular understanding in 2010, education disparities continue to be extreme. New York had the highest funding gap in the nation between districts with high and low numbers of students of color, at about $3000 per student. This has real consequences (Alliance for Quality Education 2008).

Privilege and status are sometimes expressed in attitudes toward community colleges. Students articulated both their own sense of being disrespected for attending a public university and their feeling of superiority toward groups they consider inferior. Their awareness of how they are both more and less fortunate than others provides an opportunity to educate about social stratification and structural inequality. As long as they can feel better than someone, inequality appears acceptable and they don't feel the need to question a system that ranks students by whether they are in a public or private university, attend a two- or four-year school, or are not in school at all. Leon (white male) explains, "Our butt-about jokes are about the local community college, but their [private school students'] butt-about jokes are about Brooklyn College. The community college doesn't even exist to them." Vera (white female) similarly told us, "People always say 'Oh you go to Brooklyn College, what is that, a community college?' Then there's always the community college, and you feel so much better."

While perspectives are not monolithic, most feel that they understand the reasons for differentials and why they are justifiable. The naturalization of a notion of white intellectual superiority and a lack of awareness of this presumption appeared throughout the discussions about higher education.

Police, Crime, and Justice

Many important issues relate to race, crime, and justice; a few are addressed in this research. This section explores perceptions and realities about police bias and attitudes toward the criminal justice system.

Recent assessments of racialized police bias indicate consistent evidence of discriminatory practices. "Blacks and Latinos were nine times as likely as whites to be stopped by the police in New York City in 2009, but, once stopped, were no more likely to be arrested. . . . About 1.7 percent of whites who were stopped were found to have a weapon, while 1.1 percent of Blacks were found with one. In examining the stated reasons for the stops, as checked off by police officers on department forms, the center found that about 15 percent of the stops last year cited 'fits a relevant description.'[42] In cases where police mistakenly shoot a fellow officer, "racial bias, unconscious or otherwise, played a clear role."[43]

Contradicting these realities are consistent disparate perceptions where the majority of whites believe that racial bias is limited or does not exist in police treatment and services whereas Blacks and Latinos generally believe that discrimination is practiced (Weitzer and Tuch 2005, 1017) The well-publicized incident of the police arrest of Henry Louis Gates Jr. as he was entering his own home during the summer of 2009 appeared to bring the discrepancy between perception and reality to public notice. However, it's not clear that this incident shifted these misperceptions, nor is it apparent that this led to deepening discussion about the gap between opinion and reality.[44]

Participants explained their perspectives on the issue of police bias:

> Someone in class was talking about how they got pulled over by a cop; a white boy. There was two black cops or one black cop, I don't know, he got pulled over. He was discriminated against—it goes all ways, against blacks, against whites, against Jews. It happens everywhere. You don't know if they're in the Ku Klux Klan. There are cops who are in the KKK. (Zena, white female)

> The cops were definitely wrong but I don't know if it always translates to a white on black kind of thing. A friend said he was stopped by the police. They rolled up, grabbed him, threw him up against the car. That's less than being shot and killed, but still it can be anyone. I think the cops, it's like a totally different story, they go over the limit with a lot of things. (Jacob, white male)

Such statements convey the message that students have an idea about what a criminal looks like (generally not white and educated), but they also reflect a concern about policies implemented by officers, regardless of race. "It's gone so far beyond race right now. It's everyone versus the cops. They're on the sickest power trip. If you look since the verdict, three other people have been killed by a cop. It goes so much further to the Department and Giuliani. They are not trained correctly" (Cindy, self-described as "human" female). It was said that Mayor Giuliani's first response to hearing about Amadou Diallo's murder by forty-one bullets was to question why the young man had been out at 1:00 a.m.[45] Would his response have been the same, had his own son been shot dead?

Students spoke of the excessive tendencies on the part of the police department. This kind of conversation provides an opening for dialogue about the kind of policing one might envision in a caring society. When these incidents occur within the white community, it fosters understanding about excesses of power yet also provides a rebuttal to the notion of racially targeted harassment. The *Journal of Blacks in Higher Education* reports that 4 percent of white Americans say they were unfairly stopped by the police, compared to 37 percent of Black Americans (2001b, 81).

Students are also concerned about criminal justice policies that direct police to shoot to kill or maim, as evident in this exchange:

> Think about it. If you think the guy is crazy and he can kill people, rape them, whatever, and you're the police officer, and you think he has a gun, what are you gonna do? (Leonard, white male)

> They shouldn't be trained to shoot but maybe they're afraid not to because of the race and everything. If you're a cop and you're looking for a dangerous criminal, you probably are gonna be afraid and a little edgy. If you think he has a gun, you're gonna shoot. It doesn't have anything to do with race. Wipe out the color part. You know, everybody's the same. (Jacob, white male)

In 2009, Max (Latino/white) speaks about the shooting of Sean Bell:

> The guy thinks that was a race shooting and that the black police officers were trying to be white and that's how they proved themselves. Part of me wants to be like why would you say that but then part of me is like he really strongly believes that so there's got to be something there if he feels it at least for him. I don't know. I've seen people do ridiculous things to try and fit in. I'm not sure if I am willing to believe that someone is willing to shoot someone forty times to fit in but people have done some pretty awful things to fit in.

The disparate experiences of whites and people of color are treated as if they are the same despite the vast differences in frequency and pattern as if racialized images have no consequence. In this case, racialized comparisons of invidious distinction that render some groups and individuals criminal, negligent, violent, and dangerous, yet others innocent, responsible, and safe function as another mechanism for the reinforcement of patterns. In addition to concerns about police excesses, students described how such images have been reinforced by the media and through the educational system. They were most explicitly illustrated by students of color who shared their own experiences of being subject to such bias. Fernando (Latino) explained, "One of the worst experiences that ever happened in my life was being stopped by the police. They kept saying right from the start, 'Who you gonna beat up, what kind of problems are you trying to raise. I don't like the way you're walking, what kind of drugs are you selling.' I'm like, . . . Where is all of this coming from?"

Flora (West Indian female) asks, "How could Rodney King (televised for 53 seconds), Louima (what a sadistic and sinister culture that they could get away with it), Diallo (41 shots), and Dorismond take place? Racism is drummed into white folks' heads since birth. When they are stressed, they cannot be thoughtful about their reactions."

Finally, Carl (Black Latino) tells us, "They had a notion that this Black man is a rapist and that all Black men in this area are criminals. That's in the back of their heads."

In these images, racial significance explicitly attaches to comments about police excess, reflecting internalized fear. "The Diallo case was totally related to fear. If there was no fear, I don't think that the cops would have shot him. If they did the right thing, they would have called back up instead of opening fire, which made no sense" (Leonard, white male). "In the Diallo case they were afraid of being in the neighborhood. That was part of it. They were getting a lot of pressure from Giuliani and from the higher-ups to catch this criminal. When you get pressure like that, mistakes happen. Your boss is telling you, get this done, get this done. Maybe you're gonna cut corners, you're gonna be nervous and bad things happen" (Jacob, white male).

Students also struggled with the implications and significance of the racialized structure of the criminal justice system. As in many of the comments above, students appear to resist the racialized portrayal of who uses drugs and who is a criminal, though they are unsure about why there were so many more Blacks and Latinos in prison. They are also uncertain as to whether drug use is more common in communities of color and asked for information on these topics. Without basic data and with media images that promote a "public pedagogy and representational politics that cannot be separated from a racial panic and fear over minorities, the urban poor, and immigrants" (Giroux 1999), people tend to repeat de-contextualized and depoliticized analyses rooted in individual failure and structural success.

In contrast, to popular images, FBI and National Institute for Drug Abuse (NIDA) data showed that whites are the primary consumers of narcotic drugs, although in New York State 90 percent of drug-related prisoners are Black or Latino (New York Correctional Association 1998).While African Americans and Latinos comprise about 25 percent of New York State's population, they represent 83 percent of the people in its prisons (and 92 percent of the people in New York City's jails) (Gangi, Ziedenberg, and Schiraldi 1999, 8). The following statement explains how this happens.

Blacks, whites, and Latinos all use drugs at the same rate. . . . But it's where you buy the drugs that gets you arrested. Do the police go into stock brokerage houses to bust people for cocaine? Do they go to Columbia University fraternity parties? No, they bust the people who are using drugs out on the street. . . . If whites were arrested at the same rate, we would not be building prisons. Governor Pataki would be declaring a state of emergency. (Schiraldi as quoted in Choe 1999, 14)

Furthermore, a recent study by the Office of Applied Studies, Substance Abuse and Mental Health Services Administration ". . . found that young Black adults ages 18 to 25 years old were less likely to use illicit drugs than the national average" (February 18, 2010, 3). A 2007 study of college undergraduates published in the *Journal of Ethnicity and Substance Abuse* found that young Blacks' rates of illicit drug use were substantially lower than their counterparts, with Black women having the lowest rates of all (McCabe et al. 2007). Quite different from images of Black youth usually portrayed in the media.[46]

As discussed in the section on education, funding patterns prioritizing prisons over schools were established in the 1980s and 1990s and have continuing impact. The official position about these data is that New York State neighborhoods are safer now than during the last twenty years and that the high costs of prisons are a result of New York State's commitment to inmate "programming" (Choe 1999, 14). However, funds actually are allocated to corrections operating costs and to building new prisons and not to education or programming for prisoners, particularly in upstate New York (Gangi, Ziedenberg, and Schiraldi 1999, 8). Additionally, crime rates over the last quarter century of prison buildup indicate both periods of increase and periods of decrease and do not correlate to the increases and decreases in the prison population (Gonnerman 2000) nor to the news portrayal of increasing or decreasing crime rates (Gonzalez 2004).

Why has the prison system expanded so dramatically over the last two decades?[47] Are people more criminal now; was society too lenient in the past? Is it possible that these people are no longer needed in the job market—what becomes of an educated population with no jobs? Why is it that the United States has the highest incarceration rate on the planet, with more than 25 percent of the world's prisoners (Street 2003b, 2)? One perspective not often heard is reflected in the following quote:

Why is there such bipartisan agreement on expanding police power? The answer lies in the function of the police. Cops don't arrest bosses when they lay off workers. They don't arrest politicians who take healthcare and food away from children. They don't arrest the KKK or right-wing militias who promote and commit racist violence. The politicians and their corporate bosses are anticipating an explosion of justifiable anger in response to their cutbacks. So they want more cops to keep the poor in check while they intensify their economic oppression. (Saxakali.com 1999)

This section explored attitudes and beliefs about the use of force by police and the criminal justice system in general. Strong sentiments were articulated about an overall excess use of force toward all communities; the evidence of racially discriminatory practices appeared to be simultaneously recognized and resisted. Most white respondents had difficulty in acknowledging differential treatment because their own experiences with police led them to believe that they understood the experiences of people of color. They did, however, note several concerns about structure and policy in relation to officers' lack of familiarity with the neighborhoods they patrol and about department policy that dictates "shoot to kill." Students recognized that racialized images about crime in the media arouse fear and, when combined with a quick-draw policy, have devastating consequences. However, there was little recognition among whites of the broad and devastating implications of these images for communities of color. The disconnect between everyday thinking and its material consequences allows these patterns to continue, thereby forming another mechanism for the reproduction of structural inequality.

OPPORTUNITY, EQUALITY, AND FAIRNESS

This section examines whether society is responsible for taking steps to equalize opportunity. The difference between ideals and their implementation was central to the discussions. Many comparisons were drawn about how different groups are treated (see table 5.3).

While many people may be willing to acknowledge specific inequalities or injustices, viewing them as a systemic problem is less acceptable. People may agree in principle with universal equality, but they worry that measures to equalize resources inevitably lead to having to give something up oneself. However, between 2000 and 2009 the percent agreeing that measures should

Table 5.3   If People Don't Have Equal Access to Resources, Measures Should Be Taken to Equalize Opportunity

2000		Disagree	Moderately Agree	Agree	
		6.2%	22.4%	71.4%	
2009	Strongly Disagree	Disagree		Agree	Strongly Agree
	3.8%	9.5%		56.2%	26.7%

be taken when people don't have equal access dropped from 93.8 percent to 82.9 percent. What happened? John (white male) explains, "When my great-grandparents came over, the generation had no money. It took four generations. You got to be around longer."

John conveys his opinion that while everyone should be given a fair chance, people should wait their turn, implying perhaps that Blacks and Latinos are impatient. In a discussion with white staff, feelings about whites being treated unfairly emerged as follows:

> In a lot of the offices all the new people coming in are majority black. Certain offices are mainly black. It's probably pressure from elsewhere to hire black students. I don't think these jobs pay enough. A lot of white people, who would be willing to take them, couldn't live on them. It snowballs. It depends who's doing the interviewing, who's doing the hiring. If you look around at offices, that the top person in the department is a black person, you'll see that the majority of people in there are black. Black people tend to want to hire their own, more so than white people. I think white people will hire the better-qualified person for the person, and I think black people tend to like to hire their own. (Barbara, white female)

The idea that Blacks hire discriminatorily whereas whites hire by qualifications was elaborated in the following statement that expresses an underlying and implicit belief that whites are likely to be more qualified, but Blacks are hired because of "affirmative action" or cronyism:

> White people in administration tend to hire more white people but I think they hire qualified black people just to fill the quota. It's the same way with the blacks but I think black people maybe are more so because they feel they've been down so long that they have not had the opportunities that when one black person gets in, they're going to like hire only blacks, because they do have that unit. (Doreen, white female)

Ted, a white male staff member responds,

> I don't think it's fair either way, really. White people would probably pick more qualified people and take a qualified black person but I think that black people will take black people even if a white person was more qualified. They would take the black person, to give the black person the opportunity, only to pull them in, because they have this unity thing.

Doreen continues,

> Right, they want to keep the club, because I think that's how they look at it. Like what Barbara was talking about in her office where three black people said,

"Well, you wouldn't understand." Now that more black people are in that office, they can all stand there and say, "Well, you don't understand," and not even care to explain because they all understand and you're the individual who doesn't.

In the end, Doreen tries to explain this pattern by saying, "But maybe white will hire white and Black will hire Black because that's who they feel more comfortable being with, associating with or maybe they feel like they have a better understanding of them."

The attempt to reconcile hiring patterns presumes a level playing field but whites have much more control over hiring decisions within the workforce than people of color and there is a racial concentration and a hierarchy of different sectors of the workforce. For example, nationally, among university faculty, four-fifths were white, as were 82 percent of executive, administrative, and managerial staff in 2007.[48] These numbers have not significantly changed since then.[49] The perception that whites are fair and Blacks are biased was discussed in chapter 2.

Sentiments about group segregation being "natural" do not take into account historic dynamics and relations of power. The repeated mystification of why certain groups and people tend to be in certain sectors or functions, as if it had no consequence, reinforces the pattern of stratification. The workplace negotiation about who gets what jobs and why conveys underlying tensions that are articulated through a racialized lens. In fact, historically, various occupations have often been slated for different groups, with the higher income jobs reserved for whites.

This pattern intensifies in the upper class, where the higher the income, the higher the concentration of whites (and males) (Patchen 1999, 126–38). While white men are 33 percent of the population, they are 88 percent of tenured professors, 85 percent of partners in major law firms, 95 percent of Fortune 500 CEOs, 97 percent of school superintendents, 90 percent of U.S. Senators, 99.9 percent of professional athletic team owners, and until recently 100 percent of U.S. presidents (Hahnel and Pai 2001). At all levels of employment, this pattern is significant. In less polarized sectors, competition for employment and mobility is expressed on a micro level as tensions in interpersonal relationships. In a discussion of why whites are concentrated in certain jobs rather than others, it seemed that the participants had not previously thought about or discussed it. In fact, Ted (white male) describes a realization that he came to in this discussion, yet concludes that his experience was unique. He says,

It's interesting, because as a student I took many classes, what, a hundred and some odd credits, half at Brooklyn College. I only had one black professor. I think that's really odd to me, that all of these classes and I would have only one black professor? Maybe it's because of the course, time, and sections that I chose, not being aware of who the teacher was, but I'm sure there's many more faculty which are not, you know, white.

Sally (white female staff) counters this example and provides an explanation for why whites are concentrated in certain sectors: "It's like the baseball team managers are mostly white. But I think there are just not the people out there to hire."

Continuous comparisons were evident. In this context, one can understand a belief in equality concurrent with a relative unwillingness for measures to be taken to equalize opportunity. In the focus groups, it appeared that whites feel vulnerable and resentful that measures taken to equalize opportunity could work to disadvantage them. Therefore, they would believe in the ideal (which, to their minds, might help them) but not in the measures (which they feel might hurt them).

Contrasts between how Blacks and whites, in particular, are regarded were frequently drawn in a variety of contexts, as evident in the following comments all made by white students:

> A lot of black comedians make puns in terms of white jokes and they're taken as funny, but if a white comedian tells one black joke that is a little bit far-fetched, he's gonna be a racist for the rest of his life. I don't think it's right. (Alex, white female)

> At the "Million Man March" and Louis Farrakhan, nothing happened to them, but the KKK rally was stoned. (Sharon, white female)

> I've been pulled over several times, too. Why is it that when I am pulled over it is because I have done something wrong but when a black guy is pulled over, it's because the cops are racist? (Angelo, white male)

> You have to watch what you say. When you're talking to a friend, you got to make sure he's your friend before you tell him something racist. I mean, what I'm going to say is not racist. It's like a black person saying to a black person "Hi—blank" or whatever, if a white person comes up to a black person and says the same thing, it's turning into, "Oh, what are you saying now, are you being racist? Are you saying something about me?" We have to watch what we're going to say. That's how it is in this world. If you step outside and you say something wrong, you never know what's going to happen. . . . I've seen it happen a lot of times. (Sam, white male)

White students often said they felt confused about how to act, that they didn't know when they could raise the issue of race, and when it would be okay to say "black." They feel unsure about the rules and appear resentful about possibly having to learn about how people may perceive their actions. It is as if they are saying, "Why can't we be left alone? We're not hurting anybody. We feel victimized by having to watch what we say." Doreen asks, "Why is it—I don't feel insulted if somebody says, 'Oh, he was a white guy'—why is it an issue? Why do you have to worry about what words you use—like if you say black or African American, or if you say, whatever, I mean, as long as they don't call me idiot, or a terrible name?"

Barbara responds, "I think black people have a problem. I think it's hard for them—African Americans, I think it's demeaning, or something. If I called him a n-gger—that's a definite bad thing, but if you call me—honky, well, they do have some white expressions."

In this exchange Doreen and Barbara express ambivalence about whether they object to a distinction being made about different names. This provides an opening to discuss how language is weighted with historical meaning and how whites' experience cannot be equated with that of Blacks in this country. Furthermore, the gap between believing everyone should have a fair chance and that measures should be taken might be explained by a perspective that assumes we are all starting at the same place. Whites tend to express the view that progress has taken place, so any advantaging or accommodation is now reverse discrimination to the exclusion and detriment of whites. Their resentment is apparent even as they struggle to understand different perspectives.

PRIVILEGE AND DISCRIMINATION

This chapter explored how race is understood within three specific areas of everyday living: media, education, and the justice system. Poverty is generally seen as natural and assumed. Racial inequality is most frequently believed to be the fault of unmotivated individuals and culturally weak groups. "Our society generally worships the symbols of authority, and power. We applaud those who are wealthy, and despise the poor. Individuals are all too often judged by their market value, rather than by their character as human beings" (Marable 2002).

While the ideal of equality is generally supported, measures to level opportunities are viewed as benefiting people of color and discriminating against whites. Significantly, fewer people are willing to support proactive measures, perhaps because they fear it means having to give something up. Explanations for inequality and racism are needed to keep patterns of discrimination and injustice hidden. Contradictions often emerge within one sentence. Statements such as "it's not race; it's human nature" or "it's not race; it's class" provide rationales for why poverty exists, but they don't explain racialized patterns of inequality.

Struggles about multiculturalism and diversity can distract people from talking about structures of inequality that keep patterns and structures of racialization in place all over the world. "Ours is a society that routinely generates destitution—and then, perversely, relieves its conscience by vilifying the destitute" (Ehrenreich 2002, 9). If people are ideologically prepared with an understanding of economic forces and how they influence politics, they may be more willing to understand race as a smokescreen for the elites who manipulate whites into believing that Blacks are to blame.[50]

The next and final chapter summarizes the conclusions of this research and provides an analysis of roles that higher education can play in fostering a deeper understanding of the racial dynamics of the dominant political and social system. Education for transformation involves including in the curriculum the history, struggles, concerns, and accomplishments of people of color; it also demands education about the social, political, and economic forces of history. White students clearly have some awareness of the structural causes of racial inequality but draw upon ideological explanations to place blame on individuals and groups. They are able to acknowledge injustice and inequality when it is not examined locally or for underlying causation. They appear to accept structural arguments about what is going on globally, but they feel they must act individually because they believe that if they play their cards right they can succeed. They may feel a little guilt but they don't act on it, because they feel things are not going to change. Generally speaking the system works for them, just the way it is.

Education can and should play a more sophisticated role in fostering awareness about the dynamics of power, rather than feeding people's illusions about the future. Education could engage in public discourse about the dynamics of global capitalism, corresponding racialized structures of power and subordination, and the impact that these systems have on ordinary people's lives.

The stakes are high because, as the system shifts in a downward trend, many whites who previously felt secure find themselves in increasingly precarious circumstances. Unless persuasive alternative discourse is available along with ideological explanations for what they are experiencing on an everyday basis, the dominant white supremacist explanations will continue to reign supreme.

6

Cracks in the Wall of Whiteness: Desperately Seeking Agency and Optimism

"There's no use trying," Alice said; "One can't believe impossible things."
"I daresay you haven't had much practice," said the Queen. "When I was your age, I always did it for half-an-hour a day. Why, sometimes I've believed as many as six impossible things before breakfast."

—Lewis Carroll, *Through the Looking Glass* (1995 [1871])

As participants share their perspectives about the role of race in their lives, a multitude of mechanisms become apparent. These shape their understanding of who they are, how they should conduct themselves, and what they can expect from society. Also evident are moments when openings exist that can increase awareness about the processes and patterns of racialization, racism, and inequality. These mechanisms, openings (or as I label them, "cracks"), and corresponding recommendations for academia are the subject of this chapter.

Ultimately, the study upon which this book is based sought evidence of agency[1] within the perspectives of ordinary people, particularly whites. Locating "cracks in the wall of whiteness" helps to uncover and affirm hope and optimism about the possibilities for challenging the vast historical inequalities and injustices systemically structured throughout the institutions of our society and sustained by ideological narratives that support and justify racialized patterns.

This book explores the accommodation, acquiescence, and collaboration particularly, though not exclusively, of whites with pro-system ideology and structure (white supremacy, Eurocentrism, white privilege) as well as their ambivalences and apparent sites of resistance. I place an ethnographic

203

study within the theoretical framework of political, social, and economic transitions that have occurred from the 1960s onward. This study examines white racial consciousness at a historic moment when ideological narratives that explain why inequality exists are being reformulated. Hegemonic symbols, everyday consciousness, and theoretical analysis are linked to their material manifestations. Secondly, I examine race to understand the mechanisms of privileging and subordination, and believe that the lessons can be generalized to other axes of power. For example, many of the conclusions can help us understand the dynamics of power in gender and class relations (Collins 2004). "Kurt Lewin, a famous social psychologist, once said, 'There is nothing so practical as a good theory.' A theoretical framework that helps us make sense of what we observe in our daily lives is a very valuable resource" (Tatum 1997, xi). This study sought to identify how structural patterns of inequality are held intact by the everyday thinking of ordinary people. In this way, I examined the ways that racial identity is manipulated to serve the political interests of the powerful and, through critique, can locate agency and action in service of humanity.

"Cracks in the wall of whiteness" become apparent as moments when it is possible to intervene by shifting dominant narratives and corresponding imagery enough so that a white police officer would hesitate before presuming guilt based on racialized notions of criminality, the hiring and treatment of workers would not be tainted by racially weighted notions of merit, and people would decide where to live without consideration of how many of "them" live "there."[2] In doing so, this research is framed within a vision of a world built upon just and equal relationships of shared power and community. I look to a third reconstruction that will address issues of wealth, power, human rights, nation, and the very future of the planet Earth. This may be idealistic; what are our options?

In the final analysis, this project is about dismantling the construct of racial domination and subordination and its entrenched and brutal consequences. In my mind, institutions of education in general and higher education in particular can support interventions that challenge the mechanisms that reinforce and reproduce racial processes and structures. It is urgent to find spaces to engage and place the issue of identity within a political and economic framework from the perspective of the world's peoples rather than that of the rich and powerful. As beliefs and attitudes of ordinary people and the ways they manifest themselves are individual expressions of structural realities, they can support or challenge the reproduction of structural patterns and are therefore critically important to address.

MECHANISMS OF THE REPRODUCTION
OF RACIALIZED PATTERNS

Identifying the processes by which race is constructed and reproduced on an everyday basis can provide the means to interrupt them. This section explores mechanisms that became apparent in this research, including but not limited to the narratives that shape the attitudes and beliefs held particularly, although not exclusively, by whites. While a spectrum of views exist about any one issue, most perspectives fall within a general range as most whites continuously negotiate contradictions between ideals and realities. Often evident in the control of discourse, I label them "mechanisms" because they are structured into the social fabric of everyday living and the political, social, and economic institutions that govern society. These assumptions and stereotypes prevent deconstruction of misperceptions, stereotypes, and inaccurate understandings of the social world and how it operates.

The first mechanism is the naturalization and mystification of poverty, wealth, and inequality. Students readily acknowledge that poverty exists and that racial inequality is "still" problematic, but their overall attitude is that this is "just the way things are": Inequality always has been and always will exist. They appear resigned; they have their "own problems" so there is nothing they can do. Discussions focus on the individual: they did not create the unequal conditions, so why should they be responsible for addressing them? They articulate minimal understanding about how wealth is accumulated, of the relationship between rich and poor, or the realities of privilege and discrimination. Participants were not aware of how the notion of an "American Dream" emerged, or that the criteria for having achieved the "dream" have dramatically expanded over the last several decades even while the possibility for achieving it has constricted. Little connection is made between the structural lack of resources and the vilification of people who are homeless, ill, hungry, or illiterate. These states are described as if they just happen to some people and not to others.

To the extent that the existence of poverty is acknowledged, it is explained by saying poor people lack a work ethic or that people of color use race as an excuse for their own lack of effort. Arguments are repeatedly made that claims of bias are used as a tool to blame white society for racial inequality because the opportunities for people of color are abundant. It is not just that poverty is mystified but that, for some groups, it is naturalized as if the character weaknesses of these groups are what lead to their impoverishment.

The second mechanism is the naturalization of whiteness and American identity and the invisibility of race-dominance, all of which hide the processes of privileging. Whites tend to assume that everyone has access to the same resources and receives the same treatment as they do. There is an assumption of a common American experience. Race relates only to people of color.

A significant proportion of white participants indicate that they rarely discuss or think about race and don't feel it impacts their life experience; however, they do recognize sometimes there is unfair treatment of people of color. By acknowledging racism, yet detaching themselves from its consequences (unintentionally or otherwise), whites participate in allowing inequalities to persist. How else might they say that they are aware of the role of race, yet simultaneously choose to deny or ignore it? They can receive the benefits of being white without feeling responsible to do anything about those who do not, because—the line of thinking goes—race is something that doesn't affect whites. "Colorblindness" can reduce the capacity to deal with racial patterns as has been shown—whites tend to believe that not talking about race means that racism is no longer a problem. "Interestingly, the research suggests that it is precisely when the racialized aspect of an issue or dispute is allowed to remain sublimated and below the surface that it tends to have the greatest ability to control people's opinions and actions."[3]

This mechanism functions similarly with American identity, as people born outside of the United States and people of color born in the United States are not considered truly "American." Since 2001, someone of Arab descent, even if born in the United States, may be challenged in his or her claim to an American identity. Japanese Americans whose families were resident in the United States and interned in concentration camps during the early 1940s certainly also know this experience too well. The notion that "God blessed America" as opposed to any other nation also expresses this naturalization and "Americentrism."[4] That the borders and definitions of being "white" and being "American" have changed over time, and continue to do so, is yet another expression of this process of naturalization as these identities bestow status differentially, depending on the circumstance.[5]

Another component of this naturalization of whiteness is that, once illuminated or questioned, racialized power is inverted, suggesting that whites are now the victims. Various participants speak about feeling confused, especially when they attempt to compare their experiences with those of people of color who they believe more easily receive scholarships, jobs, and other benefits. White participants also often contrast their own experiences with those of peers at private schools or colleges out of town. They express feelings of victimization, both by people who are more fortunate than they are and by people who are less so.

Many of the white participants make comments alluding to students of color such as that "they" always try to separate, raise their flags, want their history included, insist on the validity of their languages and dialects, and want "us" to worry about "their" issues such as police brutality and inequality. Several whites ask, "Isn't that divisive; aren't we all American?" In this way, national identity, linguistic distinction, activism, and protest are viewed as "a Black or Latino thing," exclusive and self-serving, while accommodation is viewed as white, inclusive, and generous. Within the context of a general belief that we have achieved racial equality, this mechanism suggests that challenges to the status quo are greedy and opportunistic.

Finally, this mechanism equates "being American" with being "from the United States," thereby marginalizing peoples throughout the Americas. Perhaps we could use "United Statesian" as more accurate terminology.

The rigid regulation of discourse is a third mechanism that reinforces and reproduces racialized patterns within the organizational structures of society. The boundaries for acceptable discussion of poverty and wealth, justice and democracy, structure, agency, and possibilities for the future exist with strict borders. Origin and development narratives about how the United States became a global power and how the social structure became racially configured are explained and rationalized in such fine detail that to question them is considered objectionable. Ideological order is considered a priority, so perceptions are treated as truths and ambivalence, ambiguity, or confusion are rendered unacceptable. Mainstream discourse presumes the vantage point of the corporate elite (such that laying off two million people is considered a moral good because it protects profits, which in turn "protects jobs"). One's status derives from one's individual positionality rather than from the perspective of society as a whole. This way, an upper-middle-class person can feel that he or she is poor in light of the wealth of the rich, and Brooklyn College students can feel victimized because they could not attend school out of town or at a private institution. They look to students from community colleges to make themselves feel better.

Sites exist in the public sphere, where this mechanism is particularly orchestrated, for example, the educational system, the media, the judicial and political arenas, and employment. Within these domains, images of equality, colorblindness, and individual and group responsibility, either for success or for failure, dominate. Misinformation and a lack of information are routinely accepted. It is therefore not unusual that poverty and wealth are mystified, or that whiteness and American identity are naturalized, as narratives presented to the public at large are to be considered "truths." The expanded criteria for achieving the American Dream, assimilation and upward mobility, are assumed virtues. Images of interracial harmony and the notion that Blacks, Latinos, and Asians have achieved equal status to whites are often portrayed in the media. This evidence is used as a means to communicate that inequality is a thing of the past. Eurocentrism is naturalized within academic curricula that perpetuate the origin and "great society" myths of the United States and white superiority.

The fourth mechanism is one that draws upon many techniques to ensure the transmission and regulation of social values and relations between groups and individuals in society. The techniques include coding of language to camouflage the racial component of policy and actions; the use of fear and silences as means of control; the use of oppositional and dichotomous ways of thinking (Brewer 1993, 16); and the strategies of public versus private personas, defense-consideration-defense, and the hard cop/soft cop technique.

As discussed in chapter 1, coding has become a useful mechanism whereby notions of work ethic, crime, standards, merit, welfare, and urban areas conjure up definitively racialized images but can be raised without the stigma of racism. "It is now possible to perpetuate racial domination without making any explicit reference to race at all. Sub-textual or 'coded' racial signifiers or the mere denial of the continuing significance of race may suffice" (Winant 1994, 19). Codes such as "crime in the streets," "states' rights," "welfare mothers," "law and order," and "urban" are used in ways such that the meaning is conveyed without the risks that explicitly racial language incurs.[6]

The use of fear as a mechanism for the reproduction of racialized patterns in society was evident in several ways. The concern that something one said might be deemed "racist" was often mentioned by white focus group participants. When race is discussed among whites, most people indicated that it is done in whites-only settings to avoid what they describe as being "misunderstood." This apprehension makes it very difficult to engage in conversations about privilege and assumptions or to critique dominant narratives, because discussions become very personalized and people become defensive. Like the clerk minding the company store, whites guard the register. Fear is also evident in the stigma against talking about these topics, because whites may feel that conversations make one vulnerable, hence the position that talking about race perpetuates racism. Most whites appear to be more concerned about being called a racist than about the impact of racism or about the possibility that they might not understand or know something. The lack of open interaction undermines the process of learning about everyday experiences. Ira Berlin, historian at the University of Maryland, said of President Obama's speech on race:

> As Obama indicated, there are lots of legitimate hurts on both sides. It is extremely easy for people to misspeak. In part, because we don't speak a lot and because we don't speak a lot you don't understand the language. People don't understand where the land mines are. They sometimes use the wrong words or are condescending or seem to be condescending when they're trying

to be honest. It's easy for people to take offense when the wrong language is used, particularly when they've got within them a lot of anger and are looking for someone to beat with a small stick. In those circumstances, it's often better to say nothing.[7]

Another way that fear is implicated in the reinforcement of racialized patterns is through the impact of hate crimes. It is not just the individuals involved who are affected, but also the establishment of boundaries for who is allowed where, and under what circumstances. Students express the sentiment that if you break the "rules," anything can happen. They frequently refer to incidents such as Yusuf Hawkins's murder or the burning down of houses of Black families who moved into white neighborhoods or of whites who socialized with Blacks. Fear of crossing "the line" functions like the terror of lynching among poor whites—setting the tone and rules for interaction. Furthermore, there is a fear of the unknown and a concern about the loss of control, power, and status, however incremental it may be for poor and working-class whites. There is also the fear of consequences that can be incurred when one resists the status quo.[8]

Another aspect of the coding, silences, and fear is the way that older generations convey social values and norms to younger generations. Children learn how to conduct themselves by observing and listening, whether to a grandparent's reaction to Bill Cosby or to a parent's offhand comment, tone, or actions. Direct conversations about race don't often occur, yet attitudes and beliefs are clearly transmitted from one generation to the next.

A weak acknowledgment of structural relationships of power sometimes occurs when, in public forums, one person says something controversial that allows others to appear to be mediators. I repeatedly observed a "hard cop/soft cop" dynamic that was apparent when people made what appeared to be contradictory statements during different parts of one discussion. In these cases, more conservative positions are voiced so others can appear to moderate even when they agree. This defuses tension while providing space for more extreme positions to be articulated. Backing down from an initial position might also reflect that people feel ambivalent about the issues being discussed. Another tendency among whites was to be defensive when accused of racism, consider the accusation, and then return to a self-defense, as though the process of consideration clears one's name. The dynamic of a defense of white innocence, consideration of responsibility, and then reversion to a defense happens frequently. Finally, it appears that when students were not sure whether something they were saying was acceptable, they spoke with a very tentative voice. By doing so, they could stay in the discussion while maintaining the option to retract their statements if an objection was raised to something they said.

The fifth mechanism is the use of racialized narratives of invidious distinction that bestow positive and superior status (benefits of the doubt) to whites and impugn negative and inferior status (presumed guilt) to Blacks, Latinos, Asians, and sometimes to groups considered "not fully" white, such as Italians, Jews, and immigrants. These narratives apply different standards to different groups and allow whites to be seen as individuals, but people of color are viewed as representatives of their race. Stated below as the polar opposites of black/white terminology, these characterizations emerge as follows:

- Whites don't murder, steal, speed, or take drugs; Blacks do them all.
- Whites are generous; Blacks want more than their fair share.
- Whites are patient and work hard; Blacks are lazy and like to complain.
- Whites are good; Blacks are bad; Latinos and Asians are invisible, in-between, and homogenous.
- Whites are inclusive and reach out to all; Blacks are exclusive and self-segregate.
- Whites are objective; Blacks exaggerate.
- Whites are peaceful; Blacks are violent.
- Whites hire by ability; Blacks hire by race.
- Whites vote by issue; Blacks vote by race.
- Whites are in positions of authority; Blacks are subordinate.
- Whites can't make "Black" jokes; Blacks can make "white" jokes.
- Whites are civic-minded and philanthropic; Blacks are activists.
- Whites run society, don't have time to complain, or to fight injustice; Blacks waste time whining rather than doing the "real work."
- Whites are realistic; Blacks are idealistic.
- Whites make mistakes; Blacks' mistakes are a sign of their poor character and values.
- Of whites, Italians and Jews appear mixed or "different"; all Blacks look alike.
- Whites are orderly and safe; Blacks are rowdy and dangerous.
- Whites are authentic and honest; Blacks are phony and manipulative.
- Whites succeed on their own; Blacks need help.
- Whites are moral; Blacks are immoral.

Narratives such as these are communicated through discrete and implicit imagery and discourse. The centering of whiteness gives whites significant and positive unearned advantage while it marginalizes, vilifies, and objectifies Blacks, Latinos, and Asians, reflecting a differential valuation of these groups. The implicit moral presumptions of whites as superior and people of color as inferior emerged repeatedly as whites described themselves as multicultural, realistic, relevant, open-minded, caring, educated, honest, and reasonable, in contrast to people of color, who were characterized as self-centered, unrealistic, irrelevant, close-minded, selfish, dishonest, and unrealistic.

At times this was blatant: "They are incompetent; we need to correct their spelling"; "Why are their national flags so important that they have to march around with them. You don't see us draping the U.S. flag over us and marching"; "We chose relevant and realistic issues, not outside concerns"; "They are imbeciles, what does police brutality have to do with BC [Brooklyn College]." Facts are rarely presented and perceptions are expressed as truths. The dearth of close social contact contributes to a lack of understanding, but the more superficial contact allows whites to say that they do know and understand what people of color experience and therefore feel justified to pass judgment. In political campaigns such as in the attacks on the public sector of the past decade, these invidious comparisons are drawn upon to garner support from whites through coded yet racialized imagery to reinforce systemic patterns.

A sixth mechanism is the belief in ideals and apparent awareness of racial inequality, but a lack of willingness to actualize the ideals or acknowledge the consequences of not doing so. Many whites openly agreed that inequality exists but hesitate to accept it as a structural or systemic problem that needs to be addressed by society as a whole. They believe that schools educate, police protect, the government directs, and, when things go wrong, it's the individual's fault. The belief that the United States is a model democracy provides a defense against assertions of inequality. The U.S. experience of European immigrants is held up like the model minority myth, to show that all people can make it if they work hard, ignoring differential factors of whether they are documented, refugees, transmigrants, educated or skilled, or traveled of their own free will, have family ties, experience discrimination, or receive transition benefits.

It appears as if acknowledging a systemic problem would too dramatically challenge assumptions (or justifications) about why some people do better than others do. This dynamic (belief and awareness of inequality but lack of willingness to recognize consequences) is constantly negotiated, depending on the circumstance (whom one is speaking to, and who is listening) and on the context, so that one individual may acknowledge and deny the impact of race within a single conversation. The tendency to avoid acknowledging the impact of inequality supports the status quo, because it prevents a thorough discussion of structure and political economy. There is an implicit disconnect between one's beliefs and the consequences or implications thereof.

Individuals who have experienced other forms of subordination based on gender, sexual orientation, or class status can often draw upon personal experience to reflect upon racial processes. However, if these experiences are not theorized in the context of power relations, they can sometimes have the reverse effect, such as in someone saying, "As a woman, I have overcome the challenges of a male-dominated society, so why can't you as a person of color overcome the challenge of a white-dominated society?" or "Class relations are worse than race." In these cases race, class, and gender are analyzed in comparison to their impacts, and different types of impact and context are viewed as the same. However, understanding relations of power and patterns of dominance and subordination from any point of entry can provide an opening for a more systemic understanding of the systemic and endemic inequalities of capitalism. A deepened grasp of the mechanisms of power and its consequences could dismantle the ideological justifications used in their defense.

To openly acknowledge white privilege would mean chaos and disassembling the "order of being" in society. Sherry Ortner, an anthropologist at Columbia University, describes this dynamic: "Actions like smoking on school grounds or dating someone of the 'wrong' ethnicity were 'seen as virtually disrupting the order of the universe'" (Glenn 2003, A13). The notion of structural inequality appeared to be overwhelming, so while people acknowledge unequal circumstances, they dismiss institutional or systemic analyses that may leave them feeling personally implicated or responsible. One senses that they feel they can acknowledge that things are not perfect, as long as it is someone else's problem. Acknowledging structural inequality implies that we, as a society, may need to do something about it. This is more of a commitment than most people seem willing to make.

Another example of the dynamic of willingness to recognize inequality but not the structural component was that participants acknowledged the role of media in shaping views but found it more difficult to identify the media's impact on the way people act. In explaining the "White Fairness Understanding Gap," Paul Street says that misleading and provocative news stories that exaggerate white suffering from affirmative action combined with images of a Black middle class give people the sense that society is now equal (2001, 9). Street says that for Blacks and other people of color, life experience counters these messages. For whites who often live in segregated environments, these media images become reality. For white students with little interaction with people of color off campus, perceptions of what most Black people's lives are like today are modeled either on Black celebrities or on Black people portrayed in the news for one or another reason, generally negative.

The divergence between an agreement with grand notions of equality, democracy, and fair treatment and the relative unwillingness to support measures to equalize opportunity (see table 5.3) is another example of whites' apparent awareness of racial inequality unaccompanied by a sense of its material implications.

The segregation of most aspects of daily living and casual interaction between whites and people of color is the seventh mechanism that reinforces racialized beliefs rather than challenges them. Students spoke about segregation on campus but felt it was due to human nature and too difficult to change. While it is apparent that contact does not necessarily increase understanding, it also does not appear to increase tension. In some ways, ironically, going to school or living in a diverse environment functions to lessen white people's sense of the need to better understand the everyday experiences of Blacks, Latinos, and Asians. The public interaction sometimes allows whites to think that they "know" and can judge the daily experiences of people of color. They make broad generalizations based on "knowing" someone they work or go to school with. Exposure thus lends itself to being used as a defense against having to examine one's own attitudes and beliefs. Students acknowledged that the visible diversity of the student body does not necessarily represent intertwining of people's lives. They agreed with the survey data, which indicated that people predominantly interact with different groups on campus but with their "own" when they leave. Positive contacts between whites and people of color are seen as personal and exceptional rather than as refutations of media stereotypes.

The eighth mechanism that contributes to the reproduction of racialized patterns of inequality and injustice is the evident "unwritten rules" that dictate the parameters for interaction between people from different groups. The rules are implicit modus operandi for intergroup relationships. They are driven by the fear of consequences or of rejection, or of pressure from family or friends, or of discomfort, or of making a mistake, or of not understanding or being understood, and by a concern about the risks involved in operating outside the bounds of assumed conduct.

These rules are taught to young children but not enforced until young adulthood, when economic pressures in a competitive labor market drive a wedge into relationships. At this point, whites often explain their job search and scholarship difficulties as resulting from an unfair advantage given to Blacks, Latinos, and Asians. However, they know that the rules dictate that they can say this privately, to their friends, but they need to be cautious in public, as racially explicit language is not considered acceptable. Other rules include that one does not bring home people of another racial group (particularly Blacks) because one's parents would not allow it or one knows it is not acceptable in the neighborhood; interact only in public and/or safe spaces; handle business as business and do not presume ideological agreement; friendliness is acceptable but intimacy is not. Internal struggles (dirty laundry) are not aired in public; they are kept within the family. It's okay to resist the rules but not to openly challenge or defy them. "Winks" and silent nods indicate agreement; explicit complicity is not necessary and in fact is not preferred as it might confer heightened vulnerability.

Just as we learn not to discuss politics or religion, we learn the boundaries for discussion of justice and inequality, lest we be forced to reckon with race (and class). Relationships are established and maintained instrumentally. Casual contact maintains a veneer of positive relationships between groups and functions as a disincentive to intergroup dialogue about tensions and segregation. For example, Catherine (white female) explains, "I thought everybody was equal and happy, like, you don't pay attention; you're only a little kid, you know, you don't pay attention to these things."

Several whites explain that they want to do the right thing but unspoken rules interfere.[9] They speak of their good intentions, making critical analysis difficult because everything is focused on the individual and the intention, rather than on the outcome patterns or the structure.

Social pressures supporting both individualism and competition function simultaneously as a ninth mechanism and reinforce historic relationships between groups of people and between individuals. Human nature is characterized as selfish, greedy, and competitive (everyone wants to feel better than someone); people prefer to stay "with their own kind" and everyone categorizes people into who is the "same" versus who is "different." In this view, interracial relationships are deemed deviant, as though the individuals couldn't find someone of their own kind to date or marry. To encourage intergroup contact and interaction is to mess with "what's normal." Explanations for overt racism include that "some people just hate."

Students describe feeling that, even if they could care for society as a whole, doing so was not practical. They say that they do not have enough flexibility and personal security to watch out for other people, and anyway, "Significant progress has been made, so why are Black people always complaining?" "It is expecting too much for us to have to take care of everyone." "It would lead to my own demise and I will end up in their place." There is little encouragement to consider what is best for the community as a whole or to think about what society as a whole should be doing to support the well-being of all its members.

This mechanism also operates to set the discussion within terms of the individual. Racism has been eliminated if everyone "gets along." Relationships between people and the social status of groups and individuals are dehistoricized, decontextualized, and personalized. With no one and nothing held responsible, the capacity of individual and group agency and the possibility for social change both deteriorate.

The illusive nature of race, expressed through ambiguities, ambivalences, and shifting borders, functions as a tenth mechanism Students express conflicting notions about race; while they realize that race matters in everyday living, it does not really exist (or at least it doesn't exist anymore). They explain why people tend to associate with their own group (human nature), and why they support the policies they do, maintaining plausible deniability about the process of their racialized thinking. Many white students express the belief that race exists only in the minds of those who keep talking about it and those people of color who want to use it for their own advantage. They explain that, while it appears that race separates people, it is really a desire for comfort, familiarity, and human nature.

In this way, the roles that race plays are fluid though definitive, tangible yet elusive. The process of racialization performs a distinct function by dividing people while remaining camouflaged. The white male who described himself as a Brooklyn American deconstructs race's role through his geographic identification with a place that holds racialized imagery, yet he still proceeds as a white male in society. In this manner, white participants provided much evidence about their attempts to reconcile their recognition that race matters with their denial that it exists. They acknowledged racialized generalizations but then made statements such as "it's not that I'm racist," "some people think . . . ," or "it's not that I think all Black people . . . ," to legitimate their statements. Ambivalence undermines the ability to engage in principled dialogue, because contradictory or incongruous beliefs often exist simultaneously. The pressure to simplify or solely deal in the realm of intentions makes it very difficult to analyze perspectives or circumstances critically. The emphasis on dichotomous and oppositional thinking (e.g., either you are or you aren't racist; either no Blacks have been upwardly mobile or all Blacks have been so) prevents sophisticated analysis of how different axes of power and subordination function and how race is structured into the fabric of society.

An eleventh mechanism is the way that resistance is stigmatized, marginalized, and racialized, with the ultimate message that things are the way they are because that's the way they should be and they won't and can't change. Students in primary and secondary schools are deemed good when they are quiet and "well-behaved." "Nice" people are deemed superior; people who "make waves" or challenge the status quo are deemed an irritation. Strict notions of what is possible are conveyed in such a way that to envision substantive social change is viewed as unrealistic, idealistic, or ignorant.

This mechanism dictates the boundaries of potential and contributes to sustaining the status quo. Students' feelings about being overwhelmed compound this perspective. They asked, "Even if you did want to do something, what could you do that would make a difference?" and asserted that there are no means to intervene in society-wide or global problems. Their heightened sense of powerlessness functions to reinforce the status quo and uphold dominant narratives and racialized discourse rather than to identity true loci of power.

Other mechanisms became apparent in 2010, for example (the twelfth), that the ideology of white supremacy is considered only to be propagated by people of European descent ("whites"), only by "racists." Racism is only real if intended. The increased visibility of persons of color in positions of power (including but not only, President Obama) functions in multiple ways to reinforce racial patterns. While their presence in the public view challenges some of the borders of a segregated society and the racial hierarchy, it also suggests that racism is a thing of the past and that we now live in a "post-racial" society. Recall William Bennett's statement on November 4 that the election of Obama demonstrates that Blacks no longer have excuses for being poor.

This mechanism also functions in that racial patterns are sometimes perpetuated by persons of color whether Black or Latino police officer such as in the case of Sean Bell, or in policies supported by individuals such as Alberto Gonzalez, Clarence Thomas, or Michael Steele. As the narrative about the culture of poverty has become increasingly entrenched in public policy and discourse, it is not uncommon for people of color to ascribe to these ideas, regardless of the actual realities about discrimination and structural inequality. In fact, the Pew Research Center has found that despite facing increasingly difficult circumstances, Blacks themselves generally believe that conditions have dramatically improved.[10] Thus, the symbolic visibility of persons of color in positions of power conveys the idea that the structure of society has in fact changed. This mechanism also provides a justification for whites as racial patterns and thinking supported by persons of color affirms their own beliefs, attitudes, and actions.

Another mechanism (the thirteenth) is the way that we are so often led to understand aspects of the social world only in dichotomous, oppositional terms. One is male or female, old or young, gay or straight, privileged or oppressed, racist or nonracist, Black or white. Rose Brewer speaks of the way that Black feminist thought is anchored in challenging these dualities by employing both/and formulations, recognizing the simultaneity of struggle and oppression, recognizing the relationality of race, class, and gender and the embedded nature of these hierarchies within our understanding of the society (1993, 16). In this way, decontextualized and dehistoricized narratives function as another mechanism supporting the status quo.

Finally, the fourteenth mechanism, that the historical and current tradition of struggle for human dignity and the common good—both in the United States and globally—is kept almost entirely out of view, functions as a profoundly disarming mechanism. That young people particularly in the United

States are kept busy with assumptions about their material needs, technological innovations, and little exposure to the notion that we exist within and part of a broader human community means there is little sense of responsibility for the well-being of those outside of our immediate circle. To the extent they are aware and interested in having impact, they are guided to "help out" (which of course, is important), but not to create anew or to transform the structures, institutions, and patterns of social life.

Whether in a diverse setting or in a predominantly white environment, the everyday experiences of ordinary people tend to reinforce these mechanisms and provide disincentives to questioning the status quo. It is deemed acceptable for whites to acknowledge racial injustice and inequality on a macro level, but less acceptable to acknowledge it in everyday living. Whites appear to be able to understand and accept structural arguments, but they act individually. In a national survey conducted by the 2001 Cooperative Institutional Research Program (CIRP) of the Higher Education Research Institute (HERI) at the University of California, Los Angeles, 30 percent of Brooklyn College students indicated that "Realistically, an individual can do little to bring about changes in society." This compares to 28.7 percent of students at four-year public colleges nationally (CIRP 2001). By 2008, this number had declined to 23.4 percent.[11]

Paul Rogat Loeb suggests that another factor in students' feelings of what he calls "learned helplessness" is the way that history is portrayed as single acts of extraordinary individuals, rather than as many small acts that support a public and visible action or movement that creates change. He cites the example of Rosa Parks and the Montgomery Bus Boycott as a part of a long-term effort that involved many people. He suggests that this perspective on history undermines people's sense of their own power and defuses the will to resist (Loeb 2001, 4).

As described in chapter 5, in a forum about the struggle for access to CUNY, and why Jewish students and organizations should be involved, Edith Everett, former CUNY Trustee, said, "In order to participate in resistance and critical action, one must believe that the whole population suffers from poverty, illness and lack of education" (1999). She urged students to take action and to believe that things can change. Is it possible that as long as they are doing well, this group of young people feels they can detach themselves from social concerns such as access to public higher education? To this question, Karen (white female) responds,

> This discussion validated my own feelings. It is not just me who feels the way things are, is unacceptable. It helps to talk; it makes me stronger. I feel surer of myself. I know my confusion and distress are reasonable. The issue of race

is better to be on the table. I really believe in that story about the starfish—if you throw back just one into the sea, you have made a difference. But you can't pressure people to talk or to be involved, so it is not easy.

Ultimately, whether it is easy is not the issue. The process of talking increases awareness, and if we do believe that there are ways to intervene, we have no choice but to attempt to do so. With these mechanisms and corresponding ideological explanations in place, opportunities to challenge structural and system-wide dominance and subordination based on race or any other constructs of power are constrained. Answers are provided up front about whom we should interact with, when, under what circumstances. Perhaps with alternative explanations and openness, we can embark upon on a new path.

CRACKS IN THE WALL OF WHITENESS

It makes me wish I had the power to cure it all. I know I can't, I'm just gonna have to sit there and take it.

—Karen, white female

Inherent in many of these mechanisms is the potential for challenging, rather than reinforcing and reproducing, patterns and structures of racialized inequality. A variety of openings for the engagement of whites became apparent in this research. This subsection will summarize these "cracks in the wall of whiteness."

Ideals

Strong beliefs in the principles of equality, justice, and democracy and expressions of caring for those less fortunate were apparent in both the quantitative and qualitative findings of this research. Students expressed pride in diversity and wanted to be part of a nation and a community where all people matter. Ambivalence emerged in the question of whether this was a realistic goal. Their general idealism, however, signifies opportunities to draw contrasts between what they believe should exist, their perceptions of what is, and the actual status of different groups of people. Students clearly recognize that understanding different languages and cultures will be a great advantage, regardless of what career or job they have in the future. To varying degrees, they are troubled by inequality and poverty and seek explanations if not solutions. Exposure to diverse perspectives provides new ways of thinking about the social world. A crack, or an opening, therefore exists.

Ambiguities and Contradictions

There were many points of contestation where students acknowledged multiple realities and incongruous attitudes. While upholding, for example, dominant narratives presenting the attacks on CUNY or public education as part of a campaign for standards, they were also aware that increases in tuition made completing their degrees much more difficult. Those who were aware of the shift in funding from education to the prison-industrial complex were upset both at legislators and at those they held responsible for the need for more prisons: generally Black and Latino youth. They frequently vacillated in their allegiances, not knowing where to place blame for their difficulties. Furthermore, the visibility of contradictory treatment of whites and persons of color provides opportunities to discuss the very structured way that race shapes the lives of people in very different ways. A vivid example is provided by the treatment of the pregnancy of Sarah Palin's daughter, Bristol. Most people would acknowledge that had this been President Obama's daughter, the situation would have been framed very differently.[12] These incongruities provide openings for more thorough dialogue to analyze the implications of holding individuals or groups, or the structure itself, responsible.

Ambivalence

A related, but additional "crack" is the uncertainty that was evident as whites navigate their own increasing financial insecurities and as they are exposed to alternative perspectives. Their uncertainty is sometimes expressed in a tentative tone or by a thinking out loud that I suggest reflects some level of awareness of the contradictions of mainstream discourse about race (and the economy) and the meaning of being white in the twenty-first century. The mechanism whereby racism, status, and morality are measured solely through polar and dichotomous concepts means that if whites are aware that they have some privilege, they hesitate to acknowledge it. Their ambivalence therefore functions as an opening, as it reveals an awareness and sense of vulnerability that can be drawn upon to heighten consciousness about current realities and future possibilities.

Knowledge and Awareness

Students reveal their recognition of contradictions within mainstream narratives. They struggle to uphold the image of the United States as the land of opportunity while acknowledging discrimination in the spheres of educational access and employment opportunities and in relationships with the police. This presents an opportunity to draw upon the awareness of individual circumstances to theorize about institutional and structural relationships of power in society. Similarly, sensitivities to or experiences with other forms of dominance and subordination (gender, language, sexuality, religiosity, etc.) can translate into a broad understanding of system-wide patterns. Intellectual and social engagement has been shown to result in powerful cognitive development, critical awareness, and sense of social responsibility, all key factors in the development of agency.

Systemic Downturns

As whites feel economic and political pressures forcing changes in employment patterns, their sense of vulnerability is heightened. While these circumstances can in fact lend themselves to further entrenching the dominant narratives about who is to blame, so do they also provide opportunities for broad-scale public engagement about global economic and political forces. An opening thereby exists to increase awareness and understanding about racism and racialized patterns of inequality.

Confusion

Similarly, the uncertainty that many whites seem to feel about why they feel vulnerable provides an opportunity to discuss structural causality. When they realized that they really did not understand how the current social organization came to exist, many whites appeared to be open to alternative narratives that perhaps have the potential to shift their basic beliefs, which tend to follow the culture-of-poverty framework.

Exposure to Diverse Experiences

Whether due to demographic changes, technological innovations, downward economic pressures, or increased visibility of persons of color in positions of power, young people today have increased opportunities for interaction with people of diverse backgrounds and experiences. While communities remain largely segregated, experiences such as in community engagement, study abroad, and volunteering and service learning present the possibility for students to interact and learn from people whose lives may be quite different from their own. Much of academia has moved to support civic engagement and these types of learning, increasingly over the last decade. While we can not assume that these experiences raise consciousness and awareness of the racial and class hierarchies, they provide opportunities to do so, particularly when combined with active reflection and analysis.

Creativity, Possibility, and New Inventions

Cracks in the wall of whiteness exist in the many formulations and inter-rogations of the tenets of the racial order that has existed over the last five hundred years. Whether it be the notion of Brooklyn Americans, wiggahs, crossover hip hop culture, multiracial identities, and unions or new aboli-tionists, there appear to be more categories and a blurring of borders compli-cating notions of race. Such formulations provide potential openings through which whiteness may be examined and possibly challenged as presumed superior and supreme.

Courage, Openness, and an Understanding of the Stakes

Throughout the discussions there were many times when someone would ask a question or provide a response that appeared to be inconsistent with their other comments. There were moments when it was clear the speaker was thinking deeply about the experiences shared by other participants and that provided a sort of rupture in the way they understood society and the positioning of different groups. While not in every discussion, in many, "aha" moments occurred where students began to understand just how inter-connected their lives were with those around them, both in the United States and globally. Each of these times provides insight into dynamics that can support the shifting of racial paradigms and willingness to challenge racial structures and institutional patterns. Tim Wise poses the questions "What if the Tea Party Were Black?" and asks us to imagine scenarios such as if "a Black radio talk show host were to predict revolution by people of color if the government continues to be dominated by the rich white men who have been 'destroying' the country."[13]

Another aspect of this crack is the extensive evidence that unequal societ-ies are unstable and in fact unhealthy, even for those with privilege. Inequal-ity fosters vulnerability, weak sense of community, and increased violence. If you have to walk home alone late at night, would you prefer to do so in an unequal society or a more equal one?[14]

Opinion polls indicate that young people are increasingly open to new possibilities. For example, 66 percent supported Barack Obama while only 32 percent voted for John McCain. Voters ages 30 and older were dividing their votes almost evenly.[15] Young people are more accepting of homo-sexuality, interracial dating, and expanded roles for women and immigrants. While 60 percent of people over 60 said that peace is best achieved through military strength, in 2009, just 38 percent of millennials agreed.[16] It appears that they more clearly understand the way their lives interconnect with others than previous generations. This is also reflected in increased interest in the political sphere and commitment to civic and social responsibility (Bush and Little 2009)

Increased Visibility and Higher Levels of Representation

Having a Black president and some greater levels of diversity and representation visible in the media and other public spaces does matter. Symbolically, these images can present this different frame as natural to young people in particular. They can present evidence of new possibilities and thereby contribute to challenging deeply embedded racialization within the structures and institutions of national and global society. They offer opportunities to raise awareness and build a movement that can push for broader social change. Furthermore, if in fact greater visibility translates to kinder interactions and more dialogue between Blacks, whites, and other communities of color, it certainly makes a difference.

At the second U.S. Social Forum in Detroit, Immanuel Wallerstein spoke of the need to recognize both the short-term goal of minimizing pain and the long-term goal of creating a world based on human dignity rather than profit. Both goals are important. Whether the short term translates into a movement to challenge the system-wide inequities and injustices is not predetermined; however, evidence of possibility demonstrates that change can happen and altering how people feel can make a difference.

None of these cracks, alone or even together, provides the impetus or the transformation necessary in everyday consciousness to spontaneously overturn structures of white supremacy. However, I suggest that by understanding the mechanisms of reinforcement and the possibilities for change, we have a better chance. We are up against immense powers and need to draw upon every individual, in every capacity that we can, to challenge and transform the patterns of inequality that have been built into both national and global history. Furthermore, the World Social Forum movement that has taken root globally and nationally on the grassroots level provides evidence of the possibility that our current uncertainty about the future can be re-centered in creating a better world.

CONCLUSION

By identifying mechanisms that function to reproduce and reinforce patterns of inequality in society, we are able to locate points of entry for broad-scale engagement about the forces that have resulted in the pressures that most whites have increasingly felt during the last three decades. This is critical to our ability to counter the dominant ideological campaign that continues to blame people of color and immigrants as the cause of the economic strain.

This section suggests ways to counter the master-narrative and disrupt current patterns of conversation about race, racism, and racialization. We must engage, not preach, as we draw upon our understanding of the experiences of subordination and dominance, discrimination and privilege, prejudice in its negative and positive forms, inclusion and exclusion. We need to analyze race through a multilayered paradigm, recognizing the intersections with class, gender, religion, national identity, and so forth, so that while it is understood as central to the maintenance of the capitalist world order, race and racialization are not re-essentialized. To do so would only recast the very same relations of dominance and privilege in a reformulated configuration.

In chapter 1 I raised several questions, indirectly answered throughout this chapter. I now explicitly articulate my conclusions: Have the political, social, and economic transitions since the 1960s led to an acute sense of victimization and of the world being stacked against white citizens, as portrayed in the media? I would answer yes, albeit with two qualifications. While the gains from the civil rights era and the social movements of the 1960s increased the visibility of the Black and Latino middle or upper class, racial inequality still exists in relatively similar proportions to that which existed in the 1960s. However, the segregation of communities (e.g., housing, education, and employment) and media images of middle-class Blacks and Latinos render the reality of racial inequality largely hidden. In schools today, roughly half of all white students attend schools that are more than 90 percent white, roughly a third of Black students attend schools where the population is more than 90 percent Black. This segregation is also reflective of socioeconomic status as one-third of all black and Latino students attend schools where more than 75 percent of students receive free or reduced lunch, where only 4 percent of white children do.[17] Furthermore, schools have become more, not less segregated and are about at the same levels as in the 1960s.[18]

However, whites consistently believe that equality has been achieved or that opportunities are so extensive that grievances about racism are now unjustified; they say that people of color blame whites merely to excuse their own lack of motivation. This conclusion is drawn from both the quantitative and qualitative data of this research project, as well as from national studies (Sack and Elder 2000, 1; Roper Center 2001, R29A; National Opinion Research Center 1998a, Question 154; Morin 2001, A1, update).

There are times, however, when whites question the discourse about who is to blame for their economic strain, and moments when the contradictions between what they think and what they observe become visible.

What role does and can education play in shaping beliefs and attitudes about race? The answer to this question is discussed below, in the section on Implications for Academia. It is my belief that educational institutions play a major role in shaping beliefs and attitudes about race. They shape whether or not students are introduced to the history, concerns, accomplishments, and perspectives of people of color. Pedagogical styles are influenced by cultural norms and practices. The presence or absence of faculty of color conveys messages about who belongs where, who has knowledge and power. That Black professors represent 3 percent or less of tenured or tenure-track positions and that faculty of color are 16 percent of total positions is symbolic of the overall power structure in U.S. society but has particular ramifications, as this pattern appears "normal" to young people.

Schools support or prevent access to opportunities for programs, dialogues, and engagement between groups. Academia provides (or does not provide) the means for intellectual exploration of the concerns and experiences that influence students' perspectives about significant issues in their lives. Education is inherently political and needs to be understood in the context of relations of power in the broader society. It plays a key role in shaping identities, orienting values, and establishing the boundaries of "legitimate" knowledge and in functioning as a key site for struggles over the meaning of race, class, gender, sexuality, ability, and other dynamics of power (Apple 2008, 254).

Interestingly, a recent study about the direction of liberal education in the United States and "What Matters Most" found that students ranked economic benefits to the individual most important, and then economic benefits to communities; broader social impact, and impact on civics and democracy last (KRC Research and Consulting 2002, 18). This is the common view: that higher education is primarily aimed at preparing students for careers, although this occurs in a socially structured manner to reproduce the class ordering of society. However, such a view forfeits the very resource that can help our society overcome the challenges of its vast inequalities—an informed and engaged public. Hence my argument about the connection between everyday thinking and the structures of social organization comes to light. It is in the power of the ordinary person that the fabric of society is either reproduced or challenged. "Higher education has the potential to be a defining institution within societies, but only if it understands the importance of its role as an independent, creative and activist force. . . . We must work to restore public understanding of why college matters—not only to students and their families, but to all of society" (Burkhardt and Chambers 2003, 1).

It is time to reclaim the moral imperative of liberal education . . . to provide students with fundamental knowledge and skills—critical thinking, communications skills, etc.—that are neither job- nor place-in-time specific. . . . It is our greatest hope for a good society. . . . It is in these connections that we find our common good . . . understand not just what we can do, but what we ought to do. (Harrington 2003, 51)

Students need opportunities to learn in environments that allow for critical analysis of their daily experiences and the application of theory learned in the classroom to their everyday world. Without opportunities for both experiential and theoretical growth, ideas remain abstract and do not bear the true power of knowledge. Ideas and facts can be forgotten after an exam or turning in a paper if they have not been integrated into an individual's life. At the same time, exposure to diversity (without opportunities to theorize the causes or significance of inequality or difference) and interactions with people from different groups (without any grappling with the meaning of democracy, diversity, power, or civic duty) make it easy to personalize an individual contact. It can comfortably be seen as an individual interaction with a nice person who may or may not be "like the rest of 'them.'"

The case for co-curricular involvement must be that it is inseparable from the curricular in the pursuit of a broad intellectual mission, particularly of higher education. It is central, not marginal; it is where ideas may be tested and experiences understood without concern for grades or retribution. Without this opportunity, it is difficult to achieve the true value of education. Students need space for intellectual engagement where the social context is discussed and personal experiences may be understood.

The greatest possibilities lie in the connection made between the agency of individuals and their ability to understand structure and system, and between the application of theory and the theorizing of application. There is a synergy in this learning process. Positive interchanges are only personal interactions unless they are understood within a framework that can reckon with the structural and institutional forces of inequality that militate against those very interactions between groups. It is through the power resident within the broad masses of people that social inequalities can be challenged. However, as long as whites see themselves allied with a power structure and the status quo, few of the true questions about how our world today is structured will ever receive adequate attention.

Whites who identify themselves with the dominant power structure do so not out of a malicious desire to impose tragic consequences on the masses of people of color throughout the world. Yet, they may want to protect what they have such that they are willing to sacrifice the possibility of working toward a greater good for all, if they need to do so to achieve a sense of security themselves. Each mechanism and narrative identified above contributes to a worldview that holds the current pattern as their only option and replicates, reinforces, and reproduces structures of inequality. If we could interrupt and expose these mechanisms, narratives, and structures, we might have a chance at building a world where hunger, homelessness, and fear of violence would no longer be an issue for so many people. What we need, Arundhati Roy, author, suggests:

> What we need to search for and find, what we need to hone and perfect into a magnificent, shining thing, is a new kind of politics. Not the politics of governance, but the politics of resistance. The politics of opposition. The politics of forcing accountability. The politics of joining hands across the world and preventing certain destruction. In the present circumstances, I'd say that the only thing worth globalizing is dissent. (Roy 2002)

We have few options other than to believe that, given the opportunity, and as part of a moral campaign for what is right and loving and good, people can care about more than just themselves. The question is, will they?

This book is about exposure and about agency. I refer not just to the everyday contact that occurs while interacting in a classroom or on a subway train, but the type that encourages and supports thorough exploration of the structures, history, and systems of assumptions, biases, and ideological presumptions about why poverty exists. I refer to poverty in general, and racialized poverty in particular, as inequality is embedded into the structures of society. There is, at this moment in time, a great need to listen, not just talk. We need to draw upon common values of safety, strength, respect for human life, and social justice. We need to foster understanding about the mechanisms of power that underlie current and past events, such as the U.S. government's response to the tragedy of September 11. Mainstream media have worked in concert with corporate interests and have generally followed the lead of President George W. Bush in framing the military response within notions of patriotism and moral righteousness. Many grassroots, youth, community, progressive, and academic groups and individuals have worked to focus current public discourse on issues of peace and justice. However, powerful forces are at work to discourage, stigmatize, and undermine voices of dissent (We Interrupt This Message 2001).

In a presentation at the African American Institute of Columbia University on 10 December 1999, Dr. James Jennings, scholar and author, argued for a change in the civic discourse about the invisibility and blaming of victims, about the true nature of policies and practices oriented to compensate for past discrimination, and about civic participation. He described mainstream discourse as a political tool used to disarm and diffuse the political power of poor and working people.

Theoretical discussions or analyses of structural inequality do not adequately expose its causes or consequences as they affect personal and daily life. Positive interactions between groups do not necessarily illuminate what must change in society, nor do they eradicate structural inequalities. It is solely through the continuous and dialectical flow of theory and practice that these two critical components can be bridged in forging a new public awareness, in particular among whites who, as a group, most vehemently defend the status quo.

Multicultural America: The System and Its Symbols

Significant differences in attitude between native and foreign-born whites were evident such that foreign-born whites appear to defend the system more consistently than U.S.-born whites do, even if U.S.-born whites appear to defend the symbols more vehemently. Perhaps foreign-born whites feel that their experience upon arriving in the United States has generally been positive. Their access, resources, and encounters lead them to view the country as a land of opportunity. They less often recognize discrimination, more often believing that all people are treated equally when applying for jobs or housing, when approached by police, and in the media. As distinguished from foreign-born Blacks, they believe more than other groups that all people can be assimilated into U.S. society, that the United States cannot be both multicultural and "American," and that eliminating remediation in the university impacts all students equally.

The defense of symbols by U.S.-born whites appears to reflect their allegiance and loyalty to the positive principles articulated as "what it means to be American" and at the same time articulates their complicity with the notion of white superiority and supremacy. National identity functions as the base for patterns of dominance and subordination that underlie all other patterns, at times contradicting, at other times enhancing the individual's status. U.S. national identity often functions like race in that the holder lives in an assumed state, white and English-speaking, from which all "others" depart. The stark images of the whiteness and maleness of the police and fire departments, construction crews, and the political administration are what being American is all about. This apartheid-like labor structure has rarely been exposed. While inequality in employment has been alluded to, it has not been widely discussed in the press. The very definition of an "American hero" is starkly racialized but rarely challenged. Discussions, then, that express the perspective that the United States cannot be both multicultural and American particularly exclude people of color, especially immigrants who have arrived in the African, Asian, and Latino diasporas of the last forty years.

Racialization has also been expressed in the relationships between West Indians, South Asians, Haitians, and African Americans. Often oversimplified as an attempt by immigrants of color to distinguish themselves from African Americans (who, in the racial order of the United States, have been viewed as the most undesirable group), this dynamic is actually much more complex. Winston James, a historian, speaks to the impatience that many West Indians have felt upon arrival in the United States when confronted with racism; one result has been a significant history of Black radicalism. He asserts, however, that West Indian activism developed along a slightly different path from that of African Americans, who had experienced racism throughout their lives (1998). James disputes the notion that relationships between West Indians and African Americans have been characterized solely by tension and argues that they have been shaped by the political contexts of different historical periods. He documents significant collaboration and interaction between the two groups (1998).

As immigration patterns shift toward increasing numbers of Latinos and Asians in the United States and as political interests attempt to use this change to their advantage, the mechanisms of race, racialization, and racism will continue to be in transition and complicated.[19] Within this present-day context as well as historically, the meaning of being American shifts continuously between something tangible and specific (place of birth, naturalization, or citizenship) and something ambiguous and constructed (belief system, loyalty, patriotism). In 2010, the passage of SB1070 in Arizona requiring police officers to stop and check the immigration status of anyone they "reasonably suspect" to be undocumented is a vivid example of both the fluidity and extremely politicized nature of belonging in present-day U.S. society. Accepted as a workforce that makes but does not draw substantive contributions to the economy, myths, and stereotypes abound that function as mechanisms for justifying discriminatory and biased actions and structures.[20]

When one claims to be an American and defines this identity as the embodiment of democracy, freedom, generosity, hard work, etc., there is an implicit assertion of superiority over anyone who does not make this claim. It is difficult to critique this concept because it is so integrally linked to individual self-worth and self-definition; questioning the founding myth creates a distressing void.[21] It was questioned in the fall of 2001, as freedom of speech and the right to dissent emerged as critical civil rights principles challenged by forces looking to impose their narrative about how such a tragedy as 9/11 could occur. CUNY Trustees were part of this ideological campaign to squelch the intellectual interrogation of the myths of America; they labeled "seditious" the faculty who raised questions about the history of U.S. foreign policy at a City College teach-in (Perez and Barrera 2001, 2).

In another example, Clear Channel Communications, a media giant that owns more than 1,100 radio stations nationally, suggested that John Lennon's song, "Imagine," should not be played in the aftermath of September 11. "Apparently, you can't afford to go around imagining 'no countries' and 'nothing to kill or die for' now, with so much killing and/or dying for your country to be done" (Masley 2001, C2). Powerful forces set forth to work to protect the unquestionably positive image of the United States and to ward off challenges or inquiry.

For native-born people in the United States, particularly whites, the influences of a primary and secondary education in the United States and various forms of media have ingrained a belief in the natural order of society and where "America" fits in. Yet, at the same time, all whites, regardless of where they were born, articulated a belief in ideals more often and more strongly than they expressed a willingness for action to be taken to ensure these ideals. A discrete calculation among whites about how to best position oneself individually was evident, with little apparent concern for the consequences for society as a whole (Street 2001, 9–11). Whites appear to take a pragmatic approach toward upholding "truths," so that what is important is not a clearly defined set of beliefs but an implicit understanding of the consequences that correspond to adopting one or another way of thinking. Otherwise, whites could be held responsible for inequality, and for them, this burden may be too great to bear (Street 2001, 11).

THE FOCUS GROUP EXPERIENCE

It's healthy to be in a situation where you're kind of forced to talk to people that you wouldn't normally be talking to. It heightens awareness.

—Dmitri, white male

Continuing the process of identifying opportunities for engagement, this section summarizes feedback that students gave regarding their experience of participating in this project's focus groups. Their comments indicated that they had not consciously thought about many of these issues before but appreciated doing so. Since no grade was assigned and no positive or negative reward given, there was no reason that they needed to say that they valued the experience.

Overall, students acknowledged that they felt uncomfortable and even put somewhat on the spot. However, they clearly valued the chance to hear diverse opinions about aspects of everyday living. Repeatedly students say that they came to talk but ended up doing more listening because they felt they had something to learn. While this was particularly true for students who participated in the mixed groups, it was also true in the all-white groups, where students were able to hear different opinions among white participants. They often express the desire to hear more, and for increased civic engagement. "It was a good experience," Allen (white male) says. "I never thought about these questions before. I don't know, it makes me think that maybe we should get more involved."

Barbara (white female) begins, "I want to be open about whatever. I want to try to bring you into my community, my white whatever world, because of the equality thing, but I don't feel like I'm being let to. Do you understand what I'm saying? I want to be more accepting."

Doreen asks, "Do Black people care as much as we seem to care whether they are accepted by us, as if we are accepted by them? I'm hearing us say 'We want to get along and things to be more equal.' Do they feel the same way? Do they want to get along or do they want to keep the segregation?"

If the only issue were segregation, perhaps the answers to the participants' questions might be simpler. Their comments, while not reflecting much understanding of the experience and impact of racial subordination in daily life, do however reflect concern and a desire for a better world. This is the essence of what I mean by a "crack in the wall of whiteness." These conversations opened the possibility of dialogue and deepened the participants' understanding of the devastating impact of racism in its personal and its institutional forms. Discussions also provided an opportunity to find common ground among people who share class or gender experiences. However, what incentives exist to motivate open discussion? I believe that our collective future is at stake; perhaps the events following 9/11 make that more apparent.

It might be useful to follow up with participants after they have a chance to reflect upon what they had heard in the focus group to note whether beliefs or opinions had changed. The very positive feedback that students expressed about hearing diverse perspectives in a "low-stakes" environment reflects the increasing awareness nationally of the role that intergroup dialogue can perform both in educational and in community settings.

"A strong democracy today requires both that citizens be engaged in civil life and that they act together in a spirit of equality and social justice. . . . Intergroup dialogue is one effective approach to addressing these concerns for a strong democracy based on diversity and justice" (Schoem 2003, 213). Engagement in the formal process of dialogue, particularly as linked to collective action, has significant potential for affecting individual communities and society at large as common interests can be recognized and acted upon. With an understanding of the connection between everyday thinking and the perpetuation of structures of inequality, this provides one vehicle for potential change.

Implications for Academia

Throughout this chapter I have discussed the significant role that education (particularly higher education) can and should play in addressing issues of social inequality that underlie the relationships and ideological framing of race in our society. I have stated with some urgency the need for collaboration between academic and student affairs so that theoretical and experiential learning can be viewed as a partnership and not as two separate pursuits. This research aimed at understanding white racial consciousness and identifying the everyday mechanisms that reproduce racialized beliefs and structures, not at proposing a diversity initiative. However, I would be remiss not to express my support for what has been shown to be the most effective strategy for promoting diversity as a core component of the academic mission. That strategy involves comprehensive and multilayered initiatives that enhance the many different structural elements, including positive campus climate, diverse staffing, inclusive curriculum, and support for students from underrepresented groups, to improve access and success as well as the quality of education provided. In this way, we can draw upon what has been described as "Academics of the Heart," in the education of the whole person and as a balance of reason and spirit.[22]

While higher education has generally emphasized the benefits of higher learning (intellectually and economically) to the individual learner, the benefit to society as a whole in enriching the quality and vitality of communities and fostering engagement in democracy and civic involvement is just as great (Schneider 1995, xiii–xiv). Additionally, while other institutions also provide opportunities that support interaction and understanding between groups, higher education is uniquely positioned, by its mission, values, and dedication to learning, to foster and nourish the habits of heart and mind that Americans need to make diversity work in daily life as a value and a public good.[23] The implication and significance of a move in this direction will necessarily be global.

In the next subsection, I summarize a few recommendations.

Co-Curricular Programming

. . . Community-based research, collaborative projects, service-learning, mentored internships, reflections on what has been learned from experiential learning and/or study abroad. All are efforts to help students make connections between scholarship and public questions, consider alternative frameworks for judgment and action, draw meaning from experience, critique theory in light of practice, and evaluate practice in light of new knowledge. All are practices that require students to negotiate their differences with colleagues and which therefore have clear implications for cultivating thoughtful and reflective forms of citizenship in a diverse democracy. (Schneider 2003, 3)

As noted above, students felt they benefited from being in an environment with people of different opinions and/or from different groups and talking about issues of race, identity, and inequality. Having a facilitator meant that there was an element of protection and safety that would not otherwise be present were a group of people who did not know each other to sit down and discuss these topics. Dialogues need to be a regular part of the college experience and perhaps in primary and secondary schools, too. They can be moderated and guided by faculty and student co-facilitators in first-year experience courses and throughout the academic career.

> Universities are places with soul and integrity, and . . . those associated with an institution know its distinctive values . . . the best institutions are open and respectful learning communities, where ethical concerns and values are easily and often discussed and where the educational programs and internal decision-making process are consistent with those values. Colleges and universities can act more proactively and imaginatively when they have to reinforce the democratic values of pluralism, social justice and civic responsibility. (Mallory and Thomas 2003, 17)

Special emphasis needs to be placed on involving white students in these types of activities because, observably, when they do not perceive a problem they are less likely to get involved. It has also been shown that "face-to-face interaction in the higher education context can play a key role in developing genuine interracial understanding and tolerance" (Alger 1997, 20), and that "dialogue about racism can be a powerful catalyst for change" (Beverly Daniel Tatum as quoted in Humphreys 2000, 14). Furthermore, "they begin to see the world through someone else's eyes. The capacity to do that comes with practice and proximity" (Humphreys 2003, 29).

Knowledge that emanates from daily experience and is then theorized, along with political and economic theory applied to everyday living, has the power to transform individuals and, in turn, society. The following quotes further demonstrate how three white students felt about the discussions. "If I'm in charge in a perfect world, I would force people to relate to each other" (John, white male). "When we were first introduced . . . I was very eager to express my own opinions. After I heard different people talking, I realized there were a lot of important things being said, and it was more important for them to be said, to try to learn more. The things that were said, they were a bit surprising to me. All of these things were going through my head. I'm going to go home and still try to digest all these things, information I got here. It was a good experience" (Craig, white male).

Jeanne (white female) explains, "This is the type of discussion that you really don't talk about outside. You talk within a group where you know it's safe to talk."

Particularly at the college level, students need opportunities to discuss their opinions and perspectives with people who disagree and with people who have had different life experiences. They need the chance to explore and examine their thinking as adults. The college years are a critical period in a person's life, when intellectual growth mandates challenge, particularly from peers. We must become masters at learning from each other, and not just hearing each other speak.

Students offered their ideas and suggestions about what is effective in heightening people's awareness of each other, particularly whites' understanding of the experiences of people of color. Marianne (white female) suggests that working side by side makes a difference: "If you're in an organization, like a club or organized group, you get along better with people. There's a sense of more understanding." Other students, such as Michael (Latino and white male), express similar sentiments: "We should establish cross club internships. Force students in the African club and the radio station to switch places for a semester. If we are segregated as leaders, there is no chance to integrate students."

Catherine (white female) agrees but also discusses the challenges of this approach:

> If I was president of Student Government I would hold events so [students] get to know each other. I personally deal with this because I go to parties. I know all the minorities and everyone's like "Wow, you know everyone." I'm like, "Why don't you come to the parties? Why, cause you're scared of minorities? What are they going to do, kick your ass?" They're like, "No; we just don't hang with them." I'm like, "So why don't you? They don't have a disease." People are uncomfortable. I was, at first, but now I'm used to it. I still feel uncomfortable but he's just a person, just because he's black doesn't mean, you know, he's going to totally come out and be like, why are you talking to me?

Etienne (Black male) articulates his ideas by saying that "Colorblindness is a possibility, but not for everyone. We need group therapy and building bridges. Group work helps."

The impact of programs that increase interaction between diverse groups of students can be extremely positive for all students. However, it is particularly valuable for white students, whose daily experiences provide them with little ammunition or reason to question mainstream images and narratives as they relate to race.

While perhaps the implicit connection between co-curricular programming and initiatives that foster personal and social responsibility is apparent, it is important to state the importance of these values in developing an engaged, compassionate, and thoughtful social community. Organizations such as the Association of American Colleges and Universities have published extensively about the positive impacts of learning environments that are not only engaged, but also emphasize social responsibility. They argue that the significant outcomes are evident in students' ability to take seriously the perspective of others, their competency in ethical and moral reasoning, and their integrity, excellence, and overall contributions to society.[24]

Similarly, hiring practices must increase the representation of people of color in all disciplines. Having faculty, administration, and staff who reflect the community as a whole brings tremendous strength to institutional efforts to address issues of racial inequality and provides long-excluded perspectives and experiences that form a significant part of the learning process.[25] If whites only take classes from white professors, the mechanisms described above will remain intact. This is not, however, to essentialize race. Simply hiring more Latinos, Asians, and African and Native Americans will not eliminate other structural imbalances, nor will it necessarily provide widespread engagement about racial domination and subordination or about the political and economic theoretical analysis that I refer to. However, it would be an important step toward inclusion and representation and increased balance in perspective on an institutional level.

Curricular Issues

Students repeatedly spoke of the classes they described as favorites, because these courses provided tools to understand current events, personal experiences, and both national and global history. Students consistently said, "We need more classes like Core 3."[26] We should expand courses dealing with social issues. One student even recommended that we eliminate another core to do this. "Core 3 opens people's minds up and makes them think about the way they think. Core 3 changed my perspective for the way I look at life. It is long, but it flies. I learned from it; I learned different points of view" (Fernando, Latino). Jenny (white female) agrees, "Classes like that reaffirm that something is there. It shows that this is not made up. There is a long history behind it. For white people, it shows that this is not made up. The only way we're gonna change is don't do the things we did in the past. If the person is willing, then they will change their mind."

Paul Montagna of the department of sociology indicated in an interview that a study of the Core Curriculum after ten years of existence revealed that the most popular course among students was Core 3. He says, "They felt it was most beneficial because it exposed them to different perspectives."[27]

Inclusion of multiculturalism in the curriculum is generally viewed as an issue of self-esteem, as individualistic enhancement for those people who have been historically left out, or as enriching whites' understanding of history. While these are important functions, multiculturalism and diversity training do not necessarily challenge structural or systemic power dynamics. I believe the biggest threat to the status quo is a broad-based understanding of the economics of social and global inequality, which includes the racialized structuring of society at all levels. It is in this context that multicultural curriculum has its most powerful impact. If education included information about how Wall Street functions, about the cyclical nature of capitalism, about deindustrialization, about profit on a global scale, and the concrete implications of these processes for real people's lives, then what was described as the "White Fairness Understanding Gap" might be narrowed.[28]

This call, for deepening the curricular emphasis on diversity and race within an economic framework, differs from most of the scholarship that focuses on politics, culture, or identity. More emphasis is needed on developing students' understanding of the nature of society from an economic perspective, which has often been marginalized within the social sciences, as group experiences are often analyzed from the perspective of a collection of individuals rather than as part of a structure. A related phenomenon is that the study of economics often falls under the division of business rather than that of social science, creating a false and problematic separation. "If multiculturalism is not going to take seriously the link between culture and power, progressive educators will have to rethink collectively what it means to link the struggle for change within the university to struggles for change in the broader society" (Giroux 1999).

> This suggests developing a pedagogy that promotes a social vocabulary of cultural difference that links strategies of understanding to strategies of engagement, that recognizes the limits of the university as a site for social engagement and refuses to reduce politics to matters of language and meaning that erase broader issues of systemic political power, institutional control, economic ownership and the distribution of cultural and intellectual resources in a wide variety of public spaces. (Giroux 1999)

Carol Geary Schneider, president of the Association of American Colleges and Universities, has been quoted as saying, "Very few courses in the contemporary undergraduate curriculum directly address democratic principles and/or aspirations" (Schneider 1999, 9). She further asked where in the curriculum are students engaged about concepts of justice, democracy, equality, opportunity, and liberty and suggested that these challenging topics belong in general education because they are integral dimensions of American pluralism and must be understood in the context of their historical connections (Schneider 1999, 9). This engagement is central to the development of civic responsibility and social awareness as a core tenet of higher education.

While most of the work on civic engagement does not speak to the issues of involvement in political projects or the world of social movements, the history of democracy in the United States alone and certainly globally is one that situates these activities squarely within the realm of liberal education and civic engagement. This may be avoided out of concern for partisanship, because of a perception that service is good, activism is problematic or is a result of efforts to sustain the status quo. Regardless of the reason, it is important to note the significant value that comes from political involvement especially aimed not only on raising awareness or affecting individuals, but also toward structural change (Bush and Little 2009).

> Learning about political institutions, issues, contexts, and practices should be an integral part of that enterprise (liberal arts education). College graduates cannot make sense of their environment and their place in it if they are politically ignorant, unskilled, and lacking in a sense of civic agency, the sense that they can work with others to solve problems that concern them—in their communities, workplaces, . . ." (Colby 2008: 8)

Overall, every opportunity to advance a broad-based and deepened understanding about the global dynamics of white supremacy, including its material impact on the lives of all people, should be pursued. This effort could cultivate a counter narrative that deals with white racism from "cradle to grave."[29] It can also provide incentive to the large numbers of white people outside the ruling class, whose acceptance of the status quo contributes to the entrenchment of the patterns of racial inequality and injustice that threaten our future, to perhaps redefine their allegiances and reconfigure their notion of "who's to blame."

Directions for Future Inquiry

Deconstructing the construct of whiteness means to take up the struggle in every arena to show how white privilege is maintained through unequal resources being allocated to schools, hospitals, and social facilities; how job discrimination functions; how environmental waste gets handled; how the death penalty and criminal justice system are administered; who gets admitted to institutions of higher education; and how narratives about crime, welfare, and affirmative action tell only part of the story. One direction for future research would be to explore specific examples of past and present-day challenges to white privilege. Social activism that addresses this idea includes the lawsuit related to the differential in funding between CUNY and SUNY; the Health Care for All Coalition, which raises the issue of unequal allocation of healthcare resources; the Same Boat Coalition; student activism to uphold affirmative action in admissions; movements against the prison industrial complex and the death penalty; and the many other community-based projects that address the privilege of whiteness.

As we document when and how challenges to racist policies have occurred, and as we analyze when and how the codes and mechanisms of whiteness have been broken, we will be able to better support future challenges to systemic white domination. For, in many ways, the subscription of most whites to the mainstream worldview increasingly does not make sense, especially as they face the effects of a global economic crisis and heightened political disempowerment. While racism has allowed the ruling elite to maintain a race-stratified labor force and has functioned as a useful tool to poor, working-, and middle-class whites as willing gatekeepers, this strategy is vulnerable during periods of economic down-turn (Kushnick 1981, 192). Fernando (Latino) recognizes this and says, "I'll be honest, even to this day, I still don't understand it. Why do people have a racist prejudice? It's the year 2000 and I don't even know what's going to happen tomorrow."

If whites do not reckon with this illogic, they will continue to live with the paradox described by James Baldwin, that "those who believed they could control and define Black people divested themselves of the power to control and define themselves" (1984, 92). Research that identifies when this pattern is challenged can help further our ability to intervene in the processes and mechanisms that reproduce and reinforce racialized structures of power.

Also emerging from this research are questions (some listed below) that require thorough study, with direct connections being drawn to concrete social change through policies and programs. If we believe in the power of knowledge and in the potential of social science research to impact society, it will be through popular engagement that we may witness shifts in the consciousness of everyday people. It is my hope that such questions provide talking points for understanding the significance of my study and the implications for future work in this area. Such queries take the conclusions of the project to the next step, where critical engagement is necessary for changing minds. Talking, reflecting, and experiencing are crucial components of that process of individual change and can impact structural patterns. The questions include but are not limited to:

How do status and quality of life impact one's perceptions about the world? How much diversity of opinion is there within families? What factors influence whites' understanding of fairness in U.S. society? What effect do programs, curricula, and policies about diversity have on belief systems?

What is the impact of consistent dialogue and intergroup interaction? Do attitudes change as a result of exposure to these types of experiences? What leads to despair? What leads to the decision to do something?

How do we theorize the racialized experiences of foreign-born whites as compared to that of foreign-born people of the African, Latin, and Asian diasporas? What are the similarities and differences in the experiences of foreign-born versus U.S.-born whites?

Each question alludes to a project in and of itself, as they relate to the role of race in everyday life, in the United States and globally, at the beginning of the twenty-first century. We need to understand the significance of the World Conference against Racism, World Social Forums, and anti-globalization movements in their challenges to white supremacy and its implicit connection to the crisis of the capitalist world system.

SUMMARY

This book suggests both concrete and theoretical implications for the centrality of agency, possibility, and change to the structuring of society, the educational system, and the perpetuation of mainstream narratives. As such, this writing is explicitly aimed at impacting public policy and contributing to the forces of change that influence structures and institutions that predominantly implement the will of the powerful. This is particularly important within post-secondary education, where students often explore "outside the boxes" of mainstream discourse and their own family's ideas and traditions. The need to forge links between student and academic affairs and to understand the critical role of praxis in learning is essential.[30] While, nationally, there is a trend in academia toward recognizing the role of community service and volunteer learning, there has also been a trend toward distance learning and enclosed "learning communities."

The implications of these developments are tremendous and need to be examined within the context of the overall mission of higher education, as many assumptions underlie structural forces that determine who is educated, about what, whom to lead, and for what purpose.[31] The implicit racialization of these assumptions is highly consequential, and the same point can also be raised in the examination of the primary and secondary educational systems, where resources are differentially allocated to various communities. Whiteness scholarship must support an interrogation of the future of academia in this light. The present work is specifically and uniquely directed to assisting in that effort.

Finally, I would like to return to the issue of agency, for if there is one central theme of this book, it is the belief that the current structures and patterns of our highly inegalitarian and unjust order can change. We must identify, cultivate, and mobilize every possible crack, and recognize and strategically utilize every contradiction, to make this happen. "If racism can change . . . it can be made to go away" (Kovel 1984, xlix, xl). We must fight to the end for the common good and for all of humanity. To give up, or to settle, leaves us defensive and vulnerable to the "chickens coming home to roost in ways that are unpredictable and uncontrollable."[32]

Scholarship that investigates whites' consciousness (or lack thereof) of their own racialized identity matters, because the link between consciousness, ideology, social practice, and structure allows us to develop the means to understand and address systemic patterns of inequality. This book provides insight into how white pan-ethnicity affects everyday perceptions that impact actions and, in turn, affect policies that reinforce patterns of racial inequality but also have the capacity to challenge them. I take my lead from a long tradition of activists and scholars who have been willing to dream.[33]

Social science research that identifies and articulates the mechanisms through which institutional inequality is maintained by the day-to-day consciousness of ordinary people has the potential to contribute to its dismantlement. We can best understand the everyday forms of whiteness as a response to a fundamental historical transformation that includes economic pressures, an extended period of conservative ideological onslaught, and increasingly limited opportunities for all peoples. Our hopes about the potential success of liberal reform have been diminished by the dramatic events of the last quarter of the twentieth century. The myth that upward mobility and the American Dream can be achieved by anyone who works hard is no longer espoused with the same vehemence and sense of truth as it was three decades ago. Instead, some communities have been criminalized and depicted as lazy, unworthy, the cause of "our" (and their own) troubles, and beyond the scope of our concerns. Many people accept this narrative, although it is clear they have many questions about it. They have been historically and are currently seduced to a position that accepts these depictions and that defends the status quo and the polarization of wealth. My research measured the effectiveness of this ideological campaign.

Reflecting on the meaning of the stories, statistics, and history revealed in this research, I ponder what our vision for humanity must be and suggest ways to utilize the venue of higher education to equip ourselves and our youth to function in today's world and to build a better tomorrow. We must listen, reflect, and develop intellectual strategies to foster the social awareness needed to challenge the history of inequality and injustice in our society. This project is dedicated to that end. The issue, once again, is agency—in the interest of humanity.

Ultimately, all we have is our desire for a better world and the strength of breath between us. If we believe in human goodness, we must fight for it, tapping every crack so that it may shatter the picture of a world that presumes some people as better and more worthy than others. All of us matter.

Afterword

The events of September 11, 2001, and after have exacerbated the global economic and political reconfigurations that were underway for the previous thirty years and described throughout this book. Writing the initial draft of the manuscript during this period heightened my sensitivity to the ways in which daily events provided further evidence of my central arguments. Here I reflect on the meaning of this project as it relates to the present time and some of the most apparent connections between my conclusions and this juncture in world history.

As has been discussed in this study, the notion of race is and has been historically crafted, manipulated, reinforced, reproduced, and rearticulated to justify the presumed superiority of white people and to distract attention from the social arrangement that concentrates power and wealth in a very small percentage of the world's population. The heightened instability of U.S. hegemony within the world capitalist system over the last two decades and the consequent vulnerability of western and white supremacy materially affect poor, working-, and middle-class people in concrete and everyday ways.

During times when ordinary people experience political and economic insecurity, ideology plays a critical role in shaping how they understand and interpret what they feel and where they place blame. Since the events of fall 2001, the structures of power have become more visible than they had been since the 1960s. Political leaders moved aggressively to dictate the terms of these interpretations, looking to justify the current social organization and their power within it. We have been told we are not at war with Islam, Muslims, Arabs, Afghanistan, or the Iraqi people, yet who is profiled, and who is bombed? Would the public reaction be the same if the suspects were British, French, or German?

Blatant war profiteering occurs in plain sight; Special Operations forces are deployed in seventy-five countries around the globe, up in number and budget from about sixty at the beginning of 2009.[1] Corporate bailouts and tax rebates now appear routine. "The 20 U.S. financial firms that have received the most bailout dollars from taxpayers awarded their top five executive officers, in the three years through 2008, pay packages worth a combined $3.2 billion. These 100 financial executives, on their way to driving the U.S. economy off a cliff, averaged $32 million each. One hundred U.S. workers making the 2008 annual average wage would have to labor over 1,000 years to make as much as these 100 executives made in three."[2] These actions are being taken simultaneous to the layoff of ever-increasing numbers of poor, working-, and middle-class people and to tripled foreclosure rates from 2006 to 2008[3]; roughly one in four households with children in the United States reported not having sufficient funds to purchase food in 2009.[4]

We live at a time when the government's primary constituency is corporate. Their interests are in direct contradiction to the interests of ordinary people in the US; ". . . increased profits are realized by showing the door to as many workers as possible, and squeezing the remainder to the bursting point. Productivity (based primarily on improvements in technology) is way up. Hiring, of course, is down. Part-time and temporary workers are in; full-time workers with benefits are out . . . " (Herbert 2003).

Despite the efforts to camouflage, disguise, and deny the implications of these events, the mainstream media have functioned to expose these contradictions, even if not willingly or deliberately. Many educators and activists struggle to bring to light the history of the United States' foreign and economic policies that form the backdrop for recent events. Such policies enabled, for example, continuous interventions in the affairs of sovereign nations over the last one hundred years, recent support for Islamic fundamentalists, and economic partnerships between the Bush and the bin Laden and Hussein families.[5]

Simultaneously, political and media leaders assert narratives about freedom and justice that cloak the economic self-interest of the most powerful in language such as "what is good for corporations, is good for us all" and "either you are with 'us' (the civilized and good), or with the 'terrorists' (the evil and barbaric)." They ostentatiously exclaim their own right to power in plain view. A McCarthy-era type of repression has emerged, attempting to conceal the facts and implications of these events and aiming to squelch dissent.[6]

The contradictions of this dominant worldview have been exposed, though not often explicitly articulated. As of October 2010, there have been 4,742 casualties in Iraq among U.S. and coalition forces and 2,116 in Afghanistan. This is more than twice the number of people who died on September 11, 2001,[7] and it appears that during that time more U.S. soldiers were killed by "friendly fire" than enemy fire.[8] At a memorial service for those who died at the World Trade Center, Rudolph Giuliani, heading one of the most racist New York City mayoral administrations in history, was seen singing "We Shall Overcome" with Oprah Winfrey at his side. The slogan, "United We Stand," reinforces mainstream narratives about our having achieved equality for all people, dismisses the systemic racialized structuring of our society and of the world-system (which, if anything, has been heightened by recent events), and stigmatizes and marginalizes voices that challenge patterns of inequality in the United States and throughout the world.

Plausible deniability, however, is an increasingly difficult argument to sustain in relation to racial inequality in particular and social inequality in general because racialized structures and their consequences are so visible. "Racial categories and racism are closely, if indirectly, related to political economic processes" (Robotham 1997) and therefore need to be understood in order to comprehend the global forces actively at work, today. "With the collapse of communism and the triumph of market relations, the grand categories of global competition have necessarily changed. What prevails in the new context is a sense of an international competition between nations and, implicitly, between 'races'" (Robotham 1997).

In Jane and Peter Schneider's study of the Mafia and anti-Mafia in Palermo, they assert that it is important to recognize that power and its tentacles are not monolithic, that "resistance movements are critical to weakening the terrorists' political shield and undermining their prestige and that . . . the world struggle against poverty and desperation is urgent" (Schneider 2001). The struggle against structural racism can also draw from these lessons. The increasing polarization of wealth witnessed during the last decades parallels intensified global impoverization. Resources are available to eradicate hunger, homelessness, and many illnesses running rampant throughout the globe. However, they are concentrated within a tiny percentage of the world's population and used to bolster and reinforce power relations rather than to serve the needs of the world's peoples. These realities need to come to the fore as their invisibility contributes to the reproduction of racialized patterns in a society that hides a brutal reality behind a shield of righteous ideals.

On Nationalism, Patriotism, and Human Nature

After 9/11, public debate about the meaning of patriotism surfaced. U.S. flags became increasingly visible and choosing to wear or fly one became a measure of one's loyalty. The meaning of being American was actively contested, and the reality of war loomed heavily in the hearts and minds of many people. Rigid notions of identity and the interpretation of history left little room for dialogue. The demand for us to "choose sides" between "good" and "evil" made it difficult to discuss alternative perspectives, as voicing dissent became grounds for suspicion, resulting in the silencing evident not only in the lives of ordinary people but also in the halls of Congress. The heroes portrayed in the media were overwhelmingly white firefighters and police officers. Raising the question of how this employment pattern came into existence and how it is perpetuated is deemed unacceptable, for it sheds light on the deeply stratified (apartheid-like) labor structure that is supposed to remain "hidden," as if we should pretend it does not exist.

Upon reflection on the meaning of this research, it becomes apparent that assumptions about national identity and its symbols are present even when not conscious or explicit. It is also clear that the dearth of open engagement in society about the meaning of concepts such as democracy, freedom, peace, and justice has real consequences because, during such periods, underlying and concealed presumptions determine what people do. Academia can and should play a more active role in developing social awareness and civic involvement by engaging society (in schools and communities) in dialogue about the kind of world we want to live in and how to make it happen. This project is inherently linked to people's sense of urgency about the need for a deeper understanding of global and local concerns as individuals, as a society, as a nation, and as members of the broadest all-encompassing community of humanity in the twenty-first century.

It is in this context that I responded to my daughter Sarafina when she said that prior to 9/11 she had really not thought about being proud to be American but the cooperation and generosity that was evident in the aftermath precipitated feelings of national pride within her. I asked whether these qualities might be "human" rather than solely "American" nature. Is it only "Americans" who can lay claim to generosity, democratic ideals, the striving for freedom, and the passion for equality? I suggest that hope ultimately resides in our ability to conceive of ourselves as members of a global society, rather than as "Americans"—all the while taking responsibility for the actions taken in our name, and with our taxes. I hold that this is similar to considering oneself as part of the human community, positioned and allied with the world's majority, yet recognizing the social realities of racism. Therein lie the particular responsibilities of whites who benefit from the presumption of white superiority.

As J. Krishnamurti, philosopher and educator, said to an American woman who had lost one son to war and wanted to know how to save her other one:

She had to cease to be an American; she had to cease to be greedy, cease piling up wealth, seeking power, domination and be morally simple—not merely simple in clothes, in outward things, but simple in her thoughts and feelings, in her relationships. She said, "That is too much. You are asking far too much, I cannot do it, because circumstances are too powerful for me to alter." Therefore, she was responsible for the destruction of her son. . . . So it depends upon you and not on the leaders—not on so-called statesmen and all the rest of them. It depends upon you and me, but we do not seem to realize that. If once we really felt the responsibility of our own actions, how quickly we could bring to an end all these wars, this appalling misery! (Krishnamurti 1975, 182)

Martin Luther King Jr. in his 1967 speech said war is a nightmare "for the victims of our nation and for those it calls the enemy." Speaking out against war was the "privilege and the burden of all of us who deem ourselves bound by allegiances and loyalties which are broader and deeper than nationalism, and which go beyond our nation's self-defined goals and positions" (Cohen 1996, vii–viii).

The nationalism of those in positions of dominance, like patriotism and whiteness, is a fabrication with real social consequence constructed solely to bestow value upon its owners. It is, as the "Race Traitors" describe whiteness, like royalty—an identity propped up to render some people more worthy and righteous than others (Ignatiev and Garvey 1996).

Now more than ever, the need to engage, to discuss, to understand different perspectives, is evident and pressing. Academia can foster these dialogues both within university settings and as part of a broader community. This is an ideal opportunity to allow knowledge to be applied to everyday living, and the knowledge of everyday living to be theorized. We have the responsibility to engage the public about the ideals of democracy, freedom, and justice, especially in relationship to the values that drive modern society and in the corresponding civic engagement that follows from valuing the common good.

On Chickens Roosting, Wizards Oz-ing, and Sharks Biting [9]

Shortly after 9/11 and along with calls for patriotism and unquestioning loyalty, the assertion was made that, to quote Malcolm X's famous statement, "It was a case of chickens coming home to roost"[10] (Haley and Malcolm X 1965, 301) was to disrespect the innocent people who died.[11] I didn't understand this and wondered, Is it not actually the reverse? Isn't understanding what led to these events showing respect to those innocent people who died? Is it not our moral imperative to investigate the structural factors that contribute to tragedy, so we might know how to prevent the further loss of innocent life? Is it not through questioning that we might come upon ways to address or even solve a problem as urgent as world peace?

The pressure against talking about "chickens roosting" bothered me until I awoke one night, mid-December 2001. Then the relationship between this concept and the processes I had just written about as reproducing and reinforcing patterns of racial inequality suddenly dawned upon me. Being told not to interrogate root causes of the tragedies of September 11 and to believe that bin Laden (or Saddam Hussein) the individual is to blame is the same kind of thinking that discourages us from understanding the true causes of poverty, injustice, and all forms of inequality. We are made to understand that either racism no longer exists, we have reached true equality (people "get along" in public, so stop whining), and causes for poverty and privilege are elusive and mysterious, or the reason equality does not exist is that some people are just plain lazy. The stigma against understanding causality in fact undermines and defuses agency and disallows any capacity we have to change disastrous and brutal patterns of inequality.

Ultimately, many whites seem to feel that it does not matter whether we have achieved equality, because whatever is just is. Explanations for what happened on 9/11 were similarly fragmented and projected responsibility everywhere but home. Why do these people hate us? "Freedom itself is under attack," President Bush announced. Our antagonists, he went on, "hate our freedoms, our freedom of religion, our freedom of speech, our freedom to assemble and disagree with each other." But as Eric Foner articulates,

"Freedom is the trump card of political discourse, invoked as often to silence debate as to invigorate it. . . . Calling our past a history of freedom for everybody makes it impossible to discuss seriously the numerous instances when groups of Americans have been denied freedom, or the ways in which some Americans today enjoy a great deal more freedom than others" (2003). We are told not to criticize or to look at history—that's mixing apples and oranges. "Osama bin Laden and Islamic fundamentalism are the problem." The United States represents goodness, generosity, democracy, superiority and freedom, so "they" (whoever "they" are) must personify evil.[12]

This dynamic functions with racism, too. One is a racist or not a racist. If not, then one must reconcile what one sees (racialized poverty) with what one thinks (everyone is equal; racial "problems" are a thing of the past), and since it is irreconcilable, the awareness is overwhelming. "Anyway, then, just forget it. I'll just mind my own business."

The link between everyday thinking and the formation and implementation of policy and the real consequences that impact the lives of all people cannot, however, be ignored. It is not about whether one is nice, or who one's friends are; it is about the structures and patterns of inequality and injustice that persist, both within the United States and on a global scale. As long as the gaze is focused on the personal and as long as the measure of racism is whether or not another person of color is brutalized in a highly publicized incident, we are prevented from structural analyses that may provide us with the power to do something about the conditions of daily living around the globe, including right here in the United States.

Thus, the tension between agency and structure is evident, for the same discourse that disallows discussions of "chickens roosting" also disallows discussion about the forces underlying inequality along all axes of power. Prohibiting inquiry both defuses and diffuses agency and makes it difficult for everyday people to reckon with their own power. It is the very same discourse that tells people that nothing can be done, that it is too confusing, that it is not their fault and really not a problem, anyway.

It appears that attention must be paid to diverting us from an analysis of "chickens roosting"—to the suppression of inquiry. Suppression of inquiry emanates from the same dynamic that allows for the perpetuation of structural racial inequality and blocks a critique of how everyday thinking permits the structural forces and patterns to be reproduced and reinforced. "'The chickens came home to roost' are dangerous words because they make connections that are necessary to transform power relations in a deeply inegalitarian world."[13] If we foster awareness and openness about white adherence to mainstream discourse about race and demonstrate the mechanisms of power that obfuscate structural inequality (utilizing race as one of many tools), we have the potential to dismantle those mechanisms for the betterment of all.

At a time of tremendous change and uncertainty, it is especially urgent that alternative frameworks for understanding both global and local events, grounded in concern for the greater good, are available to the public, to counter those that reinforce structures of dominance and to link those frameworks to action. It is important to recognize that the everyday thinking of whites can function either to support or to challenge patterns of inequality. The current vulnerability of most poor, working-, and middle-class white people provides an opportunity to educate and raise consciousness about the structural and systemic forces that pattern inequality of all sorts and racial inequality in particular. Individuals concerned with the future of our society have a chance to make a difference by providing alternative ways to interpret the political, economic, and social events that are shaping people's lives today and to bring to light the many ways that everyday forms and extraordinary forms of challenge can be successful.[14]

Let's do it.

Epilogue: How Things Change as They Remain the Same[1]

What has changed in the decade since the original research was conducted for this book? No doubt, many people (particularly those under thirty) see the world differently, and they also see a different world. There is more intergroup familiarity, greater visibility of persons of color in the public sphere (whether representative or not), an overall greater sense of vulnerability, and concerns about the future. During the election of 2008, "race" became ubiquitous in popular discourse leading to increased comfort with talking about the subject matter though not significant cross-experience dialogue. Capitalist ideology remains entrenched though there is a greater openness to questioning how we explain events such as the British Petroleum oil spill of 2010, the banking collapse, endless wars, loss of jobs and high levels of unemployment among youth, the pervasiveness of enormous student debt, and/or why communities of color disproportionately face foreclosure.

These questions are not easily answered without discussion of a political and economic system that prioritizes the accumulation of capital and quest for profits (by those with power) over protection of and regard for human life. Exploring these questions within this framework can reveal alternative explanations for inequality and ultimately to alternative solutions; however, the path forward is uncertain.

Most people are confused as dominant explanations for why poverty and racial inequality exist don't provide an adequate understanding of the current situation. They feel uneasy and insecure about their future and less sure about how to interpret the concentration of poverty among communities of color in the United States and nations globally or wealth among whites. In the absence of an explanation that makes sense, most rely on standard narratives about social mobility, personal wealth, and cultural stereotypes. Most people are less confident that Horatio Alger would get rich today, and that things do always get better and better. Many feel that it altogether possible that circumstances will become increasingly more difficult in the twenty-first century. While young whites feel increasingly insecure about their futures, high levels of continuing segregation (along racial and class lines) mean that most have little close interaction or exposure to experiences different than their own so they are unaware of the privileges they do have. Media images are taken as truths, despite their distortions, exclusions and misrepresentations.

What remains the same or is worse than in 2000 are the embedded structural realities of the racial order. This is often not evident, particularly to whites who have less personal exposure to the ways that racial discrimination operates both institutionally and interpersonally, and often without the language of race. While the greater visibility of race can provide openings for honest conversation, it has led to a more casual approach and the sense that everyone is an expert. Personal experience has become the measure of whether we are "post-racial," not facts, structural realities, historical patterns, etc. Personal cross-experience interactions and increased visibility of persons of color (including President Obama) provide a veneer that implies inequality is a thing of the past, so needs no assertive action. Individual incidences of offensive language and bias crimes are used as a proxy for dealing with "race" rather than the pervasive policies and practices that discriminate with racially devastating consequences.

Everyone's racial experience is leveled so that systemic hierarchies or institutional and historical patterns that differentiate that of whites from communities of African but also Latino, Asian, and Native Americans are rarely examined. Unquestioning belief in common misperceptions and racialized images provide a rationale for unequal and unjust patterns. Whites' misperceptions about the material existence and consequences of racial patterns have long been documented. As has been argued in this book, these mistaken beliefs serve to protect white privilege. In 2010, these misperceptions however appear also to increasingly shape the thinking of many Blacks, with a greater presence of conservatism (Bobo and Charles 2009, 246–47). These misperceptions are propagated and perpetrated by the media that has a stranglehold in defining which issues people have access to, what information they have about those issues and possible interpretations.[2] So a key challenge is figuring out ways to disseminate complete and accurate information and how to address the broader narratives about society that frame how these realities are received. Circulating facts about the persistence of discrimination in housing, education, policing, hiring, etc., must challenge discourse that conveys we are increasingly less racialized and more equal. Why should someone believe one narrative over another if their life experience does not provide validation? White privilege functions as a disincentive for people of European descent to question the mainstream discourse, as long as they receive the benefits of that privilege. However, in a system in crisis, those material "perks" are being whittled away. What prevents not only a realistic assessment of the current conditions but also a change of mind as to their cause and solution and a readiness to transform the structures of society? Which factors support that kind of tidal change, which stand in the way?

Having a Black president has reinforced the idea that anything is possible with hard work and has generated a "no excuses" narrative that denies institutional and structural realities. The economic crisis has heightened awareness that the formula for success is not entirely viable, that capitalism has weaknesses. However, the overwhelming corporate control of media (and for that matter the functioning of government and the educational system) stifles engagement of the broader context such as the function of racism in supporting the increasing concentration of wealth at the top. Racial stereotypes and assumptions provide useful rationales for why people are poor—predominantly explained in personal and/or cultural terms.

In other ways the presence of persons of color in high profile positions, particularly President Obama, reinforces the notion that there are now no boundaries to upward mobility. This makes challenging institutional patterns more difficult. The idea that poverty is a result of personal and cultural weakness further reinforces group stereotypes even as nearly all working, middle class, and poor people in the United States are in more dire straits, since communities of color disproportionately experience increased unemployment, foreclosures, etc. But this process did not begin then, nor will it end a decade from now. The question is what the future holds. Whose interests will prevail in this next era and ultimately in this next stage of human history?

While initially after the 2008 election there was greater optimism about the potential for progress, economic and political actions taken in the past year have reversed some of feeling that racism is a problem of the past. Visibility and representation do matter, but they are only factors that can contribute to challenging deeply embedded racialization within the structures and institutions of national and global society. They offer opportunities to raise awareness and build a movement that can push for broad social transformation.

While youth particularly evidence awareness of inequalities and interest in change, surveys also reveal that many continue to feel that race is taken much too seriously and that communities of color need to stop being so sensitive in everyday interactions. The assumption is that the problem with race is people perceiving it still matters when it does not so much anymore. Discussions of race continue to focus on interpersonal attitudes and rarely engage issues about structure as if we could all just get along things would be fine. If in fact, greater visibility translates to more and kinder interactions in public spaces, that does make a difference. Perhaps whites are more willing to see Black people as individuals—the body has emerged from behind the glove. This may translate to a feeling that race relations have improved.

Having high profile counter-images to the stereotypes of African Americans provides alternatives to the negative cultural portraits. However, most conversations revolve around race "relations," not equality or justice. Materially, vast racial inequality remains along almost all measures such as income, wealth, educational attainment, health care access, mortality, etc. In fact, in many cases these have been exacerbated in the last decade such that gaps in income, wealth, employment rates, access to health care, adequate food, and educational options have increased along with the downward economic push on nearly all in the United States. Ideologically, little inroads have been made in attacking the underlying presumptions of Euro-dominance and superiority. This applies in the United States and globally. Civilian casualties in Iraq and Afghanistan for example receive little notice; a Nigerian planning to blow up a plane becomes generalized as Nigerians whereas a British citizen doing the same does not bring upon suspicion of all those British.[3]

The global and national economies are in crisis. At times like this, those most vulnerable suffer the most but all are affected. Whether heightened vulnerability translates into system-wide challenge to racial inequities, injustices, and forms of domination that affect the great majority of the human population is yet to be seen. Evidence of possibility demonstrates that change can happen and altering how people feel can make a difference. However, in the big picture race is embedded within all sorts of institutions that are not easily transformed or even moderately changed. There is much work to be done for that type of change to occur.

Implications

For the system to sustain itself, "cracks" must be plugged or they will create ruptures. The media and educational curriculum are two important venues for dissemination of alternative explanations for social occurrences. These have always been sites of contestation, and at a time of heightened crisis, they are increasingly so. It has therefore been critical for those in power to work to maintain their stranglehold on our access to information. Whether it be the lack of coverage of push backs against the system such as the student strike at the University of Puerto Rico, the passage of the Domestic Workers Union Bill of Rights, or the Republic Windows workers' strike, many people are fighting back. More people are hurting yet there are also greater possibilities for mobilization. The creation of the Detroit City of Hope is another example, and there are many in Latin and South America, throughout Africa and Asia. The U.S. Social Forum that took place in June 2010 in Detroit provided an opportunity for communities to come together in efforts to address the vast inequalities that have been exacerbated over the last thirty years. Between 15,000 and 20,000 people attended, from over 1,000 organizations. Fifty "action plans" were developed on topics such as food justice, addressing poverty and gender rights. Most people in the United States are kept unaware of these struggles and achievements, for if they knew, perhaps resistance would spread.

It is for this reason that educational curriculum has been particularly contested. Who gets to tell the story of history? While this has always been a critical site for the imposition of a worldview framed by white supremacy, at a time when political, economic, and social realities are shifting, there is a contest to define what those changes mean. In whose interest will the story be told? Melissa Harris-Lacewell reminds us of the song from South Pacific, Rodgers and Hammerstein's controversial 1949 musical: "You've got to be taught to hate and fear, You've got to be taught from year to year. It's got to be drummed in your dear little ear—You've got to be carefully taught."[4]

CONCLUSION

Plus ca change, plus c'est la même chose. While there is evidence of increased awareness of race as a "social construct," most of the attitudes and views about its impact as a lived reality are moderated by numerous factors—most of which mirror the "mechanisms" I identified in chapter 6. Revisiting questions related to everyday thinking about race has been challenging at a time when everyone seems to be talking about it. It might appear that would make the task easier. However, it has been challenging because on the surface, everybody's talking about race, post-race, and weighing in on just how far we've come since the civil rights movement and the *Brown versus Board of Education* decision. Yet while changes in interpersonal relations have shifted somewhat, few can deny the continuing structural realities of racialized inequalities along nearly every indicator of social and economic well-being.[5]

There remain several obstacles to a plan for redress: Few have access to data about the living conditions of the people in United States that are patterned by race. They are greatly influenced by images and messages that convey that we have achieved equality, that all is possible with adequate motivation, that poverty is a personal problem and inequality is inevitable. As

William Bennett articulated when the vote for Obama was announced, "Well, I'll tell you one thing it means, as a former Secretary of Education: You don't take any excuses anymore from anybody who says, 'The deck is stacked, I can't do anything, there's so much in-built this and that.'"[6]

This conclusion was reached not only by this individual known for his conservative beliefs, but expressed by those such as a reporter for the African American student newspaper of North Carolina State University, in a column titled "The First Black President: No More Excuses. In reaction to the election of Barack Obama" (Reed and Louis. 2009, 97–98). She wrote:

> For so long we've used the excuse of being inherently behind because of slavery and the oppression of so many years, but Tuesday marked the end of many of the excuses, and its name is Barack Hussein Obama. Black men can no longer use the excuse that their name is Tyshawn Deon Jackson. So what! A man named Barack Hussein Obama was elected president of the United States of America. No longer can we let our situations dictate the rest of our lives.[7]

Coinciding with a barrage of messages about individual responsibility and personal liability has been the discourse about the threat of socialism, rising taxes, and government control. Whether bailing out the banks or working on health care reform, the interests of the very wealthy are presumed. This does not help the project of reducing racial inequality, nor does it improve race relations that require real and deep conversation and action about economics and capitalism, nor how race developed and is used to implement, justify, and camouflage inequality through notions of biology, culture and practices.

Conversations about whiteness and white supremacy that do not also engage discussion of the particular context within which they arose in the world capitalist system leave analysis and its implications in the realm of the personal. Heightened awareness of the continuing legacies and everyday implications of this history matters and can have significant impact on interactions between people and policies that have consequences from offense to death. If discussions are only about individual privilege, blindness, or actions, the larger more intransigent structural inequalities remain out of sight, unchallenged and unchanged.

So this is what is same and different. There is certainly a higher degree of awareness of the need to respect diversity, and perhaps greater levels of exposure or comfort in "talking about race"; however, we are still left with images of *Precious*, the reality that Black and Latino communities are hardest and most disproportionately affected in this economic crisis. If we are not even allowed to entertain conversation about a more flat distribution of wealth, because that discussion becomes identified with the defense of communism or socialism rather than a critique of an economic system that has so polarized wealth, then we can never really deal with racism, either interpersonal or institutional. It is always about defense of the system, defense of capitalism, defense of meritocracy, and never about defense of humanity, fairness, or justice.

It's time to have the conversation about economics and about a vision for a fair, just, and loving world. Ricardo Levins Morales, artist and author, suggests core values that could center a new society, including that no one gets seconds until everyone has had a first, and that the Earth is a home shared by everyone who lives here.[8] What do the exorbitantly paid corporate executives contribute to the common good? Why do we ask where the money will come from to provide health care but not where it will come to add billions to the military budget to send 30,000 more troops to Afghanistan? Until we make the connection that racism (ideologically and materially) was created and fostered to bolster an economic system centered on empowering and emboldening the most powerful, we will never understand the power that we have to make sure that the basic needs for all people are met. All people. It is time to reckon with the system and its ideologies. Otherwise it's just about individuals whose lot in life was not chosen. What we do with the position we find ourselves in personally or collectively makes all the difference.

So much has changed: more comfort in discussing race, greater exposure among young people to persons of different races, music, greater numbers of friendship, and greater awareness of structural factors leading to inequality. So much has not changed or even worsened: entrenchment of disparities— economic, political, prison incarceration, health care access, educational access. Those of us concerned about racism and racial inequality must use what has changed to leverage what hasn't, both in raising awareness and working toward changing policies, and programs that sustain racial patterns. If we only focus on structure, we miss ways that people understand and how that affects what they do.

Finally, any discussion that asserts "it's x not y" will be unsatisfying and incomplete. This applies to suggestions that one's positionality is determined only by class, only by race, only by gender, religion, sexuality, etc. In addition, Patricia Hill Collins, Kimberle Crenshaw, and Rose Brewer and others (particularly critical race theorists) have eloquently articulated the need to recognize intersectionality and guard against "oppositional, dichotomous" type thinking. That said, if we look historically and understand the emergence of the current world system that is based on white supremacy, then we need to recognize the particular role that race/racism/racialization has played for all people. It's embedded in the system.

Still further, since the mass uprisings both nationally and globally of the 1960s (sometimes referred to as the Second Reconstruction) the discourse has shifted to one that does not necessarily need explicit mention of racialized terms yet the political implications, especially given historically established patterns of structural discrimination, can reproduce and in fact expand. However, just as we no longer need the words of race to know we are talking about race, we also no longer need the rigid separation of who stands for policies that either support the racist status quo or challenges it. Hence we have Gonzales, Thomas, Rice, Connerly, etc. We cannot oversimplify the fact that "whiteness" is both real and made up so it really depends on whether you are buying into the privilege, assumed status, presumptions, etc.

If we are to overcome the very entrenched patterns that structure and organize society, we need to recognize the complexity of these relationships and how they simultaneously operate in very destructive ways yet are based on lies and fabrications that turn "wallets into guns," people without food into "lazy beggars," people including children who die from bombs, bullets, and lack of water into collateral damage, and a millionaire into "a regular and compassionate" guy." We recognize that privileging is a social dynamic, but we each have the choice to defend it or battle the system that sets up those relationships. It means very actively and nondefensively taking up the fight against racism, particularly since whites have been so led to believe that our experience is the norm—and it just isn't—regardless of our gender, religion, sexual preference, class, etc.

"The point is not so much public gaffes as it is the creation, support, and maintenance of systemic and structural inequalities."[9] While interpersonal interaction may indeed be more frequent, and persons of color more visible in positions of power, the structural realities of race are not only mostly unchanged, in some cases they have materially worsened. In addition, the appearance that race is a thing of the past makes challenging racism that much more difficult. Race is an embedded and central part of our social structure. Defeating the ideology and structure that capitalism has fostered must therefore include an assault on Euro-dominance at all levels, just as we must do as we fight for gender justice, etc. White supremacy is part of the strategy and tactics of the capitalist system, so combating it must be part of the strategy and tactics of the counter-system and the creation of a world anew. At the same time, efforts toward a better world need to be strategic, not dogmatic. We need a movement that is centered on coalition, collaboration, capacity building, creativity, and community. This is essential because we are talking about the structure and ideology, not just about the individuals who uphold them. Community and grassroots effort are the force that can make the changes for the better.

Young people today do see and experience the world differently than those a decade ago, in some ways that support the struggle to overcome white supremacy, in other ways that make that process more difficult. The assault on their minds and understanding of the world has been amplified by an educational system focused on testing and rote learning; service not activism; extraordinary debt on the level of higher education; a media that defines the terms of individual and group experience; and an overall play on fear—of immigrants—of terrorists—of socialism, etc.

The struggle is transnational such that any analysis of race must be linked to critiques of nation, empire, capitalism, gender, sexuality, labor, etc. Secondly, efforts to challenging whiteness must be connected to building community, viability, vision, and humanity. We need vehicles to disseminate real data and break the media blockade. The Applied Research Center "public service announcements" could be used as a model.

Things have changed, and they have not. More young people are asking questions about the racial order and what they can do. Shalom, who participated in the original research, describes his own transformation over the decade to a time when he is startled by the lack of awareness evident in the group of wealthy, white, upper east side high school students he took to New Orleans in 2008. He said, "It is easier to accept that poverty exists in a far-off country in the global south that you've never been to." But even more startled was he when he asked the white hotel manager if Bourbon Street was always so crazy. "He said yes, but the real reason New Orleans was still in dire straits was the lazy Black people who lie around all day drunk and steal from white people, some of whom are stupid enough to help them." Shalom also speaks of a young woman asking for subway directions at Penn Station. She asked whether it was safe, and said she was from Atlanta where they have a subway called MARTA. "Then she smiled and said that it stands for 'Moving Africans Rapidly Through Atlanta' because white people don't take the subway because it is not safe. Again, I was shocked at this stranger's comfort with being racist and making a racist remark to me as if I am in on the joke. Perhaps if I were a better person or stronger, I would have spoken up in both instances." Why are the narratives so convincing, what do they promise? Why is there so much trepidation to challenge these assumptions?

Let's take the lead from Valerie (Hispanic female) who says, "I wish I could somehow auto-correct all my failures and imperfections in regards to my mindset toward race and ethnicity, but I can't, so I'll just strive to fix myself and correct myself as I go along."

Notes

PREFACE

1. In 1984 Eleanor Bumpurs was a sixty-seven-year-old woman who was shot dead by the police when she refused to be evicted from her apartment in the Bronx. Michael Griffith, twenty-three, was beaten by a group of white men in Howard Beach and then chased onto the parkway, where he was hit by a car, in 1986. And sixteen-year-old Yusuf Hawkins was beaten and killed in 1989 by a group of about thirty white youths in Bensonhurst where he was shopping for a used car.

2. This refers to the shooting by police of Amadou Diallo in the vestibule of his apartment building in 1999.

3. Arundhati Roy, "Confronting Empire." Porto Alegre, Brazil, January 27, 2003.

ACKNOWLEDGMENTS

1. As quoted in Rodriguez (1991, xxii).

CHAPTER 1

1. The notion of the Civil Rights Movement and the period of the sixties as a Second Reconstruction has been widely discussed (Marable 1991). The centrality of opposition to white supremacy in the struggles of the sixties is well articulated in Dohrn (2001).

2. Commonly termed "white backlash," this is described as the trepidation many whites have about policies and programs that they feel are too concerned with the plight of minorities. Craig Wilder cites an early example as noted in the *New York*

Times in 1965, with the formation of the group calling themselves "SPONGE: The Society for the Prevention of Negroes' Getting Everything" (Wilder 2000, 242). This topic has been extensively explored in works such as Fine et al. (1997), Frankenberg (1997), and Kincheloe et al. (1998).

3. Grasz, Jennifer (2009). "Six-in-Ten Workers Live Paycheck to Paycheck," *Career Builder*, www.careerbuilder.com/share/aboutus/pressreleasesdetail.aspx?id=pr525&sd=9%2f16%2f2009&ed=12%2f31%2f2009&siteid=cbpr&sc_cmp1=cb_pr525_&cbRecursionCnt=4&cbsid=4c07f5ee24fa4e4c8098f244c389a3ee-330690148-wy-6.

4. The Joint Center for Housing Studies of Harvard University "The State of the Nation's Housing." www.jchs.harvard.edu/publications/markets/son2010/son2010.pdf. Accessed June 15, 2010. 1–2.

5. See page 42 for the definitions of "ordinary" and "everyday" used in this book.

6. *Washington Post*-ABC News Poll. January 13–16, 2009. www.washingtonpost.com/wp-srv/politics/documents/postpoll011709.html. Accessed 21 December 2009.

7. A recent example of this is the case of white firefighters in Connecticut who protested that they had been unfairly denied promotion because of their race.

8. MSNBC, "Income Gap between Black, White Families Grows," *Associated Press*, November 12, 2007. www.msnbc.msn.com/id/21759075/ns/business-stocks_and_economy/. Accessed December 21, 2009.

9. For an excellent discussion of the shift toward conservatism in the 1970s, see Edsall and Edsall (1991b).

10. This comment refers to an incident in which four New York City Police officers fired forty-one bullets into Amadou Diallo on 4 February 1999. They claimed that they thought he had a gun. When the case went to trial, it was ruled that their fear justified their actions and the officers were let off. This claim has often been made in incidents in which police officers have murdered unarmed individuals because of the stereotypes, particularly of young black and Latino males, as violent.

11. Jane Schneider and Rayna Rapp point out a traditional approach to anthropology: "Much of anthropology asks whether locally situated, powerless peoples— classical anthropological subjects—can exercise agency in relation to the 'structures' that would dominate them." They describe Eric Wolf's starting point as "an open-ended, unpredictable, interaction sphere, whose very fluidity among competing and often contradictory forces enlarges those possibilities for empowerment from below" (Schneider and Rapp 1995, 5). I attempt to merge these two approaches.

12. Lawrence Mishel and Heidi Shierholz state that 6.9 million jobs have been lost in this recession and 3.4 million children have lost health insurance in the Labor Day Report 2009 (Economic Policy Institute). Also see DeGraw (2010a).

13. Charles Gallagher, in a discussion of research he conducted, says, "It becomes difficult for working-class college students to think about white privilege when they are accumulating college debt, forced to live with their parents, working 25 hours a week, and concerned that K-Mart or the Gap may become their future employer" (1995, 176).

14. Howard Zinn thoroughly describes dominant "American ideology" and the way our choice of ideas is limited (1990, 1–9).

15. Steve London, "An Opportunity to Change Course" (testimony, CUNY Budget Request, New York, November 20, 2006) www.psc-cuny.org/PDF/PSCcuny-BOTbudgetTestimonyNov06.pdf.

16. Income, Earnings, and Poverty Data From the 2007 American Community Survey Table 1. Median Household Income in the Past 12 Months by Race and Hispanic Origin: 2007 www.census.gov/prod/2008pubs/acs-09.pdf. Accessed April 10, 2010.

17. Christopher provides an analysis of class dimensions and implications of the structure of the California State University system (2003, 40).

18. National Center for Education Statistics, *The Condition of Education*, NCES 2003-067 (U.S. Department of Education, 2003), table 18-1 as cited in Haveman and Smeeding 2006, 126.

19. *Greta Christina* argues that while liberal vs. conservative views are generally deemed as two interpretations, in fact the liberal perspective represents universalism, and conservatism represents the protection of privilege and should be explained in terms of those values. "Why Being Liberal Really Is Better Than Being Conservative." Alternet. www.alternet.org/authors/8504/. Accessed June 10, 2010.

20. These include, but are not limited to: Mazie et al. (1993, 281–94); Hartigan (1997, 8); Page (1998, 58, 60); Rodriguez (1999, 20); Karenga (1999, 26); McMillen (1995, 26); Page (1995, 526–28); Giroux (1997, 222); *Hungry Mind Review*: The *National Book Magazine* (1998); Stowe (1996, 69–77); Hill (1996); Talbot (1997, 116); Conley (2000b, 45); Soyinka (1997).

21. The Fourteenth Amendment "enshrined in the Constitution the ideas of birthright citizenship and equal rights for all Americans" (Foner 1998, 105).

22. During the last decade of the twentieth century, 7.6 million people immigrated to the United States: from Europe, 17.4 percent; from Asia, 38.9 percent; from North America, 33.4 percent; from South America, 6.6 percent, from Africa, 4.0 percent; and from Oceania, 0.7 percent (Kraly and Miyares 2001, 49).

23. W. E. B. Du Bois originally came up with the idea for this comprehensive study of race relations; however, his proposal was turned down by the General Education Board (GEB). Subsequently the GEB-connected Carnegie Corporation decided to fund Myrdal and not Du Bois with the implicit explanation that, despite his expertise, Du Bois was too involved with the subject (Donate et al. 2002, 227).

24. Gil Scott-Heron describes this period, "Civil rights, women's rights, gay rights; it's all wrong. Call in the cavalry to disrupt this perception of freedom gone wild. First one wants freedom, then the whole damn world wants freedom" (Scott-Heron 1992). I owe thanks to Roderick D. Bush, professor of sociology, St. John's University, for a clarifying discussion on this topic, 5 January 2002.

25. Amy Fisher was the teenager whose affair with a married man was widely publicized in the media after she shot his wife in the face (Kenny 2000, 11).

26. Brooklyn College, "Fast Facts," www.brooklyn.cuny.edu/pub/about_fast_facts.htm.

27. Handout distributed by the Office of the Borough President Howard Golden, "Fascinating Facts about Brooklyn," compiled by Borough Historian John Manbeck.

28. Borough President Marty Markowitz has launched a website exemplifying this image, www.brooklyn-usa.org.

29. U.S. Census Bureau, "Census 2000 Demographic Profile Highlights," *American Fact Finder*, http://factfinder.census.gov/servlet/SAFFFacts?_event=Search&geo_id=86000US11207&_geoContext=01000US|86000US11207&_street=&_county=&_cityTown=&_state=&_zip=11212&_lang=en&_sse=on&ActiveGeoDiv=geoSelect&_useEV=&pctxt=fph&pgsl=860&_submenuId=factsheet_1&ds_name=DEC_2000_SAFF&_ci_nbr=null&qr_name=null&reg=null%3Anull&_keyword=&_industry=.

30. Images of Brooklyn abound; for instance, the comic series "Boondocks" includes routine references. Recently, Caesar writes his own version of the song "My Favorite Things" calling it "Things that's Aiight." When Huey asks how he manages to sound cool yet a little disinterested, Caesar says, "Hey, I'm from Brooklyn" (McGruder 2001).

31. Dr. Arthur Bankoff, chairperson of the Brooklyn College anthropology department, along with two students, brought international attention to the 282-year-old Lott House in Marine Park, Brooklyn. They discovered a hidden room and items beneath the floorboards, which are considered evidence of slave quarters (Brooklyn College 2001).

32. For example, in the late 1970s, Brooklyn College had approximately sixty black faculty members; by the mid-1990s there were thirty-three (BC OIR 1994–5, 63). Figures for the 1970s are drawn from a personal conversation with Professor George Cunningham of the Africana Studies department, as historical data is difficult to retrieve. The college has information dating back to 1995; the university has information dating back to 1985.

33. Interview with Professor Tucker Farley, English department, Brooklyn College, 15 December 1999.

34. Interview with Dr. William Sherzer, department of modern languages, Brooklyn College, 6 June 2000.

35. Interview with Dr. Paul Montagna, department of sociology, Brooklyn College, 15 September 2000.

36. "The New York State public school system is starkly segregated, with nearly 30 percent of its approximately four thousand schools having student bodies in which 80 percent or more of the children are African American, Latino, or otherwise non-white, while almost half of the state's other schools have student bodies that are 80 percent or more white" (Dunn 1999, 19).

37. I draw this concept from James Scott's illuminating discussion of "everyday forms of peasant resistance" (1985, xvi).

38. Rose M. Brewer discusses the need for critiquing oppositional thinking, eschewing additive analyses, and recognizing simultaneity, historicity, embeddedness, relationality, and contextualization in James and Busia (1993, 16).

CHAPTER 2

1. For a discussion of the theory of the "culture of poverty," see chapter 1. For a clear description of the individualist framework for understanding social problems see Johnson (2008).

2. See McIntosh (1998).

3. For an overview of this history, see *ColorLines Special Edition–War on Terrorism: Profiled & Punished*. Applied Research Center. December 2001.

4. This comment refers to the benefit concerts held for the families of people who died on September 11, 2001. *The Onion* is a magazine known for political satire (2001).

5. Iraq Body Count www.iraqbodycount.org/. Accessed December 10, 2009.

6. Mr. Sherwood Johnson, director of the Brooklyn College Financial Aid Office, stated: "Need-based state and federal aid is based strictly on economic need. Race is not a factor. In analyzing the allocation of merit-based scholarships, including those designated for minorities, a disproportionate number of the total are awarded to white versus minority students based on the proportion of whites versus minorities in the overall student population." A preliminary report from the Brooklyn College Scholarship Office on funds administered through their office during the year 2000 indicates that 54 percent were given to white students. Personal communication, 27 November 2001.

7. The *Journal of Blacks in Higher Education* states, "Blacks and other minorities are now attending college at nearly the same rate as whites yet only 4 percent of the nation's scholarship money is earmarked for Blacks and other minorities." Furthermore, "Young Blacks are far more likely than young whites to come from families with low incomes. Census figures show that Black families are three times as likely to be poor as white families. The wealth gap between Blacks and whites remains greater than 7 to 1. New statistics demonstrate that financial problems are primarily responsible for keeping low-income Black students from entering and completing college. Poor Blacks are far more likely than poor whites to have no access to outside connections, friendships, or other sources of money to help them pay for college. Contrary to popular opinion, scholarships for Blacks claim a tiny pool of aid monies" (*Journal of Blacks in Higher Education* 2001a, 11).

8. For an excellent discussion of this, see Hill Collins (2004, 529–43).

9. Total loss from street robbery in the United States in 1989 was $405 million, but a single price-fixing conspiracy by oil companies cost the nation's consumers $432 million; 3.2 million burglaries accounted for a $3.4 billion loss, yet the Savings and Loan scandal cost the nation from $300 to $500 billion" (Delgado 2001).

10. For an excellent discussion of the impact of race on middle- and upper-class Blacks, see Cose (1993).

11. The New Abolitionists believe that "the white race is a historically constructed social formation. It consists of all those who partake of the privileges of the white skin in this society. Its most wretched members share a status higher in certain respects than that of the most exalted persons excluded from it, in return for which they give their support to a system that degrades them" (Ignatiev and Garvey 1996).

12. Personal conversation on 10 February 2000, Brooklyn College, New York.

13. Leonard Steinhorn and Barbara Diggs Brown describe "Wiggahs" as wannabes, white kids, often from the suburbs, who dress, talk, and act "inner-city," and cite Michiko Kakutani, who labels them "cultural tourists." They equate Wiggahs with Beatniks in the 1950s and Yippies in the 1960s, articulating a perspective quite different from that of Salim Muwakill (Steinhorn and Diggs-Brown 1999, 176).

14. Office of Justice Programs, "Homicide Trends in the U.S.," Bureau of Justice Statistics, http://bjs.ojp.usdoj.gov/content/homicide/race.cfm. Accessed January 6, 2010.

15. As of November 2008 this figure changes to 97.7 percent of U.S. Presidents. Current figures equal 94 percent of the U.S. Senate and 97 percent of Fortune 500 CEOs. For a discussion of racial bias in leadership categorization, see Rosette, Leonardelli, and Phillips (2008, 760).

16. See chapter 6 for a full discussion of these distinctions.

17. Tim Wise discusses this in his analysis of "School Shootings and White Denial." Tim Wise says, "White people live in an utter state of self-delusion. We think danger is black, brown and poor and if we can just move far enough away from 'those people in the cities' we'll be safe. If we can find an "all-American" town, life will be better, because things like this just don't happen here" (2001).

18. This widely publicized incident took place on 23 August 1989. Yusuf Hawkins, a Black teenager from Bedford-Stuyvesant, went to Bensonhurst with a friend to look at a used car, possibly to purchase. He was murdered by gunshot by a group of thirty white teenagers, disturbed by his presence in their neighborhood (DeSantis 1991).

19. Survey by CNN, "Post-election Race Relations," CNN/Opinion Research Corp. Poll, www.cnn.com/2008/POLITICS/11/11/obama.poll/index.html#cnnSTCOther1.

20. CNN Election Center 2008 Exit Polls. www.cnn.com/ELECTION/2008/results/polls/#val=USP00p1. Accessed January 15, 2010.

21. *The Many Costs of Racism* (2003) by Joe R. Feagin and Karyn D. McKinney provides an excellent examination of the consequences that racism imposes.

22. Per Dr. Hilary Gold, Dean of School of General Studies in the 1960s, then Dean of Students, and Vice President for Student Life until he retired in 1998, TLP has won twenty-nine of the thirty-three elections that took place between 1967 and 2000. Of those, twenty-six of the executive slates were all white; three included one Black, and one white student as either president or vice president.

23. For further exploration of this issue, see, for example, Perry, Steele, and Hilliard (2003); Fordham (1995); Lee (2002, A1).

24. This student club was formed in 1999, after a student leadership retreat workshop on social justice that chose to address the issue of social segregation on campus. Initially active and diverse, the group disbanded after several very successful but overly ambitious events.

25. A recent University of Michigan study found that "despite much talk about self-segregation by students of color, such students are much more likely than white students to socialize, date, and dine across the color line" (Roediger 1998, 7–8).

26. Bob Wing points out, for example, that the structure of the electoral college negates the votes of almost half of all people of color. People of color are the most consistent liberal/progressive voters in the nation, and whites constituted 95 percent

of Bush's vote, thereby essentially disenfranchising nonwhite voters. In the 1996 election, 73 percent of people with annual incomes over $75,000 voted, compared to 36 percent of those with incomes below $15,000 (Wing 2001).

27. See also Timothy Noah, "What We Didn't Overcome: Obama Won a Majority of Votes. He Didn't Win a Majority of White Votes," *Slate*, www.slate.com/id/2204251/#sb2204308. November 10, 2008. Accessed January 15, 2010.

28. The meaning attached to the flag is more thoroughly discussed in chapter 3.

29. Richard Alba speaks of the deal cut by European immigrants whereby they traded in their linguistic and cultural diversity in order to become white (Alba 1990).

30. Odegua Eko-Isenalumhe. Correspondence via e-mail dated 2 November 2001.

31. Peggy McIntosh lists these assumptions in her knapsack: 7. When I am told about our national heritage or about civilization, I am shown that people of my color made it what it is. 8. I can be sure that my children will be given curricular materials that testify to the existence of their race. 31. I can choose to ignore developments in minority writing and minority activist programs, or disparage them, or learn from them, but in any case, I can find ways to be more or less protected from negative consequences of any of these choices. 44. I can easily find academic courses and institutions that give attention only to people of my race (1992, 76–87).

32. While precise data on the demography of Greek-letter organizations was not accessible, I surveyed one staff member and three students, all of whom concurred on the following summary: Of the twelve to fifteen fraternities and sororities that have regularly been registered and active, 80 percent are approximately 95 percent white, while the other 20 percent are predominantly either Black or Latino. Of the fraternities and sororities that are 95 percent white, most are predominantly either Jewish or Italian, with a few Irish students. The other 5 percent of membership are Latino, Asian, Black, or of mixed background.

33. Peggy McIntosh's knapsack of white privilege includes: 34. I can worry about racism without being seen as self-interested or self-seeking. 27. I can go home from most meetings of organizations I belong to feeling somewhat tied in, rather than isolated, out of place, outnumbered, unheard, held at a distance or feared (1992, 98).

34. Peggy McIntosh, from her knapsack: 1. I can, if I wish, arrange to be in the company of people of my race, most of the time. I can turn on the television or open to the front page of the paper and see people of my race widely and positively represented. 24. I can be reasonably sure that if I ask to talk to "the person in charge," I will be facing a person of my race (1992, 97–98).

35. See Eileen O'Brien, *The Racial Middle: Latinos and Asian Americans Living Beyond the Racial Divide* (New York: University Press, 2008).

36. The National Opinion Research Center, University of Chicago, conducts routine surveys for the General Social Survey Project. In December 1990, findings indicated that the image of Latinos, as compared to whites, was significantly poorer, more violence-prone, and less intelligent, and suggested that Latinos more frequently live off welfare and are less patriotic (Smith 1990).

37. For a full examination of the development of the notion of race, see chapter 1.

38. Findings of the National Opinion Research Center (see note 36, above) in December 1990 regarding perceptions of Asians indicated that they were viewed gener-

ally second or third in positive attributes as compared to whites on a scale measuring rich/poor, more/less violence prone, more/less intelligent, more/less "frequently live off welfare," and more/less patriotic (Smith 1990).

39. The December 1990 findings of the National Opinion Research Center indicated that Jews are perceived as more rich, less violence-prone, more intelligent, less "frequently live off welfare," and more patriotic (Smith 1990).

40. For an in-depth exploration of these issues, see Kasinitz (1992); Jaynes (2000); Hochschild (1995); Cordero-Guzman, Smith, and Grosfoguel (2001).

41. The December 1990 findings of the National Opinion Research Center indicated that Blacks were perceived, compared to whites, as significantly poorer, more violence-prone, and less intelligent, and suggested that Blacks more frequently live off welfare and are less patriotic. In fact, over 80 percent of respondents rated Latinos and Blacks lower than whites on one or more of the five characteristics (Smith 1990).

42. An example is that anthrax terrorism is not a new phenomenon. A total of eighty-one of eighty-three criminal incidents worldwide involving anthrax in 1999 took place in the United States. Most involved white supremacists, yet it was not until the aftermath of September 11, 2001, and possible links to Iraq that this threat was made public. As it increasingly appears that a lone individual or group in the United States is behind the dissemination of anthrax, the threat is being muted once again (Blackhurst 2001, 49).

43. Despite the fact that there are 25,000 hardcore white supremacist activists in dozens of organizations, with another 150,000 supporters, in the United States today, when was the last *New York Times* article about this? Approximately ten thousand people are members of neo-Nazi groups or Ku Klux Klan–type organizations (Ward 1999, 50).

44. Whitfield questions why "young Christian white guys with crew-cuts" were not "profiled" after the Oklahoma City bombings, nor were the "Patriots who have been blowing up abortion clinics, shooting doctors, and blowing up federal buildings and exploding bombs at the Atlanta Olympics," nor were serial killers, who have also been predominantly white males. One might question why there was no full-scale investigation of the right-wing, Christian, fundamentalist white-supremacists groups that McVeigh was affiliated with, despite clear indication that he was operating not as an individual but as a representative of the right-wing tendency in the United States (Whitfield 2001, 9).

45. Media Awareness Network, "Hurricane Katrina and the 'Two-Photo Controversy,'" www.media-awareness.ca/english/resources/educational/teachable_moments/katrina_2_photo.cfm.

46. Thanks to Concessa Alfred, Phillip Goldfeder, Shalom Rosenberg, and Aldo Valmon-Clarke for helping to clarify various points within this chapter.

CHAPTER 3

1. In a fascinating discussion entitled "Citizenship Destabilized," Saskia Sassen explores these questions and others, such as whether current changes in the sociopolitics of today's world may signal an "emerging political subjectivity that partly

lodges itself outside the national, but also changes the meaning of the national." She asserts that the functionality of citizenship relates to issues such as budget allocation but that our current system needs reformulation, in the direction of being "partly denationalized" (2003, 14–21).

2. Martinez writes, "Today's origin myth and the resulting definition of national identity make for an intellectual prison where it is dangerous to ask big questions, moral questions, about this society's superiority; where otherwise decent people are trapped in a desire not to feel guilty, which then necessitates self-deception. . . . When together we cease equating whiteness with 'Americanness,' a new day can dawn" (1996, 24).

3. These questions, while asked in 1999–2000, take on a slightly new meaning since September 11, 2001.

4. CNN News, 29 November 2001, 7:00 a.m.

5. Martinez speaks of this when she says, "If ever there was a time for people in this white-dominated super-power to reject its racist contempt for 20 other American countries that happen to be of color, it is right now as Bush charges from one racist war to another . . . [and] when monumental lies have become the real weapons of mass destruction" (2003, 69).

6. In an article entitled "Oh, Gods," Toby Lester points out that new religions are born all the time. He quotes David B. Barrett, author of the World Christian Encyclopedia: "We have identified nine thousand and nine hundred distinct and separate religions in the world, increasing by two or three new religions every day" (2002, 41). Furthermore, 67 percent of the world's people are non-Christian (www.adherents. com 2003).

7. Department of Education, "DOE and Learning Leaders Sponsor Sixth Annual English Language Learners Conference," http://schools.nyc.gov/Offices/mediarelations/NewsandSpeeches/2008-2009/10222008.htm. Accessed October 22, 2008.

8. In one estimate, each firefighter's family will receive almost one million dollars, whereas families of people who were not unionized or were undocumented stand to receive little, if anything. Comparison of the severance packages of people who lost jobs as a result of this tragedy also reveals great disparities. On the one hand, the severance package for the outgoing executive director of the Massachusetts Port authority was reported at $175,000, the airlines bailout was cited at $15 billion, and the overall economic stimulus package is essentially a giant corporate tax break, whereas laid-off employees of the Hotel Employees and Restaurant Employees International Union and various airlines are reported to receive little or nothing in the form of unemployment benefits (Jackson 2001, A23)

9. Pew Hispanic Center, "Graphic: Latino Youths Optimistic But Beset by Problems," http://pewhispanic.org/reports/report.php?ReportID=118. Accessed May 10, 2010.

10. In an interesting examination of "American Values," Gerda Lerner explores the dyads of: equality and racism; open access vs. elitism; federalism vs. imperialism; individualism vs. community; and pluralism vs. nativism, among others (1997, 74–92).

11. This is similar to the trend articulated in the bestseller by Allen Bloom (1987) in which he decries the decline of American common values.

12. John Sakata, "The Voting Habits of Young Adults," CBSNEWS, www .cbsnews.com/stories/2007/12/13/politics/uwire/main3617392.shtml and Circle, "Youth Turnout Rate Rises to at least 52%," Tufts University, www.civicyouth. org/?p=323. Accessed April 12, 2010.

13. International Institute for Democracy and Electoral Assistance. United States. www.idea.int/vt/countryview.cfm?CountryCode=US and U.S. Census Bureau. Voting and Registration in the Election of November 2008. www.census.gov/hhes/www/ socdemo/voting/publications/p20/2008/tables.html. Accessed January 20, 2010.

14. Brian Montopoli, "237 Millionaires in Congress," CBS News, November 6, 2009. www.cbsnews.com/8301-503544_162-5553408-503544.html. Accessed January 21, 2010.

15. Elizabeth Martinez speaks of the origin narratives that every society creates "to explain that society to itself and the world with a set of mythologized stories and symbols." She explores the U.S. origin narrative in detail (1996) and attributes this labeling to Roxanne Dunbar Ortiz.

16. See the forthcoming book by Melanie Bush and Roderick Bush. 2001. *Tensions in the American Dream: Rhetoric, Reverie or Reality*. Philadelphia, Pa.: Temple University Press.

17. Isabel Sawhill, "Economic Mobility: Is the American Dream Alive and Well?" *The Brookings Institution*, www.economicmobility.org/assets/pdfs/EMP%20American%20Dream%20Report.pdf.

18. See for example, studies done by the Center for the New American Dream "More of What Matters" (2005), Sarah Roberts, "New American Dream: Survey Confirms that Americas Overworked, Overspent and Rethinking the American Dream," www.newdream.org/about/pdfs/PollRelease.pdf, and the Change to Win American Dream Project surveys.

19. For a summary of who receives scholarships, see chapter 2, note 4.

20. Working Together Always (WTA) is one of the two Brooklyn College student government organizations discussed in chapter 2.

21. An exploration of the history and meaning of the "Pledge of Allegiance" is available at Teachingforchange.org. As of 17 October 2001, the New York City Board of Education unanimously adopted a resolution to require all public schools to lead students in the pledge at the beginning of every school day and at all school-wide assemblies and events (Wyatt 2001, D1).

22. Bill Moyers, "Bill Moyers on Patriotism and the Flag," *NOW With Bill Moyers*, PBS, February 28, 2003. www.pbs.org/now/commentary/moyers19.html. Last accessed January 1, 2010.

23. Reported in *The Autobiography of Malcolm X* (1965, 399).

24. In 2007, 36.8 percent of the NY city population is reported as foreign-born. U.S. Census Bureau, "American Community Survey 2007," American Fact Finder, http:// factfinder.census.gov/servlet/IPTable?_bm=y&-context=ip&-reg=ACS_2007_1YR_ G00_S0201:001;ACS_2007_1YR_G00_S0201PR:001;ACS_2007_1YR_G00_ S0201T:001;ACS_2007_1YR_G00_S0201TPR:001&-qr_name=ACS_2007_1YR_ G00_S0201&-qr_name=ACS_2007_1YR_G00_S0201PR&-qr_ name=ACS_2007_1YR_G00_S0201T&-qr_name=ACS_2007_1YR_G00_

S0201TPR&-ds_name=ACS_2007_1YR_G00_&-tree_id=307&-redoLog=true&-_
caller=geoselect&-geo_id=16000US3651000&-search_results=01000US&-for-
mat=&-_lang=en. Last accessed January 1, 2010.

25. Interestingly, of the U.S.-born whites, only one-third of those who were born
in New York City had completed a bachelor's degree, as compared to three-quarters
of those who had moved to the city from elsewhere in the United States (Mollenkopf,
Kasinitz, and Waters 2001).

26. Personal communication with Professor Donald Robotham, The Graduate School
and University Center of the City University of New York (1 December 2000).

27. By 2008, immigrants from Europe are estimated as 12.5 percent of the total
foreign-born population. Census.gov. Table 3.1 Foreign-Born Population by Sex,
Age, and World Region of Birth: 2008. www.census.gov/population/socdemo/for-
eign/cps2008/tab3-2008.pdf. Accessed January 15, 2010.

28. This event occurred on 4 February 1999 in the Bronx, New York. Four police
officers, searching for someone who had committed a rape, came upon Mr. Diallo in
the vestibule of his home. They testified that he reached for a gun, which then in their
minds justified shooting forty-one bullets, nineteen of which entered his body. It was
later discovered that Mr. Diallo was reaching for his wallet to provide identification.
Mayor Rudolph Giuliani characterized attention to this incident as "obsessive media
concern" and "frenzy" (Barry 1999). Massive protests against police brutality and
racism followed, for it was widely recognized that, had Diallo been white, the shooting was highly unlikely to have occurred.

29. From an illuminating discussion with Dr. Leith Mullings, CUNY Graduate
School, 21 September 2001. This is a complex issue; for a fuller examination see
Bobo (2000, 186–202); Smith and Seltzer (2000); Steinberg (1995, 190–2); Gallic-
chio (2000).

30. Particularly noteworthy are the works of Basch, Schiller, and Blanc (1994);
Cordero-Guzman, Smith, and Grosfoguel (2001); and Jaynes (2000).

31. An excellent discussion of the complexities of oppositional actions in schools
can be found in Sevier (2003).

32. For a partial list of U.S. military interventions from 1890 to 1999, including
approximately one hundred incidents, see Zoltan Grossman, "A Century of U.S. Military Interventions: From Wounded Knee to Afghanistan," Znet (2003).

33. For an excellent analysis of implicitly racial messages in media, see Benjamin
DeMott, *The Trouble with Friendship* (1998 [1995]).

34. Mary Sykes Wylie, Has the American Dream Become Our Nightmare? Psy-
chotherapy Networker. July 3, 2010, www.alternet.org/story/147384/. Accessed on
July 6, 2010.

35. July 1, 2010. Volume 46, Issue 26, Page 1.

CHAPTER 4

1. Amy Liu, Sylvia Ruiz, Linda DeAngelo, John Pryor. Findings from the 2008
Administration of the College Senior Survey (CSS): National Aggregates. Coopera-

tive Institutional Research Program. Higher Education Research Institute. Graduate School of Education & Information Studies. University of California, Los Angeles. June 2009. 19.

2. Harris, as cited in (Pyne 2003). An interesting irony is that Harris explains the lack of generalization about all whites being terrorists after the bombing in Oklahoma City by saying, "Most people know white guys." As the rest of this chapter discusses, the treatment of whites is not the same as that of people of color. I assert that this generalization did not occur because everyone knows a white guy but more likely because of the racialized depictions of "invidious distinction" that are so common in our society.

3. Part of the Brooklyn College Core Curriculum, "People, Power and Politics" "provides an introduction to the social sciences through the study of power, authority, and social organization in American society" (Brooklyn College 1994, 75).

4. "Friends friends" was Andrew's phrase to distinguish from a less familiar "friend."

5. For an exploration of how racial identity development occurs, and how the commonly cited segregation in school cafeterias symbolizes one aspect of this, see Tatum 1997.

6. See chapter 2, endnotes 6 and 7, for information about scholarship distribution by race.

7. Joe Feagin, past president of the American Sociological Association, at the annual conference, 2000.

8. For a thorough discussion of the process of becoming "white" on the part of European immigrants who at one point in history were designated otherwise, see Brodkin (1998), Ignatiev (1995), and Ashyk, Gardaphe, and Tamburri (1999). While not specifically addressing the issue of "passing" as individuals, these works illuminate this point from the perspective of groups as a whole.

9. W. E. B. Du Bois describes this concept (1979, 700).

10. An interesting exploration of this topic can be found in Young (2001). Young describes the disappointment of a growing number of scholars that "rather than curbing racism, cyberspace may be perpetuating racial stereotypes for some users."

11. Jeffrey S. Passel, Wendy Wang and Paul Taylor. "One-in-Seven New U.S. Marriages is Interracial or Interethnic." Pew Research Center. June 4, 2010. http://pewsocialtrends.org/assets/pdf/755-marrying-out.pdf. Accessed June 4, 2010.

12. "Prom Night In Mississippi, "One Town. Two Proms. Until Now," www.promnightinmississippi.com/the-film. Accessed January 2, 2010.

13. Joseph Carroll, "Most Americans Approve of Interracial Marriages," *Gallup*, www.gallup.com/poll/28417/most-americans-approve-interracial-marriages.aspx. Accessed January 2, 2010.

14. See Patrik Jonsson, "Louisiana Interracial Marriage Case Reviews Southern Stereotypes," *The Christian Science Monitor*, www.csmonitor.com/USA/Politics/The-Vote/2009/1017/louisiana-interracial-marriage-case-revives-southern-stereotypes. Accessed January 2, 2010.

15. From an illuminating conversation with Professor Donald Robotham, CUNY Graduate School and University Center, department of anthropology, December 4, 2000.

CHAPTER 5

1. Polling Report, Inc. and polling/sponsoring organizations. www.pollingreport. com/race.htm. ABC News/*Washington Post* Poll. January 12–15, 2010. Accessed May 19, 2010.

2. For example, see Thomas Shapiro, "New Study Finds Racial Wealth Gap Quadrupled since Mid 1980's," *Institute on Assets and Social Policy*, May 17, 2010. http://iasp.brandeis.edu/pdfs/Racial-Wealth-Gap-Press-Release.pdf. Accessed May 20, 2010.

3. Polling Report, "Race and Ethnicity," www.pollingreport.com/race.htm. Accessed May 19, 2010.

4. Devah Pager and Bruce Western, "Race at Work: Realities of Race and Criminal Record in the NYC Job Market." NYC Commission on Human Rights conference held on December 9, 2005 at the Schomburg Center for Research in Black Culture. www.nyc.gov/html/cchr/pdf/race_report_web.pdf. Accessed September 30, 2007.

5. Bob Herbert, "Blacks in Retreat," *The New York Times*, January 18, 2010, www.nytimes.com/2010/01/19/opinion/19herbert.html. Accessed January 18, 2010).

6. Black Job-Seekers Hide Race For "Corporate America," January 10, 2010. National Public Radio. www.npr.org/templates/story/story.php?storyId=122416323. Accessed January 15, 2010.

7. Urban Justice Center et al. 2010. "Submission to the UN Universal Periodic Review Ninth Session of the UPR Working Group of the Human Rights Council 22 November–3 December 2010." April. www.hrpujc.org/documents/HumanRightto-WorkClusterReportFinal.pdf. Accessed May 1, 2010.

8. Economic Mobility Project. 2010. "Summary of Findings." www.economicmobility.org/assets/pdfs/EMP_findings_summary_definitive.pdf. Accessed May 25, 2010.

9. For a thorough examination of the role of race in the perpetuation of poverty, see Kushnick and Jennings (1999), Jennings (1994), and Hartman (2001).

10. The National Opinion Research Center at the University of Chicago conducts routine surveys for the General Social Survey Project. As reported by Krysan (2002, table 3.4A), "Explanations for Inequality."

11. Pew Research Center, "Blacks Upbeat about Black Progress, Prospects: A Year After Obama's Election," January 12, 2010, http://pewresearch.org/pubs/1459/year-after-obama-election-black-public-opinion. Accessed May 20, 2010.

12. Ibid.

13. Many factors impact the structure of society—representation is just one aspect. For example, one might conclude that G. W. Bush's cabinet was diverse and that white supremacy has seen its day. However, if we analyze the policies supported, one can see that the interests being served sustained the racial status quo.

14. Susanne Craig, David Enrich, and Robin Sidel, "Banks Brace for Bonus Fury," *The Wall Street Journal*, January 11, 2010, http://finance.yahoo.com/career-work/article/108554/banks-brace-for-bonus-fury?mod=career-salary_negotiation. Accessed May 20, 2010.

15. *Forbes*, "In Pictures: Richest 25 American Billionaires," www.forbes. com/2010/03/09/united-states-richest-people-warren-buffett-michael-bloomberg-billionaires-2010-gates_slide.html, Carmen DeNavas-Walt, Bernadette D. Proctor, and

Jessica C. Smith, "Income, Poverty and Health Insurance Coverage in the United States: 2008," U.S. Census Bureau, www.census.gov/prod/2009pubs/p60-236.pdf; *Federal Register*, Volume 74. No. 14. January 23, 2009. 4199–4201.

16. Peck, Don. 2010. "How a New Jobless Era Will Transform America." *The Atlantic*. March. www.theatlantic.com/magazine/archive/2010/03/how-a-new-jobless-era-will-transform-america/7919/. Accessed May 20, 2010.

17. Jackson, Derrick Z. 2006. "Soldiers die, CEOs prosper." *The Boston Globe*. August 30. www.boston.com/news/globe/editorial_opinion/oped/articles/2006/08/30/soldiers_die_ceos_prosper/. Accessed May 18, 2010.

18. Bybee, Roger. 2010. "Bunning 'Shamelessly Intensifies National Experiment in Stress.'" *In These Times*. www.inthesetimes.com/working/entry/5636/bunning_adds_to_national_experiment_in_stress2/. Accessed May 20, 2010.

19. Wamhoff, Steve. 2009. "The Bush Tax Cuts Cost Two and a Half Times as Much as the House Democrats' Health Care Proposal." Citizens for Tax Justice. September 8, www.ctj.org/pdf/bushtaxcutsvshealthcare.pdf. Accessed January 20, 2010.

20. Ibid.

21. The very notions of government and taxation have long been contested. In its ideal state, as described in the Preamble to the Constitution, one function of government is to promote the general welfare. The implication is that taxes should support government assistance to the less fortunate (Zinn 1990, 158).

22. Email correspondence May 21, 2010.

23. "Media has long been feeding Americans a steady diet of misleading and provocative news bites. Exaggerating the extent to which whites have suffered from affirmative action, this coverage has interacted toxically with nearly three decades of relative income stagnation and decline for masses of white Americans to stoke the fires of white racial illusion" (Street 2001, 9).

24. The notion of the civil rights movement and the period of the sixties as a second reconstruction are discussed in chapter 1. See Allen (1990), Bush (1999), Harding (1980), and Louis (1970).

25. Madrick, Jeff. 2007. "Goodbye, Horatio Alger." *The Nation*. January 21. www.thenation.com/article/goodbye-horatio-alger. Accessed January 20, 2010.

26. Ibid.

27. "Between 1988 and 1998, funding to New York State prisons increased by $761.3 million, while funding for education was decreased by $615 million. People of color and nonviolent offenders were hit hardest by this shift. The cost of keeping the state's nonviolent drug offenders in prison as a result of the Rockefeller Drug Law roughly matches that of the education funding decrease. More African Americans have entered prison for drug offenses than have graduated from SUNY every year since 1989 and almost twice as many Latinos were incarcerated for drug offenses as have graduated from SUNY in 1997. The costs of housing per prison per year is $30,000, roughly that which would cover tuition for nine students at SUNY or CUNY" (*Black Issues in Higher Education* 1998, 12).

28. Martin, Hayley Bisceglia. 2010. "UCOP: Prison Funding Swap Not Likely." *The Guardian*. The University of California, San Diego. 14 January. www.ucsdguardian.org/news/ucop-prison-funding-swap-not-likely/. Accessed May 24, 2010.

29. Charles. 2010. "U.S. households struggle to afford food: survey." Reuters. January 26. www.reuters.com/article/idUSTRE60P65N20100126. Accessed January 26, 2010, and AFP. 2009. "Half of U.S. kids depend on food stamps during childhood: study." November 2. www.google.com/hostednews/afp/article/ALeqM5huS1aDImykHCJxUuyNW-fbMSAbMA and Goldstein, Amy. 2009 "America's economic pain brings hunger pangs." *Washington Post*. November 17. www.washingtonpost.com/wp-dyn/content/article/2009/11/16/AR2009111601598. html?wpisrc=newsletter. Accessed May 25, 2010.

30. Op. cit. Madrick.

31. See endnote 2.

32. Drum Major Institute. 2009. "Fact Sheet: Immigrants' Economic Contributions" http://drummajorinstitute.org/library/report.php?ID=104; Congressional Budget Office. 2007. "The Impact of Unauthorized Immigrants on the Budgets of State and Local Governments." Congress of the United States. December. www.cbo.gov/ftpdocs/87xx/doc8711/12-6-Immigration.pdf; Capps, Randolph and Michael E. Fix. 2005. "Undocumented Immigrants: Myths and Reality." The Urban Institute. November 1. www.urban.org/url.cfm?ID=900898. Accessed May 19, 2010.

33. Lewin, Tamar. 2008. "College May Become Unaffordable for Most in U.S." *The New York Times*. December 3. www.nytimes.com/2008/12/03/education/03college. html. Acessed January 21, 2010.

34. "The greatest beneficiaries of open enrollment were not Blacks and Puerto Ricans as it is portrayed, but white ethnics, particularly Catholics who had not been able to earn admission to senior colleges prior to 1970. . . . The real upheaval at CUNY, then, was not due to the beginning of open enrollment in 1970 but to the financial crisis that gripped New York in 1975" (Glazer 1998).

35. In 1970, CUNY was 74 percent white, 16.9 percent Black, 4.8 percent Hispanic, 2 percent Asian/Pacific Islander, and .2 percent American Indian. By 2000, incoming freshmen in bachelor's programs in CUNY were 33 percent white, 22.5 percent Black, 25.6 percent Latino, and 18.4 percent Asian/Pacific Islander (CUNY Office of Institutional Research and Analysis 2000, table 1).

36. Catherine Rampell, "SAT Scores and Family Income," *The New York Times*, August 27, 2009, http://economix.blogs.nytimes.com/2009/08/27/sat-scores-and-family-income/. Accessed January 21, 2010.

37. While many factors contribute to success on SATs, two are particularly significant. Having the resources to enroll in a review course and doing so can greatly increase scores. In an e-mail of 26 November 2001, Pete Guzik, assistant director of Online Course Engine of The Princeton Review, states, "We offer a guarantee of 100 points for a full course." Additionally, SAT scores are strongly correlated with family income, therefore reflecting a bias against women, low-income, and minority students in the structuring of the test (Arenson 1999, B7).

38. Sandra Mathison, "The Accumulation of Disadvantage: The Role of Educational Testing in the School Career of Minority Children," in The Promise Of Education: Child Poverty in America Today, ed. Barbara A. Arrighi and David J. Maume (New York: Praeger Press, 2007), 66–79.

39. While this remains the case, there is controversy about how to understand the underlying factors. Catherine Rampell, "SAT Scores and Family Income," *The New York Times*, August 27, 2010, http://economix.blogs.nytimes.com/2009/08/27/sat-scores-and-family-income/. Accessed May 23, 2010.

40. Gomstyn, Alice. 2008. "Top Colleges Mum on Legacy Admissions." ABC News. April 11. http://abcnews.go.com/Business/IndustryInfo/story?id=4626882&page=1. Accessed May 25, 2010.

41. Recent Supreme Court rulings have brought this issue to light. Some schools (e.g., Texas A&M) have decided to abolish the practice of legacy admissions. However, to a large extent this practice is justified as a mechanism to "build a sense of continuity and tradition" on campus and "keeps alumni donors happy" (Traub 2004, 21).

42. Baker, Al. 2010. "New York Minorities More Likely to Be Frisked." *The New York Times*. May 12. www.nytimes.com/2010/05/13/nyregion/13frisk.html?scp=3&sq=police%20bias&st=cse. Accessed May 24, 2010.

43. Baker, Al. 2010. "Bias Seen in 'Police-on-Police' Shootings." *The New York Times*. May 26. www.nytimes.com/2010/05/27/nyregion/27shoot.html?emc=tnt&tntemail0=y. Accessed May 26, 2010.

44. Talking Points Memo, "The National Discussion on Race: Henry Louis Gates," http://tpmcafe.talkingpointsmemo.com/talk/blogs/rmrd0000/2009/07/the-national-dicussion-on-race.php. Accessed May 26, 2010.

45. "Open Line Talk Show," KISS FM, Brother Mtume, 25 November 2001, 9:30 A.M.

46. Blow, Charles M. 2010. "Tyler Perry's Crack Mothers." *The New York Times*. February 26. www.nytimes.com/2010/02/27/opinion/27blow.html?emc=eta1. Accessed February 26, 2010.

47. Marable spells out the extent of this expansion: "From 1817 to 1981, New York had opened 33 state prisons. From 1982 to 1999, another 38 state prisons were constructed. The states' prison population . . . (in) 1971 was 12,500. By 1999, there were over 71,000 prisoners in New York State correctional facilities." In the United States the numbers have grown from 187,500 in 1974 to 711,700 in 1991 (2002).

48. National Center for Education Statistics, "Employees in Degree-granting Institutions, by race/ethnicity and primary occupation: Fall 2007," *Institute of Education Sciences*, U.S. Department of Education, http://nces.ed.gov/fastfacts/display.asp?id=61. Accessed May 27, 2010.

49. PR Newswire Association LLC. A United Business Media company. 2010. "New Survey of Corporate Hiring: Black and Latino Executives Falling Further Behind." March 25. www.prnewswire.com/news-releases/new-survey-of-corporate-hiring-black-and-latino-executives-falling-further-behind-89105902.html. Accessed May 22, 2010.

50. Thanks to Dr. Donald Robotham for a clarifying discussion about this topic on 4 December 2000.

CHAPTER 6

1. Agency is a social science term that refers to an individual or group's capacity to consciously choose one set of actions versus another. It is similar to

free will or deliberate action and often refers to the ability to act in one's own interest.

2. Such everyday discrimination is well documented, for example, in studies that have found that when resumes of qualified Black and white job applicants were sent to employers, whites had a 21 percent higher chance of being contacted for an interview, received a 16 percent higher chance of getting a job offer, and were given more hours and higher pay, and resumes with white-sounding names received 50 percent more callbacks than did those with Black-sounding names (Street 2003a).

3. Tim Wise, "We Have a Black President, But That Doesn't Resolve the Deep Racism Built into the American Psyche." AlterNet. June 17, 2010. www.alternet.org/vision/147204. Accessed June 18, 2010, and Bonilla-Silva (2009).

4. See Michael Schwalbe, Afterword: "The Costs of American Privilege," In *Beyond Borders*. Ed. Paula Rothenberg (New York: Worth Publishers, 2006).

5. An interesting exploration of "Americanism" can be found in Chittister (2003).

6. Janny Scott, "What Politicians Say When They Talk About Race," *New York Times*, March 23, 2008, www.nytimes.com/2008/03/23/weekinreview/23scott.html?_r=3&scp=1&sq=shelby+steele&st=nyt&oref=slogin. Accessed March 6, 2010.

7. Ibid.

8. Thanks to Loretta Chin for expanding on the ways fear is implicated, per personal communication.

9. Walter O. Weyrauch has also referred to the notion of unwritten rules in relationship to the legal academy, in Wildman (1998, 9).

10. Pew Research Center, "Blacks Upbeat about Black Progress, Prospects: A Year After Obama's Election," *Social and Demographic Trends*, http://pewsocial-trends.org/pubs/749/blacks-upbeat-about-black-progress-obama-election. Accessed June 1, 2010. Glen Ford, "Black Realities and Black Delusion in the Age of Obama," Pan-African News Wire, http://panafricannews.blogspot.com/2010/05/black-realities-and-black-delusion-in.html. Accessed June 6, 2010.

11. Pryor, J.H., Hurtado, S., DeAngelo, L., Sharkness, J., Romero, L.C., Korn, W.S., and Tran, S. (2008). The American freshman: National norms for fall 2008. Los Angeles: Higher Education Research Institute, UCLA.

12. Tim Wise, "This is Your Nation on White Privilege," Red Room, www.redroom.com/blog/tim-wise/this-your-nation-white-privilege-updated. Accessed September 13, 2008. Accessed October 30, 2008.

13. Tim Wise. 2010. "What If the Tea Party Were Black?" AlterNet. www.alternet.org/story/146616/what_if_the_tea_party_were_black. Accessed April 26, 2010.

14. Kate Pickett and Richard Wilkinson, "Hey, America: It's Time to Redefine the 'Good Life,'" AlterNet, www.alternet.org/story/145827/hey%2C_america%3A_it%27s_time_to_redefine_the_%22good_life%22 February 26, 2010. Accessed March 2, 2010.

15. Pew Research Center, "Millennials: A Portrait of Generation Next. Confident. Connected. Open to Change," February 2010. http://pewsocialtrends.org/assets/pdf/millennials-confident-connected-open-to-change.pdf. Accessed June 6, 2010.

16. Ibid.

17. Tim Lockette, "The New Racial Segregation at Public Schools," AlterNet, www.alternet.org/rights/145553?page=1. April 25. Accessed February 5, 2010.

18. Ibid.

19. See Nancy Foner (2001a), Waldinger (1996), Prashad (2000, 38–39), Bobb (2001, 212–38).

20. Heidi Beirich, "Getting Immigration Facts Straight," Southern Poverty Law Center, www.splcenter.org/get-informed/intelligence-report/browse-all-issues/2007/summer/paranoid-style-redux/getting-immigrat. Accessed June 10, 2010.

21. For an outstanding exploration of founding myths, see Martinez (1998).

22. The philosophical underpinnings of this draw on Aztec culture. Laura I. Rendon describes the five key features in "Academics of the Heart," About Campus (July–August 2000): 3–5.

23. Frank Wong, late chair, American Commitments, national panel, Association of American Colleges and Universities, as quoted in Humphreys (2000).

24. Eric L. Dey, "Should Colleges Focus More on Personal and Social Responsibility?" Association of American Colleges and Universities, www.aacu.org/core_commitments/documents/PSRII_Findings_April2008.pdf. Accessed June 4, 2010.

25. Anthony Lising Antonio's "Diverse Student Bodies, Diverse Faculties" provides an excellent discussion of challenges in and proposals for establishing and maintaining a diverse faculty (2003).

26. Core 3: "People, Power and Politics" is part of the Brooklyn College Core Curriculum and " . . . provides an introduction to the social sciences through the study of power, authority, and social organization in American society" (Brooklyn College 1994, 75).

27. Paul Montagna, professor of sociology, Brooklyn College, interview by author, 15 September 2000.

28. From a discussion with Don Robotham, professor of anthropology, CUNY Graduate School and University Center, 1 December 2000 and Street (2001, 9–11).

29. Joe Feagin, professor and president of the American Sociological Association (ASA), used this phrase at the annual ASA meeting in 2000.

30. In a recent article Noel J. Chrisman says, "When anthropology is able to promote the synergy of theory and practice, we will be a mature discipline." See "Toward a Mature Anthropology," Anthropology News (2002): 4–5.

31. See Christopher (2003) for an excellent examination of these forces within the California system of higher education.

32. The Afterword explores this idea more fully; the phrase was spoken in personal conversation with Rod Bush, 28 December 2001.

33. Particular thanks to Robin D. G. Kelley (2002), who challenges us to think like poets, unconstrained by the limits of mainstream narratives claiming that peace, justice, equality, and freedom are unrealistic and idealistic fantasies.

EPILOGUE

1. Thanks to Matt Birkhold and the Adelphi/St John's Universities delegations to the U.S. Social Forum for this language.

2. FAIR: Fair and Accuracy in Reporting. Issue Area: Narrow Range of Debate www.fair.org/index.php?page=7&issue_area_id=56 and Harvey Wasserman There's nothing mainstream about the corporate media" *Free Press*. February 9, 2008. www. freepress.org/columns/display/7/2008/1632. Accessed January 15, 2010.

3. Quoting Nigerian-American professor of political science at the City University of New York, Mojubaolu Olufunke Okome, Nico Colombant. 2010. "US Scholars Dissect Nigerian Threat." 07 January. VOA News.com www1.voanews. com/english/news/africa/west/US-Scholars-Dissect-Nigerian-Threat-80963482.html. Accessed January 15, 2010.

4. Melissa Harris-Lacewell 2010. "You've Got to Be Carefully Taught." The Nation. June 28. www.thenation.com/article/youve-got-be-carefully-taught. Accessed June 30, 2010.

5. Charles Blow's op-ed in the *New York Times* references numerous related studies (2009)

6. Neiwert, D. (2008). "Bill Bennett: Obama's win means 'You don't take excuses anymore' from minorities." *Crooks and Liars*. from http://crooksandliars. com/david-neiwert/billbennett-obama-wins-means-no-more. November 5. Retrieved December 17, 2008.

7. Lynch, Kara (2008). The first black president: No more excuses. Nubian message: the African-American voice of North Carolina State University since 1992. Retrieved December 16, 2008, from www. ncsu.edu/nubian/?story=287. November 15.

8. Ricardo Levins Morales. 2010. Float Like a Butterfly, Sting Like a Bee A political ecology of change June 21. www.zcommunications.org/float-like-a-butterfly-sting-like-a-bee-by-ricardo-levins-morales. Accessed June 21, 2010.

9. Melissa Harris-Lacewell. 2010. "What Reid's Race Gaffe Tells Us About Inequality." The Nation. January 12. www.alternet.org/rights/145087/what_reid%27s_race_gaffe_tells_us_about_inequality/. Accessed January 15, 2010.

AFTERWORD

1. Karen DeYoung and Greg Jaffe. 2010. "U.S. 'Secret War' Expands Globally as Special Operations Forces Take Larger Role." *The Washington Post*. June 4, 2010. www.washingtonpost.com/wp-dyn/content/article/2010/06/03/AR2010060304965. html? Accessed June 5, 2010.

2. "America's Bailout Barons" by Sarah Anderson, John Cavanagh, Chuck Collins, Sam Pizzigati, www.ips-dc.org/inequality. Accessed June 12, 2010.

3. http://pewresearch.org/pubs/1220/home-ownership-trends-blacks-hispanics. Accessed June 12, 2010.

4. www.frac.org/pdf/food_hardship_report_2010.pdf . Accessed June 12, 2010.

5. For details, see International A.N.S.W.E.R. (Act Now to Stop War & End Racism), www.InternationANSWER.org; Hatfield 2001; and Helmore 2003.

6. A recent campaign has called for "intellectual diversity" legislation to rein in what they perceive to be a liberal bias in academia (Horowitz 2004; Fish 2004).

7. www.cnn.com/SPECIALS/war.casualties/. Accessed June 12, 2010.

8. In Afghanistan since 2001, there have been 1,223 coalition deaths, of whom 675 were Americans, many of them killed by friendly fire www.cnn.com/SPECIALS/2004/oef.casualties/. Accessed April 5, 2009. More U.S. soldiers have been killed in Iraq since the war was declared "over" by George Bush in May 2003, than during the formal battle.

9. "Wizards Oz-ing" refers to the presentation of the Wizard of Oz as a mysterious power until the curtain was pulled back and his true identity discovered. "Sharks biting" refers to the idea that the recent increase of shark attacks is the result of sharks being fed up with the invasion of their waters.

10. Malcolm X contended, "Retaliation in self defense was a natural reaction and normal response of human beings whose dignity was not publicly recognized and respected in the nation of their birth." He spoke of impending disaster because he did not believe that America could continue to exploit the poor and weak, in the United States and abroad. In reference to the assassination of John Kennedy, he said, "chickens coming home to roost, never did make me sad; they've always made me glad. The seeds that America had sown—in enslavement, in many things that followed since then—all these seeds were coming up today; it was harvest time" (Cone 1993, 182–84). In addition to but separate from an analysis of al Qaeda and Osama bin Laden, the historical record of military and imperialist interventions by the United States throughout the globe needs to be examined, interrogated, and understood by the U.S. public. This does not signify a celebration of tragedy. It is respect for humanity.

11. Notable criticisms about using this phrase include that of Christopher Hitchens, who said, "Loose talk about chickens coming home to roost is the moral equivalent of the hateful garbage emitted by Falwell and Robertson and exhibits the same intellectual content" (2001). The National Leadership of the NAACP pulled back the president of the Durham NAACP for writing a scathing indictment of U.S. policies. He was told to make no more statements on the topic (Herald Sun 2001). Marc Cooper said that this phrase was "morally repugnant and politically unviable, this sort of demagogy can only render the left irrelevant" (2001).

12. This pattern of polar morality strikingly resembles the racial narratives of invidious distinction described in chapter 6.

13. In a discussion on 18 December 2001, Roderick D. Bush, professor at St. John's University, said, "These are dangerous words that got Malcolm X suspended from the Nation of Islam, hunted by assassination squads of more than 200 men; tracked, followed and plotted against by the FBI and the CIA; and ultimately shot before a firing range in public."

14. Evidence of this momentum can be found in the recent World Social Forums, in the antiglobalization movement, in massive global antiwar demonstrations, and at the World Conference against Racism in 2001.

Bibliography

Alba, Richard D. 1990. *Ethnic Identity: The Transformation of White America*. New Haven, CT: Yale University Press.

Alger, Jonathan R. 1997. "The Educational Value of Diversity." *Academe* (January–February): 20–23.

Allen, Robert L. 1990. *Black Awakening in Capitalist America: An Analytic History*. Trenton, NJ: Africa World Press, Inc.

Allen, Theodore. 1994, 1997. *The Invention of the White Race*. Vols. 1 and 2. London: Verso.

Ancheta, A. 1998. *Race, Rights and the Asian-American Experience*. New Brunswick, NJ: Rutgers University Press.

Ani, Marimba. 1994. *Yurugu: An African-centered Critique of European Cultural Thought and Behavior*. Trenton, NJ: Africa World Press, Inc.

Antonio, Anthony Lising. 2003. "Diverse Student Bodies, Diverse Faculties." *Academe*. Bulletin of the American Association of University Professors (November–December): 14–17.

Antonio, A.L., M.J. Chang, K. Hakuta, D.A. Kenny, S. Levin, and J.F. Milem. 2004. "Effects of Racial Diversity on Complex Thinking in College Students." *Psychological Science*, 15: 507–510.

Apple, M. W. (2008). "Can schooling contribute to a more just society?" *Education, Citizenship and Social Justice*, 3, no. 3: 239–261.

Arenson, Karen W. 1997. "Measure Seeks Campus Workfare Jobs, but City Balks." *New York Times*, 6 August, B3.

———. 1998. "Critics Fear Role of Politics in CUNY Plan." *New York Times*, 8 May, B1.

Aries, Elizabeth. 2008. Interview by Scott Jaschik. *Inside Higher Ed*, 12 September, 2008. http://www.insidehighered.com/news/2008/09/12/aries.

Ashyk, Dan, Fred L. Gardaphe, and Anthony Julian Tamburri, eds. 1999. *Shades of Black and White: Conflict and Collaboration between Two Communities*. Selected

Essays from the 30th Annual Conference of the American Italian Historical Association. Staten Island, NY: American Italian Historical Association.

Association of American Colleges and Universities. 2001b. "Statement from AAC&U in the Wake of *The Nation*al Tragedy" 18 September. www.aacu-edu.org (accessed 15 December 2001).

Avenoso, Karen. 1998. *From Savage to Negro: Anthropology and the Construction of Race, 1896–1954*. Berkeley: University of California Press.

Baker, Lee. 2001. "Profit, Power and Privilege: The Racial Politics of Ancestry." Paper presented as part of a public workshop on "Local Democracy . . . An Uncertain Future," University of North Carolina, Chapel Hill, NC, 2–3 March. Online at www.unc.edu/depts/anthro/talks/demohome.htm (accessed 8 December 2001).

Baldwin, James. 1984. "On Being 'White' . . . and Other Lies." *Essence*, April, 90–92.

Banton, Michael. 2000. "The Idiom of Race." In *Theories of Race and Racism: A Reader*, edited by Les Back and John Solomos. New York: Routledge.

Barry, Dan. 1999. "Giuliani Says Diallo Shooting Coverage Skewed Poll." *New York Times* on the Web, 17 March. www.nytimes.com.

Barstow, David, and Diana B. Henriques. 2001. "Gifts to Rescuers Divide Survivors." *New York Times*, 2 December, A1.

Basch, Linda, Nina Glick Schiller, and Cristina Szanton Blanc. 1994. *Nations Unbound: Transnational Projects, Postcolonial Predicaments, and Deterritorialized Nation-States*. Langhorne, Pa.: Gordon & Breach.

Bashi, Vilna. 1999. Review of *Crosscurrents: West Indian Immigrants and Race* by Milton Vickerman. *American Journal of Sociology*: 890–92.

Bell, Lee Anne. 2002. "Sincere Fictions: The Pedagogical Challenges of Preparing White Teachers for Multicultural Classrooms." *Equity and Excellence in Education* 35, no. 3 (September): 236–44.

Berger, Maurice. 1999. *White Lies: Race and the Myths of Whiteness*. New York: Farrar, Straus & Giroux.

Binder, Frederick M., and David M. Reimers. 1995. *All The Nations under Heaven: An Ethnic and Racial History of New York City*. New York: Columbia University Press.

Blackhurst, Chris. 2001. "Anthrax Attacks Now Being Linked to U.S. Right-Wing Cranks," 21 October. Online at http://news.independent.Co.uk/world/Americas/story.jsp?story=100635.

Blassingame, John, ed. 1982. *The Frederick Douglass Papers*. New Haven, Conn: Yale University Press.

Blauner, Bob. 1972. *Racial Oppression in America*. New York: Harper & Row.

Bloom, Allen. 1987. *The Closing of the American Mind*. New York: Simon & Schuster.

Bobb, Vilna Bashi. 2001. "Neither Ignorance nor Bliss: Race, Racism and the West Indian Immigrant Experience." In *Migration, Transnationalization and Race in a Changing New York*, edited by Hector R. Cordero-Guzman, Robert C. Smith, and Ramon Grosfoguel. Philadelphia: Temple University Press.

Bobo, Lawrence D. 2000. "Reclaiming a Du Boisian Perspective on Racial Attitudes." *Annals of the American Academy of Political and Social Science* (March): 186–202.

Bobo, Lawrence D. and Camille Z. Charles. 2009. "Race in the American Mind: From the Moynihan Report to the Obama Candidacy." *The ANNALS of the American Academy of Political and Social Science* 621, no. 1: 243–259.

Bonilla-Silva, Eduardo. 2010. *Racism Without Racists: Color-Blind Racism & Racial Inequality in Contemporary America*. Third Edition. Lanham, MD: Rowman & Littlefield Publishers.

Brewer, Rose M. 1993. "Theorizing Race, Class and Gender: New Scholarship of Black Feminist Intellectuals and Black Women's Labor." In *Theorizing Black Feminisms: The Visionary Pragmatism of Black Women*, edited by S.M. James and A.P. Busia. London: Routledge.

Brodkin, Karen. 1994. "How Did Jews Become White Folks?" In *Race*, edited by Steven Gregory and Roger Sanjek. New Brunswick, NJ: Rutgers University Press.

———. 1998. *How Jews Became White Folks and What That Says about Race in America*. Piscataway, NJ: Rutgers University Press.

Brooklyn College. 1994. "Bulletin of Undergraduate Programs, 1994–1997." Vol. 63, no. 1 (June).

———. 2001. "Archaeology Department Garners World Attention." *Around the Quad* 7, no. 1 (Fall).

Brooklyn College Office of Institutional Research (BC OIR). 1999. "Brooklyn Neighborhoods Profile: Income and Show Rates." Marketing Research Information Series, 12 April.

Burkhardt, John, and Tony Chambers. 2003. "Kellogg Forum on Higher Education for the Public Good: Contributing to the Practice of Democracy." *Diversity Digest* 7, nos. 1, 2: 1–2.

Bush, Melanie E. L., and Deborah L. Little. 2009. "Teaching toward Praxis and Political Engagement." *Engaging Social Justice: Critical Studies of 21st Century Social Transformation*. Studies in Critical Social Sciences. Fasenfest, David, editor. Leiden: Brill. 11–36.

Bush, Roderick D. 1999. *We Are Not What We Seem: Black Nationalism and Class Struggle in the American Century*. New York: New York University Press.

———. 2001. "The Domestic Costs of the War on Vietnam: The Great Society and the Civil Rights Movement." Paper presented as part of a seminar on "The Human Costs of War," 24 October. St. John's University, Jamaica, Queens, NY.

California Newsreel. 2003. "RACE—The Power of an Illusion." VHS. Companion website www.newsreel.org/guides/race/quiz.htm.

Carroll, Lewis. 1995 [1871]. *Through the Looking Glass and What Alice Found There*. New York: William Morrow.

Challenger, Douglass. 2000. "The Difference Dialogue Makes: Teaching through Student-Led Forums on Race." *Diversity Digest* (Winter): 10.

Chang, Mitchell. 2000. "Diversity Requirements and Reducing Racial Prejudice," *Diversity Digest* (Winter, 1 November). Online at www.diversityweb.org/Digest/ (accessed 15 December 2001).

Childs, Erica Chito. 2009. *Fade to Black and White: Interracial Images in Popular Culture*. Lanham, MD: Rowman and Littlefield.

Chittister, Sister Joan. 2003. "I Give Up: What Is Americanism?" From Where I Stand. *National Catholic Reporter*, vol. 1, no. 16, 15 July. Online at http://nationalcatholicreporter .org/fwis/pc071503.htm (accessed 15 July 2003).

Choe, Stan. 1999. "The Fund-a-Mentality Difference Between Prisons and Schools." *Black Issues in Higher Education* (7 January): 12.

Chou, Rosalind, S., and Joe R. Feagin. 2008. *The Myth of the Model Minority: Asian Americans Facing Racism*. Boulder, CO: Paradigm Publishers.

Chrisman, Noel J. 2002. "Toward a Mature Anthropology." *Anthropology News*, April, 4–5.

Christopher, Renny. 2003. "Damned If You Do, Damned If You Don't." *Academe Online* 89, no. 4 (July–August). www.aaup.org/publications/Academe/2003/03ja/ 03jatoc.htm (accessed 1 March 2004).

Chronicle of Higher Education. 1994. "Notebook." 13 April, A31.

Citizens for Tax Justice. 2001. "Profiteering in the Name of Patriotism." With the Institute for America's Future. Advertisement in *New York Times*, 15 November. Online at www.ctj.org (accessed 13 January 2002).

City University of New York OIRA. 2000. Table 1. "Trends in the Race/Ethnic Composition of First-Time Freshmen Entering CUNY Baccalaureate Programs: Fall 1999 to Fall 2000," 13 November.

Clarion Staff. 2001. "City College Teach-In at Center of Storm." *Clarion*: Newspaper of the Professional Staff Congress/City University of New York, December, p. 5.

Clegg, Roger. 2000. "Why I'm Sick of the Praise for Diversity on Campuses." *The Chronicle of Higher Education,* 14 July, p. B8.

CNN News. 2008a. Survey by Cable News Network and Opinion Research Corporation, January 14–17, 2008. iPOLL Databank, The Roper Center for Public Opinion Research, University of Connecticut. http://www.ropercenter.uconn.edu/ipoll.html (accessed 22 November 2008).

———. 2008b. Survey by Cable News Network and Opinion Research Corporation, November 6–9, 2008. iPOLL Databank, The Roper Center for Public Opinion Research, University of Connecticut. http://www.ropercenter.uconn.edu/ipoll.html (accessed 22 November 2008).

Cohen, Cathy J. 2004. "Deviance as Resistance: A New Research Agenda for the Study of Black Politics." *Du Bois Review* 1, no.1: 27–45.

Cohen, Joshua, ed. 1996. *For Love of Country: Debating the Limits of Patriotism*. Boston: Beacon Press.

Colby, Anne. 2008. "The Place of Political Learning in College." *Peer Review*. Spring-Summer: 4–8

Collins, Chuck, Alison Goldberg, and Sam Pizzigati. 2010. "Shifting Responsibility: How 50 Years of Tax Cuts Benefited the Wealthiest Americans." *Wealth for the Common Good.* http://wealthforcommongood.org/wp-content/uploads/2010/04/ ShiftingResponsibility.pdf.

Collins, Chuck, Chris Hartman, and Holly Sklar. 1999. "Divided Decade: Economic Disparity at the Century's Turn." 15 December. United for a Fair Economy, online at www.ufenet.org/press/divided_decade.html (accessed 8 June 2000).

Collins, Patricia Hill. 2004. "Toward a New Vision: Race, Class and Gender as Categories of Analysis and Connection," in *Oppression, Privilege and Resistance: Theoretical Readings on Racism, Sexism and Heterosexism*, edited by Lisa Heldke and Peg O'Connor, 529–543. New York: McGraw Hill,

ColorLines: Race Culture Action. 2001. "War on Terrorism: Profiled & Punished." Special Edition. December. www.arc.org/C_Lines/CLArchive/CL2001.12.html.

Cone, James H. 1993. *Martin & Malcolm & America: A Dream or a Nightmare?* Maryknoll, NY: Orbis Books.

Conley, Dalton. 2000. "Learning Whiteness." *New York Times Magazine*, 16 July, 45.

Cooper, Anna Julia. 1998. "Woman versus the Indian." In *The Voice of Anna Julia Cooper*, edited by Charles Lemert and Esme Bhan. New York: Rowman & Littlefield.

Cooperative Institutional Research Program (CIRP), of the Higher Education Research Institute (HERI). 2001. University of California, Los Angeles, "Fall 2001 Survey of Freshmen: Brooklyn College," December.

Corbett, Sara. 2009. "A Prom Divided." *New York Times,* May 21, 2009. www.nytimes.com/2009/05/24/magazine/24prom-t.html?scp=1&sq=A%20Prom%20 Divided&st=cse.

Cordero-Guzman, Hector, Robert Smith, and Ramon Grosfoguel, eds. 2001. *Migration, Transnationalism and the Political Economy of New York*. Philadelphia: Temple University Press.

Cose, Ellis. 1993. *The Rage of a Privileged Class*. New York: HarperCollins.

Cote, Joost. 2009. "Education and the Colonial Construction of Whiteness." *Australian Critical Race and Whiteness Studies Association* e-journal. Volume 5. 1. 1–14.

Cox, Oliver Cromwell. 1948. *Caste, Class & Race: A Study in Social Dynamics*. New York: Monthly Review Press.

Crain, William. 2003. "Open Admissions at the City University of New York." *Academe*: Bulletin of the American Association of University Professors. July–August, 49.

Cutting, Hunter. 2000. "Media and Race: Talking the Walk." In *Race and Public Policy*, edited by Makani N. Themba. Oakland, Calif.: Applied Research Center.

Darder, Antonia, and Rodolfo Torres, eds. 1998. *The Latino Studies Reader: Culture, Economy and Society.* London: Blackwell.

Davey D. 2001. "An interview with Congresswoman Barbara Lee." The FNV [Friday Night Vibe] Newsletter. Online at www.rapstation.com (17 September).

DeGraw, David. 2010a. "The Economic Elite Have Engineered an Extraordinary Coup, Threatening the Very Existence of the Middle Class." *Alternet*. February 15, http://www.alternet.org/economy/145667/.

———— 2010b. "The Richest 1% Have Captured America's Wealth—What's It Going to Take to Get It Back?" *Alternet.* February 17. http://www.alternet.org/story/145705/the_richest_1%25_have_captured_america%27s_wealth_--_ what%27s_it_going_to_take_to_get_it_back.

Delgado, Richard. 2001 [1995]. *The Rodrigo Chronicles: Conversations about America and Race*. New York: New York University Press.

Delpit, Lisa. 1998. "The Silenced Dialogue: Teaching Other People's Children." *Harvard Educational Review* 65, no. 3: 391.

DeMott, Benjamin. 1998 [1995]. *The Trouble with Friendship: Why Americans Can't Think Straight about Race.* New Haven, CT: Yale University Press.

Dervarics, Charles. 2008. "More than Half of Campus Hate Crimes Involve Race." *Diverse Issues in Higher Education.* http://diverseeducation.com/artman/publish/article_11996.shtml.

DeSantis, John. 1991. *For the Color of His Skin: The Murder of Yusuf Hawkins and the Trial of Bensonhurst.* New York: Pharos Books.

DiLeonardo, Micaela. 1999. "'Why Can't They Be Like Our Grandparents?' and Other Racial Fairy Tales." In *Without Justice For All: The New Liberalism and Our Retreat from Racial Equality,* edited by Adolph Reed Jr. Boulder, CO: Westview Press.

Diversity Web. 1998. "The Campus and the Public Diversity Poll: Executive Summary." University of Maryland. Online at www.inform.umd.edu/diversityweb/NewsRoom/diversitypoll.html (accessed 13 July 2001).

———. 2001. "Campus-Community Connections." December. Online at www .diversityweb.org/Leadersguide/CCC/Community_response/student_poll.html.

Dohrn, Bernadine. 2001. "Sixties Lessons and Lore." *Monthly Review* 53, no. 7. Online at www.monthlyreview.org/1201dohrn.htm (accessed 17 December 2001).

Dominguez, Virginia R. 1994. *White by Definition.* New Brunswick, NJ: Rutgers University Press.

Donate, Gaston Alonso, Corey Robin, Roberta Satow, and Alex Vitale. 2002. *People, Power and Politics.* Boston: Pearson Custom Publishing.

Douglass, Frederick. 1970 [1855]. *My Bondage and My Freedom.* Chicago: Johnson Publishing Company.

Drake, St. Clair. 1990. *Black Folk Here and There: An Essay in History and Anthropology.* Vol. 2. Los Angeles: University of California Center for Afro American Studies.

Du Bois, W. E. B. 1961 [1953]. *The Souls of Black Folk: Essays and Sketches.* Greenwich, CT.: A Fawcett Premier Book.

———. 1970 [1940]. *Dusk of Dawn: An Essay Toward and Autobiography of a Race Concept.* New York: Schocken Books.

———. 1979 [1936]. *Black Reconstruction in America: 1860–1880.* West Hanover, MA: Atheneum Publishers.

———. 1986 [1903]. "The Souls of Black Folk," In *W.E.B. Du Bois: Writings,* edited by Nathan Huggins. New York: Library of America, 358–547.

———. 1991. *Darkwater: Voices from within the Veil.* New York: Kraus-Thomson Organization, Limited.

Dunn, Christopher. 1999. "Challenging Racial Discrimination in the Public Schools of New York State." *Equity and Excellence in Education* (December): 19–24.

Dyer, Richard. 1997. *White.* London: Routledge.

Edsall, Thomas Byrne, with Mary D. Edsall. 1991. "When the Official Subject Is Presidential Politics, Taxes, Welfare, Crime, Rights or Values, the Real Subject Is Race." *Atlantic Monthly,* May, 53–86.

Ehrenreich, Barbara. 2002. "Hobo Heaven." Review of *Down and Out, On the Road.* by Kenneth L. Kusmer. *New York Times* Book Review, 20 January, 9.

Eibach, Richard, and Joyce Ehrlinger. 2006. "'Keep Your Eyes on the Prize': Reference Points and Racial Differences in Assessing Progress Toward Equality." *Personality and Social Psychology Bulletin* 32, no. 1: 66–77.

Eibach, Richard, and Thomas Keegan. 2006. "Free at Last? Social Dominance, Loss Aversion and White and Black Americans' Differing Assessments of Progress towards Racial Equality." *Journal of Personality and Social Psychology*, 90: 453–467.

Ellison, Ralph. 1970. *Going to the Territory*. New York: Random House.

Emerson, Michael O., Karen J. Chai, and George Yancey. 2001. "Does Race Matter in Residential Segregation? Exploring the Preferences of White Americans." *American Sociological Review* 66 (December): 922–35.

Espiritu, Y.L. 1992 *Asian-American Panethnicity*. Philadelphia: Temple University Press.

Farkas, Steve, Ann Duffett, and Jean Johnson with Leslie Moye and Jackie Vine. 2003. "Now That I'm Here: What America's Immigrants Have to Say about Life in the U.S. Today." *American Educator* (Summer): 28–36.

Feagin, Joe R. 2006. *Systemic Racism: A Theory of Oppression*. New York: Routledge.

———. 2009. *The White Racial Frame: Centuries of Racial Framing and Counter-Framing*. New York: Routledge.

Feagin, Joe, and Clairece Booher Feagin. 2003. *Racial and Ethnic Relations*. Upper Saddle River, NJ: Prentice-Hall.

Feagin, Joe R., and Karyn D. McKinney. 2003. *The Many Costs of Racism*. Lanham: MD: Rowman & Littlefield.

Feagin, Joe, and Hernan Vera. 1995. *White Racism*. New York: Routledge.

Feagin, Joe, Hernan Vera, and Pinar Batur. 2001 [1995]. *White Racism*, 2nd ed. New York: Routledge.

Fine, Michelle, Lois Weis, Linda C. Powell, and L. Mun Wong, eds. 1997. *Off White: Readings on Race, Power, and Society*. New York: Routledge.

Fish, Stanley. 2004. "'Intellectual Diversity': The Trojan Horse of a Dark Design." *Chronicle of Higher Education*, 13 February. http://chronicle.com/free/v50/i23/23b01301.htm (accessed 19 February 2004).

Foner, Eric. 1998 [1990]. *The Story of American Freedom*. New York: W.W. Norton.

———. 2003. "Rethinking American History in a Post 9/11 World." *Liberal Education* 89. no. 2. (Spring).

Foner, Nancy, ed. 2001a. *Islands in the City: West Indian Migration to New York*. Berkeley: University of California Press.

———. 2001b. *New Immigrants in New York*. New York: Columbia University Press.

Ford, Richard T. 1999. "Race and Recognition: Critical Race Theory Comes of Age." *CommonQuest* 3, no. 3 and 4, no. 1: 102–105.

Fordham, Signithia. 1995. *Blacked Out: Dilemmas of Race, Ethnicity and Success at Capital High*. Chicago: The University of Chicago Press.

Frankenberg, Ruth. 1993. *The Social Construction of Whiteness: White Women, Race Matters.* Minneapolis: University of Minnesota Press.

Frankenberg, Ruth, ed. 1997. *Displacing Whiteness: Essays in Social Change and Cultural Criticism.* Durham, NC: Duke University Press.

Franklin, H. Bruce. 2003. "Under Attack for 150 Years." *Clarion*: Newspaper of the Professional Staff Congress, Summer, 10. City University of New York.

Freeman, Greg. 2001. "Misperceptions May Be Holding Back Race Relations." *St. Louis Post-Dispatch Inc.,* 15 July, Five Star Lift Edition, C3.

Gallagher, Charles. 1995. "White Reconstruction in the University." *Socialist Review* 24, nos. 1 & 2: 165–87.

Gallicchio, Marc. 2000. *The African American Encounter with Japan and China: Black Internationalism in Asia, 1895–1945.* Chapel Hill: University of North Carolina Press.

Galston, William A. 2001. "Can Patriotism Be Turned into Civic Engagement?" *Chronicle of Higher Education*, 16 November, B16.

Gangi, Robert, Jason Ziedenberg, and Vincent Schiraldi. 1999. "New York State of Mind: Higher Education vs. Prison Funding in the Empire State, 1988–1998." The Justice Policy Institute. www.cjcj.org/jpi/nysom.html (accessed 28 March 2001).

Gilmore, Brian. 2002. "Stand by the Man: Black America and the Dilemma of Patriotism." *The Progressive* 66, no. 1 (January): 24–27.

Giroux, Henry. 1983. "Theories of Reproduction and Resistance in the New Sociology of Education: A Critical Analysis." *Harvard Educational Review* 53, no. 3 (August): 257–93.

———. 1997. "Rewriting the Discourse of Racial Identity: Towards a Pedagogy and Politics of Whiteness." *Harvard Educational Review* 67, no. 2 (Summer). Online at www.edreview.org.issues/harvard97/1997/su97/m97giro.htm (accessed 17 December 2001).

———. 1999. "Substituting Prisons for Schools." *Z Magazine*: A Political Monthly. Online at www.zmag.org/zmag/zarticle.cfm?url=articles/ april99giroux.htm (accessed 16 December 2002).

Glazer, Nathan. 1983. *Ethnic Dilemmas 1964–1982.* Cambridge, MA: Harvard University Press.

———. 1998. "Enroll On." *The New Republic*, 11 May.

Glazer, Nathan, and Daniel Patrick Moynihan. 1963. *Beyond the Melting Pot, The Negroes, Puerto Ricans, Jews, Italians and Irish of New York City.* Cambridge, MA: Massachusetts Institute of Technology.

Glenn, David. 2003. "High-School Confidential." *Chronicle of Higher Education*, 8 August, A13–14.

Gonnerman, Jennifer. 2000. "Two Million and Counting." *Village Voice*, 23–29 February. Online at www.villagevoice.com/issues/0008/gonnerman.shtml (accessed 25 February 2000).

Gonzalez, Juan. 1999. "Damning CUNY Report Hides Success Stories." *Daily News*, 8 June, 10.

———. 2004. "The Hidden History of Discrimination in Media." Public Lecture at Brooklyn College, 24 February.

Gorelick, Sherry. 1981. *City College and the Jewish Poor: Education in New York, 1880–1924*. New York: Schocken Books.

Gouldner, Alvin W. 1979. *The Future of Intellectuals and the Rise of the New Class: A Frame of Reference, Theses, Conjectures, Arguments, and a Historical Perspective on the Role of Intellectuals and Intelligentsia in the International Class Contest of the Modern Era*. New York: Continuum.

Gregory, Steven. 1998. *Black Corona: Race and the Politics of Place in an Urban Community*. Princeton, NJ: Princeton University Press.

Grossman, Zoltan, "A Century of U.S. Military Interventions: From Wounded Knee to Afghanistan," Znet, 20 September 2001. Online at www.zmag.org/crisescurevts/interventions.htm (accessed 7 July 2003).

Hacker, Andrew. 1992. *Two Nations: Black, White, Separate, Hostile, Unequal*. New York: Scribner's Sons.

Hahnel, Jesse, and David Pai. 2001. "Affirmative Action: 13 Myths Promoted by the Right." A flyer from The Center for Campus Organizing. Online at cco@igc.org (accessed 15 December 2001).

Haley, Alex, and Malcolm X. 1965. *The Autobiography of Malcolm X*. New York: Ballantine Books.

Halpin, John, and Karl Agne. "State of American Political Ideology, 2009: A National Study of Political Values and Beliefs." Center for American Progress. http://www.americanprogress.org/issues/2009/03/political_ideology.html.

Hamourtziadou, Lily. 2007. "The Price of Loss: How the West Values Civilian Lives in Iraq." *Iraq Body Count*. www.iraqbodycount.org/analysis/beyond/the-price-of-loss.

Harding, Vincent. 1980. *The Other American Revolution*. Los Angeles: Center for Afro-American Studies.

Harris, Fredrick. 2008. "The Obama Candidacy and Black America's Shifting Identities." *Focus Magazine*, December (Vol. 36/5). http://www.jointcenter.org/publications_recent_publications/focus_magazine/2008__1/december/the_obama_candidacy_and_black_america_s_shifting_identities.

Harrison, Faye. 1998. "Introduction: Expanding the Discourse on 'Race.'" *American Anthropologist* 100, no. 3 (September): 609–31.

Hartigan, John Jr. 1997. "Complicating Whiteness." *Anthropology Newsletter* 38 no. 8 (November): 8.

———. 1999. Racial *Situations: Class Predicaments of Whiteness in Detroit*. Princeton, NJ: Princeton University Press.

Hartman, Chester, ed. 2001. *Challenges to Equality. Poverty and Race in America*. Armonk, NY: M.E. Sharpe, Inc.

Hartmann, Roy. 1998. "We Caucasians Would Prefer to Ignore Our Preferences." *The Riverfront Times*, 17 April. Online at multc-ed@umdd.umd.edu.

Harvey, Jennifer, Karin A. Case, and Robin Hawley Gorsline. 2004. *Disrupting White Supremacy from Within: White People on What We Need To Do*. Cleveland, OH: Pilgrim Press.

Haveman, Robert, and Timothy Smeeding. 2006. "The Role of Higher Education in Social Mobility." *The Future of Children* 16, no. 2, 125–150.

Herbert, Bob. 2003. "Despair of the Jobless." *New York Times*, 7 August. <Online at www.truthout.org/docs_03/printer_080803G.shtml (accessed 7 August 2003).

Hightower, Jim. 2001. "Wave Our Flag." *AlterNet*, 16 October. Online at http:// alternet.org/story.html?storyid=11732.

Hitchens, Christopher. 2001. "Against Rationalization: Minority Report." *The Nation*, 8 October.

Hobsbawm, Eric. 2003. "Only in America." *The Chronicle of Higher Education*, 4 July, B7–B9.

Hochschild, Jennifer L. 1995. *Facing Up to the American Dream: Race, Class and the Soul of The Nation*. Princeton, NJ: Princeton University Press.

Honig, Bonnie. 2001. *Democracy and the Foreigner*. Princeton, NJ: Princeton University Press.

hooks, bell. 1995. "Representations of Whiteness in the Black Imagination." *Killing Rage: Ending Racism.* New York: Henry Holt..

Horowitz, Murray M. 1981. *Brooklyn College: The First Half-Century*. New York: Brooklyn College Press.

Horton, Harold W. 2000. "Perspectives on the Current Status of the Racial Climate Relative to Students, Staff and Faculty of Color at Predominantly White Colleges/ Universities in America." *Equity and Excellence in Education*, December, 35–37.

Hughes, Langston. 1990. *The Ways of White Folks.* New York: Alfred A. Knopf.

Humphreys, Debra. 1998. "The Impact of Diversity on College Students: The Latest Research." AACU and the Ford Foundation Campus Diversity Initiative. Washington, D.C. Online at www.diversityweb.org/Leadersguide/DREI/student_briefing. html (15 December 2001).

———. 2000. "Reasons for Hope: Promising Practices from the Campus Diversity Initiative." Association of American Colleges and Universities. Report. Online at www.aacu-edu/org.

Hungry Mind Review: *The Natio*nal *Book Magazine*. 1998. No. 45 (Spring issue, "Whiteness: What Is It?"). Macalester College.

Hyde, Cheryl. 1995. "The Meanings of Whiteness." *Qualitative Sociology* 18, no. 1: 87–95.

Iceland, John, Kimberly A. Goyette, Kyle Anne Nelson, and Chaowen Chan. 2009. "Racial and Ethical Residential Segregation and Household Structure: A Research Note." *Social Science Research* 39, no. 1, 139–47.

Ignacio, Emily Noelle. 2008. "Pro(fits) of a future not our own: Neoliberal Peframing of Public Discourse on Social Justice." In *Transnational Perspectives on Cutlure, Policy and Education: Redirecting Cultural Studies in Neoliberal Times*. Edited by Cameron McCarthy and Cathryn Teasley. New York: Peter Lang. 159–179.

Ignatiev, Noel. 1995. *How the Irish Became White*. New York: Routledge.

———. 1998. "Abolition and 'White Studies.'" *Race Traitor*, February. Online at www. postfun.com/racetraitor/features/whitestudies.html (accessed 23 August 1999).

Ignatiev, Noel, and John Garvey, eds. 1996. *Race Traitor*. New York: Routledge.

Institute for America's Future and Citizens for Tax Justice. 2001. "Profiteering in the Name of Patriotism." Advertisement in *New York Times*, 15 November. Online at www.ctj.org (accessed 13 January 2002).

International Institute for Democracy and Electoral Assistance. n.d. United States Voter Turnout from 1945 to Date. Online at http://idea.int/vt/country_view.cfm (accessed 7 July 2003).

———. n.d. "Turnout in the World–Country by Country Performance." Online at http://idea.int/vt/survey/ voter_turnout_pop2.cfm (accessed 7 July 2003).

Isaacs, Julia. 2007. "Economic Mobility of Black and White Families." The Brookings Institution. http://www.brookings.edu/~/media/Files/rc/papers/2007/11_blackwhite_isaacs/11_blackwhite_isaacs.pdf.

Isaacs, Julia B., Isabel V. Sawhill, and Ron Haskins. "Getting Ahead or Losing Ground: Economic Mobility in America." The Brookings Institution. http://www.dianahacker.com/resdoc/p04_c10_s2.html#22.

Jackson, Derrick Z. 2001. "Buckingham's Lucrative Landing: United We Stand, Except at the Unemployment Line." *Boston Globe*, 31 October, A23.

Jacobson, Matthew Frye. 1998. *Whiteness of a Different Color: European Immigrants and the Alchemy of Race*. Cambridge, MA: Harvard University Press.

James, Winston. 1998. *Holding Aloft the Banner of Ethiopia: Caribbean Radicalism in Early Twentieth Century America*. New York: Verso.

Jaynes, Gerald D., ed. 2000. *Immigration and Race: New Challenges for American Democracy*. New Haven, CT: Yale University Press.

Jennings, James. 1985. "A Look at Black Studies Today." *Forward Motion* 4, no. 4 (February–March): 10.

———. 1994. *Understanding the Nature of Poverty in Urban America*. Westport, CT: Praeger.

———. 1999. Presentation at the African-American Institute at Columbia University, 10 December.

Johnson, Allan G. 2008. *The Forest and the Trees: Sociology as Life, Practice and Promise*. Philadelphia: Temple University Press.

Johnson, Tammy. 2010. "Racing the Statehouse: Advancing Equitable Policies." *Applied Research Center*. February 18. http://www.arc.org/content/view/1859/56/.

Johnston, David Cay. 2007. "Report Says That the Rich Are Getting Richer Faster, Much Faster." *New York Times*, December 15. http://www.nytimes.com/2007/12/15/business/15rich.html?_r=1.

Journal of Blacks in Higher Education. 2001a. News and Views, "Information on Minority-Targeted Scholarships," report of the United States General Accounting Office, B251634, January 1994. No. 32 (Summer): 11.

———. 2001b. "Vital Signs," no. 32 (Summer): 81.

Kaiser, Cheryl R., Benjamin J. Drury, Kerry E. Spalding, Sapna Cheryan, and Laurie T. O'Brien. "The Ironic Consequences of Obama's Election: Decreased Support for Social Justice." *Journal of Experimental Social Psychology*, 45 (2009). http://faculty.washington.edu/ckaiser/Kaiser_2009_Journal-of-Experimental-Social-Psychology.pdf.

Kaplan, Esther, and Alisa Solomon. 1995. "Correcting Papers: The CUNY Protest You Didn't Hear About." *Village Voice*, 4 April, 11–12.

Karenga, Maulana. 1999. "Whiteness Studies: Deceptive or Welcome Discourse?" *Black Issues in Higher Education* 16, no. 6 (13 May): 26.

Kasinitz, Philip. 1992. *Caribbean New York*. New York: Cornell University Press.

Katz, William Loren. 1997. *Black Legacy: A History of New York's African Americans*. New York: Simon & Schuster.

Kaufman, Scott Barry. "Obama is President So Racism is over. Right? How Voting for Obama Can Increase Racism." *Beautiful Minds*, Psychology Today, http://www.psychologytoday.com/blog/beautiful-minds/200902/obama-is-president-so-racism-is-over-right.

Kelley, Robin D.G. 2002. "Finding the Strength to Love and Dream." *The Chronicle of Higher Education*. June 7. http://chronicle.com/article/Finding-the-Strength-to-Love/2544/

Kenny, Lorraine Delia. 2000. *Daughters of Suburbia: Growing Up White, Middle Class and Female*. New Brunswick, NJ: Rutgers University Press.

Kincheloe, Joe L., Shirley R. Steinberg, Nelson M. Rodriguez, and Ronald E. Chennault, eds. 1998. *White Reign: Deploying Whiteness in America.* New York: St. Martin's Press.

Kogler, Hans Herbert. 1999. "New Arguments for Diversifying the Curriculum: Advancing Students' Cognitive Development." *Diversity Digest* (Summer): 12.

Kovel, Joel. 1984. *White Racism: A Psychohistory*. New York: Pantheon Books.

Kraly, Ellen Percy, and Ines Miyares. 2001. "Immigration to New York: Policy, Population and Patterns." In *New Immigrants in New York*, edited by Nancy Foner. New York: Columbia University Press.

Krase, Jerome. 1999. "The American Myth(s) of Ethnicity." In *Shades of Black and White Conflict and Collaboration between Two Communities*: Selected Essays of the 30th Annual Conference of the American Italian Historical Association, edited by Dan Ashyk, Fred L. Gardaphe, and Anthony Julian Tamburri. Staten Island, N.Y: American Italian Historical Association, 103–16.

KRC Research and Consulting. 2002. "National Leadership Dialogue Series: Higher Education's Role in Serving the Public Good," October. Kellogg Forum on Higher Education for the Public Good. Online at www.kelloggforum.org/NDLSmaterials/KRC_ summit_presentation/KRC_summit_presentation.pdf (accessed 14 August 2003).

Krishnamurti, J. 1975. "On War." *The First and Last Freedom*. New York: Harper & Row.

Krysan, Maria. 2002. "Comments on the 2002 Update to Racial Attitudes in America: Trends and Interpretations Revised Edition," April. Table 3.4B, Perceptions of discrimination, white respondents. Online at http:tigger.cc.uic.edu/~krysan/ writeup. htm (accessed 5 July 2003).

Kushnick, Louis V. 1981. "Racism and Class Consciousness in Modern Capitalism." In *Impacts of Racism on White Americans*, edited by Benjamin P. Bowser and Raymond G. Hunt. London: Sage Publications.

Kushnick, Louis, and James Jennings, eds. 1999. *A New Introduction to Poverty: The Role of Race, Power and Politics.* New York: New York University Press.

Lavin, David E., Richard D. Alba, and Richard A. Silberstein. 1979. "Ethnic Groups in the City University of New York." *Harvard Educational Review* 49, no. 1 (February): 53–92.

Lazarre, Jane. 1996. *Beyond the Whiteness of Whiteness.* Durham, NC: Duke University Press.

Leacock, Eleanor. 1971. *The Culture of Poverty: A Critique.* New York: Simon & Schuster.

Lee, Felicia R. "Why Are Black Students Lagging?" *New York Times.* 30 November 2002, B1.

Lemert, Charles, and Esme Bhan. 1998. *The Voice of Anna Julia Cooper.* New York: Rowman & Littlefield.

Leonardo, Zeus. 2009. *Race, Whiteness, and Education.* New York: Routledge.

Leonhardt, David. 2009. "Income Inequality." *New York Times*, 21 August 2009. http://topics.nytimes.com/top/reference/timestopics/subjects/i/income/income_inequality/index.html?scp=24&sq=wealth%20share%20at%20top&st=cse.

Lerner, Gerda. 1997. *Why History Matters: Life and Thought.* New York: Oxford University Press.

Lester, Toby. 2002. "Oh, Gods!" *Atlantic Monthly*, February, 37–45.

Lewin, Tamar. 2001. "Growing Up, Growing Apart: Fast Friends Try to Resist the Pressure to Divide by Race." Part of a series, How Race is Lived in America. *New York Times*, 25 June, A1.

Lewis, Oscar. 1961. *The Children of Sanchez: Autobiography of a Mexican Family.* New York: Random House.

———. 1966. *La Vida: A Puerto Rican Family in the Culture of Poverty.* San Juan and New York: Vintage.

———. 1969. "Author's Response to Culture and Poverty: Critique and Counter-Proposals." *Current Anthropology* 10, nos. 2–3 (April–June): 189–92.

Lipsitz, George. 1998. *The Possessive Investment in Whiteness: How White People Profit from Identity Politics.* Philadelphia: Temple University Press.

Livingston, Andrea, John Wirt, Susan Choy, Stephen Provasnik, Patrick Rooney, Anindita Sen, and Richard Tobin. 2003. "The Condition of Education 2003." National Center for Education Statistics. U.S Department of Education. Institute of Education Sciences NCES 2003–067.

Loeb, Paul Rogat. 1999. *Soul of a Citizen: Living with Conviction in a Cynical Time.* New York: St. Martin's Griffin.

———. 2001. "Role Models for Engagement." *Diversity Digest* (Summer):4.

Lopez, Ian Haney. 2006 [1996]. *White by Law: The Legal Construction of Race.* 10th ed. New York: New York University Press.

Lords, Eric. 2001. "Outrage Continues over Fraternities' Racially Offensive Costumes." *Black Issues in Higher Education* (6 December): 10.

Louis, Debbie. 1970. *And We Are Not Saved: A History of the Movement as People.* Garden City, NY: Anchor.

Mallory, Bruce L., and Nancy L. Thomas. 2003. "Promoting Ethical Action through Democratic Dialogue." *Change: The Magazine of Higher Learning*, September–October, 11–17.

Marable, Manning. 1991. *Race, Reform, and Rebellion: The Second Reconstruction in Black America, 1945–1990.* Jackson: University Press of Mississippi.

———. 2002. "Abolishing American Apartheid, Root and Branch." Presentation at the Symposium on Racism in San Francisco, 25 July.

Martinez, Elizabeth. 1996. "Reinventing 'America.'" *Z Magazine*, December, 20–25.

———. 1998. *De Colores Means All of Us: Latina Views for a Multi-Colored Century*. Cambridge, MA: South End Press.

———. 1999. "Beyond Black/White: The Racisms of Our Time." In *Rethinking the Color Line: Readings in Race and Ethnicity*, edited by Charles A. Gallagher. London: Mayfield Publishing Company.

———. 2003. "Don't Call This Country 'America': How the Name Was Hijacked and Why It Matters Today More Than Ever." *Z Magazine*, July–August, 69–72.

Marx, Anthony. 1998. *Making Race and Nation: A Comparison of South Africa, The United States and Brazil*. New York: Cambridge University Press.

Masley, Ed. 2001. "Imagine Giving Peace a Chance through Song." *Pittsburgh Post-Gazette*, 20 September, C2.

Mathison, Sandra. 2003. "The Accumulation of Disadvantage: The Role of Educational Testing in the School Career of Minority Children." *Workplace: A Journal for Academic Labor* 5, no. 2. www.louisville.edu/journal/workplace/issue5p2/mathison.html (accessed 22 July 2003).

Matsuda, Mari J., Charles R. Lawrence III, Richard Delgado, and Kimberle Williams Crenshaw. 1993. *Words That Wound: Critical Race Theory, Assaultive Speech and the First Amendment*. Boulder, CO: Westview Press.

Mazel, Ella, ed. 1998. *"'And Don't Call Me A Racist!' A Treasury of Quotes on the Past, Present and Future of the Color Line in America."* Lexington, MA: Argonaut Press.

Mazie, Margery, Phyllis Palmer, Mayuris Pimentel, Sharon Rogers, Stuart Ruderfer, and Melissa Sokolowski. 1993. "To Deconstruct Race, Deconstruct Whiteness." *American Quarterly* 45, no. 2 (June): 281–94.

McCabe, Sean Esteban, Michelle Morales, James A. Cranford, Jorge Delva, Melnee D. McPherson, and Carol J. Boyd. "Race/Ethnicity and Gender Differences in Drug Use and Abuse among College Students." *Journal of Ethnicity in Substance Abuse* 6, no. 2 (2007): 75–95.

Mcgruder, Aaron. 2001. "Boondocks." www.ucomics.com (accessed 10 December).

McIntosh, Peggy. 1992. "Unpacking the Invisible Knapsack: White Privilege." *Creation Spirituality* (January–February). Also published in Peace and Freedom (July–August 1989): 10.

———. 1998. "White Privilege and Male Privilege: A Personal Account of Coming to See Correspondences through Work in Women's Studies. In *Race, Class and Gender: an Anthology*, edited by Patricia Hill Collins and Margaret L. Anderson. Belmont, Calif.: Wadsworth, 76–87.

McIntyre, Alice. 1997. *Making Meaning of Whiteness: Exploring Racial Identity with White Teachers*. Albany: State University of New York Press.

McIntyre, Robert. 2001. "Supply-Siders Go to War." *The American Prospect*, 19 October, 9. Online at www.ctj.org/html/prospect.htm (accessed 12 January 2002).

McMillen, Liz. 1995. "New Field of 'Whiteness Studies' Challenges a Racial 'Norm.'" *Chronicle of Higher Education.* (8 September) Online at http://chronicle.com (accessed 10 December 2001).

MetLife. "The 2009 MetLife Study of the American Dream: Rebooting the American Dream. Shifted. Altered. Not Deleted." Online at http://www.metlife.com/assets/cao/gbms/studies/09030710_AmDreamHighlights_v5.pdf.

Mollenkopf, John. 2001b. Report to the Council of Chief Academic Officers and Chief Student Affairs Officers of the City University of New York. Minutes of the Meeting (October).

Mollenkopf, John, John Kasinitz, and Mary Waters. 2001. "Chutes and Ladders: Educational Attainment Among Young Second Generation and Native New Yorkers." The Center for Urban Research: City University of New York. Paper presented at the ICMEC Conference on New Immigrants in New York City. CUNY Graduate Center, November.

Montagu, Ashley M. F. 1945. *Man's Most Dangerous Myth: The Fallacy of Race.* New York: Columbia University Press.

Moore, Joan, and Raquel Pinderhughes. 1993. *In the Barrios: Latinos and the Underclass Debate*. New York: Russell Sage Foundation.

Morgan, Edward S. 1975. *American Slavery, American Freedom: The Ordeal of Colonial Virginia*. New York: W. W. Norton.

Morrison, Toni. 1992. *Playing in the Dark: Whiteness and the Literary Imagination*. New York: Vintage Books.

Moynihan, Daniel Patrick. 1965. *The Negro Family: The Case for National Action*. Washington: U.S. Department of Labor.

Mullings, Leith. 1978. "Ethnicity and Stratification in the Urban United States." *Annals of the New York Academy of Sciences*, no. 318: 10–22.

———. 1995. "Racism Remains Pervasive." *New Politics* 5, no. 3 (Summer), issue 19: 31–34.

Muwakill, Salim. 1999. "Aaron the Wiggah." *CommonQuest*, vol. 3/4, no. 3/1: 67.

Myrdal, Gunnar. 1964 [1944]. *An American Dilemma.* Vols. 1 and 2. New York: McGraw-Hill.

Nakayama, Thomas K., and Judith N. Martin, eds. 1999. *Whiteness: The Communication of Social Identity*. London: Sage.

The National Center for Public Policy and Higher Education. 2008. "Measuring Up 2008: The National Report Card on Higher Education." http://measuringup2008.highereducation.org/print/NCPPHEMUNationalRpt.pdf

National Opinion Research Center, General Social Survey. 1998a. "Question 154." University of Michigan. Online at www.icpsr.umich.edu/GSS/rnd1998/merged/cdbk/bksimp.htm (accessed 22 November 2001).

———. General Social Survey Project. 1998b. "Question 266." University of Chicago. Online at www.icpsr.umich.edu/gss/rnd1998/merged/cdbk/racdif4.htm and racdif2.htm and racdif1.htm (accessed 22 November 2001).

New York Times. 1999. Editorial, "The Journey to 2000." 31 December. A20.

Nussbaum, Martha. 1996. "Reply." *For Love of Country: Debating the Limits of Patriotism*. Edited by Joshua Cohen. Boston: Beacon Press.

———. 2001. "Can Patriotism Be Compassionate?" *The Nation*, 17 December, 11.

O'Brien, Eileen. 2001. *Whites Confront Racism: Antiracists and Their Paths to Action.* New York: Rowman & Littlefield.

O'Leary, Cecilia Elizabeth. 1999. *To Die For: The Paradox of American Patriotism.* Princeton, NJ: Princeton University Press.

Omi, Michael, and Howard Winant. 1994. *Racial Formation in the United States.* New York: Routledge.

Onion. 2001. "UN Report: 70 Percent of World's Population Could Use All-Star Benefit Concert," 7 November. www.theonion.com/onion3740/all-star_benefit_concert.html> (accessed 12 November 2001).

Orleck, Annelise. 2001. "Soviet Jews: The City's Newest Immigrants." In *New Immigrants in New York,* edited by Nancy Foner. New York: Columbia University Press.

Osajima, K. 1993. "The Hidden Injuries of Race." In *Bearing Dreams and Shaping Visions,* edited by L. Revilla, G. Momura, S. Wong, and S. Hune. Pullman, WA: Washington State University.

Page, Ava, Amanda Petteruti, Nastassia Walsh, and Jason Ziedenberg. "Education and Public Safety." Justice Policy Institute. http://www.justicepolicy.org/images/upload/07-08_REP_EducationAndPublicSafety_PS-AC.pdf.

Page, Helan. 1995. "White Privilege and the Construction of Racial Identity." *Current Anthropology* 36, no. 3 (June): 526–28.

———. 1998. "Understanding White Cultural Practices." *Anthropology Newsletter* 39 no. 4 (April): 58, 60.

Painter, Nell Irvin. 2010. *The History of White People.* New York: W.W. Norton & Company.

Patchen, Martin. 1999. *Diversity and Unity: Relations between Racial and Ethnic Groups.* Chicago: Nelson Hall Publishers.

Perez, Luis, and Edward Barrera. 2001. "CUNY Chancellor Softens Stance on Free Speech," *Kingsman,* 15 October, 2.

Perry, Theresa, Claude Steele, and Asa Hilliard III. 2003. *Young, Gifted and Black: Promoting High Achievement among African-American Students.* Boston, MA: Beacon Press.

Petteruti, Amanda, and Nastassia Walsh. 2008. "Moving Target: A Decade of Resistance to the Prison Industrial Complex." *Justice Policy Institute.* www.justice-policy.org/images/upload/08-09_REP_MovingTargetCR10_AC-PS.pdf.

Picca, Leslie, and Joe Feagin. 2007. *Two-Faced Racism: Whites in the Backstage and Frontstage.* New York: Routledge,

Podur, Justin. 2003. "Revolutionizing Culture, Part One: Michael Albert Interviews Justin Podur." Znet, 15 July. www.zmag.org/znet.htm (accessed 11 August 2003).

Pollock, Mica. 2008. *Everyday Antiracism: Getting Real About Race in School.* New York: The New Press.

Postel, Danny. 2001. "Outsiders in America." *Chronicle of Higher Education,* 7 December, A12.

Prashad, Vijay. 2000. *The Karma of Brown Folk.* Minneapolis: University of Minnesota Press.

Price, Hugh B. 1995. "Where Do We Go From Here? *Replacing Racial, Ethnic and Gender Preferences.*" New Democrat (May–June): 19.

Professional Staff Congress, CUNY. 2001a. News Bulletin (February). Sources: CUNY Budget Office, National Center for Public Policy and Higher Education.

Pyne, Solana. 2003. "Making Enemies." *Village Voice* online, July 9–15, 2003 (accessed 10 July 2003).

Quinnipiac University. 2009. "U.S. Voters Disagree 3-1 With Sotomayor On Key Case, Quinnipiac University National Poll Finds; Most Say Abolish Affirmative Action." www.quinnipiac,edu/x1295.xml?ReleaseID=1307. Accessed 17 October.

Rasmussen, Brigit Brander, Eric Klinenberg, Irene J. Nexica, and Matt Wray, eds. 2001. *The Making and Unmaking of Whiteness*. Durham, NC: Duke University Press.

Reed, Wornie, and Bertin Louis. 2009. "'No More Excuses': Problematic Responses to Barrack Obama's Election." *Journal of African American Studies* 13, no. 2. 97–109.

Rendon, Laura I. 2000. "Academics of the Heart." *About Campus*, July–August, 3–5.

Rieder, Jonathon. 1985. *Canarsie: The Jews and Italians of Brooklyn against Liberalism*. Cambridge, MA: Harvard University Press.

Rivera, Amaad, Jeannette Huezo, Chiristina Kasica, and Dedrick Muhammad. 2009. "State of the Dream 2009: The Silent Depression." *United for a Fair Economy.* http://www.faireconomy.org/files/pdf/state_of_dream_2009.pdf

Robotham, Donald. 1997. "The Wealth of Races: The Political Economy of Race and Globalization." Paper delivered at the New York Academy of Sciences, 13–14 March.

Rock, Chris. 1999. Bigger and Blacker. Home Box Office Video. Warner Productions. First skit. Videocassette.

Rodriguez, Clara E. 1991. *Puerto Ricans Born in the U.S.A*. Boulder, CO: Westview Press.

———. 2000. *Changing Race: Latinos, the Census and the History of Ethnicity in the United States.* New York: New York University Press.

Rodriguez, Clara E., Aida Castro, Oscar Garcia, and Analisa Torres. 1991. "Latino Racial Identity: In the Eye of the Beholder?" *Latino Studies Journal* 2, no. 3: 33–48.

Rodriguez, Roberto. 1999. "The Study of Whiteness." *Black Issues in Higher Education* 16, issue 6 (13 May): 20.

Roediger, David. 1994. *Toward the Abolition of Whiteness: Essays on Race, Politics and Working Class History*. New York: Verso.

———. 1998. *Black on White: Black Writers on What It Means to be White.* New York: Schocken Books.

———. 1999 [1991]. *The Wages of Whiteness: Race and the Making of the American Working Class.* New York: Verso.

———. 2005. *Working toward Whiteness: How America's Immigrants Became White. The Strange Journey from Ellis Island to the Suburb.* New York: Basic Books.

Romer, Nancy. 1999. "The CUNY Struggle: Class and Race in Public Higher Education." *New Politics* 7, no. 2 (Winter): 47–56.

Roper Center at University of Connecticut, Public Opinion Online. 2001. Conducted by Gallup Organization on 11 June. Accession Number 0383148, Question ID: USGALLUP.01JLY11, R29A.

Rosette, Ashleigh Shelby, Katherine W. Phillips, and Geoffrey J. Leonardelli. 2008. "The White Standard: Racial Bias in Leader Categorization." *Journal of Applied Psychology* 93, no. 4: 758–777.

Roy, Arundhati. 2002. "Shall We Leave It to the Experts?" Online at www.outlook-india.com.

———. 2003. "Confronting Empire." Porto Alegre, Brazil, January 27, 2003. www.zmag.org/content/showarticle.cfm?SectionID=51&ItemID=2919 (accessed 28 January 2003).

Ryan, Joseph. 1973. *White Ethnics: Their Life in Working Class America.* Englewood Cliffs, NJ: Prentice-Hall.

Saad, Lydia. 2007. "Black-White Educational Opportunities Widely Seen as Equal: Americans Favor Merit over Racial Diversity for College Admittance." *Gallup.* http://www.gallup.com/poll/28021/BlackWhite-Educational-Opportunities-Wide-ly-Seen-Equal.aspx#2.

Sack, Kevin, and Janet Elder. 2000. "Poll Finds Optimistic Outlook but Enduring Racial Division." *New York Times,* 11 July, A1, A23.

Saez, Emmanuel. 2009. "Striking it Richer: The Evolution of Top Incomes in the United States (Update with 2007 Estimates)." *Pathways,* August 5. http://elsa.berkeley.edu/~saez/saez-UStopincomes-2007.pdf.

Sanjek, Roger. 1998. *The Future of Us All: Race and Neighborhood Politics in New York City.* Ithaca, NY: Cornell University Press.

Sassen, Saskia. 2003. "Citizenship Destabilized." *Liberal Education* 89, no. 2 (Spring): 14–21.

Saxakali.com. 1999. "As American as Apple Pie: History of Police Brutality." Online at http://saxakali.com/Community Linkups/NYCBDED3.htm (accessed 12 March 1999).

Saxton, Alexander. 1990. *The Rise and Fall of the White Republic: Class Politics and Mass Culture in Nineteenth-Century America.* New York: Verso.

Schaefer, Richard T. 1995. *Race and Ethnicity in the United States.* New York: HarperCollins College Publishers.

Schneider, Carol Geary. 1995. *American Pluralism and the College Curriculum: Higher Education in a Diverse Democracy.* Washington, DC: Association of American Colleges and Universities.

———. 1999. "Democratic Principles and the Undergraduate Curriculum." *Peer Review* (Fall): 7–9.

———. 2003. Introduction. *Peer Review* (Spring): 3.

Schneider, Jane. 2001. "Department of Anthropology, the Graduate School and University Center, City University of New York." Department communication, 12 December.

Schneider, Jane, and Rayna Rapp, eds. 1995. *Articulating Hidden Histories: Exploring the Influence of Eric R. Wolf.* Berkeley: University of California Press.

Schoem, David. 2003. "Intergroup Dialogue for a Just and Diverse Democracy." *Sociological Inquiry* 73, no. 2 (May): 212–27.

Schor, Juliet. 1998. *The Overspent American: Upscaling, Downshifting, and the New Consumer.* New York: Basic Books.

Scott, Daryl Michael. 1997. *Contempt and Pity: Social Policy and the Image of the Damaged Black Psyche 1880–1996.* Chapel Hill: University of North Carolina Press.

Scott, James C. 1985. *Weapons of the Weak: Everyday Forms of Peasant Resistance.* New Haven: Yale University Press.

Scott, Janny. 2003. "The Changing Face of Patriotism." *New York Times* Week in Review, 6 July, 1.

Scott-Heron, Gil. 1992. "'B' Movie." Reflections. Bertelsmann Music Group Company. Compact Disc.

Secours, Molly. 2001a. "Beware Black Areas: Real Estate Gambit a Sign We Must Do More." *Nashville Tennessean*, 10 December. Online at www.tennessean .com/opinion/nashville-eye/archives/01/11/11185776.shtml (accessed 20 December 2001).

———. 2001b. "Nashville's Pioneering a Path against Racism." *Nashville City Paper*, 20 December. Online at www.nashvillecitypaper.com/index.cfm?section_id=9&screen=news&news_id=4208 (accessed 20 December 2001).

———. 2001c. "Riding the Reparations Bandwagon: A White Woman's Perspective." *Nashville City Paper*, 2 March. Online at www.mdcbowen.org/p2/rap/secours.htm (accessed 2 March 2001).

Sevier, Brian R. 2003. "Ways of Seeing Resistance: Educational History and the Conceptualization of Oppositional Action."*Taboo* 7, no. 1 (Spring–Summer): 87–107.

Shapiro, Thomas M. 1998. *Great Divides: Readings in Social Inequality in the United States.* London: Mayfield.

Shaw, Wendy S. 2007. *Cities of Whiteness.* New Jersey: Wiley-Blackwell.

Shipler, David K. 1997. *A Country of Strangers: Blacks and Whites in America.* New York: Alfred A. Knopf.

Sklar, Holly. 1997. "Imagine a Country." *Z Magazine*, July–August, 65–71.

———. 2003a. "Imagine a Country." *Z Magazine*, May, 53–59.

Sleeper, Jim. 1990. *The Closest of Strangers: Liberalism and the Politics of Race in New York.* New York: W. W. Norton and Company.

Smedley, Audrey. 1993. *Race in North America.* San Francisco: Westview Press, Inc.

———. 1998. "'Race' and Construction of Human Identity." *American Anthropologist* 100, no. 3 (September): 690–702.

Smith, Chip. 2007. *The Cost of Privilege: Taking on the System of White Supremacy and Racism.* Fayetteville, NC: Camino Press.

Smith, Daryl G., Guy L. Gerbick, Mark A. Figueroa, Gayle Harris Watkins, Thomas Levitan, Leeshawn Cradoc Moore, Pamela A. Merchant, Haim Dov Beliak, and Benjamin Figueroa. 1997. *Diversity Works: The Emerging Picture of How Students Benefit.* Washington DC: Association of American Colleges and Universities.

Smith, Robert C., and Richard Seltzer. 2000. *Contemporary Controversies and the American Racial Divide.* Oxford: Rowman & Littlefield.

Smith, Tom W. 1990. "Topical Report 19: Ethnic Images," National Opinion Research Center, December. www.icpsr.umich.edu/gss/rnd1998/reports/t-reports/topic19.htm (accessed 18 November 2001).

Smith, Tom W., and Paul B. Sheatsley. 1984. "American Attitudes toward Race Relations." *Public Opinion*, October–November, 14.

Song, Miri. 2001. "Comparing minorities' Ethnic Options: Do Asian Americans Possess 'More' Ethnic Options than African Americans?" *Ethnicities* 1, no. 1: 57–82.

Soyinka, Wole. 1997. Chairman of the Editorial Board. "The White Issue," *Transition: An International Review* (by Kwame Anthony Appiah and Henry Louis Gates Jr.) 7, no. 1 (January), issue 73.

Stafford, Walter. 1992. "Whither the Great Neo-Conservative Experiment in New York City." In *Race Politics and Economic Development: Community Perspectives*, edited by James Jennings. New York: Verso.

Steinberg, Stephen. 1995. *Turning Back: The Retreat from Racial Justice in American Thought and Policy*. Boston: Beacon Press.

———. 1999. "Occupational Apartheid in America: Race, Labor Market Segmentation and Affirmative Action." In *Without Justice For All: The New Liberalism and Our Retreat from Racial Equality*, edited by Adolph Reed Jr. Boulder, CO: Westview Press.

———. 2001. *The Ethnic Myth: Race, Ethnicity and Class in America*. Boston: Beacon Press.

Steinhorn, Leonard, and Barbara Diggs-Brown. 1999. *By the Color of Our Skin: The Illusion of Integration and the Reality of Race*. New York: Dutton.

Stowe, David. 1996. "Uncolored People: The Rise of Whiteness Studies." *Lingua Franca* (September–October): 70–77.

Street, Paul. 2001. "The White Fairness Understanding Gap." *Z Magazine*, October, 9–11.

———. 2003a. "Behind the Smoking Gun: Notes from Chicago on Racism's Persistent Significance." Znet, 7 May. www.zmag.org/Znet.htm (accessed 28 July 2003).

———. 2003b. "The." Znet, 18 July. www.zmag.org/content/showarticle. cfm?sectionID=308-ItemID=3585 (accessed 16 August 2003).

Takagi, D. Y. 1992. *The Retreat from Race: Asian American Admissions and Racial Politics.* New Brunswick, NJ: Rutgers University Press.

Talbot, Margaret. 1997. "White Trash Girl." *New York Times Magazine*, 30 November, 116.

Tanaka, Greg. "The Elephant in the Living Room that No One Wants to Talk About: Why U.S. Anthropologists Are Unable to Acknowledge the End of Culture." *Anthropology and Education Quarterly* 40, no. 1 (2009): 82–95.

Tatum, Beverly Daniel. 1997. *Why Are All the Black Kids Sitting Together in the Cafeteria? And Other Conversations about Race.* New York: Basic Books.

Tell, Shawgi. 1999. E-mail to the Mult-cul@ubvm.cc.buffalo.edu list, July.

Thomas, Shaun A. 2009. *Beyond Crime Quantities: A Multilevel Analysis of the Relative Prevalence of Interracial Violence*. PhD dissertation, Louisiana State University.

Thompson, Becky. 2001. *A Promise and a Way of Life: White Antiracist Activism.* Minneapolis: University of Minnesota Press.

Tochluk, Shelly. 2008. *Witnessing Whiteness: First Steps Toward an Antiracist Practice and Culture.* Lanham, MD: Rowman & Littlefield.

Tolerance.org. 2001a. "Bias 101: Hate in Higher Education." *Tolerance in the News*, November 2001. www.tolerance.org/news/article_tol.jsp?id=331.

———. 2001b. "Hate in the News." Hate Goes to School. www.tolerance.org/ news/ article_hate.jsp?id=312.

Traub, James. 2004. "The Pull of Family." *New York Times* Magazine. 29 February 2004, 21–22.

Tuan, Mia. 1998. *Forever Foreigners or Honorary Whites? The Asian Ethnic Experience Today.* New Brunswick, NJ: Rutgers University Press.

Uchitelle, Louis. 2003a. "Blacks Lose Better Jobs Faster as Middle-Class Work Drops." *New York Times,* 12 July, A1, C14.

———. 2003b. "The Perils of Cutbacks in Higher Education." *New York Times,* 10 August. Online at www.nytimes.com/2003/08/10/business/yourmoney/10view. html (accessed 10 August 2003).

Valentine, Charles A. 1968. *Culture and Poverty.* Chicago: The University of Chicago Press.

Waldinger, Roger. 1996. *Still the Promised City: African-Americans and New Immigrants in Postindustrial New York.* Cambridge: Harvard University Press.

———. 2001. "Rethinking 'Race.'" *Ethnicities* 1, no. 1: 19–21.

Wallerstein, Immanuel. 2001. "America and the World: The Twin Towers as Metaphor." Presentation at the Charles R. Lawrence II Memorial Lecture, Brooklyn College, December 5. Online at www.binghamton.edu/fbc/iwbkln02.htm (accessed 10 December 2001).

Ward, Eric. 1999. "White Supremacy in the USA." *Searchlight* (May): 50.

We Interrupt This Message. 2001. "Reframing Debate in the Wake of WTC and Pentagon Suicide Plane Bombings." www.interrupt.org/911pj.html.

Weitzer, Ronald, and Steven A. Tuch. "Racially Biased Policing: Determinants of Citizen Perceptions." *Social Forces* 83, no. 3 (2005): 1009–1030.

Wellman, David. 1993. *Portraits of White Racism.* Cambridge: Cambridge University Press.

Wessler, Seth. 2009. "Race and Recession: How Inequity Rigged the Economy and How to Change the Rules." *Applied Research Center.* http://arc.org/downloads/2009_race_recession_execsumm.pdf.

Wetherell, Margaret, and Jonathon Potter. 1992. *Mapping the Language of Racism: Discourse and the Legitimation of Exploitation.* New York: Columbia University Press.

Whitfield, Edward L. 2001. "The Timothy McVeigh Silence Is Loud and Profound." *News of the Black Radical Congress (BRC).* elwhit@earthlink.net.

Wilder, Craig Steven. 2000. *A Covenant with Color: Race and Social Power in Brooklyn.* New York: Columbia University Press.

Wildman, Stephanie M. 1996. *Privilege Revealed: How Invisible Preference Undermines America.* New York: New York University Press.

———. 1998. "The Dream of Diversity and the Cycle of Exclusion." In *Trotter Review*: Focus on "Diversity, Pedagogy and Higher Education: Challenges, Lessons and Accomplishments, edited by James Jennings. Boston: University of Massachusetts.

Williams, Lena. 2000. *It's the Little Things: The Everyday Interactions that Get under the Skin of Blacks and Whites.* Orlando, FL: Harcourt.

Williams, Patricia J. 1999. "The Auguries of Innocence." *Nation,* 24 May, 9.

———. 2001. "Disorder in the Court." *Nation,* 10 December, 11.

Wilson, Reginald. 1995. "Racial Tensions on Campus." Review of Battling Bias: The Struggle for Identity and Community on College Campuses, by Ruth Sidel and

"Generation at the Crossroads: Apathy and Action on the American Campus," by Paul Rogat Loeb. *New Politics* 5, no. 3 (Summer), issue 19: 178–82.

Wiltse, Charles M. 1965. *David Walker's Appeal*. New York: Hill & Wang.

Winant, Howard. 1994. *Racial Conditions: Politics, Theory, Comparisons*. Minneapolis: University of Minnesota Press.

———. 2001. *The World Is a Ghetto: Race and Democracy since World War II*. New York: Basic Books.

Wing, Bob. 2000. "The Structure of White Power and the Color of Election 2000." *ColorLines*, Spring. www.colorlines.com (accessed 7 December 2001).

Wise, Tim. 2001. "School Shootings and White Denial." AlterNet, 6 March. www.alternet.org/print.html? StoryID=10560 (accessed 6 March 2001).

———. 2002. "Racial Profiling and its Apologists." *Z Magazine*, March, 40–44.

Wray, Matt, and Annalee Newitz. 1997. *White Trash: Race and Class in America*. New York: Routledge.

Wyatt, Edward. 2001. "Board Votes to Require Recitation of Pledge at Public Schools." *New York Times*, 18 October, D1.

X, Malcolm, as told to Alex Haley. 1965. *The Autobiography of Malcolm X*. New York: Ballantine Books.

Yancy, George. *Black Bodies, White Gazes: The Continuing Significance of Race*. Lanham, MD: Rowman and Littlefield, 2008.

Young, Jeffrey R. 2001. "Scholars Question the Image of the Internet as Race-Free Utopia." *Chronicle of Higher Education*, 21 September 2001. Online at http://chronicle.com (accessed 10 December 2001).

Yun, G. 1989. A *Look Beyond the Model Minority Image: Critical Issues in Asian America*. New York: Minority Rights Group, Inc.

Zachary, G. Pascal. 2002. "The New America: How Immigration is Transforming Our Society." *In These Times*, 21 January, 22–23.

Zia, Helen. 2000. *Asian American Dreams: The Emergence of an American People*. New York: Farrar, Straus and Giroux.

Zinn, Howard. 1990. *Declarations of Independence: Cross-Examining American Ideology*. New York: HarperPerennial.

———. 1995. *A People's History of the United States 1492–Present*. New York: HarperPerennial.

Index

About the Author

Dr. Melanie E. L. Bush is currently an associate professor of anthropology and sociology at Adelphi University (Garden City, NY) and was employed at Brooklyn College from 1990–2005. She obtained an undergraduate degree at McGill University in Montreal and advanced degrees at the City University of New York. Dr. Bush is coauthor of a forthcoming book entitled *Tensions in the American Dream: Rhetoric, Reverie or Reality?* (with Dr. Roderick D. Bush, St. Johns University), has published numerous articles in scholarly journals, and presented at a range of conferences, universities, and community settings both nationally and internationally. Dr. Bush has been active for over three decades in community struggles such as for full employment, education, women's rights, and against racism and academic projects for peace, justice, and the common good.